# Palgrave Studies in Literary Anthropology

**Series Editors**
Deborah Reed-Danahay
Department of Anthropology
The State University of New York at Buffalo
Buffalo, NY, USA

Helena Wulff
Department of Social Anthropology
Stockholm University
Stockholm, Sweden

D1351422

This series explores new ethnographic objects and emerging genres of writing at the intersection of literary and anthropological studies. Books in this series are grounded in ethnographic perspectives and the broader cross-cultural lens that anthropology brings to the study of reading and writing. The series explores the ethnography of fiction, ethnographic fiction, narrative ethnography, creative nonfiction, memoir, autoethnography, and the connections between travel literature and ethnographic writing.

More information about this series at
http://www.palgrave.com/gp/series/15120

Ellen Wiles

# Live Literature

The Experience and Cultural Value
of Literary Performance Events
from Salons to Festivals

*For Syd*

# Series Editors' Preface

***Palgrave Studies in Literary Anthropology*** publishes explorations of new ethnographic objects and emerging genres of writing at the intersection of literary and anthropological studies. Books in this series are grounded in ethnographic perspectives and the broader cross-cultural lens that anthropology brings to the study of reading and writing. By introducing work that applies an anthropological approach to literature, whether drawing on ethnography or other materials in relation to anthropological and literary theory, this series moves the conversation forward not only in literary anthropology, but in general anthropology, literary studies, cultural studies, sociology, ethnographic writing and creative writing. The "literary turn" in anthropology and critical research on world literatures share a comparable sensibility regarding global perspectives.

Fiction and autobiography have connections to ethnography that underscore the idea of the author as ethnographer and the ethnographer as author. Literary works are frequently included in anthropological research and writing, as well as in studies that do not focus specifically on literature. Anthropologists take an interest in fiction and memoir set in their field locations, and produced by "native" writers, in order to further their insights into the cultures and contexts they research. Experimental genres in anthropology have benefitted from the style and structure of fiction and autoethnography, as well as by other expressive forms ranging from film and performance art to technology, especially the internet and social media. There are renowned fiction writers who trained as anthropologists, but moved on to a literary career. Their anthropologically inspired work is a common sounding board in literary anthropology. In the endeavor to foster writing skills in different genres, there are now courses on ethnographic writing, anthropological writing genres, experimental writing, and even creative writing taught by anthropologists. And increasingly, literary and reading communities are attracting anthropological attention, including an engagement with issues of how to reach a wider audience.

*Palgrave Studies in Literary Anthropology* publishes scholarship on the ethnography of fiction and other writing genres, the connections between travel literature and ethnographic writing, and internet writing. It also publishes creative work such as ethnographic fiction, narrative ethnography, creative non-fiction, memoir, and autoethnography. Books in the series include monographs and edited collections, as well as shorter works that appear as Palgrave Pivots. This series aims to reach a broad audience among scholars, students and a general readership.

Deborah Reed-Danahay and Helena Wulff
Co-Editors, Palgrave Studies in Literary Anthropology

**Advisory Board**
Ruth Behar, University of Michigan
Don Brenneis, University of California, Santa Cruz Regina Bendix, University of Göttingen
Mary Gallagher, University College Dublin
Kirin Narayan, Australian National University Nigel Rapport, University of St Andrews
Ato Quayson, University of Toronto
Julia Watson, Ohio State University

# Acknowledgments

Thank yous—there are just so many. My research entailed hundreds of conversations at and beyond live literature events, and I am grateful to every person who has taken the time to speak with me, and to every producer who has given me access to their events—particularly Paul Burston and Peter Florence. Thank you to Helena Wulff for encouraging my literary anthropological explorations early on with such kindness and enthusiasm. Thank you to Mary Al-Sayed, Madison Allums, and Elizabeth Graber at Palgrave, for bringing this book into being. The book emerged from my doctoral research which was funded and enabled by the UK's Arts and Humanities Research Council, and I am very grateful to my supervisors, Claire Squires and Katie Halsey. Thank you to the Royal Anthropological Institute for honouring me with the Firth Award for this project. Thank you to Arts Council England for awarding me funding to found my own experimental live literature project, and to Sarah Sanders and Gemma Seltzer for their insights. Thank you to Peter Francis and Louisa Yates of Gladstone's Library for inviting me to perform at your festival, and for a scholarship that allowed me focus on writing at a distance from small children. That said, I was grateful to come home to gather up said children and read aloud to them—a daily live literature performance that I treasure. Thank you to my parents for their constant support, encouragement, and creative forms of Zoom entertainment for their grandchildren during lockdown. Thank you to Jude Law for reminding me that you really never know what will happen when you start an ethnographic research project. Thank you to David Wiles, Sarah Polcz, Rachel Louis, and Helen Hanson for taking the time to read drafts of this book and offering such helpful comments. Thank you to Peter McDonald, Michael Hughes, Lisa Zunshine, Helen Taylor, Deirdre Mask, Michael Jackson, Alisse Waterson, Matthew Rubery, Helen Taylor, Margherita Laera, and Anna Kiernan for your generosity in reading the manuscript and offering such warm endorsements. Syd, you snagged the dedication for many, many good reasons.

# Praise for *Live Literature*

"A pitch-perfect guide to the live literature scene."
—Matthew Rubery, *author of* The Untold Story of the Talking Book *(2016), and Professor of Modern Literature at Queen Mary University of London*

"Ellen Wiles's fascinating and engaging new book on live literature beautifully reveals how the seemingly personal act of reading can be transformed, and even enhanced, through performance."
—Deirdre Mask, *author of* The Address Book: What Street Addresses Reveal about Identity, Race, Wealth, and Power *(2020)*

"A hugely insightful and entertaining survey of the live literature scene: what it is, who it's for, and why it matters. Full of brilliant analysis and fascinating vignettes, it is sure to be standard work on the subject for years to come."
—Michael Hughes, *novelist, author of the award-winning novel* Country *(2018), and Creative Writing Lecturer at Queen Mary University of London*

"Literature is often thought of as an intensely inward, individual experience—the slow, silent immersion in a book which has the potential to transform how we see ourselves, others and the world. Yet, as *Live Literature* shows, it is for numerous groups and communities across the world now a powerful public experience as well. Creatively blending autobiographical reflection, anthropological 'thick description', and literary analysis—in a mode she calls 'experiential literary ethnography'—Ellen Wiles uncovers what it means, for authors and audiences, to bring the written word to life as speech and performance today. *Live Literature* is not only a ground-breaking contribution to contemporary cultural studies. It is a stylish and engaging counter to the cynics and doomsayers who are, as ever, prematurely waving literature's final death notice."

—Peter D. McDonald, *author of* Artefacts of Writing: Ideas of the State and Communities of Letters from Matthew Arnold to Xu Bing *(2017), Professor of English and Related Literature at the University of Oxford*

"In this bold, wide-ranging book, acclaimed author Ellen Wiles makes a convincing case for live literature as a crucial cultural practice of the 21st century—a practice that includes 'bodies, voices, performance, places, spaces, emotions, and communities, as well as individual intellects and judgments.' Combining literary criticism, sociology, cognitive science, and journalism (e.g., her account of the celebrated Hay Festival), Wiles brings us a compelling report from the future of literature that is already here."

—Lisa Zunshine, *author of* Getting Inside Your Head: What Cognitive Science Can Tell Us about Popular Culture *(2012), Bush-Holbrook Professor of English at the University of Kentucky*

"Literary festivals and salons come alive in this charming book packed with writers, readers, performers and audiences revealing the very human desire for shared cultural encounter. Ellen Wiles has crafted a reading experience that is fun, evocative, intelligent and informative, offering a gifted writer's vivid descriptions and an anthropologist's keen analysis."

—Alisse Waterston, *author of* Light in Dark Times: The Human Search for Meaning *(2020), and Professor of Anthropology at The City University of New York*

"In Covid times, with Zoom and digital culture replacing real experiences, this book is an inspiring and heartening reminder of why live literature matters. Collective human engagement with writers, in literary festivals and salons, is analysed here by a writer passionately and personally engaged with her subject. The accounts of author-performers' appearances and reader-audiences' responses make for a powerful argument that we mustn't allow live literary events to die."

—Helen Taylor, *author of* Why Women Read Fiction: The Stories of Our Lives *(2019), Emeritus Professor of English at the University of Exeter, and the first Director of the Liverpool Literary Festival*

"At a time when public life has been curtailed and we are increasingly concerned with the alienating effects of social media, Ellen Wiles' riveting account of live literature events reawakens us to the emotional connectiveness and sense of community that are fostered by participation in face-to-face art performances. *Live Literature* is an eloquent testimony to the ways in which the life of art entails the art of life."

—Michael Jackson, *Professor of World Religions, Harvard University; poet, novelist, and author of* The Paper Nautilus *(2019)*

"Ellen Wiles' book *Live Literature* breathes new life into scholarship of contemporary literary culture with this richly nuanced, highly readable foray into the world of the spoken word. Wiles' ethnographic approach is fresh, thoughtful and engaging. This is an essential addition to the expanded field of publishing and the literary industries."

—Anna Kiernan, *author of* Post-Digital Writing: Cultures and Contexts *(2021), Publisher at The Lit Platform, and Director of the MA in Creativity at the University of Exeter*

*Live Literature* takes you on a vivid journey visiting literary festivals and salons across the UK. More than a book reader, you'll feel like a theatre spectator in front of a skilfully directed performance featuring many characters, sub-plots and scene changes. Wiles' experiential ethnographies are an outstanding contribution to the fields of literary anthropology and performance studies.

—Dr Margherita Laera, *Senior Lecturer in Drama and Theatre,*
*University of Kent*

Cover image: a photograph by Chris Scott of 'Whisky Galore', a book sculpture inspired by the Compton Mackenzie novel, created by The Secret Book Sculptor, who granted permission for use of the image via The Scottish Book Trust. For more information about the secret book sculpture project in Scottish Libraries, and a map of where to find them, see the Scottish Poetry Library's website.

# Contents

# 1

# Prologue: Live in a Library

Conversation burbles among the waiting audience who have packed out a spacious Victorian drawing room. Darkly-polished wooden floors are laid with Persian rugs, the walls are lined with tempting fiction spines, and the room boasts not one but two fireplaces, one of which is now lit and flickering on this chilly February morning. I shimmy my way through to the front, and perch on a bench under a side window next to a poet who is also going to perform today. Glancing outside, I see a few more people hurrying through the dove-grey mizzle towards the entrance.

My novel, *The Invisible Crowd*, only came out last year, but it is already starting to feel like old and insignificant news in the publishing world, as the flurries of new fiction releases keep on coming and piling up on each other, like endless fresh snowdrifts, including runaway bestsellers and major literary prize winners, so I'm grateful to have been invited to perform here in what will be my first live literature event of the year, and curious to find out what this little festival will be like. There are about eighty people in the audience, I'd say, all of whom appear to be white, and about two thirds of whom are women, of varying ages and dress styles, and with varying accents, from the chatter I can overhear.

© The Author(s), under exclusive license to Springer Nature
Switzerland AG 2021
E. Wiles, *Live Literature*, Palgrave Studies in Literary Anthropology,
https://doi.org/10.1007/978-3-030-50385-7_1

I have an hour's session to fill by myself today, which gives me much more scope than the standard festival format, and allows more time for readings from the novel. I remember my surprise when, before my first ever literary festival appearance, I was firmly told by the chairperson that there would be no readings *at all*, as if their inclusion would be an indulgence.

After an introduction by one of the festival hosts, I thank her and smile out at the audience as I introduce myself and my novel, and register several smiling faces in return. I outline the main characters and the polyphonic structure, and explain that it was inspired by a case I worked on years back when I was a barrister, then talk for a few minutes about the effect the case had on me, and the political and media narratives around immigration and asylum that I wanted to explore through fiction. People seem to be listening intently enough, and I don't spot any frowns that suggest displeasure rather than concentration. I relax, a little.

In order to give people a good sense of the various voices in my novel, I've planned to read from five sections, each of which involves a different point of view. I have prepared a PowerPoint presentation with a different photographic image to project for each one, which I hope will help to focus attention, distinguish each scene from the next, and make the event experience feel a little more performative. I launch into the readings, doing my best to make the delivery engaging, and to speak clearly and at a moderate pace, and attempting to render a subtle difference between the various characters' voices. I experiment by reading a section from the chapter that's narrated by Joe, a Lincolnshire bin man, which I have never performed from at an event before, and I even brave a slight accent—and thankfully I don't fluff it. At least, to my knowledge. In fact, I get some laughs in places that I'd meant to be funny, which is encouraging. The readings seem to be flowing, and there is still a sense of intensity in the room… I don't spot anybody drifting off, anyway.

After the readings, I speak briefly about the value of the fiction, the novel as a form, and reading as an activity. The audience mmmm collectively at one of my favourite Ursula K. Le Guin quotes: 'We read books to find out who we are.'[1]

To change gear, and involve the audience in a more unexpected exercise, I invite them to co-read a poem on a theme of migration by Ruth

Padel, from her marvellous collection, *The Mara Crossing*—some lines from which became an epigraph to the novel. I propose that each person reads one line aloud, before passing the baton along to the person next to them, and so on. Several people look surprised at this development, some whisper to each other, and some furrow their brows to read intently as if I've just landed them with an impromptu exam. I'm going to be judged for this, I see; I hope it will work. I read the first line aloud, then nod to the woman on the right of the front row, who reads her line with panache. The man next to her follows, and, one by one, the distinct quality of each voice in the room rings out—voices that I wouldn't necessarily have heard if I hadn't risked this exercise, and they all vary in accent, volume, pace and tone, though I detect quite a few local accents. I notice the different approach that each person takes to their performance: most relish the opportunity, some look slightly bemused but eager, one man reads in a monotone like a computer dictation, one woman, for whom English is not a first language, stumbles awkwardly, and one shy woman is barely audible. By the end, I feel as if I have a small but visceral sense of each person, and the poem has come alive for me in a new way. In fact, the activity seems to have shifted the collective mood. What had been an audience displaying remarkably focused attention on me has become a relaxed group of fellow performers.

I invite questions. Several hands go up, and I am surprised that the first few people begin by telling me that they had already read my book and loved it; I didn't necessarily expect anyone here to have read it yet. Another couple say they will definitely read it after hearing me speak, which comes as a relief. Questions span topics from research processes to the technique of writing different voices to immigration policy, and adaptation, and I answer as best I can. "I wondered if you'd thought of sending it to a film or TV company—it would make a terrific six-part series", one woman says, beaming, at which I have to grin wryly and explain that my agent has put it out there but there has been no take-up as yet, but add that, if there happen to be any film producers in the audience, the book could be their oyster. Laughter ripples: *as if.* At the very end, when my hour is just about up, a tall woman seated towards the back, with silver, neatly-curled hair, and a serious face, puts her hand up. "I'm sorry", she says, "but I can't let this go unsaid…"

And then she stops. A pause extends, then swells. People shift awkwardly in their seats. Some look around at her, wondering what she's about to say; others glance at each other. My stomach lurches; she must have taken issue with the politics I've alluded to around the book, I think, and perhaps want to point out to me that we can't let everyone in who claims to be a refugee, and ask, pointedly, whether I don't think we need to draw a line. This kind of thing has happened before, and I don't mind it—in fact I enjoy encountering a range of reactions to the content what I've written, if not to the quality. But it seems like a shame for an event that has otherwise been so enjoyable—for me, at least—to end on a sour note. Still, I tell myself, at least *some* people here have indicated that they enjoyed the book and this event, and even if this one person has hated all of it—and even if most fiction readers out there never even heard of my little novel—and even if nobody ever buys a copy again—then at least it exists, in print, and has had a brief moment in the sun. That's something.

But then I notice that the woman is crying. Her face has gone beet-root. She's pausing, it seems, because she's struggling to speak. Finally, she says, in a croak: "I'm sorry, I was just so moved by what you just read, and it was so wonderful, I just had to tell you."

And I find myself nearly welling up too, because I am so taken aback and touched, and it feels like a moment that epitomises the best I could have hoped for in writing the book—to have that sense of my work connecting on a deep emotional level with just one reader, who I've never met before, and probably won't ever meet again. In an instant, it makes up—at least temporarily—for all the years spent crafting and revising, the stresses of pitching and failing, the pressures of publication and reviews and sales numbers and publicity efforts and endless private, self-derogatory comparison with novelists who are all clearly far more talented, successful and savvy than I am. And it is especially lovely for this to be happening now, at a live event, among an audience that seems to be so engaged.

So I thank this woman in the audience, whose colour has now faded to rhubarb, and tell her that it really means a lot to me for her to have said that. Inwardly, I resolve to do more myself to share my own responses to books and art that I've loved with their makers, even if not in a live or public forum … But I also can't help myself wondering, from a live literature research perspective, to what extent this woman's response was genuinely determined by the content of the sections of the novel I just read aloud, and if so which ones, and why—or whether it came out of the way I performed the readings, or how I framed the novel in the talk—or just the experience of being here at this festival, and in the emotionally-receptive mood she woke up in today—or whether I just remind her of a long-lost niece—and whether she has already read my novel, or plans to read it—and, if she hasn't read it yet, but buys it after this event, whether she will actually go on to read it or whether it will just sit on her shelf for a while then end up in a charity shop, and if she does read it, whether the silent reading experience will match up to what she felt about it in this session—and how much fiction she usually reads, and what kind of books she likes, and how many literary festivals and events she has been to before, and what she felt about them, and what drew her to come here today, and where she lives, and who she's come with, and what her occupation is…

But I can't ask her any of these questions. This is not the time or place for a research-oriented conversation, and I have to wrap this session up.

As the rest of this book will reveal, though, I have asked similar sorts of questions of many other participants in live literature events in which I was not performing, and not just reader-audiences but also author-performers—and their answers have been varied, unexpected, thoughtful, enlightening, hilarious, and baffling.

# 2

# Speaking of Writing This: What, Why, Where, How

## Greeting

'Hello and welcome to this live literature event!'.

Genuinely: welcome. If 'words are events',[1] as Ursula K. Le Guin says they are, then it is an event each time that an assemblage of words is published, and each time that a paragraph is read. When it comes to live performance, that 'eventness'[2] is magnified. By exploring 'live literature' in this book, I will be focusing on events like the one I described in the prologue: live performances of and about literature for audiences that take place in shared physical spaces, such as literary festivals and salons.

Live literature has exploded this century.[3] It has become a central part of contemporary literary culture and the publishing industry—not just in the UK, where I live, but across the globe. And yet its impact is often underestimated, even by those in the literary world. As a subject of research it has largely been neglected. When this dawned on me, several years back, it became clear that someone needed to write a book about it.

But this has turned out to be a very peculiar time to release such a book—and, ironically, a highly opportune time. As this book was on the

© The Author(s), under exclusive license to Springer Nature
Switzerland AG 2021
E. Wiles, *Live Literature*, Palgrave Studies in Literary Anthropology,
https://doi.org/10.1007/978-3-030-50385-7_2

point of going into production, most of the world was placed under lockdown due to the Coronavirus. Almost all live literature events planned for 2020–2021 have been cancelled, or adapted for digital streaming, as have countless other performances across art forms. Right now, it feels strange even to contemplate being part of a live event—up close to so many other breathing bodies. But, in a way, that makes the project of this book even more resonant. This feels like a vital moment in which to reflect extra carefully about how and why live literature—and other embodied, arts-based experiences—matter to us. What do they offer that digital screenings can't? Once we return to a version of normality, should special efforts be made to fund and support live literature and other live arts-based events, even in the face of economic recession, now that there is so much available to stream online? If so, why? What makes these events meaningful and valuable?

Until now, live literature events have tended to be viewed rather narrowly by the literary industry and by scholars as functional sites for bookselling and publicity, as well as audience entertainment. But one of the initial impulses behind this project was my sense that there was surely more to them than that. Why have literary events become so popular and widespread in the twenty-first century? How does the trend relate to digitalisation—aren't the two antithetical? To what extent has live literature shaped literary culture? Does it materially affect the ways in which books and authors are interpreted and valued? Has it changed the roles of the author and the reader? Does performing at live literature events affect the ways in which authors write books? What do reader-audiences get out of live literature events? How far do reader-audiences' experiences diverge from each other, and from the experiences of author-performers? Does participation create meaningful communities, beyond the temporary physical gathering of bodies? What makes a live literary event enjoyable, meaningful and *memorable* for its participants? How can the experience of live literature be researched and communicated in a way that reflects its various qualities, layers, effects, and impacts?

Delving into questions of experience is inevitably a complex task. It is especially complex in the context of a live arts-based event that is attended by a large audience (or audience*s*, at a festival like Hay) and delivered by multiple performers. The nature of human experience and perception is just so incredibly multifaceted—especially in relation to literature and the other arts, when aesthetic elements are all mixed up with other multi-sensory, emotional, social, intellectual, cultural, geographical elements. So what are the best ways of researching and understanding participant experience at a live literature event, and any other arts-based event, come to that? And how to communicate the *value* of that participation? Is there a way of researching and writing about experience that reflects not only the variety of participants including audiences and performers—but also the complexity of their individual *and* collective experiences?

In this era of economic instability, funding cuts, and data dominance, it is vital for all arts and culture initiatives that seek to survive and thrive to be able to prove the value and impact of the particular event or experience that they offer. Consequently, cultural value has become a hot topic of research over the last few years. I have devised a new approach to researching and writing about live literature in this book that that aims to encompass multiple, complex elements of participant experience in order to reveal its cultural value in a meaningful way. I call it experiential literary ethnography.

In a nutshell, an experiential literary ethnography is a narrative crafted to *evoke* participant experience through creative writing techniques while also *examining* that experience. Reading an experiential literary ethnography should make you feel a bit like the writer has brought you along to a particular event with them, so that you too are immersed in it as a co-participant. You are prompted to notice a plethora of sensory, spatial and physical elements of the event experience as well as taking account of its content; you become actively involved in various informal conversations with other participants on site about their experiences and opinions; and you are led towards certain insights and reflective conclusions that collectively reveal key aspects of that event's identity, meaning and value.

# Plotting

For the rest of this chapter, I will tell you a bit about my background and perspective; sketch a portrait of the contemporary live literature scene and its historical backstory; discuss some of the recent developments in neuroscience and literary and cultural studies that illuminate the value and significance of live literature in the twenty-first century; introduce some key terms, including a couple that I've invented; and summarise what I'm doing in this book that's new.

Next, I will bring you along with me to two contrasting live literature events: the giant that is the **Hay Festival** in **Chapter 3**; and the intimate LGBTQ+ event that is the **Polari Salon** in **Chapter 4**. There you'll be able to listen into conversations I had in situ with author-performers including Colm *Tóibín*, Andrew O'Hagan, and Simon Armitage, prominent critics such as Gaby Wood and Alex Clark, and bookselling maestro James Daunt. There's even a cameo chat with Jude Law. These are all woven into conversations with reader-audiences, and my own descriptions, insights and reflections.

**Chapter 5** is where I go into the theory. I will expand on my distinctive approach to researching and writing about live literature, and why I have devised **experiential literary ethnography** as a means of investigating this subject. I will sketch out the landscape of relevant literary-cultural research to date, and explain how my ethnographic approach and interdisciplinary perspective contributes something genuinely new. I will set out how experiential literary ethnography works, talk about some of the theories and precedents underpinning it, and outline its key advantages and limitations. I will explain how it can be used more widely by arts organisations and scholars to demonstrate the cultural value of arts events. In **Chapter 6**, key insights from the book are combined with some wider observations and moulded into a conclusion; and a short Coda, in **Chapter 7**, offers an imaginary inhabitation of a legendary author-performer in action.

# Point(s) of View

I will take a moment now to talk a bit about my background, in order to shed light on my perspective on live literature, and my approach to researching and writing about it.

Firstly, I come to the subject as an enthusiastic reader of fiction, as well as a novelist and researcher. This perhaps predisposes me to be interested in live literature events—though, as this research reveals, not all fiction readers feel this way; some loathe the very idea of them!

My initial inspiration to start thinking about the significance of live literature events came back in 2013 when I attended the first ever literary festival to take place in Myanmar. I was living and working there as a human rights lawyer at the time, soon after the momentous beginning of the country's hopeful 'transition towards democracy', while also working on my own novel. Keen to find out about Burmese writing and literature, I went along to the festival, where I made friends with some local writers, and went on to attend locally-organised 'literary talks' with them—another form of live literature event which, I learned, functioned as a hotbed of resistance under censorship. Those encounters inspired me to write my first ethnographic book about literary culture in that country: *Saffron Shadows and Salvaged Scripts: Literary Life in Myanmar Under Censorship and in Transition* (2015). That book features extended interviews with Burmese writers from three generations, paired with new translations of their work, all contextualised by my own descriptive observations and reflections on how literature and literary life in the country was shaped by—and shaped—the political situation.

When I returned to the UK, I decided to start a PhD on live literature, in order to explore the relationship between literary events, books, readers, writers, voice and performance in more depth. Over the course of my live literature research I participated in hundreds of live literature events—mostly in the UK, but also beyond—and spoke to hundreds of participants. This process was helped by the fact that I was living in London, where there are multiple literary events happening every night of the week.

In 2014, early on in the course of this research, I ventured into the realm of live literature practice as a curator and director. I had been mulling over the lack of performative experimentation and cross-arts collaborations the live literature events that I had been to so far, in comparison with many theatre and live art performances I was attending at the same time—and so I decided to found my own experimental project: Ark. Ark set out to stage immersive short story performances in library and gallery spaces involving new commissions and cross-arts collaborations.[4] I curated each show around a theme, designed it in such a way as to maximise the experience of the audience as they moved around the, and brought together a set of diverse author-performers, actors, dancers, illustrators, musicians and other artists. Funded by Arts Council England, I put on shows in a small community library, a large public library, and the gargantuan British Library, and I was then commissioned to create more shows. I don't dwell on the Ark project in any more detail in this book—you can find out more about it on the website[5]—but it has shaped my perspective on the potential for more performative iterations of live literature, and also on the practical realities—and difficulties—of producing live events, as well as writing for and performing in them.

Since my first novel, *The Invisible Crowd*, was published in 2017, I have had another relevant role as an author, and an author-performer, of fiction—but you already know this from the prologue. Since the novel came out I have performed extracts from it, and spoken about it, at many live literature events, both live and online. That process has given me another set of insights into the experiences and perspectives of author-performers. My novel has also been read as a work of ethnographic fiction by anthropologists, in how it represents the cultural and systemic realities of the immigration and asylum system in the UK.[6] As such, it represents a strand of literary-ethnographic writing that I advocate for in this book.

Finally, I have past lives as a barrister and as a musician. These might seem entirely tangential—but I am sure that they have shaped my interdisciplinary approach and my outlook. My training in legal writing, for the purposes of courtroom advocacy, has made me particularly conscious of crafting writing in such a way as to have maximum clarity and persuasiveness when read aloud. My musical training, on the other hand, has made me sensitive to the rhythm, sounds, and affective qualities of language. Anthropologist Ruth Finnegan has pointed out that a sustained focus on orality when studying literature tends to lead to the conclusion that language and music are intimately intertwined.[7]

As Ursula K. Le Guin put it: 'The basic elements of language are physical: the noise words make, the sounds and silences that make the rhythms marking their relationships. Both the *meaning and* the beauty of the writing depend on these sounds and rhythms'.[8] That insight underpins this book.

## Live Literature: Some Contemporary Scene-Setting

Live literature has exploded this century.[9] It has spread across the UK—where my research has been focused—to most cities, towns, villages and remote islets you could name; and globally, too, to the point that live literature has now become not only an integral part of the global publishing industry, but a genre in its own right. While there were many earlier iterations of live literature, it was not until this century that literary festivals[10] and other forms of literary event[11] proliferated exponentially, forming a new wave, and that the term 'live literature' became common currency.[12]

The term 'live literature', and the phenomenon, are part of a wider preoccupation with 'liveness' across the arts and culture, which has gone hand-in-hand with the exponential rise of digitalisation. This shift has been most talked-about in relation to the music industry, and largely attributed to the sharp decline in album sales effectively forcing musicians to get up on stage to make an income[13]; but it affects all art forms.

Live literature can usefully be understood as an umbrella term encompassing a wide variety of live events in which literature is in some way performed. The funding body Arts Council England ('ACE') defines it, unofficially, as including any live performance events, including digital events, where the producer considers literature to be the dominant art form presented.[14] There is no clear evidence of when the term live literature came into common usage, and it does not appear in the current OED—though, according to ACE, it became commonly used in the late 1990s when literary festivals began to proliferate. Taking a longer view, versions of what are considered 'live literature' in the twenty-first century long predate the common understanding of literature itself. In Europe, since the late seventeenth century, the term 'literature' has been understood, primarily, to refer to lettered text, 'often printed in book form',[15] and has been approached with a textual focus throughout the history of literary studies—but anthropologists engaging with diverse literary cultures further afield have long viewed 'literature' as having a much broader scope.[16]

Many people, upon hearing the term 'live literature', immediately associate it with the literary festival. While literary festival formats vary, and the term 'literary festival' is not defined by the OED either, probably due to its relatively late arrival on the festival scene,[17] a literary festival is widely understood to be a meta-event[18] with a primary focus on literature—that is, an event that feature books, writing and words.[19] Different producers use various iterations of the term—'book festival', 'literature festival' and 'writers festival' being a few.[20] They are usually held on a single geographical site, where multiple individual live literature events are staged, the majority of which can be characterised by a standard format that involves a live on-stage conversation involving a chairperson and a panel of two or three author-performers, short reading(s) from their fiction, and an audience Q&A session.

Literary festivals are often seen as showcases of the places in which they are staged: a means of putting their heritage and cultural capital on the map.[21] Since 2011, for instance, Singapore's Government has run the Singapore Writers Festival, which has as its mission 'to not only present the world's major literary talents to the people of Singapore, but also to promote new and emerging Singapore and Asian writing to a wider public'[22]—and to demonstrate the country's status as an Asian and a global hub, in relation to its economic competitors; Shanghai, Beijing and Hong Kong all host literary festivals too. Most global literary festivals began life in the twenty-first century, including those held in Somaliland, East Africa; Galle, Sri Lanka; Accra, Ghana; Jaipur, India; Paraty, Brazil; Dubai; and even the Rock of Gibraltar. In the UK, and elsewhere, literary festivals have now diversified to form part of cross-arts festivals; notable British examples are Latitude Festival in Suffolk and Wilderness Festival in Oxfordshire, which feature literary tents, as well as theatre, cabaret, comedy and multiple music stages.

But there are many other forms of live literature besides the literary festival. They range from conversation-oriented literary events to all kinds of other literary performances, some of which have roots in theatre or performance art,[23] including word-based events where no physical books are involved. Live literature events usually involve verbal performance and embodied audiences—but not always. For instance, in one 'Live Writing' series, writers used digital technology to project and publish their writing as they composed, as a live public performance.[24] In another event I attended at an art gallery, text was projected digitally onto a wall along with imagery as a form of silent live 'telling'.[25] Live literature events also range vastly in scale between book shop readings, featuring a handful of people in a small room, to events in grand theatres or public spaces—like a performed reading of *The Iliad* that I attended in the British Museum foyer, which migrated physically to the Almeida Theatre, and was streamed online to over 50,000 people.[26]

Within the live literature scene, performed poetry is a long-established cultural practice. Poetry has always been more closely associated with orality and music than fiction, and consequently poetry-in-performance has been researched and written about more widely than fiction-in-performance.[27] Performed poetry incorporates the sub-genre of 'spoken word', or 'performance poetry'—terms that refer to poetry composed primarily for verbal performance rather than the page, and that also tends to have a rap-influenced aesthetic.[28] Writers working in this genre often hone their craft through competitive 'slam' nights. But 'spoken word' has increasingly crossed over into 'page poetry' publication during the last five years. In the UK, some 'spoken word artists', notably Hollie McNish and Kate Tempest, gained fame through YouTube, and went on to be published by top literary imprints: a form of recognition that has caused some controversy and division among poets.[29] The distinction between page and stage, though, has become increasingly blurry within literary culture, as live literature has evolved.

This has been spurred on as diversity has become more actively debated and advocated, particularly in terms of race, but also class, sexuality and gender. There has been increased exposure over the last five to ten years of how writers of colour have long been excluded from traditional publishing, along with the forms and styles that they often espouse, and how they continue to be excluded. Diversity in publishing is increasing, but not fast enough.[30] Important research into diversity is being produced by Melanie Ramdarshan Bold,[31] Anamik Saha[32] and others—but much more needs to be done, both in scholarship and in practice.

The performance poetry or spoken word scene, partly because of its links with rap, and partly because its accessible slam event formats, has always been more diverse than the 'page' scene. Several live literature projects have focused on giving platforms to underrepresented authors, often by encompassing these forms. A notable example is Speaking Volumes, founded by Sarah Sanders and Sharmilla Beezmohun after they left roles at PEN International[33]; they have gone on to produce many live literature events featuring literature in translation, including by European writers in the UK, and frequently showcasing writers of colour. Projects like this are vital to increase the diversity of live literature, and of literary culture in general.

Live literature also includes the newly-revitalised genre of literary salons: a smaller, more intimate form of event than the literary festival. Several of the contemporary literary salons were initially founded by writers seeking to create a network to promote and perform from their own and friends' new books, but have since expanded to draw in significant audiences. The most well-known in the UK salon is Damian Barr's, which brings in the country's biggest literary names; but there are many others, including Polari: the LGBTQ+ salon that I explore in depth in this book. Publishers soon cottoned on to the new popularity of the salon when it re-emerged, and have now begun hosting their own; 4th Estate a literary imprint of HarperCollins, is an example.[34]

Popular literary entertainment nights, staged after dark, have also populated the live literature landscape over the last two decades. Some feature competition between author-performers, akin to the slam events that have long underpinned spoken word. Literary Death Match,[35] for instance, founded in the USA in 2006 and then brought over to the UK, became a popular example.[36] Other literary entertainment nights feature live music performances alongside performed fiction readings;

one such event is the Book Slam, a 'shindig' co-founded by a novelist and a musician.[37] Again, publishers soon caught on to the potential of this live event concept; the literary publisher Faber, for instance, launched the Faber Social[38]: an informal event involving performed readings and sometimes live music, often hosted in bars and festivals.

Live literature includes oral storytelling, which has remained the lynchpin of literary culture in many parts of the world. Storytelling has increased vastly in popularity in Western countries over the last two decades, alongside other forms of live literature, spearheaded by The Moth[39]: a US-based event series founded in 1997—just one year before Hay—which also involves a competitive slam element.[40]

Some labelled as theatre performances can also be seen as forms of live literature. These events tend to be focused around extended prose monologues or storytelling elements, and to be staged, often in theatre spaces, in performative ways, without reference to printed texts. The show *Gatz*,[41] created by Elevator Repair Service, is a rare example of a novel, *The Great Gatsby*, performed in its textual entirety in a single show, by actors, as a play. Daniel Kitson's off-kilter, interactive monologue-based work[42] is a contrasting example of theatre crossing into both comedy and live literature; another is Ross Sutherland's experimental poetic, live performances, that meld memoir with analogue video of pop culture classics.[43] Theatrical adaptations of novels can be hugely successful; the staged version of *The Curious Incident of the Dog in the Night Time* is just one example—but most participants would regard such productions as pure theatre.

Live literature can also manifest itself as live art or performance art events, which are often held in gallery spaces among visual and performance art communities, and where performances often interact in creative and visual ways with printed texts. One of the most experimental examples that I have experienced was 'Plastic Words', hosted by the gallery Raven Row in London: a series of events, including live literary performances, curated by a group of artists and writers, that set out to 'mine the contested space between contemporary literature and art', and reflect on the 'overlaps, parallels, tangents and interferences between them'.[44]

A fascinating series of events that I used to attend in London was 'Homework': a 'night of literary miscellany' created by a group of performance poets, whose work was expanding into other forms of literature, including fiction, theatre and scriptwriting.[45] Each night was curated around a theme, for which they would each produce new, experimental work for performance, often involving live interactions with other media like PowerPoint and video or props. Staged in the retro Bethnal Green Working Men's Club in the trendy part of East London, Homework always opened with an entertaining cult film quiz to get the audience interacting and to cultivate a deliberately playful vibe. While seriously experimental in the work produced, the author-performers actively encouraged the audience not to receive their work too seriously.

Once I began to research live literature I noticed how few and far between such creative approaches were. Curious about the possibilities for combining art forms and pushing the performativity of live literature through curation, I founded my own small experimental live literature project, Ark.[46] Soon after that, a similar project called Story Machine, supported by the Writers' Centre in Norwich, staged an immersive show in a warehouse featuring short story performances in conjunction with other art forms, with audiences given the option to choose the order of stories and to navigate themselves around the space.[47] Echoing the *Gatz* concept, in 2015 the Southbank Centre staged a complete performance of *Moby Dick*, unabridged, over four days, produced by a company called The Special Relationship, directed by the writer Jared McGinnis,[48] who feels strongly that, when it comes to literary events, 'the event's the thing'.[49]

All around the UK, particularly in the bigger cities, there are now plenty of live literature events and genres and experiments evolving and overlapping and interacting with each other and with other art forms. In Edinburgh, UNESCO City of Literature, for instance, Neu! Reekie!, an artist collective-turned- 'literary production house', stages events that it describes as a 'delicious feast of spoken word, music, animation and film fusion' involving a 'wild mixture of different performers and styles as well as an enthusiastic audience'.[50]

In many ways, live literature is diversifying and evolving in more performative and experimental directions, as well as expanding. That being said, ACE's live literature specialist admitted to me that they did not get as many genuinely experimental and performative live literature proposals as they would like, partly because such events were seen as hard to market, compared to theatre, for example. This tends to be because many people tend to automatically associate live literature with the conversation-based event format that dominates at literary festivals.[51]

## Live Literature: A Backstory

That was a rough sketch of the contemporary live literature scene in the UK. But as I alluded to earlier, live literature has far deeper, wider-reaching roots than that, extending back before the twenty-first century, before books began to be published as pretty printed objects, and beyond 'Western' literary-cultural practices.

Live literature can be said to have had a deep significance across all human cultures for as long as our species has had language, in the form of storytelling. Every one of us tells stories to each other as a way to connect and to forge relationships, communities, and, as individuals, to underpin and understand our place in the world. Oral narrative has been held up by linguistic anthropologists as 'constitutive of social life'[52]—and fictional storytelling, in particular, as an 'ability that defines the human species even more than the use of language'.[53]

Oral prose-poetry dates back to before the ancient Greeks, with *The Iliad* and *The Odyssey* both being based on more ancient legends,[54] while the oral performance of short prose fiction is recorded as far back as 100 BC, in the form of the lost *Milesiaka*.[55] The literary competitiveness that marks out many contemporary literary events with 'slam' elements was present among the ancient Greeks.[56] Classicist Rosalind Thomas argues that most of their literature took place 'in situations of contest or antagonistic exchange',[57] and that, by focusing on texts documented in writing, scholarship has tended to marginalise the fundamental role of performativity in the social meaning of those texts.[58]

Performativity was central to Roman literary culture, too; 'in Cicero's day authors ready to launch their newest work would gather friends at home or in a public hall for a spirited recitation or reading. Audiences would cry out when they liked a particular passage. Nervous authors enlisted their friends to lend support, and sometimes even filled seats with hired "clappers".[59] Evidence from Sumeria to India reveals oral literature's historic role in communicating both mythology and 'news', before the use of writing.[60]

After Gutenberg and the development of the printing press during the fifteenth century, reading aloud remained a core part of Western European literary culture. This persisted during the growth of the print publishing industry, which generated new business-focused events; the Frankfurt Book Fair began in the mid-sixteenth century.[61] It was only after a widening of access to printed books that silent reading began to be a common practice.[62] By the eighteenth century, when the novel emerged and bloomed as a literary form in Britain, literacy rates were still fairly low, and books were expensive and not necessarily easy to come by. Reading novels aloud to groups, largely made up of family and friends in domestic settings, remained a popular pastime, and continued across socio-economic groups well into the nineteenth century.[63] As several of Jane Austen's novels illustrate, skill at this practice was considered an 'art'[64] and highly valued—to the point of being considered a way to judge the reader's character, and even their soul.[65]

Literary salons, which Jürgen Habermas singled out as a key ingredient in the rise of the liberal and democratic public sphere,[66] became widespread in the seventeenth century and grew further in the eighteenth century alongside book clubs, reading parties, coffee houses and accessible political journalism.[67] The salons often involved performed readings of new works of literature by notable authors before publication of the text, and by emerging authors seeking networks, audiences and patrons, and extended discussions about literature, 'literariness'[68] and society. Meanwhile, reading parties were a popular and more class-diverse form of event, where participants would gather socially to read aloud from published texts, not usually in the presence of the author.[69] Both were a significant part of European cultural life until the mid-nineteenth century, when they were—until recently—thought to have died out.[70]

In last two decades of the eighteenth century, there was an 'explosion of writing and publication',[71] when books and other periodicals became radically cheaper and easier to access.[72] This corresponded with the rise of Romanticism across the arts, with its emphasis on individuality, feeling and inspiration as opposed to classical form and order, elevating the persona of the artist in society. By the nineteenth century, when serial publications of novels became popular, prominent authors of fiction were able to reach much wider readerships. They also began to take a more active role in the public sphere[73]—in part by performing readings from their work at events, helping to generate still-wider audiences. Dickens's staged readings of his novels, which lasted up to three hours at a time, packed out theatres and halls in London and on tours throughout Britain and America, with audiences numbering up to 2000.[74] Having trained as an actor, Dickens would edit his texts for performance, and rehearse them extensively, hundreds of times, learning them largely by heart, to maximise the impact of his delivery, while also employing his own lighting and stage manager: evidence of the value he placed on the performativity of these events.[75] The effects were striking; his performed readings triggered dramatic physical and emotional responses from his audiences, from fainting to sobbing and fighting over who could touch his props.[76] Dickens gave so much energy to these performance tours that they are said to have hastened his death.[77]

Meanwhile, though, the practice of silent reading in domestic spheres spread, as books' ownership and availability increased.[78] According to Walter J. Ong, this wider move from sonic orality to silent engagement with printed books was a kind of 'silencing', and effectively removed the body from literature.[79] Critiquing Ong's take on this, Steven Connor has pointed out that silent reading also involves an embodied 'inner sonorousness',[80] including 'inner speech'[81]—an experience the poet Denise Riley has explored philosophically as a 'feeling of hearing',[82] and which is borne out by contemporary neuroscience: MRI scanning has revealed that silent reading stimulates the auditory cortex.[83]

Still, the nineteenth century did see social practices of embodied, verbal literary performance diminish significantly in Western cultures. Dickens would prove to be not only exceptional as a performer of his own fiction, but an exception to this wider shift. This was reflected in education systems. Until the late nineteenth century, oratory pervaded school and university curricula, reflecting the social and cultural value allotted to public speaking, which was seen as a core skill underpinning civic life,[84] but it largely died out after that in the UK. I remember vividly the ceremonial experience of being admitted to the 'Utter Bar' in 2007, as a brand new barrister, and being struck by the importance of the 'utterance' to all forms of education in centuries past—in contrast to most of my years of school and university, where the written word was central, and silent reading and writing were the primary modes of engaging with it. This may now be starting to change. At Stanford University, for instance, where entrepreneurialism is at the heart of the culture in the region, first year students all take a course in public speaking—but this is unusual, certainly in the UK.

As book production industrialised and commercialised, individual silent reading increased still further. Broadly speaking, from the mid-nineteenth century to late twentieth century, a reader's typical experience of literature and literary culture would involve buying a printed book or borrowing one from the library, and, after the completion of silent reading, perhaps some limited communal sharing of that experience, through comparable private conversations or joining a subscription book club.[85]

As for a typical author: after handing their manuscript over to their publisher, they were largely free to retreat to the desk and work, silently—or so it is often assumed—on the next book. This, in part, was because authors tended to have more sustainable incomes than they do now,[86] and also because the expectation of their role, within literary culture, was primarily to write books. From the twentieth century onwards, agents became books' gatekeepers and the advocates of most fiction in relation to print publishers; print publishers were the gatekeepers and advocates in relation to bookselling; booksellers promoted and distributed the books to readers; and literary critics were respected authorities on books' quality.[87]

The late twentieth century ushered in a range of new literary events, including festivals. The Cheltenham Literature Festival was launched decades earlier than most, in 1949.[88] In the 1970s, publishers started putting on experimental events to promote reading and literacy, like London's Bedford Square Book Bang in 1971.[89] Bookshop-based literary readings for fiction writers became popular in the USA in the 1970s too.[90] The emergence of such events was linked to changes in the structure of the publishing industry and specifically the marketing of literature[91]: the 1970s was a decade characterised by a significant intensification in the marketing activity surrounding fiction, in the wake of an increase in financing available to publishing, alongside conglomeration and globalisation. A new wave of marketing, including through live events, significantly affected literature's reception.[92]

A couple more book festivals launched in the 1980s—notably the Edinburgh International Book Festival in 1983, and Hay in 1988. This corresponded with the beginning of an era of 'corporate buyouts, mergers' and 'downsizing' across the publishing industry[93] in the 1980s–1990s, as globalisation accelerated and digitalisation crept in. Transnational 'book days' were invented in the mid-1990s—UNESCO's World Book and Copyright Day is an example, inaugurated in 1995.[94] The mid-1990s also marked the arrival of a little start-up online bookstore called Amazon.

In twenty-first century it is hard to imagine a world without Amazon. A now-ubiquitous household name,[95] the company has transmogrified into a gargantuan publisher, producer and global retailer of innumerable other products. Amazon now owns Goodreads: a social reading site where non-professionalised readers can comment upon, review, promote and share their reading, and it has dominated in the evolution e-books and self-publishing to become part of the mainstream.

Meanwhile, a profusion of blogs, vlogs and other social media have become significant contributors to literary-cultural conversation,[96] alongside the traditional literary press.

All these changes have contributed to profound shifts in the structure and power dynamics of literary production, creating new economic imperatives for the industry's stakeholders. Authors' incomes have plummeted, partly due to e-book piracy; in 2018, the average income of an author in the UK was £10,500—more than £5000 below the lowest sustainable income—with only one-third of all authors able to make their living from writing, and women authors' incomes just 75% that of their male counterparts.[97] Publishers are generally doing better than authors; but they, along with specialist physical booksellers, have become increasingly David-like in their quest to keep competing with Amazon's Goliath[98]—though the global conglomerate publishing groups appear resilient.

This has caused the roles of all stakeholders in the publishing industry to change in fundamental ways: booksellers have been forced to become curators, baristas and event hosts; publishers have had to step up their role as publicists; agents have had to increase their editorial role to fill the gap; critics have become marginalised as taste shapers; audiences have become online critics and live audiences; and authors have had to become self-publicists and performers.[99]

## Choice Bombardment: Digitalisation and Curation

In this competitive, digitalising environment, among the mass proliferation of information and entertainment available online, it has become harder than ever to promote and sell books effectively—to capture the attention of readers and direct them to a single title or author when they are bombarded with so much choice. This brings me to one important function of live literature and a likely cause of its rise: as a form of curation.

Curation, defined by Michael Bhaskar at the outset of his 2016 book on the subject, means 'using acts of selection and arrangement (but also refining, reducing, displaying, simplifying, presenting and explaining) to add value'. All live literature events are forms of curation; any literary event producer makes a curatorial choice in selecting works of fiction and authors to feature.

In comparison with the curation offered by booksellers in any bookshop, the selection at a live literature event is smaller, more targeted, and more comprehensive. The reader-audience is introduced to each text and/or author involved in some depth over the course of an event.

All forms of curation have become more important in a digital age involving a greater-than-ever mass of available information, art and sources of entertainment.[100] Since the arrival of the behemoth that is Amazon, the impact of curation is magnified. Amazon and other online bookstores offer a near-infinite choice of reading material, in forms ranging from hardback and paperback to e-Book and audiobook. Any individual book becomes a needle in a gigantic haystack.

Potential readers have instant access to a myriad of other literary sources online too, including literary podcasts, book blogs and BookTube videos,[101] in addition to online literary articles and traditional literary criticism.

Face-to-face contact with audiences through live events clearly helps to promote and sell copies of books, both physical and digital. Publishers and authors know this, and it is evidenced—in part, at least—by the significant spike in book sales at the big literary festivals.[102]

The extent to which participants experience live literature events as a form of curation, though—is debateable, and is most certainly under-explored. In this book, I will show that most reader-audiences do not choose to participate in a live literature event primarily as a way to pick which titles to buy or read. There are many other important elements of the experience that they value.

For authors, performing at live events is often seen as a platform to make their work stand out from the rest and as a way to help the publisher to sell more copies. Live literature can also be a useful source of money at a historical moment when, partly due to digitalisation, most authors' incomes are plummeting.[103] Despite this, many of the major literary festivals have regularly asked authors to perform free of charge. This has begun to change in the UK, after public revelations that certain major festivals had been inviting authors to perform without offering them fees, and then turning a profit—this prompted a vigorous campaign by the Society of Authors in 2015, spearheaded by author Philip Pullman.[104] But this situation and debate both point to a wider underlying undervaluing of the labour and skill of authors as performers in live literature events—and to a general a neglect of the performative and aesthetic elements of live literature events. This seems likely to be the result of an assumption on the part of the literary industry that live literature's value mostly lies in its economic impact by making certain key authors and titles more publicly visible. It also indicates that a lack of attention has been paid to live literature's value as a form of literary experience.

In this book, I argue that participant experiences at live literature events have more significance, value and impact for literary culture than is often assumed—including in the ways that those experiences shape reader-audiences' interpretations and evaluations of the texts presented on stage, and shape author-performers creative outputs and perspectives. This makes live literature events into uniquely powerful forms of curation, which can have far deeper and longer-lasting effects than other forms of publicity or marketing, or the placement of a book face-out on a bookshop shelf—welcome though such placement is for any author.

## The Science of Experience in a Digital World: Attention, Liveness, Performance, Value

We are experiencing a 'crisis of attention' in the digitalising twenty-first century—certainly according to philosopher Martin Crawford, who has emphasised the emotional stress that individuals endure as a result of digital technologies that constantly force them into a battle over where to direct their attention.[105] The 'time–space compression'[106] of contemporary life, including the rapid digitalisation of media and communications, means that an abundance of information and content can be delivered to anyone on the globe in seconds. This, Crawford argues, is causing our 'mental lives' to become 'fragmented' to the point that 'what is at stake often seems to be nothing less than the question of whether one can maintain a coherent self' rather than 'just flitting about'.[107]

The notion of a 'crisis' of attention is problematic now that digitalisation is so integral to our lives. We need to accept that we now live in an 'attention economy', or, as Yves Citton characterises it, an attention 'ecology',[108] in which attention has become a more precious and limited resource—but also a resource that is more difficult to manage for those seeking to capture it.[109] As Philip Tassi puts it, because 'digital convergence' has transformed us into 'continual transmitters and receivers of information of all kinds' on smartphones and other devices,[110] it is harder than ever for communicators, including artists and writers, 'not only to establish contact but also to attract the attention of and hold the interest of the recipient'.[111]

Fiction reading has been profoundly affected. Sven Bikerts has argued that, in a 'saturated digital media environment', a particular type of literary reading has been lost forever', as the 'single-track concentration' of reading has been 'hijacked' by the 'restless, grazing behaviour of clicking and scrolling'.[112] But, as Brian Glavey has suggested, this cultural shift can be seen as a 'double-sided coin' for writers, and for the health of arts and culture: while it is now a greater challenge to fight for the attention spotlight, this has made many artists focus on trying to capture the essence of experience, often with fertile creative results.[113]

Of course, capturing the attention of an audience has been a concern of writers and speakers ever since Aristotle's *Rhetoric*—but digitalisation has significantly raised the stakes. The attention ecology that we are living in reinforces the value of curation across all forms of culture, including the arts and literature. Audiences need extra help to choose what to focus on and engage with.

The attention ecology is also said to have led to an increase in the cultural value of live, embodied experiences, relative to digital alternatives. Futurologist James Wallman has persuasively argued that the materialism of the twentieth century has been replaced by experientialism in the twenty-first.[114] This has increased the economic value of experiences that involve the body as well as the mind. A premium has been placed on experiences that succeed in immersing people in the present moment and in a particular place or story—and in creating lasting memories.

All this helps to explain the contemporary preoccupation with liveness throughout arts and culture, including literary culture. Live events require that people engage with the present moment, at least conceptually. It also helps to explain the new cultural buzzword: 'immersive'. This descriptor is increasingly used for arts events and experiences of many different kinds. It refers to events that seek to drench participants' attention in an all-encompassing live experience, both in the 'now' of the event itself, and beyond, in the form of memory. The term 'immersive' highlights the intensity of the experience and suggests its experiential value. An example of the immersive event trend is the stellar rise of Punchdrunk[115]: a theatre company that stages highly interactive, site-specific performances, in which each audience member often determines the 'narrative' of their experience. Another is Secret Cinema[116]: an organisation that creates immersive live audience experiences in found spaces around screenings of classic films. Both attract huge audiences.

Many performance studies researchers have long argued that live, embodied performances have a special quality that makes them distinct from digital-only forms—but there was plenty of heated debate in that field as digitalisation became more mainstream. Back in 1993, Peggy Phelan famously claimed that: 'Performance's only life is in the present. Performance cannot be saved, recorded, documented... once it does so, it becomes something other than performance'.[117] Philip Auslander dismissed that idea out of hand in his 1999 book on liveness, in which he rejected any substantive differences between 'live and mediatized cultural forms'.[118] But nine years later, Erika Fischer-Lichte countered Auslander with a powerful, nuanced argument for the distinct value of live performance that involves the 'bodily co-presence of actors and spectators' in a particular place and time. This process, she argued, creates 'feedback loop' between participants, whereby the presence and continual reactions of the audience to the performance turns them into active co-creators, along with the main performers, which allows the performance to feel spontaneous,[119] and creates a kind of community among participants'.[120]

Recent neuroscience has confirmed the validity of this feedback loop idea in live, embodied performance, and has revealed still more about the distinctive impact that live performance has on participants, particularly in the context of events involving storytelling and the communication of ideas.

Another neuroscientific revelation of the past decade is that practice of reading fiction—silently, it is assumed—significantly improves readers' Theory of Mind: the ability to empathise with another person's emotions and reactions.[121] New evidence suggests that this translates to fiction performed at live, embodied events—even that the impact of this process is heightened, now that so many of our normal, everyday communications are digital. This is because live, embodied events that engage with audiences' emotions have been shown to be considerably more effective and impactful than other forms of communication, including digitally-screened events.

Tali Sharot discusses much of this emerging research in her book, *The Influential Mind* (2017). She points out that the 'tsunami of information we are receiving today can make us even less sensitive to data'.[122] As a result, data 'is often not the answer when it comes to changing minds' or in making an impact on people's value systems, in comparison with forms of communication that engage their *emotion*. This finding, Sharot admits, came initially as a 'terrible blow' to the scientist in her.[123] Live, embodied interactions with human speakers that engage with participants' emotions have been proven such effective forms of communication. This is partly through an incredible, hidden process of brain synchronisation. MRI scanners have revealed that, as individuals listen to powerful speeches as part of a single audience, their brains 'tick together', including in the regions that process emotion and enable empathy—thus proving that the performance does *more* than just capture people's attention,[124] which is already difficult enough in the attention ecology.

The impact of live, embodied performance may be further enhanced by the work of mirror neurons. Mirror neurons are claimed by some scientists to cause us to 'feel what other people feel' while watching them speak, and thus enable us to 'respond compassionately to other people's emotional states'.[125] In the context of live performance, they effectively work to 'couple' audience members with performers[126]: the psychological state of the listener equates to that of the speaker, making it more likely that the listener will process incoming information in a similar manner to how the speaker sees it'.[127] When listening to a story that involves the expression of emotion, through tone of voice and content, listeners' neural activity patterns first begin to match, and then anticipate what the storyteller is going to say, enabling even better comprehension and engagement.[128] This makes it more likely that, by communicating in a way that engages emotions in a live performance, a performing speaker can persuade an audience to adopt their point of view, and to value what they are saying.[129]

These neuroscientific insights, produced over the last decade, have required a major revision of widely held beliefs in relation to human biology. Mirror neuron activity patterns reveal that our ability to empathise is a 'building block of our sociality'.[130] The proven centrality of emotion to our decision-making makes clear that our evolution has simply not kept pace with our technological developments. Our brains are 'still designed to transmit emotions to each other more quickly and easily than rational ideas'.[131]

Just being present in an audience at a live event, alongside other bodies, has also been proven to affect our responses and values in *collective* ways. Audiences observe and respond to the emotional reactions of others around them, as well as the performer on stage, and this process shapes how the entire group receives and evaluates what is being performed. As Sharot explains it: our 'brains operate according to the rule that what is desired by others is likely valuable'.[132] A group of scientists and psychologists at UCL, led by Joseph Devlin, have made fascinating discoveries about the impact of live, embodied performance events on audiences, including that audience members' hearts beat together when they are engaging in the experience.[133] They are pioneering various technologies to explore different psycho-biological reactions that are suggestive of impact and value of live event experiences, including cardiac activity, blood pressure, electro-dermal activity and electroencephalographic activity, and measurements of motor behaviour such as facial expression changes and body movements.[134]

This all supports Le Guin's observation about live literature: that 'oral performance is a powerful bonding force' that 'bonds people physically and psychically',[135] creating a 'community of body and mind'[136]; and that, therefore, 'listening is not a reaction, it is a *connection*. Listening to a conversation or a story at an event, we don't so much respond as join in – we become part of the action'.[137]

Neuroscience has also shed light on how and why author-performers value their experiences of performing at live literature event: the activity triggers *reward* mechanisms in the brain. Brain imaging has now shown that 'the opportunity to impart your knowledge to others is internally rewarding'—so, when authors get the chance to 'communicate their pearls of wisdom to others' through performance, their 'brain's reward centre' is 'strongly activated'.[138] Audience reactions at live events—like laughter, applause, and questions—materially enhance the impact of the performance experience.[139]

Conversely, where an author-performer does *not* receive an observable response at a live event, it can feel acutely disheartening. Le Guin describes her own experience of this with typical acuity through the example of a reading she once gave in Santa Barbara:

> They had no lights on the audience, so I was facing this black chasm, and no sound came out of it. Total silence. Reading to pillows. Despair. Afterwards the students came around all warm and affectionate and said they'd loved it, but it was too late, I was a wreck. They'd been so laid back or so respectful or something they hadn't given me any response, and so they hadn't been working with me, and you can't do it alone.[140]

This shows how the dynamics of an event, and of the audience participation, can materially alter an author-performer's relationship with her own literary text, and affect her sense of worth and identity as an author.

## Literature Beyond the Book

In the light of all this new science on participant experience at live events, and the fact of live literature's growth in contemporary culture, it might seem bizarre that live literature has barely been researched or written about, until very recently.

One reason for this is probably that literary studies as a discipline has long been focused on—even obsessed by—the text,[141] at the expense of the author, and certainly ideas about voice and orality.

The first scholars who looked at literature in terms of orality were anthropologists in the 1970s, who produced studies of oral storytelling in cultural contexts beyond the white-dominated, economically-privileged cultures of the 'West'.[142] Some of these anthropologists, like Ruth Finnegan, tried to persuade literary studies scholars to take orality seriously in relation to 'Western' literature too, but nothing much changed.[143]

In the early 2000s, sociologists began to pay attention to the emerging phenomenon of literary festivals in Western countries—but most of those studies were ultimately dismissive of festivals' literary-cultural value, effectively writing them off as low-brow commercialised arenas for publicity and celebrity encounters.[144]

Since then, publishing studies has emerged as a sub-field of sociology, and studies of festivals have become more nuanced and less snooty, and have incorporated more qualitative research. Millicent Weber's book on literary festivals is the most notable example, and it makes a strong positive case for their cultural significance.[145]

The field of literary studies, though, has broadly remained distant from such developments in what are seen as 'other' disciplines. This is partly due to a legitimate sense that such studies, particularly sociologically-oriented studies that are focused on data, tend to neglect literary texts, which, in their view, literature should be all about.

But it does not have to be this way.

## Listening Bodies: New Perspectives on Literature and Readers

In the last few years, the significance of the human body for literary reception has slowly begun to be taken on board by some literary scholars, along with linked issues of attention, experience and phenomenology.[146] Poet Denise Riley has reflected on more neuroscientific evidence that confirms something she had long suspected: that silent reading remains closely linked to speech. People not only hear 'internal voices' while reading silently,[147] they 'subvocalize', making tiny movements in the mouth using the muscles involved in speech. Riley calls this evidence of the inherent 'sociability of language'[148] which 'throws us back on the materiality of words'.[149]

The audiobook boom over the last few years—another change accelerated by Amazon, who own Audible—has triggered dynamic new research which demands that literature be understood differently, and that more attention be paid to the voice and performance. Matthew Rubery's landmark history of the 'talking book' offers fresh, new ways of thinking

about literature, and many of his insights point to meaningful interpretations of literary texts, as well as illuminating aspects of literary
culture.[150]

Audiobooks have long been dismissed by literary scholars with
'hostility',[151] Rubery claims, on the basis that listening was seen as
a 'lesser form' of experiencing fiction than silent reading—but early
audiobook listeners' letters reveal that they were intensely engaged with
narrators' voices and delivery styles, and that this significantly affected
their reception of literary texts. One letter to an audiobook producer,
from a blind reader in the mid-1970s, argues forcefully that narrators should *not* 'impose' their own 'interpretations' on the reading, but
should instead allow blind people to find their 'own meanings' in the
text, in a comparable way to sighted people—which rules out attempts to
'act' characters, imitating, for instance, male or female voices. A 'straight
reading, in a normal tone of voice, at a normal speed' was said to be the
ideal.[152]

Audiobook producers issued directions to their narrating actors along
similar lines.[153] The US Library of Congress issued their own set of
guidelines directing narrators to read in a way that was '(a) appropriate
to the book, (b) sympathetic but not exaggerated, (c) restrained but not
stilted or mechanical, (d) attentive to the sense of the book and skilful
in securing proper emphasis'[154]—placing weight, here, on seeking to
convey an *authorial intention* of the meaning of a text through its oral
delivery, in a way that is clearly intended to apply to narrators other
than the author. More letters revealed the positive impact that a good
'reading' could have—including that good narrators made books 'come
alive', and making the listeners 'think about a book's language in a new
way', by bringing out 'even the smallest, most obscure, most elusive and
most subtle nuances'.[155]

Rubery argues that audiobook narrators materially 'influence a story's
reception' through factors like 'accent, cadence, emphasis, inflection,
pitch, pronunciation, resonance, pace, tone, and any eccentricities that
stand out'. These sonic details *matter* for interpretation'.[156] Each individual human voice is as unique as a fingerprint,[157] except it has more
impact; humans have an innate ability to distinguish and interpret subtle
characteristics that make each voice unique—and voice quality can have

an emotional impact 'at a gut level'.[158] Many listeners quoted by Rubery express their strong feeling that an author's voice offers a 'more accurate reading than could be gained from the page alone'. They believe that they can 'detect the author's personality through tones, inflections and vocal mannerisms kept off the printed page'.[159]

Not all authors are deemed successful audiobook narrators of their own work, though—either by reader-listeners, or even by themselves. Toni Morrison apparently found Faulkner's drawling renditions of his own novels 'horrifying'.[160] Dylan Thomas, renowned as a narrator of his own work, opined on the subject too, warning of 'the twin perils of mawkish, melodramatic readings on the one hand, and flat, detached readings on the other hand'.[161]

Le Guin vividly describes her experience of witnessing Dylan Thomas performing his poetry live on stage:

> You know the Caedmon tape of him reading at Columbia in 1952? I was there at that reading, and you can hear me – in the passionate silence of the audience listening to that passionate voice. Not a conspiracy of silence, but a participatory silence, a community collaboration in letting him let the word loose aloud. I left that reading feeling two feet above the ground, and it changed my understanding of the art forever.[162]

Her description here illustrates incisively how the experience of hearing a literary text performed as part of an embodied live performance, in a physical space, can have a profound effect: it can change how the person values a text or author, how they perceive and participate in literary culture.

The experience can affect author-performers, too. Le Guin confessed, with typical self-deprecating wit, while describing her experience of recording her audiobook, *Gwilan's Harp*: 'I had to read it in my own God-given croak; and in the corner of my mind, all the while, Dylan Thomas was weeping softly'.[163]

Perhaps these new developments indicate that a burgeoning change is finally in progress: a new understanding of literature in the twenty-first century as an assemblage of cultural practices that exist, and have value, beyond the page and the screen—that always involve bodies, voices, performance, places, spaces, emotions, and communities, as well as individual intellects and judgements.

## Authors as Performers

It is not only scholars and publishers who have neglected to think much about the experience of participants at live literature events until now—this is true of authors, too, and the literary community of which they are a part.

One illustration of this is the way in which small live literature events are often referred to as 'readings', and live up (or perhaps down) to that description. Poet and multidisciplinary artist, Steven J. Fowler, has written about his growing awareness of the culture of 'readings':

> When I was to read for the first time in public... I immediately felt, along with painful nerves, I was *performing* the act of reading. It struck me immediately that everything from the tone of my voice, the clothes I wore, the content (and length!) of my introduction utterly changed the impression of my actual poem and its semantic meaning. This is a fact so obvious to be meaningless or revelatory. To me it was the latter.

However, he soon became aware, after attending 'poetry reading after poetry reading', 'how extraordinarily formal and full of pretence, the notion was' in literary culture more widely, and how *'utterly uninterrogated as a thing'*.[164]

Many authors of fiction identify the core of their role as being the act of writing—in the sense of silently composing texts to be read on the page, as opposed to creating texts for vocal narration or performance. The prospect of performing those texts at live events often gets neglected, and this can lead to unpleasant surprises.

In Robin Robertson's edited collection, *Mortification: Writers' Stories of Their Public Shame* (2003), poets and novelists describe their experiences of their public-facing activities, including live literature events, focusing on incidents of humiliation—and there are many. Jonathan Coe begins his contribution with a rhetorical echo of his brief: '*One* story, of a bad experience in front of the reading public? Just the one? That's impossible'.

Many of these humiliations are caused by arriving at an event to find a negligible audience—which is almost always a consequence of the lack of attention given to the event experience by producers, and not the fault of the disappointed author. Coe and several others describe travelling long distances and getting psyched up to perform at an event that is ultimately attended by just one or two people.

But there is also a sense that many authors simply don't feel comfortable with the expectation to perform, even—especially—when they *do* get the chance to perform at well-attended events. John Banville writes about speaking at the same event as a Pulitzer prize-winning author, and feeling convinced that people there were only tolerating him as a necessary appendage to the other author—and then, at the book signing, being approached by just three customers, one of whom confided: 'I'm not going to buy a book… but you looked so lonely there, I thought I'd come and talk to you'.[165]

Author John Lanchester tells of how he once accidentally offended a group of other, more famous members of a panel he was part of at a literary event, by intimating that he was the only one who had actually written his own book. He uses this as a springboard to fume at the entire culture of live literature events on the basis that they foreground the author rather than the text:

> The truth is that the whole contemporary edifice of readings and tours and interviews and festivals is based on a mistake. The mistake is that we should want to meet the writers we admire… that meeting them in the flesh somehow adds to the experience of reading their work. The idea is that the person is the real thing, whereas the writing is an excrescence or epiphenomenon. But that's not true. The work is the real thing, and it is that to which readers should direct their attention.[166]

The Nobel Prize-winning author J. M. Coetzee has made clear that he shares this view. Coetzee is notorious for avoiding all forms of publicity particularly events and publications for which he is expected to participate in discussions, and offer opinions about matters of and beyond his fiction. In his speech on receiving the Nobel in 2003, he critiqued the idea of the author as a 'sage' who could 'offer an authoritative word on our times'; that idea might have been present at the time the Nobel Prize was inaugurated in 1901, he argued, but was 'dead today'—and he would, in any case, 'feel very uncomfortable in the role'.[167] He proceeded to write a semiparodic, quasi-autofictional novel exploring this idea.[168] Peter McDonald, an expert on Coetzee, has called his approach a deeply-rooted philosophical and ethical one; Coetzee has 'dedicated his life to defending literature as a legitimate mode of public intervention in its own right, not to escape the burden of history or politics but to confront them on his own resolutely literary terms'.[169]

Essentially, this is an argument that literature—texts—must stand on their own two feet, and must be respected and valued for what they are.

But how many authors can afford to step out of the public eye these days and refuse to participate in live literature events? Should they? Would this be better for literary culture, and for readers?

In his contribution to the *Mortification* collection, Simon Armitage takes a very different view: he calls live literature events the 'human interface between writing and reading'[170]; and now, as the UK's Poet Laureate, he has spoken of his sense of responsibility as an artist to engage with the public.[171] There will be more from Armitage in Chapter 3, when I speak to him at the Hay Festival.

As live literature becomes more and more prevalent, attitudes are changing, and authors are speaking out more about live literature practices, as well as participating in them—but it is still very rare to encounter authors writing or speaking about live literature events as *performances*.

Will Self, a notably dynamic performer at live literature events—while also being a notably derisive cynic about the publishing industry and about his readers and audiences—has opined in strong terms about what it takes to perform well in this context:

> I've always understood that my fiction of extreme mental states, genital transformations, and the linkage of mental illness to social change, would prove a tough sell, and I've also understood that it would be me who'd largely have to do the selling, so I've worked hard at understanding which passages will come across well when read – comic set pieces usually, but

not always – and how to introduce these passages in such a way as to hold an audience's attention.

But the truth of the matter is that if you are a shy, blushing, Proustian recluse for whom the least sound is exquisite torture, you'll never be able to wake up and smell the coffee being served up in the bar adjacent to the windy yurt where you're being called upon to declaim. Reading one's own work aloud to an audience requires the ability to gauge their reaction, while at the same time affecting complete nonchalance. Basic rules on projecting and stage presence can be acquired, but these must be honed by years of experience.[172]

When I came across this piece I was struck by how rare it was for an author to write about their experience of live literature, using performance-focused terms like 'stage presence'. But I also wanted to interrogate more carefully whether Self was right: that a successful live literature performance is only possible if you happen to be a very self-confident author who has trained and honed their actorly skills for years, as he has.

## 'Reading' vs. 'Performance' vs. 'Listening'

As part of my quest to reframe the way in which live literature is perceived, and to interrogate its value as a performance experience, I have use two hybrid terms throughout this book: 'author-performers'[173] and 'reader-audiences'. These might seem like common-sense terms, but I have not seen them used before.

In many live literature contexts, when 'authors' read aloud from their texts to 'audiences', this activity is usually referred to in the literary community a 'reading', rather than a 'performance'.[174] This no doubt links to the historical value allotted to the activity of silent reading as a more 'advanced' way of engaging with literature,[175] and also indicates a lack of emphasis or value placed on the performance element of the activity. In contrast, members of the reader-audience tend to refer to this person as the 'speaker', or even the 'talker'. The term 'author-performer' highlights the fact that authors do become performers at live literature events, both in discussion and Q&A sessions, and when they read aloud from their books, and that this function has value; and yet their role and identity as authors remains integral.

The other participants at live literature events are usually referred to as 'audiences'. My alternative term, 'reader-audiences', is meant to highlight the relationship between the performance experience at an event and the relationship that each member has, or may go on to have, with the literary texts and authors featured on stage.

## So What's New?

Insofar as anything is truly original, this book seeks to do several original things.

It is the first book about live literature.[176] It is the first to focus on live literature events featuring fiction, and the first to consider the views of both view reader-audiences *and* author-performers at events. (As I have mentioned, it is the first to use those labels.) It is the also first to look at the cultural value of live literature events in terms of participant experience.

It proposes an original approach to ethnographic writing, in the form of experiential literary ethnography, and explains how this approach works, and why it has the potential to be widely applicable in practice as a way to reveal the cultural value of arts and culture events for the benefit of diverse audiences.

This book should offer some fresh insights, whether you are reading it as a festival-goer, a scholar, an author-performer, an event producer, a publisher, an arts funder, a bookseller, or a keen fiction reader. Most importantly, I hope it makes for an enjoyable reading experience.

# 3

# The Hay Festival: The Remote Welsh Field That Stages the Global Publishing Industry

## Day One

I have to sprint to make my train from London. Sitting back in my seat, allowing my breath to slow, I watch the city sprawl and recede, then pull out my laptop. A couple of hours later, I change onto a smaller train that chuffs through an ever-greener landscape, and dip into a book. I get off at Hereford, and after an hour's wait in a pool of sunlight, contemplating a concrete supermarket, I change again onto a bus that winds along snaking roads towards the swell of the Black Mountains. Finally, the bus pulls up at my destination: a little grey stone town in a valley at the foot of a steep bluff, on the banks of the River Wye, at the border of England and Wales.

There is a sign to a Norman castle, but I drag my case the other way, along a miniature high street and past a sparse supermarket. So far, so pleasantly unremarkable, you might think, if you happened to find yourself here—until noticing that, for such a small town, it bulges disproportionately with bookshops. There are about thirty of them, mostly second-hand, for a population of 1500—that's about one bookshop per twelve households.

© The Author(s), under exclusive license to Springer Nature Switzerland AG 2021
E. Wiles, *Live Literature*, Palgrave Studies in Literary Anthropology,
https://doi.org/10.1007/978-3-030-50385-7_3

Outside this little town, in the direction of the Brecon Beacons, lies a field, which is my actual destination. An innocuous stretch of grass for most of the year, as fields tend to be, at the end of May it transforms, rising like a giant pop-up book into a literary festival that looms mountainously in the literary-cultural landscape, attracts some of the world's biggest names in literary and popular culture, hundreds of thousands of visitors, and has spawned sister festivals in thirty countries around the world. One of the 'Big Four' literary festivals, alongside Cheltenham, Oxford and Edinburgh, Hay is one of the biggest, in the UK and globally. In 2018, 273,000 tickets were sold at the Welsh edition of Hay for 800 events: an increase of 18,000 over 2017.[1] Literary festivals have grown over the last twenty years to the point that there are now said to be over 350 in the UK and Ireland alone,[2] and 450 across the English-speaking world.[3]

The sun has nearly set by the time I find the house where I'll be renting a tiny room for a festively-high price. I check in and head out to get a bite to eat at the pub around the corner, which is brim-full with people. Most, I suspect, are festival-goers, and I wonder how locals feel about the deluge.

## Day Two

The next morning, I find myself part of a slow stream of people trickling along the narrow pavement out of town towards the festival site. The breeze quickens as space opens up, and I zip my jacket up at the neck. We pass several front gardens set up as cafes selling Welsh cakes, instant coffee, sandwiches, old books and magazines, battered toys and other jumble; those living on the route who haven't taken the opportunity to rent out their houses at premium rates aren't going to miss the change to reap the benefits of this annual pedestrian stampede.

I wonder afresh what to expect at this festival: just how festive will it be, and how literary?[4] As an ardent reader since childhood, I remember the first time I heard the phrase 'literary festival'. It triggered a multicoloured vision of a verdant space populated by carnivalesque tents, in which my favourite authors, alive and historic, would be reading aloud, talking about characters from their books so vividly that the characters might materialise any minute and leap up to enact certain scenes and riff on their backstories, showing me more of themselves... others filled with silent readers lying on giant beanbags engrossed in paperbacks... some resonant with live music, all lyrics somehow connected with books... the outdoor areas scattered with people gathering for impromptu book clubs under trees and drinking and dancing on the grass... the atmosphere would fizz with a 'collective effervescence',[5] and we would all feel as if we had escaped normal society for a while to take part in a creative and playful ritual,[6] to experience a 'time out of time'.[7]

Approaching the site, I remind myself that it won't actually be like this. Fictional characters are unlikely to materialise, for one thing. And I have done enough research to have a reasonable idea of what I might find—though I am quite sure that, like most places you travel to after reading the guidebook version, the reality will be different to the mind's eye preview.

The Hay Festival changed its name from a festival 'of literature' to a festival 'of ideas' in the late 1990s, but is nevertheless regarded as, not only the most famous of literary festivals, but the epitome of a literary festival, format-wise. This entails being held among a collection of tents in a field, where simultaneous, individually-ticketed and conversation-based events are staged, the majority of which involve a chairperson and a panel of two or three authors (or just one author, if that author is particularly famous), in which those authors converse about their newly-published books with a chairperson, read a passage aloud from their books and then answer questions from the audience.

Literary festivals are part of the **'festivalisation' of culture**.[8] Festivals are everywhere now, ranging from film, theatre and mime, in the arts, to food, drink and cycling.[9] They were traditionally conceived of by anthropologists and historians as ritualistic, short-term events, in which members of a community affirm and celebrate shared bonds through encounters and exchanges that transcend the mundanity of everyday life.[10] But more and more contemporary festivals have begun func-tioning as forums for performances framed around expressions of taste, cultural identities and lifestyle practices, and are now often designed to attract tourism.[11] Scholars have increasingly come to consider them as revealing polyvocal sites of cultural exchange[12]—but many have critiqued the way in which they have been 'McFestivalized' as their popularity has led to them being driven by commercial imperatives.[13]

There are various causal theories about festivalisation. One is that, 'in a world where notions of culture are becoming increasingly fragmented' due to globalisation, festivals become an important way of 'communicating something meaningful about identity, community, locality and belonging'[14]—and are increasingly rare 'collective manifestations in an era of growing individualism'.[15] They are considered to be part of the contemporary monetary economy, as well as the 'symbolic economy', as places to deal in cultural capital, and—last but not least—the attention economy.[16] Hay's local economic impact is said to have totalled more than £70 million from 2015 to 2018.[17] Festivals' popularity can clearly be seen as products of the new 'experientialism', whereby the bombardment of online information and the abundant availability of material things have caused people to feel 'stuffocated',[18] and to value 'real', embodied experiences, that create 'real' memories, more highly.

As I approach the crowd of giant white tents, I wonder: how far do literary festivals like Hay draw participants because they feel 'stuffocated' with their materialistic lives and crave a physical collective experience? Or is it more about the books, or about the authors and personalities on the programme?

Colourful flags and celebratory bunting flutter ahead mark the entrance, and a huge banner announces the HAY FESTIVAL above the strapline, *Imagine the World*, with several large sponsorship logos displayed alongside it, most prominently *The Telegraph's*.[19] Large, white marquees rise up behind. In the entranceway, I pause to look into a thrumming box-office tent, and a *Telegraph*-branded tote bag is waved at me: free with today's paper. I accept one, take a programme from another steward and walk on through.

I circuit the site to find my bearings. Not a difficult task, it turns out; in comparison with most music and cross-arts festivals I've been to, this site is exceedingly neat and geometric, with all the tents arranged in an orderly manner around a large rectangle of metal walkways. It might be situated in a muddy field, but no wellies are necessary. It feels slightly reminiscent of a trade show I once went to in London's Exhibition Centre—but the regular glimpses and constant sense of the hills and trees around the site are a reminder of Hay's distance from urban centres of commerce. Greenery pervades the site, too, albeit in a manicured iteration of the surrounding countryside. In between the walkways are perfectly mowed lawns dotted with deck chairs and picnic benches for audiences to relax, mingle and read. In the centre of one lawn is a quaint shepherd's hut on wheels, advertising itself to would-be writers[20]—in which audiences can sit and perhaps order a replica if so inspired and sufficiently deep-pocketed. Another lawn features a giant, multi-coloured HAY sign that children can climb on and be photographed, ideally smiling widely, and in the sunshine—which is looking doubtful today. There's a shop selling Hay Festival merch, an Oxfam second-hand bookshop, and a Festival Bookshop selling the new titles of featured authors and presenters. The latter is huge: big enough not only to contain all the books featured at the festival, but also to accommodate the all-important post-event book signing queues. Food and drink options are plentiful; there's a food hall-style tent, a fancy restaurant tent, several cafes, a tapas bar... Wait, is that the towering form of Stephen Fry walking past the press tent?

A watch check: it's time to meet **Director** Peter Florence, so I weave through the increasing crowds back to the entrance—and there he is. A genial man with a dark beard and a resonant voice, friendly while also being unmistakably in charge, Florence welcomes me warmly and introduces me to some of the others on the Hay team. Like Florence, most of the full-time staff have been doing this job for years, from when the Festival was in its infancy. He has to dash off for something, but Revel Guest, Hay's vivacious octogenarian **Chair**, leads me through to the Green Room for a longer chat.

The **Green Room** is furnished with comfy sofas, chairs around tables adorned with vases of flowers and pictures on the walls. It has a bar serving tea, coffee, biscuits and wine, and helpful volunteers hover at the edges, ready to guide author-performers to their events. Few are here yet, as the day is just beginning, but I can see that, as people pour into the site, it will function as a comfortable oasis amidst the fray. I imagine the ghosts of literary greats from festivals past—Rushdie,

Morrison, Angelou—clinking invisible glasses, exchanging literary gossip and ideas, safely out of the public view yet actively being seen by each other.

I ask Guest about the **founding** of the Hay Festival, and the story I'd heard that it was dreamt up around the Florences' kitchen table in 1987. 'Oh yes', she says. 'And it was very small, almost like a little *party* in the beginning'. Guest is no stranger to a good party; aptly named, she is known for hosting glamorous revelries during the festival week for Hay's most famous author-performers at her mansion, sponsored nowadays by GQ Magazine and Land Rover. You wouldn't guess this to meet her out of context, though; she dresses simply and talks to me pleasantly and directly, as if she were telling me about a local fête she happens to run. As a long-time friend of the Florences, involved with the festival from the start, she told me more about how the concept was born.

The actors Norman Florence and his wife Rhoda Lewis, with their then 23-year-old son Peter, fresh out of RADA, began brainstorming ideas for a happening in their town. Since they were based in the world's first '**book town**'[21]—invented by Richard Booth, an eccentric owner of the Norman castle, who opened a clutch of bookshops there in the 1960s and declared himself King and his horse Prime Minister in 1977—it made sense to capitalise on that. They came up with the concept of 'The Hay-on-Wye Festival of Literature and the Arts'.[22] The first edition featured fifteen events[23] that took place in the back rooms of pubs, with tickets sold from a friend's caravan, but the following year, Peter Florence persuaded playwright Arthur Miller, famous by then for his marriage to Marilyn Monroe, to be the star guest—though only after making some effort to explain the location. 'Hay-on-Wye?', Miller apparently asked. 'Is that some kind of sandwich?'[24]

**Starry literary names** piled in, and authors and their agents began to lobby passionately for slots. Most prize-winning and bestselling authors in the English language, as well as many of the best-known translated authors, have gone on to appear at Hay: J. K. Rowling, Martin Amis, Margaret Atwood, Derek Walcott, Mark Haddon, Ben Okri, Ian McEwen, Zadie Smith, Carol Ann Duffy, Hilary Mantel, Michael Morpurgo, Muriel Spark, P. D. James, Orhan Pamuk, Dave Eggers, Michael Ondaatje, Doris Lessing, Edna O'Brien—to name a few. The most famous guests began to be put up in the local five-star hotel complete with helipads and to fraternise at the five-star parties.[25] When one Hay audience member once put up her hand to ask literary super-agent, Ed Victor,[26] how they could get their book in front of him if they were not on that glamorous party circuit, he replied: 'You don't'[27]—an indication of the **exclusivity** that was soon perceived to surround the Festival and the wider publishing scene.

The Festival garnered *Sunday Times* **sponsorship** in 1990 and sparked international interest; *The New Yorker* began flying teams over to debate *Times* journalists on stage. It moved into its own field site where it would have room to expand further. Bill Clinton arrived in 2001 to speak about conflict resolution and delighted the organisers by calling Hay "The Woodstock of the mind": a catchphrase they quote still.[28] But Clinton's appearance, and its £100,000 price tag,[29] sparked controversy about the Festival's core identity, substance and integrity as a 'literary' event in a debate that still continues, nearly two decades later. It was triggered by an article by Steven Moss published shortly after the 2001 Festival, in *The Guardian*, titled 'Making Hay',[30] with the bye-line: 'what happened to the books?'[31] 'What', he asks, 'was [Clinton] doing for Hay, which since its foundation in 1988 has established itself as the leading literary festival in the country?' He quotes the novelist Robert Edric as arguing that the way Clinton and Paul McCartney 'dominated' that year's festival 'marginalises writers and changes the nature of the event', posing the rhetorical comparison: 'Would Glyndebourne have circus clowns because it made good sense to entertain people in between concerts?' What was unique about Hay, Edric felt, was 'being eroded', in a context where 'everything else is easily available outside Hay' but 'good literature isn't'. 'It's sad', he concluded, 'because Hay has always set **the standard** for literary festivals'. He did not spare audience members from criticism, alleging **hypocrisy**: 'if you want to go and see Paul McCartney, don't pretend that it is a literary occasion'.

There are many assumptions embedded in these words that invite further reflection, not only on Hay's role, moral or actual, in 'setting the standard for literary festivals', but also a normative question about **what a 'literary festival' is and *should* be**, and what literary festival audiences' true vs performed **motivations** are—the implication being that, for many audience members, the function of attendance as a form of **cultural capital**[32]—a badge of cultural achievement to show off to one's friends—is more important than any aspect of the experience itself, and bears no relation to the amount of 'good literature' they actually read. This perspective on the literary festival was adopted by the earliest sociologists to consider it; they condemned literary festivals as uncritical sites of mass cultural production—effectively soulless places for fawning over celebrity books and bestsellers.[33]

The 'case for the defence' for the injection of **celebrity** into literary festivals, Moss proposed, could be reduced to one word: 'buzz'—or raising **literature's profile**.[34] This was seen as an overwhelming positive by some authors and critics.[35] Others were more ambivalent. Novelist D. J. Taylor felt that the embrace of celebrity was 'inevitable' for wider **economic** and cultural reasons that have forced literature 'to sing for its supper' as a 'branch of the **entertainment** industry', since the old days of thirty Bloomsbury adherents sitting in a tent are gone'[36]—a reference, perhaps, to the Bedford Square Book Bang of the 1970s.[37]

Revel Guest speaks to me with abounding enthusiasm and energy about Hay, its history and evolution, its global expansion, and their plans to found new Hay Festivals around the world in the years ahead. They have a close-knit production team, but Peter, she explains, firmly, has always been in charge of the programming. Before long she too is called away, and I head back outside.

The sky is now dense with cloud and there's a distinct chill in the air. I head to one of the cafes for coffee and peruse the programme. It's still early, and the first events are only just about to start, but the site is already buzzing. I sip my cappuccino, pull out my pen, and prepare to start circling events I'd like to go to. It feels a bit like perusing the *Radio Times* at Christmas; in fact, after the late politician, Tony Benn, started going to the Hay Festival, he pronounced that it had 'replaced Christmas'.[38] I knew there would be a lot of events within this **meta-event**, but still find myself surprised by their profusion. There are ten tents, a couple with a capacity of 1200, all lined up back-to-back with events, many featuring well-known authors and household names who have written books. A lot of the most appealing events—to me, at least—are running concurrently or overlapping; Hay is a festival with considerable 'density'.[39]

In principle, Hay's density should heighten its participants' sense of **collective participation** and **liminality**, as Victor Turner put it: the 'feeling of entering into another world' at a festival.[40] This in turn is said to heighten audiences' **attention**[41] over a concentrated space–time frame.[42] A festival's density can also be fuel for its audience's anxiety, though, surely—how to pick which events to go to? For each reader-audience member, choosing a selection of events is a bit like plotting a choose-your-own-adventure-story; it will end up forming a narrative arc of the festival in your memory. Sitting here with the **programme**, reading all the event blurbs, cross-checking and weighing up, my eyes start to spiral. A few other people in the café are actively looking at their programmes too, and one middle-aged couple at another table are hunched over a copy with furrowed eyebrows, exuding all the tension of an important exam.

After finishing my coffee, I get up to have a people-watching stroll around the site, to get more of a sense of who's here bright and early. Many, like me, are strolling around, several chatting with a friend or family member. Several people had already told me, in the course of my research among reader-audiences at events, that they had never been to a literary festival and had no inclination to, since they were sure it would be full of 'posh, middle-class white people'—or 'smankers' (smug, middle-class, etc.), as journalist Decca Aitkenhead encapsulated her preconceptions of Hay's audiences back in 2010 in an article for *The Guardian*.[43]

From my brief visual and aural survey of the **demographic** here, people are pretty much all **white**. Most are casually dressed—and the majority appear to be middle-class. There are probably **more women** than men, which fits with the evidence about literary festivals discussed by Helen Taylor in her excellent book, *Why Women Read Fiction* (2019)[44]—but not vastly more. There are numerous grey heads, but significantly more younger people than I had expected, and a good mix of **regional backgrounds** too, from the accents I can pick up through passing snippets.[45] In her 2010 article, Aitkenhead describes Florence as responding 'crossly' to her suggestion that the festival was too white and middle-class. He countered: 'We're interested in people who are interested in stories, and that isn't a middle-class thing. What this *is* is a great crucible for experimenting. There's something about being here in a field that makes everyone more at their ease than anywhere else. Being in a field is a big leveller. It doesn't matter if you're the president of the USA, or a sixth-form wannabe poet. That you're in a field is the big thing'.[46]

When I first read this, I winced at what sounded like a dismissal of **diversity concerns** in the light of clear evidence of diversity deficits within the wider publishing industry, which have not gone away[47]; such deficits affect perceptions, not just of festivals like Hay, but of other literary events, and literature in general. They cause marginalised groups, particularly people of colour, to feel and to be unfairly excluded from literary culture, and that ultimately makes literary culture less representative, culturally relevant and meaningful. Since 2010, Hay has evidently made efforts to increase the racial diversity of authors on stage, even if it still has a long way to go to be representative of the wider population. As someone with a mixed-race family, the issue of diverse representation has personal importance to me, as well as clearly being a key issue within contemporary literary culture that urgently needs to be addressed in order to make it fairer, more relevant and more dynamic. Festivals, particularly the big ones like Hay, clearly have a vital role to play in catalysing change.

Still, right now, sitting here on the Hay Festival site, breathing in the fresh, clean air scented with cut grass in this enclave among rugged hills, so far from the city, with only thin canvas separating bodies seated in events from the wide-open sky, I relate in a new way to Florence's point about shared **field-solidarity**. There is a palpable sense here that most participants have, like me, made an attenuated journey to this out-of-the-way place from many different corners of the country, and even the globe, for the sole reason of being part of the same event, assembled together, in this tiny patch of field. There is a visceral energy and power in that.[48] I am keen to find out more about how this sense of physical collectivity translates to the diversity of reader-audiences here—in terms of their literary tastes, habits and values, as well as their demographic characteristics.

**Class**-wise, it seems clear that most reader-audiences at Hay must be quite well-off if they are coming from faraway and staying for the whole festival. The Festival site is free to enter, but all events are individually-priced, and some, featuring the biggest names, are priced at over twenty pounds, multiples of which add up steeply. **Cost** of tickets would be a significant determining factor in my own event choices if I hadn't generously been given a pass to assist with my research. There are plenty of tickets for events on offer for around ten pounds, reflecting lesser-known names, but even the cost of those would be significant if you wanted to buy several per day over the course of the ten days of the Festival. Added to that, accommodation in Hay at Festival time can be very expensive. Even the 'glamping' is pricey,[49] and the unpredictable Welsh weather puts many people off sleeping under canvas.

The individual event-based **ticketing model** is the same for all literary festivals that I've come across. It contrasts with the model for most music and cross-arts festivals; for those meta-events, the ticket price covers entry to the festival site and all individual events, so audiences are free to drop into whatever they feel like without pre-booking. I wonder whether this difference is linked to literary festivals' close connection to **bookselling** and sales accountability; or to the fact that literary events are usually seated, since they are fairly long and require concentration, and audiences are not (generally) expected to dance through them. To some extent, the typical literary festival ticketing compromises the liminality of the festival experience: at festivals where there is a single ticket for weekend entry to the site, audiences can **flow** between events as and when they feel like it, and this changes the dynamic and the sense of **freedom in the experience**. I have been to many festivals with the single festival-entry ticket model, including Port Eliot: another rural festival, staged in a beautiful estate in Cornwall featuring a castle, woods, walled gardens and a tidal river, which started out as a literary festival but evolved into a cross-arts festival that includes a series of literary events.[50] Not only is that site a larger, more topographically-varied and loosely-arranged space to wander around in than Hay's; but the sense of being able to dip into any event (or even the river) gives it a spontaneous feel.

I spot someone I recognise on a deck chair, far-removed from the green room, tall, slim, black-haired—yes, it's **Jo Glanville**, Director of **English PEN**: an NGO that supports writers at risk, freedom of expression and literature in translation.[51] She will be chairing several international fiction events over the next few days. I go over to introduce myself, and happily she's very welcoming, so I sit cross-legged on the grass to chat to her. I am slightly surprised to hear her opinion about the rise of literary festivals: it is 'utterly baffling'. 'I'd be very interested if you find out the key to their popularity', she adds. 'I think the literary event in itself is a really *peculiar* thing, because, just because someone can **write** a book, it doesn't mean that they can stand and *talk* about it, and talking about the book in **public** isn't the same as reading a book which is a very *private* act… and when you're reading a great piece of literature, we all know what an *extraordinary* experience that is… you enter some extraordinary *world*, and you *leave* your real world to enter this other world'. I'm intrigued by the way she evokes the idea of otherworldly liminality, just as Victor Turner described it. 'And obviously, aesthetically, depending on what you're reading', Glanville continues, 'you're enjoying extraordinary *language*… So the concept of a festival, actually – and the popularity of events where a writer is standing up and speaking – is actually *really* baffling to me. It's a conundrum! The **paradox** of literary festivals'.

She shakes her head, reflectively. 'You know, I *love* books', she continues, 'and have always loved books, but before I started doing this job that has brought me into this sort of world I wouldn't *ever* go to something like this!' She mulls over this statement, as if unsure of its accuracy. 'Well, I would very *occasionally* go to see a writer speak if I thought they were somebody really *amazing*… Of course there's the whole tradition of, the great writer being a kind of **oracle**, a *visionary* or something, and so maybe there's a sense of people wanting to **learn** from *them* about how things are, or trying to understand life?'.

I head back into the Green Room, where I spot the prominent literary scholar and critic **John Sutherland**[52] chatting to **John Crace**, the journalist who had already become well-known for his bitingly satirical 'digested read' column in *The Guardian*, which brilliantly compresses renowned novels to a few pithy and absurdist paragraphs.[53] They are lined up to do a double-act event about Jane Austen later in the day. When I mention that I am researching live literature, Sutherland's eyes gleam. 'It would be very interesting to look at it as a post-World War Two phenomenon', he says. '**After the War**, there was a big interest in the arts, which led to the founding of the Arts Council [in 1946], and then Harvey Wood started the Edinburgh Festival [in 1947]', which was all about creating a new post-war identity for the city and forging cultural bonds.[54]

Crace jumps in. 'I think starting with *Dickens* is a better place, because of the idea of performance... When I first came here though, it wasn't as much of a performance as it is now. I was *amazed* by how many writers had *no* on-stage presence. You know, they were supposed to sell books, but they could put a glass eye to sleep! I thought that was a real problem'.

Sutherland nods, considering this, but decisively rejects the proposition. 'Still, I'd be more inclined to start with World War Two, in terms of festivals. There was a huge burnout amongst the professions, so they all took early retirement, with pensions that were very generous, and were well-read, and literary festivals *throve* on that. I think that's now been replaced by a different constituency, by **the *reading group* constituency**, who aren't so well-read, but still enjoy reading... Some of them make admissions, in front of thousands of people, like: "I'm reading this book but am only half-way through!" There's also the fact that the book industry has fallen under huge pressure to sell books, so the literary festival acts as an engine for that... And to keep authors happy, you know – offer them a chance to speak in front of 2000 people and they burst into spontaneous applause'. Crace bursts into spontaneous laughter at this. 'I'd be genuinely interested to hear your conclusions',

Sutherland says, grinning and turning to me. 'I don't know whether this all inflates egos and creates false currency values, or really adds something for readers'.

'I think the fact that a lot of writers still don't perform well', Crace interjects, 'is still a big problem with some literary festivals – you know, if you're paying eight quid for an event, you want to be entertained'. 'Slightly instructed as well', Sutherland chips in.

This exchange pointed to an **existential question** I wanted to ask about Hay, and of all literary festivals: how far are they performance events; or educational events; or marketing events; or meet-your-hero opportunities; or social opportunities; or literary experiences?

It is time for me to head to the first event I've circled in my programme, which is lined up for one of the smaller tents, named the 'Starlight Stage': a conversation between **Philip Gross**, the T. S. Eliot prize-winning poet, and artist Valerie Coffin Price. They collaborated to create *A Fold in the River*: a **poetry and art** book inspired by the Welsh River Taff. Gross used to live by and walk regularly along this river, and transformed his journals into a poetry collection. For this book, Price retraced his routes to develop prints and drawings, and the result was published by Seren: a small indie press.

The tent is prettily decorated with a web of tiny fairy lights over the ceiling, and the stage is painted black. A gentle, slight and bearded persona on stage, Gross reads softly but engagingly from his poems, which are moving, exquisite and seem particularly apt for the geography and climate of Hay:

> Enough now. Wind back the reel;
> spool in the river, right up to the source
> which is no one where
>
> unless you hold it cupped
> in the all-angled lens of a raindrop – that
> or the quivering globe of all this
> for the most part sea…

Price's projected illustrations make the experience of listening to the poems more immersive, reflecting their spirit and helping focus our attention. After a sequence of readings by Gross, Price eagerly introduces her work, and the two take turns in explaining how the project developed. Gross speaks somewhat hesitantly, but articulately, warmly and in a calmer manner than his illustrator. While not a charismatic performer, in the extrovert sense, he is clearly more used to speaking in front of audiences. The event is not chaired, and this seems to give it an intimacy and informality, but also a slight awkwardness in turn-taking. Most of their conversation is about process: their respective processes of making and their collaboration.

After the event, I speak to **Stan and Kira**,[55] a British-American couple in their mid-thirties, who are married and both work in Christian ministry. I ask how they found the event. 'Fascinating', Stan tells me, beaming. 'Especially hearing about the ways people produce art. I have been interested in music before, but poetry is a bit of a side thing for me'. Kira tells me that she'd studied English, and had come to Hay a couple of times before—and always tries to see at least one poetry event as well as fiction. Neither had heard of Gross or Coffin before seeing their names on the programme. 'What I loved', Kira says, was 'the fact that both of them were so *absorbed* in this river, even though it doesn't sound like a particularly beautiful one'. They both enjoyed the 'play-off' between poetry and images in the event, and in the concept of the book.

I ask Kira whether she goes to literary events outside the Hay Festival. 'No – but I would like to', she says. 'There aren't many around us', Stan adds. When I ask what they felt they gained from hearing a writer like Gross reading his work aloud at an event, rather than reading it themselves on the page, Kira says that the *meaning* is clearer, for her. 'Sometimes you don't understand something until you hear someone read from it'. Because she hasn't read Gross's poetry before, it is impossible to know how her understanding of the texts he performed might have changed had she done so—but her sense of **enhanced comprehension** is definite. The point raises an interesting question: how much does an audience's **interpretation** of a text, that was originally meant for the page, change in the context of the factors at play in a live reading by its author?

Stan jumps in: 'True, though that can equally limit a thing. I mean, the writer reading aloud gives you *their* understanding of a work, but there are legitimate other understandings… But I don't mind that, because there are so few chances to hear most poems read aloud, really, and it's a great thing'.

Stan observes that Gross had a 'speech twitch'—which isn't 'a *negative*', he adds, hastily, a little embarrassed, as if he'd been caught out being malicious, 'but I found it interesting that poetry can be a profession, even for someone who has an issue with speaking'. The implication here is that oral delivery is an assumed core part of a poet's work. And this comment alludes to another point about live literary performance: the ***fragility* of the performer** and the inevitable sense of **risk** that attaches to a writer in reading aloud at an event like this, when they are hoping to win over an audience to their work, but risk putting them off reading it. Does such fragility in performance in fact ***endear*** a writer to an audience, generating empathy, and a sense of **authenticity**, perhaps, rather than a slicker presentation? Or is **charismatic performance** always more likely to engage, making the writer's performance role more akin to a professional actor's? To what extent do facial tics and expressions, in combination with other non-lexical elements of speech, such as intonation (paralanguage), body language (kinesics) and the implications of the physical space (proxemics), affect an audience's reception of a text, and evaluation of its author?

I ask Stan and Kira what their Hay highlights had been in the past, and Kira doesn't hesitate: 'Oh, **Toni Morrison**![56] Her reading from her novel was remarkable – she's so insistent, and there's a real *rhythm* to it, and so it felt to me like: unless you're reading it like that, you're reading it *wrong*'. I am intrigued by Kira's emphasis on rhythm: a word and an idea that is most commonly associated with music and poetry, but clearly applies to performed readings of fiction too.

Morrison herself felt like that about her work, Stan adds: 'I actually listened to her reading her audiobook of *Beloved*, after she said to us, at the event, that someone else had done it first, and had done it "all wrong". So it was interesting to hear her read it, and to hear her opinions… But in some ways *she* wasn't that clear to me over *audio*… so it cuts both ways. It can be a play-off between authenticity and quality'.

This word 'authenticity' has already come up many times in my participant conversations about live literature. It has multiple potential meanings in this context that intrigue me: how far does it relate to an interpretation of the author's text, based on their literary intention; or to an authenticity of persona that the writer is projecting; or to an authenticity of emotional experience on the part of the audience?

As we part ways, Kira and Stan tell me they are heading to the bookshop to look up Philip Gross's books, and I head back to the Starlight Stage for to the next event that I've circled in my programme.

This fiction event is billed as featuring 'two international superstars', the Danish short story writer Dorthe Nors, who has a new collection out titled *Karate Chop*, and German-Austrian novelist Daniel Kehlmann whose new novel, *F*, is about art, money and brotherhood. It is going to be chaired by Daniel Hahn, author, translator and Chair of the Society of Authors.

The audience seats are about two-thirds full as the three take their places on the stage. They look around the same age: mid-forties. Hahn introduces the two authors, mentions that he will ask them to read at some point so audiences can get a 'little flavour' of their writing, and assures the audience that they will have plenty of time for questions.

He comments on how 'odd' it is that, 'as a chair of these events', you have the 'task' of 'finding things in common between the books'—the first of several ironic meta remarks about literary festival events that he will make during the session. The programme does not explicitly link these two authors as writers in translation, but they clearly are staged together as representatives of the small percentage of writing in translation featured. Hahn points out that, in many ways, their books could not be more different. He describes Kehlmann's new novel *F* as 'big and generous and full of things and stuff', whereas Nors's books, collections of short stories, are 'thin and spare, and give the reader lots of things to fill in, lots of gaps'. Focusing on Kehlmann's writing style, he describes it as 'mischievous and funny', and then quotes various reviews that contradict that characterisation. He hones in on Nors's writing, describing her stories as 'potent, compact and so cleverly put together', like 'devastating little detonations'. While reading one of them at home, he admits, he actually 'shouted out' at something near the end: a personal confession that links the orality of this event to an embodied oral element of reading the texts on the page.

Each author is then asked to talk about their **writing process**. Kehlmann talks, with measured confidence, about how messy his is, and how he often thinks that a book is not going to work and puts the manuscript aside, before coming back to it. 'I abandon a lot of material – I have a lot I could sell to these archives', he jokes. Hahn moves onto the intricate structure of Kehlmann's novel and asks how far this was planned. Kehlmann says he deliberately wanted to try writing a book where he *didn't* know the answers—though, on the other hand, he was very interested in structure, and so, for this novel, he chose to explore the same day narrated by three different brothers, whose perspectives would sometimes overlap. There was a lot he *didn't* know as he was writing, though, and he wanted to try to write a character-driven novel and see how the characters led him.

Hahn interjects here to recount an anecdote from an event he chaired, which he calls 'typical of a literary festival', in which an audience member asked: 'what is plot?', and the author answered: 'plot is the wake a character leaves behind them'. People around me nod, and I note that this anecdote subtly makes the audience aware of their part in a cultural community of literary festival events, extending beyond the time and space of this festival; and also of Hahn's own literary and festival-chairing expertise, in being able to insert relevant authorial quotes from past events organically into this one.

When asked how she ended up writing so concisely, Nors said it 'just happened'; she started off writing novels, but they got thinner and thinner: 'I think I distilled my way into my own language'. She recounts a moment when someone commented to her: 'the way you speak, you're perfectly suited to short fiction', and she thought *go to hell!*—but then wrote a short story and felt something happening. It was 'blissful'. She went on a retreat on a remote Danish island and suddenly she had written seven stories, and it was 'like being in love'. 'I think I found myself, my own voice'. This anecdote, spoken in her sharp, knowing tones, resonates with the substance of her comment about her literary style—that she has just joked about rebuffing before embracing.

Nors points to a part of Kehlmann's novel which could be taken out as a 'wonderful short story'. But Kehlmann responds that, unlike her, he always tries to start out writing in a minimalist way, but somehow ends up with 300-page novel—drawing out a pleasing reverse symmetry that doesn't seem to have been planned when programming these two on the same panel.

They discuss the **difference between novels and short stories** further. Nors says that she likes to 'find the voice of a character and have them reveal stuff – it's like you're walking in the mist, and then a face appears and reveals something, and then it's gone again, and you're left with an experience, which can be profound'. Hahn jumps in here to draw another link, pointing out that both their books are 'about people presenting certain versions of themselves'. He springboards off this point to tell the reader-audience: 'that's **why *fiction is great***: we're allowed to see a truth about the characters that isn't otherwise revealed to anybody'. Again, this is a neat way of locating this event in the broader sphere of fiction and its cultural value, emphasising, for the reader-audience's benefit, a reason why their presence matters.

A conversation about the nature of happiness follows. Nors quotes an Australian magazine article in which the journalist can't understand why Denmark is judged to be one of the world's happiest countries— 'when you look into Danish people's eyes' [spoken with a sinister edge; prompts audience laughter]. Kehlmann is invited to comment on the darkness of his characters in *F* and talks about one of his narrators, Eric, who has strange, almost 'psychopathic tendencies'. Hahn quotes a line of Eric's back to Kehlmann: 'I invent almost everything I tell people'— and this leads to a discussion about the relationship between fiction and lies in 'real life'. 'If you're a novelist, you're expected to get up on stage and justify everything you do', Hahn comments, tartly: another meta commentary upon the **relationship between live literature, fiction and authorship**.

After beginning on a new track about '**themes**' that appear in both books, Hahn breaks off and comments, 'I find myself asking about *themes* in these books, although nobody really talks about themes…': yet another meta statement about literary festival events. He then proposes that common 'things' in both these books are 'things' that don't happen in the story itself, but are acknowledged in the telling, and suggests that this gives them more drama. Nors responds that, in her case, leaving 'things' unsaid in a fictional narrative is characteristic of 'Danish minimalism'. She expands upon the 'natural minimalism of the Danish language' compared to English, given its smaller vocabulary: it leaves more interpretation gaps for readers and listeners, she explains, and 'you can put in your own emotions'; but that causes problems of translation down the line. Hahn takes this opportunity to acknowledge the translators of both books, as: 'also brilliant people'. Nors sums up the effect of her minimalist aesthetic on readers' emotions with typical brusqueness: 'I can get into their heads, then kick them in the stomach'.

At this, Hahn looks out at the audience and faux-anxiously points out that they should 'still read this book', prompting audience laughter: yet another meta-reference, this time to the marketing element of the festival at which they are all performing.

Hahn asks Kehlmann if he'd like to read a bit from *F*. Kehlmann moves across the stage to stand at the lectern. He tells us he's chosen a section narrated by Eric, describing him waking up in the morning. 'I've already been hearing the sobbing for some time. [Kehlmann's voice here, on the word *time*, takes on a deep tone, a resonance that hadn't been present in his conversational voice, signifying the move from performed conversation to performed reading.] I was having a dream, but now I come out of the dream, I hear that the sobbing is coming from the woman next to me... I lie there motionless. How long can I pretend to be asleep?... [The pitch variation of his voice is much greater than in speech, and the volume varies more too. The pace is slow enough to be clear, but still sounds natural.] The morning sun pushes through the slats of the blinds, drawing fine lines on both the carpet and the wall... I push back my blanket and get up. As I'm groping my way down the hall the memory of the dream returns. No doubt about it, it was my Grandmother... She was determined to tell me something...'.

Kehlmann **performs** with vigour and humour and, while the reading is longer than I had expected, lasting for about fifteen minutes, it keeps me absorbed throughout. By the end, I am keen to read more about this strange and repellent character. As Hahn then points out: 'you get from this reading a strong sense of the shifts in tone in the novel', and things that are funny, surprising and 'a little bit upsetting'.

Hahn asks Kehlmann about the **experience of reading words aloud** when they are not actually the words he's written, but the translator's. Kehlmann admits that he is 'painfully aware' of his accent, but says he likes to read from the English version because: 'generally, if I had the choice, I would always prefer to do public readings from other people's books [audience laughter], so in a way a translation is that, so I like that. It also feels cool and glamorous to be translated into English. But if only I had the accent!'.

Hahn invites Nors to read. 'We're going to get a *whole story!*', he proclaims to the reader-audience, in confiding but exuberant tones, making clear that this is something rare, something special; the norm at Hay, and other literary festivals, is a reading of a very short excerpt from a new novel. 'That's the good thing about writing short, short stories', Nors comments, as she moves to the lectern. 'So, I'm going to read a story called "The Winter Garden"'.

Like Kehlmann, Nors leaves a pause to mark the transition from conversation to reading. 'The Winter Garden', she repeats. [She reads the title the second time with a raised voice, in a heightened, orating tone.] 'It was the night the comedian X died... he was taken to the hospital where it was said that he died on arrival. It was 3ʳᵈ of September 1980 and I remember it because it was the night my mother and father decided to tell me that they were getting divorced. [Her reading style is fluid and clear, delivered at a fairly fast pace but not rushed. While she has a Danish accent she sounds fluent in English in a way that Kehlmann does not, quite.] This was announced during dinner and somewhere inside me I think I was relieved. It sounds harsh but when my mother told me I think all I did was put down my fork...'.

The story evolves as a portrait of the narrator's father, and the divorced woman, 'Margit'—pronounced with a snide edge—who found out that he was divorced, sized him up and preyed on him. To the narrator's outrage, she had a son, who would stare solemnly at them from the couch and stick out his tongue when their father wasn't looking. At the end of the story, the narrator sticks their tongue out at the father when he isn't looking.

'How brilliant – and a bit brutal!', Hahn comments, at the end. He then opens the event up to the **audience** for **questions**, and a couple of hands go up.

The first person chosen to ask a question stands up. A shy-sounding white middle-aged woman, she thanks them for the readings and says she came here because she'd heard Kehlmann on the radio, and wanted to choose one of his books for a mixed gender, British book club that meets in the pub. 'Which one would you recommend?' I try to guess how many other reader-audience members at Hay are book group scouts. Quite a few, probably. Kehlmann isn't keen to pick just one from his back catalogue.

The next audience member, an older, balding man, asks Nors whether she found it much more difficult to get short stories published than novels—a hopeful writer, perhaps. 'Well, the publisher normally doesn't go: hooray!', Nors tells him, with a grin. She explains she was published in American magazines first, then got scouted, and there they have a much stronger short story tradition, so it went well for her after that— but concedes that all shorter forms have to struggle a bit. 'But that's okay – a book doesn't have to be sold in millions to be important'. Hahn points out to the audience that Nors was the very first Danish writer to have a short story in *The New Yorker*, and Nors smiles with understandable pride.

The third questioner, an anxious-sounding slim younger-middle-aged woman, asks, in a somewhat protracted way, as if she is working out what to say as she goes along, how both authors know when to stop editing, and how much feedback to take on board. Kehlmann answers first: 'Well, when you have a deadline, that's it. But as time passes I do have this kind of satisfying experience that the things you feel you need to edit and polish get less and less…'.

'And at some point you need to let it go', Nors cuts in, brusquely. 'If you still want to edit at the point you go to the publishers, you should probably not publish'.

'There must be personality types, though', Hahn says, sympatheti-cally—'I know with my process, I edit and it gets better and better, then at some point it starts getting worse and worse'.

'Also it takes a certain narcissistic personality to say: oh, this is really good!', Kehlmann adds, prompting audience laughter.

Hahn ends the event with a strong urge to the audience to read both books, before inviting their applause for the author-performers.

Back in the Green Room, I track **Hahn** down. A quietly-spoken man off stage, and dressed in muted colours, he is open to sharing his views with me, and we sit on one of the sofas. I ask him what he thinks about literary festivals generally. 'They help in a lot of ways', he says, thought-fully—'not only building conversations around books but also helping get books to people who wouldn't ordinarily see them otherwise. For writers, though, they are a double-edged sword. They are potentially exciting, but also potentially problematic... because I think writers are also *expected* to be able to do live things as well as having the *opportunity* to. When you publish a book now, the **expectation** from your **publisher** is that you'll be prepared to do a **road show** which means not just having the time but also... being *comfortable* getting on stage in front of lots of people – a sing a song, do a dance, tell a joke sort of thing. There are some people who find that comes very naturally to them and enjoy it, and some who probably don't and yet have to do it anyway. It's part of the job now I think'.

I ask Hahn whether, in his view, the usual literary festival event format for adults, such as the one at the event he just chaired, works well as a way of bringing a book to life. 'It all depends on the book, the audience and the site', he says, then muses, 'I do tend to like having readings... but not at the beginning. I'm not convinced by those events where you say "**sit down, shut up**, I'm going to read to you now". They're a bit *cold*. I think most of us don't have the habit of being read to very much, unless people listen to **audiobooks** a lot – we sort of lose that habit, so it's not a very easy thing to do'. But audiobooks are becoming much more popular, I want to say... Hahn continues: 'I tend, as a matter of choice when I chair events, to have a point where I say, "do you know what I think would be nice, actually, it would be nice to have a little bit of the book read" [spoken in a revelatory tone, as if he'd spontaneously come up with the idea], and then it can be part of an illustration of something, an introduction to a conversation about the texture of the language or whatever it might be – but it can be *embedded* and it feels *live*, like a living thing, rather than being a sort of presentation'.

I am interested in this reference to **liveness** relating to the lack of a *script* in a literary event: to the notion of **improvisation through conversation**; in contrast to an author reading 'live' as opposed to on screen or via a recording. 'But it depends on the kind of writing', Hahn adds. 'Take the event today with Daniel Kehlmann – I've heard him before, so I know he's very good at reading aloud. I wouldn't normally trust someone with a fifteen-minute reading as it wouldn't suit everyone. But then I don't think some writers are very comfortable with having a *conversation* which is natural and organic and unscripted. There are some who like to hold onto their book and do their thing. So a one-size-fits-all is difficult'.

In general, Hahn adds, literary festival **audiences' expectations** have 'shifted in the direction of conversation'. 'There was a time', he tells me, 'when the expectation was, especially at certain kinds of events, that they would get a twenty-minute reading, twenty minutes of questions about themes – "your novels are about family a lot; tell me about family" – and then a twenty-minute Q&A. Now, audiences expect something *more* live, in a funny way, which is less predictable – which is a conversation. So, one of the reasons having two writers is quite *nice*, is because, as a writer, you can't just do your regular thing, but you and the audience get something you can't get in any other way: a conversation between two authors and a chair that hasn't happened before and can't happen again. And you want it to feel like a *spontaneous* conversation, rather than a pre-packaged thing… I'm sure people would be disappointed by going to something where someone just reads to them for 55 minutes – unless they're *really* good, in which case it's amazing what you can get away with'. I am curious about the extent to which reader-audiences share his view about the ideal ratio of conversation to readings, and resolve to look into it.

Hahn elaborates on why, in his view, literary festivals have become so much more popular over the last twenty years. 'Readers now have **expectations of *access*** – an interest in getting a little bit more, some kind of *insight*. It's a little bit celeb-y – you get to be in a room with someone amazing – this year, here, say, with Ishiguro, with someone you admire'.

Since he is a representative of the Society of Authors, I ask Hahn about the controversy over authors increasingly being expected to perform at literary festivals for free, which has been described as 'iniquitous' by Philip Pullman and led to a campaign for fees to be required.[57] 'It's difficult', Hahn says, visibly tensing, 'because on one hand you can say *only do the ones you want to* – but if my publisher was to say *we've got you a gig at a superstar festival that doesn't pay anything*, they would have an absolute fit if I were to say: *no, I'm going to pass on the opportunity of being in a tent with 2000 people*. It's something publishers still see as being of value. Not so much value that they will invest their money in it so much. But of some value. Of profile I think. Rather than direct sales'. He pauses. '**Book sale statistics**' per event at festivals 'don't actually tell you very much', he adds. That said, Nielsen BookScan has now begun tracking sales at Hay and at Edinburgh International Book Festival, after the head of the PFD[58] literary agency, Caroline Michel, made the case that festival book sales were now such an important part of sales figures that it would be 'crazy' not to count them.[59] 'There are certainly some festivals I know who are very proud of their '**conversion rate**' – but I'm not sure you could measure it in a way that's meaningful', Hahn says. 'As an author', he explains, 'you'd have to be in a 2000-seater and selling very well for it to be worth the money, directly. But you hope that some people who saw the event will buy a book later, maybe months later when they see it in a shop and remember they quite enjoyed it and wonder what it's like... it's **impossible to quantify**'.

I ask Hahn for his views on festivals' **audience diversity** and how that affects reading practices. 'There are festivals and there are *festivals*', he answers and begins telling me enthusiastically about one he was involved with in London called **Pop Up**. It works with 'a certain kind of **community** and certain kinds of kids, that are not the same as Henley or Cheltenham where there are lots of regulars who read regularly and often come from a... similar background...' This indirect phrasing, evading the words race and class, is indicative of the awkwardness of representing more established literary events as a regular chair and author, while also being asked to critique them.[60] 'One of the things Pop Up does that I think is different', Hahn continues, 'is its dynamic and active **school-based programme** that involves writers going to schools and running workshops. At the end of that there will then be a festival which brings together children who've been through a programme already… It's a way of making people who *don't* feel like going to see a novelist in Cheltenham town hall is for them that *this* may be a thing that is real for them'. The **format** of Pop Up and other **children's festivals** is different from mainstream adult festivals and events too, he explains. 'They're much more **interactive** and much more engaging… the writers create an experience, so the festival becomes something much more immersive and creative, rather than "shut up I'm going to read to you"'.

I note Hahn's repetition of the phrase 'shut up' in relation to an adult author reading, implying that the audience is being forced into submission—and also the reference to children's events being more 'immersive' than adults' events. It is true that children's events tend to be far more performative, with the use of props and images by authors being common.

This is something that I've noticed too, while I've been attending live literature events frequently as part of my research, and something I've wondered about. **Immersiveness** has become an increasingly popular characteristic of live events in the wider 'adult' arts culture, with events like Secret Cinema drawing audiences into an immersive theatrical world around the film being screened, through actors and props in specially-selected locations. Hay is not 'immersive' on that aesthetic and performative level—and I wonder why more literary events do not seek to be so. (This line of inquiry will lead me to found my own experimentally-immersive live literature project.)[61]

On the other hand, Hay is immersive in the sense of being presented in a single rural site far from most people's normal lives and offering a series of engaging events. The use of **tents** creates a sense of immersion through its differentiation from the usual building structures in which people usually work, play and live—the thin separation of the canvas from the sky and the elements makes it feel different. That difference is heightened when a rainstorm hits, and performing voices rise to compete with the rumble of pitter-pattering drops.

When I ask Hahn how, **as an author**, he has found the experience of reading his work aloud in festivals like Hay—I fully expect the reticence he has just expressed in relation to author readings to continue. It doesn't. 'I love it!', he says, with unabashed enthusiasm. 'My stuff is slightly odd though, because most of my work, certainly at the moment, is translation, so it's work that is written by me but also not by me... I think if something works to read, it tends to work to read *aloud*, because I think we read aloud in our heads even if we're reading silently – or at least I do. So when it comes to **reading** '*aloud* **aloud**', in public, it's been road-tested somehow. And I like reading – and being on stage'. I am struck by the apparent disjunction between his repeated idea of audiences being made to 'shut up and listen' to readings, and his own delight in giving readings as an author-performer.

How does he choose the sections he likes to read '*aloud* aloud', and does he finds certain types of writing work particularly well? 'There are', he says, musingly, but 'I don't know how to characterise them. There's one paragraph of one of my novels that I translated years ago, that I think is my single favourite read-aloud thing; it's only a paragraph, and almost requires no context at all, but it's amazing.... It's basically an extended metaphor, which really shouldn't work because it's so audacious, in a way. It's a guy saying: I met this man... and the paragraph describes what the man was like, but it's so complicated... he says, *I used to have this turtle, and he used to like listening to Leonard Cohen, and he used to look really happy when you turned it on and really sad when you turn it off* ... It just shouldn't work! And yet it's the most beautifully constructed thing... But I usually just read the first two pages or whatever'.

Hahn admits to thinking ahead about the prospect of reading aloud at future events at some points while he's writing. 'When you're doing the first edit, and you think: actually, there's a two-page set piece here and it's clever and it's got two good jokes in it and a nice shape and doesn't require reading the whole novel in or the rest to have an impact... so yes, I do think about it'. This points to a level of **interconnection** between the culture of **live literature** and the practice, style and even the **content of creative writing** among contemporary authors.

The **green room** has filled up, and with a lot of recognisable faces. James Rhodes is laughing at one of Stephen Fry's jokes, Louise Brealey is sitting with Kirsty Logan, Malorie Blackman is conferring with her publicist, and Sandi Toksvig appears to be happily sandwiched between what I suspect are members of her team on the sofa. The bundling-together of big literary names in this behind-the-scenes space at Hay has led to gossip-worthy interactions in the past. Paul Theroux and V. S. Naipaul, for instance, had a fifteen-year feud after Theroux discovered a book he had given to Naipaul, inscribed 'with love', was up for sale for £1000, and hit back by publishing a memoir damning their friendship, whereupon Naipaul called Theroux's work 'tourist books for the lower classes'— until, in 2011, Ian McEwan decided the Hay green room was the place to brave bringing these two male egos back together.[62] (It worked.)

I spot the literary journalist and event chair **Alex Clark**, and ask if she would mind sharing her thoughts about live literature. 'I remember coming to Hay twenty years ago and it was a lot smaller then – there were not many literary festivals', she recollects. 'But in the last *few* years there has been an IMMENSE explosion'. She goes on to muse over various potential causes. I ask whether, as a reader, as well as a critic and interviewer, she is affected by hearing a writer read their texts aloud. She ponders. 'There is definitely something that *happens* when you hear a writer reading from their own work, however much you've enjoyed or not enjoyed the book; it's a... different experience. Now some writers are *brilliant* at reading, some just read in a very straightforward way, and some are not very performative, it's not their most comfortable thing – but I think whatever it does, it *does* bring you some kind of **different perspective on the text**. You hear a nuance, you hear what the *author intended*, and it's a good *guide* **to intention** – just in an *inflection* even, or the emphasis on a word – and you often find you haven't read it that way yourself when you just read it on the page'.

'As a chair, it is difficult to talk about prose style and language, though', she admits '– those aspects of writing which are what make fiction writers fiction writers, and distinguish one writer from the other – without seeming too abstract for people to really get a handle on what you're saying. It can go slightly into the ether; one risks sounding pretentious. It's very difficult I think, with novels, when they are brand new, to talk about them *at all*, in a way... If I say, "your character *x*", it means nothing to anyone in the audience; and if it's got any kind of suspense issue you don't want to spoil it. So I do think there's **an issue with** ***how* you *talk* about a novel**. And I think that's often why, in a festival setting, you do see a **lower take-up for fiction**. When there's a very clear *issue* that can be talked about, *that* will get audiences coming along'. Hence the utility of discussing themes, I suppose, remembering Hahn's commentary. 'Of course, when it's a really beloved or popular author, who's enjoyed significant success, like Hilary Mantel – you know she will always sell out every event she does', Clark points out. 'Or someone really beloved, like Ali Smith. But it *is tricky* for fiction'. Clark's viewpoint manifests the same apparent paradox to that of Glanville: both have a key role in chairing fiction events; yet view them as being inherently problematic.

I seize a moment to speak with **Jane Austen** expert **John Mullan**, whom I knew had written about Austen 'road-testing' her novels by reading drafts aloud at home—a process her brother had termed '**gradual perfor-mances**'.[63] He warms to the subject of live literature and points out how important reading aloud was for many of Austen's characters, reminding me how important the **social practice of reading aloud** was for wider society. 'Austen's name was made, in part, by reading aloud', he adds. 'George Eliot and her partner, George Henry Lewis, read Austen aloud to each other, and Lewis wrote about it afterwards and said, that's the *real* **test of a greatness of a writer**... when you read aloud you can't skip bits, and you see that every word matters'.

I ask whether Mullan thinks that, as the social practice of reading aloud died out, as a private leisure pursuit, it changed the nature of prose. He pouts. 'That's a big question to answer. There are writers who didn't write in a culture where reading aloud was common but whose work comes to life when read aloud. Joyce's *Ulysses*, for example – bits of that are fantastic when read aloud! And make a kind of *sense* read aloud which they don't on the page. I think some of Virginia Woolf... *To the*

*Lighthouse* is fantastic read aloud… it's actually very funny but you don't *realize* it quite until you hear it read aloud. You might research this: what evidence *is* there that novelists read aloud as part of the writing process?'.

This conversation reminds me of the self-flagellating accounts I've heard of novelists who have had to read their entire books aloud for the very first time in the context of audiobook recordings. Audiobook producer Dougal Patmore once described, on radio, witnessing authors reading their own work and 'cursing themselves' for 'how complicated and lengthy their sentence structure was. To paraphrase one author, it was: *I wouldn't write like this again, having read it all out loud*'.[64] On the same programme, author **Michael Hughes** said that reading his own novel aloud for the audiobook was 'transformative'; he had been unprepared for 'having such an intimate relationship' with his own words. 'Every single word of it you're experiencing *physically* in a way you never do while you're writing… I was just a wreck afterwards'. The experience caused him to rethink his literary style and aesthetic choices: 'I set myself the task of actually trying to write as people speak'.[65] His latest novel, *Country*, is particularly dynamic in its evocation of spoken dialect in Northern Ireland.

At live literature events, in contrast to audiobook recordings, author-performers can select the most 'speakerly' sections of their work and can edit them easily. I have noticed a lot of writers at live literature events hastily crossing through sentences in pencil, just before going on stage to read—and I have done this myself. But still, I wonder now: how common is this experience, among author-performers at live literature events, of feeling uncomfortable about re-encountering their work as they read it aloud? How often, as the audiobook experience did for Hughes, does this change the nature of their future writing?

Across the green room, I spot the bestselling children's author, **David Almond**. A gently-spoken man in his sixties, Almond has eyes that wrinkle at the corners and greets me in warm tones. 'I love all aspects of writing, including reading', he tells me, beaming. 'And there's a particular frisson when you get up to read in front of live audiences, and you get questions and answers – it's very stimulating to me as an author'.

Does he write with live audiences and reading aloud in mind, I wonder? 'I always **write for sound**. I write for *sound*', he repeats, so that the word rings on in my ears. 'So wherever I'm writing, in order to get something to work properly, I'll *beat* it, I'll [here he clicks his fingers, four times], you know?' I'm surprised and enchanted by this idea emerging from his fingertips—and what it reveals about the musicality of his literary aesthetic. 'And I think all writing should be like that, it should be *poetic*', he continues '– so I'll often say, you know, if a sentence is working, on the page, the way to find out what's wrong with it is to speak it aloud; and if you can't speak a sentence aloud very well it's probably a sign that something is wrong inside a sentence. So the connection between the human voice and the words on the page I think is – *really* – close – and we often forget that'.

Orality also determines how Almond selects passages to read aloud at events. 'I choose something which – speaks out well, which is rhythmical, which is poetic, which is powerful, which contains strong images – that's what I *try* to do. Writing for young people, you're always reminded that you're as close to oral storytelling as you are to books on shelves... And reading isn't just to do just with the brain, it's not just to do with the conscious mind; when children learn to read and to write it's a *physical* thing. Writing is a physical act. People think it's to do with the brain – it's not, **it's about the *body*.** We learn to write through the body by using our hands. It's not just about the abstraction of print. And in my events I like to talk about the process – I show notebooks and talk about how I go about making books – notes, scribbling, playfulness, and then I read and I like to have lots of questions'. I am struck by how Almond's keen awareness of embodiment clearly affects both the performance of his work and the nature of the writing itself. To my disappointment, I discover that I've just missed his event.

I ask Almond how he thinks that questions and conversations about his process around the live readings add to his audiences' experiences of his texts when they read them later on. 'I think it helps readers to understand that writing on the page is the product of a very human act, in some ways a very *ordinary* act', he says. 'The danger of the printed page is that it looks perfect. It's almost *untouchable*. But if you somehow involve people in the process of writing, they understand that what seems to be perfect is actually not, that **we are imperfect beings**. And one of the purposes in all of my talks is to make people feel able to be *creative*'. This is an interesting perspective: the idea that a goal of a literary event is to unleash **creativity in the audience**, not by making people in awe of the celebrity writer-as-oracle, as Jo Glanville and Daniel Hahn alluded to; but the opposite: making them see their flaws, their ordinariness and their humanity.

Does Almond think that people respond to his work differently having heard him talk about his process and read from his books? 'I think they do', he says, with quiet certainty. 'I get a lot of people come up and talk to me afterwards and say: it **helped me to *understand*** your work through hearing it spoken'—as Kira described earlier, from an audience perspective—'and also that they've understood the ***nature of literature***, writing, by seeing things like scruffy notebooks'. He also believes that an audience's experience of witnessing David-Almond-the-author reading from his work at a live event is fundamentally different from an actor reading the same text. Again, for him this comes down to sound. 'It's because I write in my own ***rhythm***, and I write in a kind of *northern* rhythm. And I like reading my own work aloud – a lot of writers don't – and I think I do it well, that I'm a good reader... I think my accent and the nature of the words *feed* each other, and the rhythms – I read in the rhythms of the book, and I think other people who read my work, they sometimes slip the rhythms slightly, and miss the beat. Which goes back to sound again'. Again, this reminds me of the ways in which Stan and Kira talked about rhythm as being vital to their experience of Toni Morrison's performance.

I am curious to hear more of Almond's thoughts on the relationship between contemporary novels and oral storytelling. 'It goes *way* back', he says, 'and a thing I try to do when I'm writing is to be ***ancient***, as well as to be very modern. You know, to actually accept that I'm part of a tradition that goes back **pre-*literature***, right back to people in caves telling stories... it's good to see books on shelves, but we have to remember that it comes from something much rawer and wilder'.

Finally, I ask why he thinks there has been such an increase in live literature events and festivals. 'I think **people want *authenticity***', he answers, decisively. That word, again, I note. 'Seeing, hearing, touching.

You know, there's one theory that we're becoming more digital and ever more remote, but that comes at the same time as this huge burst of literature festivals, drama festivals, performance festivals, philosophy festivals... and I think people don't really *want* a purely *abstract* world. Because we're *physical* beings, we're flesh and blood, and I think that's what it is'.

As I head outside I feel somehow more alive in my own skin, and I resolve to read Almond's books.

Outside, the sun is shining and plenty of people are soaking it up on the lawns and at picnic tables. As I pass a slight, middle-aged woman sitting alone with a book, she glances up to look around, and I ask whether she would mind telling me about her experience at Hay. A quietly spoken person from Cheshire, she works as a legal publisher and has been coming to the Festival regularly for over twenty years. 'I read English Literature at university, so that's always been my core, even though I trained as a lawyer'. Since arriving yesterday, she's seen a session on dyslexia, 'with a Cambridge professor, and that was marvellous... there seems to be a higher level of diagnosis, and I have a young child... and her theory I think is a very *very* interesting one... And I went to one this morning on the Disraeli marriage, which was great – I mean, I had no idea – I knew he'd purportedly married for money but there was love there as well, and they packed a lot into their marriage, and she was a very *very* enlivening speaker. And the next one I'm going to is a writer I know nothing about, called Andrew O'Hagan. And then tonight it's Sally Wainwright, because she's a good scriptwriter. I tend to **mix obscure authors and celebrity ones**. Nothing too heavy, and nothing too frothy either'. Many would take issue with the word 'obscure author' in the context of a Hay stage, I think—but Elsa's sense, as a self-proclaimed literature lover and Hay regular, that there are plenty of 'obscure' authors here to discover, offers a counterpoint to literary professionals who dismiss this festival on the basis of its celebrity dominance.

I ask Elsa how she chooses her fiction events. 'I mostly try to discover new authors, now. I go with my gut when I'm reading the programme. There'll be something in the little write-up which snags me. And I think; ooh [high], interesting – that's an interesting hook. Normally something to do with emotions [embarrassed laugh], because, you know, I always loved the 19<sup>th</sup> century novels. And the big story. And the big emotional core. So if there's something of that ilk in the write up, I'll book it'. I ask why she's less inclined now to go to events with writers she already knows. 'Well, it's about **exposing yourself to the new** isn't it?', she asks, rhetorically. As for whether she tends to buy the books afterwards: 'only if the talker really *charms* me, and draws me in so that I think: yeah, I *will* buy their new book [decisive]'. I'm intrigued by this term: '**the talker**', and the use of 'charm' in verb form, suggestive of a spellbinding power that certain authors wield over their audiences.

Does the experience of seeing the author reading aloud from a book affect how she reads it on the page later? 'I see them as… separate…', she says, uncertainly. 'But there might be a page the writer reads where I think, oooh, I like the *sound* of that. There was one last year: he was so eloquent, and cerebral, and quietly spoken, and *impressive* as an author, that even though I wasn't sure about the book at first, I found his talking about it and reading from it definitely influenced me – so much that **I bought it, and even bought it as presents** for people, actually! So in that case the two really **interlocked** – the **experiences of** *being here* **and** *reading*'. I'm intrigued that this memory of sound is what she linked to her decision to buy the physical book.

What else draws her back to the festival so regularly? I wonder. 'It's set in the most *stunning* countryside', she says, 'so, although I went to Cheltenham and Oxford a couple of times, to me they just didn't feel the same…. Going into a kind of draughty *room* to hear an author, you feel as if you could be anywhere. Whereas here it's kind of quirky, eccentric – it's – I personally feel this festival is *unique*, and that's why I come back every year'. She grins, a little mischievously. 'I would also say – it probably sounds a bit pathetic – but I also **leave behind my family** for these few days! And I'd say… it's almost the *highlight of my year* [reflective]. It's also somewhere where as a woman, as well, you can just hang out by yourself [high pitch – a revelation]. And that's quite rare as well, having a friendly place, a friendly festival, where you can do that. But I think we all get ground down by work. And also I've got a very young daughter. And all of those things, you know, they're great… But actually, to plug into something else, where you're *submerged* **in ideas**, and other lives... and I tend to book a *lot* of talks, things I'm naturally interested in, but also things I know nothing about. I come away feeling enlivened, inspired... I feel like I've had a massive ***injection***! Which wears down over the 12 months that pass until the next time'. I'm interested in her choice of embodied language here—the word 'submerged' suggesting a step beyond 'immersion', taking her out of her normal environment entirely; and the word 'injection' suggesting an internal transformation, running through her blood. 'But it – it just opens your mind!', she carries on, beaming. 'It's a cliché but it really, really does, because – I can't think of any other environment or setting where your mind is dipped into something, many things, that are completely different. Sure, you can go to the occasional talk, and you can look around your local bookshop which is always a pleasure. But actually it feels amazingly indulgent, and wonderful, to be able to be exposed to these minds and ideas, and to have it in such a concentrated dose. And then of course, like I'm doing now, you get to hang out, and totally relax, and think through what you've just seen or what you're going to see and look at the book.... I mean, it's sublime! It really is. And so I don't bother with any of the other festivals, having gone, in the past, to them... I just, kind of, I'm not a literary festival guru, I'm **just a Hay guru**'.

Her choice of the word 'guru' here brings to mind the notion of the festival as a form of contemporary secular **pilgrimage**, which is now the subject of increasing study,[66] largely in the context of tourism, and again following in the footsteps of **Victor Turner**.[67] In the light of the decreasing role of religion in the UK and in many parts of the globe, the concept of making a 'pilgrimage' to Hay and to other literary festivals has become a resonant one. There is a quality of reverence, not only in Elsa's words, but in a lot of other discourses I have encountered about Hay that reflect that idea.[68] Hay's now-long-term centrality to literary culture, its remote location, the ritualistic quality of the annual collective gathering of audiences with writers and the literary establishment in such a remote geographical space, renders it a kind of literary mecca.

Some literary festivals expressly describe themselves as pilgrimages,[69] and the 'literary pilgrimage' to the fictional settings of classic novels has become a commercial form of tourism beyond the remit of the literary festival.[70] Elsa's emphasis on the significance of Hay's rural location for her—in particular her point that even beginning the long train journey felt like a pleasurable element of the festival experience—resonates strongly with the pilgrimage concept, which entails journeying physically away from everyday life to a destination for the purposes of spiritual transformation. While being hard-to-reach might on first glance appear to be a *negative* characteristic of Hay, in a contemporary culture in which value is often defined by speed and convenience, the experiential value of its remote rural location is actually heightened. As Maggie Kerr, Hay's Development Director, put it in a brief conversation we had there near the ticket office: 'Other festivals with city centre locations have to compete with other things, which makes it hard to create a sense of place and **atmosphere**'.

On the subject of journeying to remote places for literary purposes, the next event I've circled is poet **Simon Armitage** talking about his new prose **memoir**: *Walking Away: Further Travels with a Troubadour on the South West Coast Path*, with Stephanie Merritt as chair. The memoir recounts a long walk that Armitage arranged, punctuated by performed readings of his work, in return for donations and accommodation, and culminating in this book of prose and poetry: a process that can be viewed as a live literature event itself—in a very different form to Hay. Armitage's headshot in the Hay programme depicts him with a pen between his teeth.

The event is staged in one of Hay's biggest tents, and it is packed out. After the two settle themselves on stage and wait for enthusiastic applause to die down, Merritt introduces Armitage, who's dressed in dark jeans and a dark shirt. 'Many of you will have read the first volume', she tells the audience—referring to his first memoir, of a different walk—thus assuming a general knowledge of Armitage's work on their part, perhaps through his previous appearances at Hay.

Armitage nods. 'I walked this route as a **troubadour**, passing a sock around and asking people to pay what they thought I was worth', he explains: a converse model to the literary festival ticketing structure. 'I virtually promised myself never to do such a thing again. [The audience laughs, knowingly. Armitage has a laconic, mellow, almost self-deprecatory tone of voice, and speaks gently and assuredly in a measured rhythm with a distinct Yorkshire accent.] But a couple of years later, I just started getting itchy feet, a bit restless… I started thinking of it a bit like **testing my reputation as a poet, and also poetry's reputation**, in a way. Would people come out on a wet Wednesday in Wensleydale for a reading? [He speaks so naturally, and un-performatively, somehow, that this alliteration and assonance seems entirely natural.] It started to dawn on me that I really should have put this to the test in a region further from home'.

'Where did the troubadour idea originally come from?' Merritt enquires. 'I'm just not that comfortable with being a writer that just sits at home all the time', he replies. 'Otherwise I'm going to end up writing poems about my *study wall*'. [He separates these two last words fractionally; this is a poet experienced in delivering words with the right timing, and the audience laughs, appreciatively. Beyond the comic image of a collection of poems about a blank wall, his underlying point about the work of a writer being to connect with people, with society, as he is doing now, seems to resonate. It is also a distinct counterpoint to Hahn's description of the tension felt by writers who crave solitude to write but are called upon by publishers to read at commercial events.]

'I was trying to imagine a walk that was contrasting in many ways to the first', he explains. 'So the Pennine way, it's upland, it's northern, it's interior, it's *terrible* [audience laughs], it's grim… When I'd finished it, someone in a book described me as the Eeyore of walking, I'd moaned about it *that much*. [More laughter. There is a melancholic quality to Armitage's speaking voice, even when he isn't 'moaning'. His frequent jokes, funny and incisive, are all delivered with a near-dead-pan tone, in the manner suggested by his profile picture.] So I imagined this one as walking along sunny beaches for 250 miles', he continues. 'I'm not that familiar with the coast, the language of the coast, its diction, its rhythms' [nice literary metaphors, lightly dropped in] '… so to do something along the coast of the south west, going through lots of tourist areas, appealed'.

Intrigued by what might happen if he competed with other tourist entertainments, he decided to stay in a Butlins holiday camp at the start of the walk. 'I mean, that could have been a whole book', he adds [again, dead-pan]. The audience laughs loudly, and he pauses to mark the transition to reading and then opens his copy of the book.

'The outward appearances are not encouraging. [His voice doesn't change much here, though his tone becomes fractionally more dec laratory.] After guest check-in, I'm directed towards a place called Strawberry Square, in an area labelled Plantation Quay, which seems to be an area of apartments somewhere between Swiss chalet and mock Tudor in design. Varnish is peeling from the window frames, the outside walls of each block are stencilled with large, Soviet style letters, lots of men are wearing premier league football shirts with their own surnames printed on the back [audience titters], and in a female voice, an uninterrupted stream of abuse and profanities issues from a ground floor flat. This isn't my first time at Butlin's. In the 70s, we bought a family day pass and spent 7 or 8 hours on the rides and in the swimming pool… I remember the straggly barbed wire face that marked the perimeter, that my dad said wasn't to stop people getting in, but to deter escapees' [the audience laughs fulsomely.]… At one stage I find myself in the staff quarters, ranks of distinctly dilapidated barracks beyond the last supermarket, spookily quiet except for a tinny portable radio playing capital FM…' [His poetic sensibility is evident from his evocative language, including the sonic and rhythmic qualities of his lists of names, yet there is nothing overtly poetic about the delivery; it comes across as a slightly heightened version of the way that Armitage would normally speak.]

'I had tortured myself with the idea of giving a reading at Butlin's [the audience titters], pitting myself against an eighties comedian, an ex-game show host, or army sweetheart, to **see if poetry could hold its own against the massed forces of light entertainment**. [More knowing titters; a juxtaposition to how many will probably see the event they are in now.] But instead of going head to head with *A Tribute to the Music of Olly Murs* [high-pitched laughs] – that was actually on that night [this comment is clearly off-script, and prompts more laughs] – … I'd taken a cowardly sidestep, and opted for a more literary opening night'. He proceeds to describe the venue, away from the main Butlins site, at which he finally decided to perform, and paints a vivid picture of an unconventional live literature event that jabs further at the themes of class divisions, celebrity and entertainment: themes that have been the subject of heated media debates in relation to Hay.

Merritt asks him to talk more about the idea of supporting himself through his words, and he compares it with busking. 'I've always thought of **poetry as a very portable art**', he adds. 'I don't like to think about it as something static. I mean, I was a probation officer in a former life, and I've always wanted to be someone out there and doing things, and I didn't want to give that up just to sit in a garret. I've also always been somebody who's written about things that are right in front of me, but for that to keep happening you have to keep changing the scenery. And I think my style of writing, in non-fiction in particular, is to look at things that are familiar and see them as a stranger'—something, I reflect, that ethnographers often try to do, too, as well as novelists. 'Travelling is one way to continue to have these encounters. In terms of the financial aspect to it [he chuckles to himself] – yeah, there's something... *impish* or mischievous in me that wants to be able to prove that I could get by on my wits, if you like. I wouldn't *recommend* it as a way of trying to earn a living... I totted it up and it came up under the living wage.... But the richness, the profit, comes in the encounters'.

His project clearly drew audiences not just through the performances themselves, but through his pre-existing reputation as an author-performer. This much is revealed by Raynor Winn in her memoir, *The Salt Path* (2018), which recounts the walk that she and her critically-ill husband Moth took along the very same route at the very same time, due to unexpected homelessness. During their walk, strangers kept on mistaking Moth for Armitage with great excitement—one rich man even inviting them to stay at his rental house overnight as a result: a situation that led to Moth busking one summer day in St Ives by reciting *Beowulf*, the only poem he knew by heart, to the surrounding crowds, until he was moved on.

Armitage offers a fascinating evocative description of a very different kind of live literature event to Hay, showing how the 'form' can be stretched to less overtly literary and commercial contexts, in a way that tests the connective possibilities of literature between strangers, as a form of radical social encounter. I can't help noticing how his description of the context around his near-Butlins performance reflects what

I am seeking to explore in writing ethnographically about Hay and other live literature events: how elements of the experience—such as the surrounding, space, sense of time, event structure and aesthetics—work together holistically to generate the meaning and value of the event for participants.

After audience questions, Merritt announces: 'we've come to the end of the session', and is just directing the audience to the bookshop and is on the brink of inviting them to applaud… when she stops short, remembering something. 'Oh yes, the poem!', she says. 'Have we got time?' Armitage asks her, one eyebrow raised. 'Yes, yes!', she replies, so he rises again, then pauses, again, to mark the start of What is the seaa reading.

> What is the sea? The sea is sleep…. Dockheaded fish, and transparent brine-blood creatures loll and glide in its depths… Boneless life forms tur inside-out in its dreams but it sleeps… Who is the sea?

[There is a new quality of silence in the audience, now, as they listen.]

> Why is the sea? Because it sleeps… Sleeps like a drunk… its feet on the pillow of reefs and shallows… its head where light never breaks… face down in the sand… I know this… I know this… I am the land.[71]

[Solid applause].

It now seems almost inconceivable that the event wouldn't have ended with this poem, which seems to have walked the event back home to the text.

I find Armitage afterwards and ask him if he'd mind sharing his thoughts about the **relationship between oral performance and literary text on the page**. 'I think it's a very complicated relationship', he says, reflective and more serious, now, than he had been on stage. 'When I started getting involved with poetry and literature I saw the two things as being very separate: that literature lived in books on the page, and it was certainly written for that purpose – and my understanding was that that was how most people received poetry and *wanted* to receive it'. I wonder how common this is: an authorial assumption that a publishing convention equates to an audience preference or demand. 'I had a fairly purist view about it', he continues, 'that poetry lived on the page, and that readings were a kind of day out, little sort of *excursions* [small laugh.] But readings have become a big part of my life, and I'm more inclined now to think of books as just another aspect of poetry'. He could substitute 'literature' for 'poetry' here, it occurs to me, given that he's just published and a book of prose.

'And certainly poetry will have predated this thing that we call literature and certainly books, and poetry's origins go back to ancient theatre, to sacred rites, to the campfire...' He's echoing Almond now. 'To the troubadours, the performance was a crucial aspect. Probably *the* crucial aspect. So I think: yeah, there might've been a time where I was a bit shy about talking up the poetry reading; but I see it as a *task* now, and I *enjoy* it. And I like the idea that you've in some way got a **responsibility to be publicly** *accountable* **for your work**'.

This is a new angle in my conversations, this idea of live literature events being a form of 'responsibility' and 'accountability'—a perspective that links with Armitage's background as a former probation officer. 'I like going to see readings, listening to people reading, connecting their personality, their voice and their verbal mannerisms with their work', he continues. 'I think it can have a humanising effect as well. A demystifying effect. I also think that **poetry lends itself very much to the event**, to the reading, in a way that prose doesn't always', he reflects, anticipating my next question. 'You go to see an event about a novel and they have to spend up to ten minutes explaining the storyline, the character development, and then you know, they can read something that can, on occasions, be very *page-bound*. Whereas poetry by nature is a very small thing, that often doesn't get to the right-hand margin, or to the bottom of the page, and I think the intro around it and the preamble can really work in concert with the actual thing'.

'You have to really *attend* when you listen to a poem', he continues. 'And so little bursts of conversational discussion, I just think suit – well, I'm hesitant about using the word *performance*... but certainly the *reading*'. I ask him to expand on this **'reading/performance' distinction**. He grins, wryly. 'I think there used to be a thick black line between the two things, and I think that line's becoming – more of a fuzzy line these days. But I think if you start talking about *performance*, there are expectations it will be something theatrical and rehearsed – and I like to think that what theatricality might be is in the *words*. And I think most poets I listen to have a fairly dead-pan **delivery style**. And I assume that's because they want to *trust* the words and to trust the idea that the words will do the work for them. Then there are I think other poets whose... their whole project is about performance; that is where they see their poems as existing and living, and they devise whole performance strategies... That's performance with a big P'. This idea of letting the words do the work reminds me of recent research on the history of audiobook narration.[72] The **spoken word scene**, he says, is 'incredibly vibrant... I do think it's **enlivened the poetry scene** and it's made more page-bound poets consider what they're offering.'

I refer Armitage back to something he said earlier that when he started off as a poet he thought of it more as a medium for the page, but that as time's gone on that's changed—and I ask whether that has affected the way he writes. 'No... at least, I'm **wary of the idea of the reading as a sort of *test bed***', he explains, 'because the response you get, the reaction you get to a poem, when it's audible or visible, isn't necessarily the way you're affecting someone's *mind*, and you can't really see *that* response. And I think if you *did* start writing just for that environment, you might end up going for the cheap laughs and the instant reaction. So I would hope that there isn't *too* much of a relationship'. I nod, recalling how many fiction writers have spoken to me about selecting passages that are likely get laughs. 'There have been two or three occasions when I've sat down with that in mind, thinking I could do with something a bit lively and rhythmical that will work in the middle of a reading', he admits.

Recalling John Mullen's question to me about whether many writers read aloud while they write, I ask this of Armitage, and am surprised when he hesitates, perplexed. 'I don't *think* so', he replies eventually. 'That'd be a form of insanity! [He laughs.] I think occasionally I try a line out. But I probably do it in my head; I don't speak it aloud'. He shakes his head and grins sheepishly. 'At the event, that was the very first time I'd read that poem about the sea, and I realised I hadn't quite figured out how to deliver it'. He looks genuinely embarrassed at this confession.

'You know, I was inching my way through it'. I tell him, honestly, that I thought it was beautifully read, and that to have a reading was a lovely way to end the event—particularly with the idea of going to sleep as a form of ending in that particular poem. 'Yeah – it was a nice way to end', he says, looking relieved, as if my opinion mattered, despite his vast experience relative to my own and his apparent confidence on stage. 'I prefer to finish with a poem rather than a question. Finish on your own terms really'.

Armitage considers it vital to **balance questions and readings** at literary events. 'I've been to some festivals in parts of the world where the *last* thing they want you to do is read any of your work, and it's almost *rude* to ask do it…. What they want is to hear you interviewed, or they want you to sit on a panel and talk about the death of the novel, or the religion in society, or something topical and political'. I ask why he thinks that is. 'I don't know whether festivals know what they're doing, or whether they're pandering to the cult of personality, or whether they think that people can read your work wherever they like, in their own time, but they only get one chance to hear you talk about *other* things. Or maybe there've been too many terrible readings [laughs] – people reading for an hour without a break'.

I am interested in whether his experience of reading from his prose book has been different to reading from his poetry, for which he is much better known. 'It took me a while to adjust, actually', he says. 'I hadn't read from this book before – it was the first time. I started the first sentence thinking there'd be a line break, thinking it was poetry, and forgetting it was prose! It took me a while to relax into it. I tend to read poems with a little more emphasis and intensity. But I daresay I'll get used to it in a little while. Also, as this was the first event I'd done around the book, I haven't got used to the conversation I'll have around the book – **the *patter***, if you like. I don't feel very familiar with the book yet; I haven't looked at it since the last proofs, 4-5 months ago'.

Does he enjoy that **process of rediscovery** of his work at events, I wonder, or wish he could go back and re-edit, or just move onto the next project? 'It's quite nice', he replies, 'because you forget the creative processes you've gone through. And I fucking hate proof reading! I can't bear it. And it's the kind of reading... you're essentially reading for *mistakes*. And that level of attention you've got to give to your own work feels... I don't know. There's something immodest about it' [he laughs, faintly embarrassed].

Reflecting back on his comment about novelists' need to spend more time explaining their work at festival events, I ask: 'Do you think prose can ever work well in this context?' 'Absolutely I do', he responds, with certainty. 'But I think the same about that as I do as about poetry.... that **writers can't any more just *turn up***. You've got to **think** about it, maybe ***practise*** a little bit, choose carefully which bits you're going to read and which bits you're not... And, don't take this the wrong way, but *poetry* can be *boring* for people – I mean, some people find it *incredibly* boring, and I think if you get it wrong it can be a terrible thing. If it's too dense and clotted...it can be very alienating. And I think prose in that sense can be more engaging and welcoming. We're more familiar with it. Our experience of written language tends to be prose'.

As I walk away, I spot a couple of women I'd seen in the audience for Armitage's event. It turns out that one of them is a children's author, **Liz Kessler**, who did an event the previous night, and she is with Laura, her partner. They're in their 50s and 40s, respectively. I ask what they thought about it. 'I really enjoyed it', Laura glows. 'It was – I'm not very *literary*, and I'm not into poetry *at all* – but I wanted to go because I'm doing a walk, along the coast path... And I think he's just – a nice guy! And it was entertaining and *interesting*, and I've got the first book but I haven't read it yet but I will be doing, and we will be getting the second one!' She seems to reflect, head tilted up. 'I mean, the poem he read just then was *absolutely* beautiful' Laura says, smiling dreamily. 'And it makes me think, ooh! *Poetry*! [laughs]'. 'It changed your view about it?', I ask. 'Yeah! Yeah' [revelation].

'And what did you think about it?', I ask Liz. 'I think he's just got this really lovely **manner** where he's very dry, and quite droll, but he's *so funny*. And he has these little moments that you kind of feel building up, and he says something funny at the end...I thought it was great. Really nice. And he's fab. Go Simon! And **he's northern**! [They both laugh]. Sorry, that's a private joke', Liz tells me, then adds: 'Laura's got this theory that all the people she gets on with best are northern'. 'Oh dear, well I won't last very long then', I say. Jocular though they are, their comments emphasise how much accent, as a vocal quality, can impact upon audiences' reception of an author-performer's work, and their wider evaluation of it. This links back to the idea of authenticity that has been coming up so frequently in my conversations, and to the role of regional identity in judgements about authenticity.

I ask Liz how much she enjoys hearing authors read prose aloud in comparison with reading them on the page. 'I do read a lot, and I like reading a book and getting into it…', she says, 'but I think there's something quite *special* about hearing an author read *their own work* – it **brings it to *life***. And especially something like this, I think, which is a non-fiction, autobiographical piece, where he's talking about his experience – hearing him say it just puts you almost in the place he was… hearing his words saying it, it's – so powerful. Really'. I ask whether she thinks it is much more powerful hearing him read live as opposed to, say, in a YouTube video. 'Oh *yes!* There's a connection, especially with this book – there's a connection because he's talking about intimate meetings with people'.

Laura chips in. 'He's got that beautiful voice and that beautiful regional accent… and hearing those words as he's saying them, is like hearing how he imagined them. Do you know what I mean? Because it's *his voice*. And it makes it really special'. Liz agrees. 'With his accent, it's like you're hearing it coming straight from his mind because you're hearing it from his voice'. Laura agrees, enthusiastically. 'It's his *voice*', she repeats. 'It's similar with David Almond – he's amazing', she adds. 'Even though it was prose', Liz chips in, now talking about Armitage again, 'he made it very poetic because he's got a very beautiful way of… his *language* is very beautiful, and it [his prose] *sounded* quite like reading a poem, in a way when he read it'. Laura agrees, nodding: 'Yeah, yeah…' Again, I am intrigued to hear this emphasis on the **sound and musicality** of voice as a recurring element of reader-audience experience.

Laura looks at me, confidingly, and lowers her voice. 'I've heard various people read while we've been here. And quite naughtily, actually, I've said to Liz, "oh I didn't like the way she read that", or "I didn't like the way he read that" – you know, I've pointed out the ones I didn't like'. 'So who didn't you like?', I ask, grinning, but Liz jumps in hastily. 'Nooo we're not saying that, we're not saying that!' 'Or, why didn't you like the way they read?', I rephrase. Laura answers: 'Because they just sort of **read their words with no passion** – it was just sort of like eurghlur-blurlurlurlurlurlur [in a monotone], and I just didn't feel it? I think that's the difference'. Liz nods, firmly. 'Yep: I think if someone's going to read, then that's part of the whole point of it, that you're hearing the *feeling* in their voice'. 'Especially when *they've* written it!', Laura adds. 'Surely they should – if anybody's going to read it well, *they* should!'.

It is mid-afternoon. I take a break, leave the festival site and stride up the hill to look down on the town, nestled among such lush greenery, beneath the soft arcs of the surrounding landscape. I breathe the sweet air deeply and watch a squirrel scamper up a tree trunk. It's so quiet up here, so peaceful. Not a person in sight. The white tents below, where the festival continues, look so tiny from up here beneath the puffy clouds, so anonymous. You'd never guess, if you didn't know, that thousands of people, ideas and coffees were circulating inside them. A crow caws lazily, accompanying a trilling blackbird.

Back down in the fray, I queue then file into the vast hive that is the tent about to host Booker-winner **Kazuo Ishiguro**, who'll be talking to BBC presenter **Martha Kearney** about his new novel, *The Buried Giant*. It's long been sold out. Kearney and Ishiguro arrive and take their seats on the stage to a barrage of applause. He greets the audience modestly and waits for the interview to begin, fluttering his eyelashes. It appears oddly disproportionate to have such a tiny, still person at centre stage in such a vast tent, though his image is projected up onto a big screen for those at the back.

'Ish has managed to combine great literary success with great popularity amongst readers which is a holy grail for authors… his books have sold more than 5 million copies around the world', Kearney announces. Her use of this pet name for Ishiguro surprises me, but conveys a sense of his public presence and wide appreciation, popular as well as critical—*there is a reason that this event is so big*, it implies. 'Today I want to explore some of the themes in his books as well as his very individual prose style'. She begins by asking how he came to write about ogres and dragons in *The Buried Giant*, which makes the book appear so different to his previous novels. 'You haven't been involved in that world yourself I assume', she grins.

'I backed myself into a corner', Ishiguro says, smiling modestly. He's got a quiet voice that matches the stillness of his body language, sitting motionless in his chair, but the audience seems to grow extra quiet in response, as if all ears are being tilted towards the stage. 'I couldn't get my story to work for ages, and in that corner were ogres and pixies.... I do get into those kind of desperate phases with all of my novels. People think I must have some kind of routine, but it's a fluke – I haven't got it figured out. With this one, I had this story, and kept putting it in different times and places, even different genres... it was only when I finished I thought: Oh, there's ogres and things in it! Will this be an issue? And then people started saying: "Oh [markedly disappointed tone]. I liked *Never Let Me Go*, but I've heard your new book's got dragons and ogres in it – I'm not sure I want to read it." I've been shocked by the sheer prejudice that exists against ogres [delivered straight; audience laughs]. It's just an imaginary thing, amongst other imaginary things... I think people are mistaking a characteristic of a genre as the *essence*. In the end I became quite militant on behalf of my ogres and pixies. They're really just extras in my novel – I hired them, but they did a good job and I stand by them. People are terribly preoccupied about certain **genre lines**. I think maybe as a book culture, a reading culture, we've got ourselves into a bind when we take genres too seriously... most genre boundaries are relatively recent things that were **created by the book industry to help market the book to different demographics** of the reading public. I think there are such things as genuine genres, but most of what we call genres, the stuff that's written on the top of bookshelves in bookshops, is a marketing exercise created relatively recently.[73] Someone told me recently that horror had finished, and people were going around moving those books to thriller and sci fi [audience laughs]. I'm **against the imagination police**... we should be very careful of ogre prejudice'.

As these comments allude to, genre has a significant impact on way in which literature is marketed and valued: a fact that is reflected in the Hay programme, which features very few events showcasing books that are obviously marketed as genre fiction, except by authors who, like Ishiguro, have critical recognition as authors of 'literary fiction'. The limiting effect for authors is an issue that has been raised by many who have managed to transcend genre categories through work that has been received as 'literary fiction', including Margaret Atwood, Neil Gaiman and Ursula K. Le Guin.[74] There are now, though, an increasing number of literary festivals that are genre specific.[75]

'I had ogre prejudice', Kearney gamely admits to Ishiguro and the vast assembly [audience titters], 'but now I've thrown it away… and I've realized a lot of this book is actually about an idea about society's attitudes to memory or painful memories – didn't you think initially that the story could have taken place in Bosnia or Rwanda?' Ishiguro nods. 'I admit that's where it started'. He talks about the difference between individual and social memories, and compares the impulse to suppress memories in a long marriage to the impulse for a society to suppress atrocities. 'Is it better to remember?', he asks, looking out to the crowd.

Kearney goes on to ask about parallels within his earlier work. He talks about how, as a young writer, his peers were very political, and, it being the Cold War era, people adopted strong, badge-wearing positions on issues. 'When I wrote *Remains of the Day*, I think I kind of assumed that, as young people do, that if you got your political and moral values right, at a certain stage, you'd be able to steer a good course through your life… I think that was the unexamined assumption behind those book…. As I got a bit older, into my 40s, I started to think that was a naïve way to think about life'. Kearney nods and looks at her notes. 'You said as you get older you realise that principles can be precarious – you can be picked up by a wind and dumped down somewhere else…' Ishiguro raises his eyebrows and shakes his head a fraction. 'That's remarkable – when did I say that?' [audience laughs loudly] He appears like the epitome of a wise **sage**, sitting with such poise, speaking quietly but commanding reverence from all these people, including the renowned yet assiduous, eager interviewer, and gently making light of the entire situation, including his own persona as represented in the media. 'Yes, I think those earlier books were flawed', he says. 'But I'd still *recommend* them to people. [audience laughter] – another knowing reference to the marketing purpose behind the event'.

She tries to get her own back: 'You've also said that writers tend to peak early'. He smiles wryly. 'Yes, when I was in my early thirties, my wife and I were researching this… we were surprised that most significant novelists tended to peak before they were 45 – it was slightly alarming… Now that I've got older, I'm reluctant to accept this thesis. I'm now searching desperately for examples [audience laughter; he waits a fraction] … of people ahead of me – examples of *late style*… there's the Neil Young model where you just keep doing what you always did, with just as much enthusiasm… Or you can do the kind of distilled, concise summary of the things you were doing before… novellas, where everything is very pared down… like Philip Roth's *Nemesis*….'

Kearney jumps in here: 'But *you're* not the retreater – you reinvent yourself with each book! I can't believe you're going to become a minia-turist'. She links his reference to the 'pared down' model of late style with a quote from critic James Wood in the *New Yorker* about Ishiguro's literary prose style in general: 'Wood said you have "prose of provoking equilibrium, sea-level flat with unseen fathoms below"… I wonder how much rewriting there is to get it down to that. 'As for the flat style with stuff underneath', Ishiguro replies, evenly [audience laughter] – I can't say it as well as Wood does – but when I first started to write that's just what came out. And I wasn't aware of it being a style. I just wrote in the best way I could. And it was only when I started to publish, that I started to read these reviews that said things like that, right from the start… Except, it was also apparently quite a novelty that someone with a Japanese back-ground was writing in English, so they tended to use metaphors like a *Japanese pond*, with *carp* [loud audience laughter] – essentially saying the same thing. And I thought: Oh! **Maybe this *is* a quality I have in my style**. I started to take credit for it. You know, I'd say: "Yes, yes, you have to work very hard to achieve that, and do a lot of rewriting" [more audi-ence laughter]. But **to be honest it's just how my voice came out**. When I started *The Remains of the Day*, it's the first time I went in *conscious* that that was how people would see my natural voice: as a quiet surface with these emotions rumbling underneath. And I thought that should also be deployed in the writing – what the stories were *about*. I became *self-conscious* courtesy of the *responses* I got to a thing I was doing *uncon-sciously*. So *The Remains of the Day* is about someone who wants to keep a very controlled surface and to keep things under the surface, and by implication an English society that wants to do the same thing'.

This fascinates me—not just the fact that Ishiguro never used to see his prose in the way it was characterised, and how much of that characterisation seemed to be inflected with a racial stereotype—but how much this characterisation of his prose style is reflected in the way he is presenting himself live, now: so calmly, with such unruffled demeanour, subtly wry and self-deprecating, yet clearly armed with acerbic wit. This observation taps back into a seam running through many of my live literature conversations: how often there seems to be a **relationship between the idiolect of vocal speech and the substance of the writing produced**; and how this connection—real or perceived—gives rise to a **sense of authenticity**.

When Kearney 'opens up' the event for audience questions, I am struck that she has at no point asked Ishiguro to read from the novel. I suspect that he must have had a say in this, given his profile, and the obvious weight accorded to this event within the Festival. Could it be that he is self-conscious about how his work is received through readings, or that he prefers that the work is encountered in full on the page? Or does he simply not enjoy giving performed readings, and prefer offering his experience and opinions to the audience in conversation?

I am reminded of **J. M. Coetzee**, who avoids all live events—particularly those in which he is expected to offer opinions, as a kind of sage, on matters ranging far beyond his books—on the basis that it is philosophically important for literature to stand on its own terms. A decade and a half after Coetzee's Nobel Prize speech addressing this issue, the idea that any author—particularly one who has been awarded significant prizes like Ishiguro or Coetzee—would *not* be in high demand to perform a sage-like role at major literary festivals today, is inconceivable. The pendulum of literary culture has clearly swung against Coetzee for the time being; but, as Peter McDonald perceptively suggests, his stance can be seen as either a 'last gasp from a bygone era' or as a form of radical literary 'activism', countering the 'opinionising that the industry favours'.[76]

A late middle-aged white man from the audience is selected to be the first questioner for Ishiguro, and asks earnestly, with an Essex accent: 'I read *Artist in the Floating World* about a month ago and I'm still savouring it, so I'd like to thank you. What I'd like to ask is: is everything transitional, or if not, what is the rock you anchor to?' Ishiguro pauses, as a few people in the audience titter, then bats it back: 'In my writing life or my personal life?' He doesn't pause quite long enough to allow a response. 'In my personal life', he says, 'I've been with the same woman for 36 years, so I suppose I have to *grudgingly* admit she's the rock'. Kearney hoots at this. 'She's here by the way! You will pay for that!' Ishiguro smiles a little. 'Since we're in a *literary* context here'—perhaps a gentle way to make a point about what he feels audience questions at literary festivals *should* be about—'I think it's hard to find something constant to cling to in my writing life. Martha implied I'm quite *promiscuous* about... genre...'—she grins a little at this—'and I don't quite know *how* you write a novel. It always feels like a strange random series of luck and chance that the last one got finished. But... I think I do have some themes and concerns that I do quite strongly recognise as my own territory'.

A young woman, maybe 18, wearing glasses, a flowery top and a ponytail, asks in a quavering voice: 'I found your thoughts on genre really interesting, the idea that it's a product of the publishing industry. I wanted to ask whether you ever think about genre when you're writing or if it's something you disconnect from'. 'I do think about genre and it can be quite stimulating', he answers, 'but, perhaps I'm quite naïve or silly, but my book tends to be recognised in some genre I wasn't even thinking of...'.

A long-white-haired, bearded man, wearing a collared t-shirt, asks, with a Cornish accent: 'Are you aware of, or do you have any thoughts about, the fact that *Remains of The Day* is used on a business administration course?' Ishiguro raises his eyebrows; he had not heard this, but smiles, amused and offers a thoughtful response. A smiley woman in her forties with red hair gets the final turn and asks whether *The Buried Giant* is going to be turned into a film, adding: 'because I really want to see the ogres!' Unsurprisingly, it has been optioned already, and Ishiguro offers his view that filmmakers shouldn't see themselves as translators of books, but should feel free to make their own work.

As the event ends, the applause is thunderous. Ishiguro has been a highly **compelling** speaker, despite—and perhaps because of—his **understated** style of speaking and expressing himself. I enjoyed the event, but am left wishing that it had included a reading from the new book so that I could have got a sense of the text.

As everyone gets up to pile out, mostly to head to the bookshop to join an anaconda-like book signing queue, I talk to two white women in their mid-fifties who had been sitting in front of me, and are clearly friends. Katherine is from Hampshire and works in publishing, while Sarah lives locally and has a software business and a plant nursery. Katherine speaks of the event in an almost dreamlike tone. 'He was so self-effacing…', she says, a small smile playing on her lips, to which Sarah nods, reflectively. 'And witty!', adds Katherine. 'And had this way of talking about serious issues…'.

'Frustrating though', chips in Sarah, somewhat sternly, 'because he would talk about themes and then not *illustrate* them'.

'Right…', Katherine says, sounding unsure.

'Examples from his books!', Sarah explains. 'He'd say something and then not back it up. **I like *readings***'.

I'm intrigued that they echo my own thoughts so quickly. I ask if they've read his books already, and both laugh their assent, as if it were a silly question. '*The Buried Giant, Never Let Me Go, Remains of the Day…*', lists Sarah. 'We're **big fans** of his work – and we've both heard him at Hay before… ten years ago now, when he was talking about *Never Let Me Go*'. I ask whether they think they got something new out of hearing him speak about his new book. 'Ooh yes', Katherine says—'I'm going to go back and re-read it and some of his old ones!'.

'Do you think it will *change* the way you read or think about the books, having now seen him live?' I ask. Sarah jumps in: 'Definitely – I want to go back to re-read things to see how his comments on his creative process influenced how I read it before – you get **an insight into *how* he constructed it**'. I ask whether that insight mainly comes from conversation, but she replies that in her view, readings are important for that too. 'Last year I saw Hanif Kureishi read the first paragraph of his recent book and it was *great*. You've got that... *angry man* [laughs] coming through... so yes'. 'It depends on whether they're a *good* reader or not though', Katherine chips in, 'because not all of them are, are they?' Sarah laughs. 'Some are *terrible* at presenting their own work, and others are not, so I.... it depends. If you've got a Simon Armitage type, who's poetic, it's great...' Katherine nods at this. 'And I suppose if you go to read a book again, you've got his *voice*...', she says, prompting a vigorous nod from Sarah. 'Yes – if I went to read *Remains of the Day* now I would have *his* voice in my head while reading it', Katherine says, happily. 'Yes, me too!', cries Sarah. 'That does give it a different flavour', Katherine continues. 'A different dimension', Sarah adds.

'Do you usually choose fiction events at Hay?' I ask. 'Well, we're off to Martin Reese next, and Germaine Greer', Katherine says. 'She goes to a lot of the politics stuff, and I go to a lot of the literary stuff', Sarah explains—but Katherine isn't so sure about this characterisation. 'I'd say I do a mixture. I *do* do some of the sciencey ones'. Sarah nods. 'Yeah. I did Gavin Francis last year, about the Antarctic. That was brilliant. But that was great *literature* actually! His ways of *describing* ice. If you haven't read his book, read it! Just describing a landscape as *alien* is like fiction, in a way'. I ask whether they think they'd have discovered many of writers they've seen if it wasn't for Hay. 'I wouldn't', Sarah says, emphatically. 'I bought the book before I went to see Gavin Francis, because I saw the programme and thought, that looks interesting, so I went to buy the book, read it, and then came'.

Katherine takes a different approach: 'I have to say, I'm going to see people that I already know about, so I look at the programme... I suppose I'm coming from a bit further afield, so I have to have more motivation, be more committed to whoever I'm going to see... So yeah, Kazuo Ishiguro, Germaine Greer, Martin Reese – they're **all people I'd known of** *before* coming to Hay. I think I'm like that with buying books too. I tend to buy known names. Even though I work in publishing, and publishing non-names!'.

'Would either of you be interested in going to events that were purely author readings, of fiction or poetry, without the discussion element?', I ask. Neither look horrified, yet neither look keen either. 'I think **you**

**want the discussion** actually', Sarah concludes, finally, and Katherine agrees.

In the evening, I go along to a Christy Moore concert on the site—part of the Hay programme involves musical events in the evening, after the daytime programme that is mostly filled with spoken words. After such a long day of concentrated listening to words in speech form, it feels like a welcome release to listen to melodic, harmonised lyrics about raving fishermen, goddesses and winter paths, with no analysis, no questioning and no mediating of emotional experience.

I realise I haven't eaten and it's late, so I head back into town to find food. I wander past several gastro pubs and festival pop-up stalls and bars. Inevitably, the success of the festival has changed the town of Hay-on-Wye as well as the wider literary cultural landscape; the boost to its economy[77] has caused the place to gentrify considerably. Not thoroughly, though. On a corner at the bottom of town, I stop at a hole-in-the-wall chip shop—a reminder that much of life here during the rest of the year is as mundane and ordinary as anywhere else. Hot, greasy and salty, the first chip hits the spot. I sit in the dark on a picnic table by the river to eat the rest, listening to the rush of water and the rustle of breeze through leaves.

## Day Three

The next morning the sun is bright, the air is warm, the lawns on the site glow emerald and lots of people are milling around, drinking coffee and eating pastries. I wander around to speak to a few people, trying to approach as diverse a range as I can.

Tim is a young guy with spotty cheeks who seems to be walking aimlessly around the site. He tells me he is 23 and lives in the Valleys an hour away. He has just got here for the first time to check out what's happening and has **no idea what to expect**: an indication that it is not just the bookish who come as 'pilgrims' to Hay intent on seeing particular events, but local, curious people too.

Dave, 50, from Cheshire, is a business writer, here with his family; they've come for a whole week for the last six or seven years and don't plan to stop. '**Hay's like Christmas for us**', he says, echoing Tony Benn. 'It's an *immersive* experience, because you're dropped in a field in the middle of nowhere and – we've been to Cheltenham Festival as well, and that's different because you're in a town and you can come and go. Here there's no other things to do, **not usually any wifi, and no phone signal**. You don't feel like you need to check email or work...' I note this emphasis on an escape from the digital, which seems to be pivotal, for him, to a sense of liminality, perhaps, and to achieving the experientialist aim of being able to devote his complete attention to the experience. 'And you can just throw yourself into this complete range of topics and subjects – I mean, this is rare for me, right now, to have an hour where I'm not at a talk and can actually read'. I note his use of the word 'talk', rather than 'event', and also wonder how many reader-audience members value silent reading time—*not* talking—as an integral part of the literary festival experience.

Not wanting to interfere in that precious hour-long slot for too long, but curious, I ask him what he's reading. 'For once, it's fiction!', he says and explains that he only reads fiction on holiday. He doesn't tell me what the book is, though, and I can't see from the back cover. 'I tend to go for science, history, philosophy events – the non-fiction stuff', he tells me. 'My wife goes off to the fiction, my daughter goes to the YA [young adult fiction], and then we get together at the end of the day and talk about it! [upward inflection – he grins, serenely]. And it's just, you know, **that week where you sort of have a different type of** *life*'.

'And what's the appeal of hearing a writer read from their book live, as part of that?', I ask. 'Well', he muses, 'in terms of non-fiction, there are not so many presenters that read from their books – and I very rarely buy the *books* I go to the talks on either, because they just do presentations. I've just been to a presentation from Carole Black for instance, talking about ill health in the work place... She just did a PowerPoint presentation. And I quite like that. So for me, it's not – it sounds strange saying this at a *literary* festival – **it's not necessarily about the books; it's about the** *topics*. You've got experts in their field talking about a topic'. I reflect that Dave is exactly the kind of person who might have been envisaged during Hay's rebrand as a 'festival of ideas'.

After a bit more strolling, I speak to a smartly dressed lady with a perfect grey-brown perm and pearl earrings perusing a programme. Her name is Diana, and she tells me, in a slightly anxious tone, with an aristocratic accent, that she is from Cheltenham, where she is very engaged in the festival, but is mainly concerned about protecting the gardens there during the festival period; in her view, they should just host the festival in buildings. She is at Hay for the second year running and appreciates how very well-organised it is; how events here start *on time*. She fixes me with a steely glance as she says this, as if she can tell that I'm the kind of person who's late for things. I ask what kinds of events she enjoys going to at literary festivals. 'Well **I** – ***don't*** **read** *fiction* [decisive]. I think humans who sort of live life are far more interesting than someone else's imagination of what, er, life is about. It's their *perception* of life. Now I've worked at CAB [Citizens Advice Bureau] for 14 years, so I've *seen* life, and no one needs to tell *me*, really, what life is about [laughs lightly]. And today, um, I have a scientific background, you know, and I've been to see… could we recreate a mammoth. I've just been listening to someone who survived as a Jew, Auschwitz, and someone asked a question which *I* wanted to ask, but having gone through the lecture I thought no I *can't* ask the question, but then *he* asked the question!' I made a commiserating noise and asked what draws her to attend talks at live events like this rather than reading books about those same subjects. 'Well, **I went to that event today to ask him the *question*.** *I* was going to ask the Israeli-Palestinian question: that was my motive. I don't *read* about the war'.

I am fascinated by this admission—that, essentially, her primary motivation for going to a literary festival event was to have her own voice heard publicly while asking a particular political question, about which she clearly felt strongly and yet did not read—to the point that it was frustrating for that intended question to have been pre-emptively asked by a 'competitor' in the reader-audience—and that, whatever answer was eventually given to the question by the author-performer, it was of negligible importance to her in comparison. This brings home to me the value that some reader-audience members clearly allot to the **Q&A**

**session**, as **the most overt element of interactive participation** in the live event. The reversal of power relations involved at this point, and the opportunity for any reader-audience member to contribute is a **democratic** gesture, and it is this element in particular that, to me, makes the event comparable to a Habermasian **public sphere**, as Giorgi suggested: a rare phenomenon in the context of an era defined by fractured, mediated narratives about politics and society and by increasingly digitalised interactions.

At a picnic table, looking at *The Telegraph*, I find an elderly man called Clive. His wife has been to every single Hay Festival but one, he tells me, proudly, and he's been coming too since 1989. They live in a local village. He's a scientist who spent his working life in Surrey. He talks about how Hay *used* to get people like Clinton, and brilliant debates chaired by people like Jon Snow, but now it's 'declined somewhat'—by which I assume he means that there are less celebrity names. I ask what he enjoys most about the festival now. 'Well, it's a combination of **stimulation**, **time with friends**, and... we like **the area**'. His wife is the one who's really 'interested in *literature*', he explains; she first came with a local literature club. 'I think she used to pick up a couple of library books on the way back from school, *daily* [he laughs]. So she's well-grounded and founded in the literary, and loves all those events'. Echoing my conversation with Dave, this again reflects the evidence that women in general are more likely to read fiction than men.[78]

I'm heading back to the green room when I spot bookseller **James Daunt**, founder of the Daunt chain of bookshops, who would imminently become the new CEO of Waterstones: the largest high street chain in the UK. I ask whether he'd mind speaking with me, and we take a seat in a corner. He tells me that the **live literature scene has changed a lot** over the course of his career, and feels that this was partly to do with the **'evolving maturity of bookselling'**. 'Difficult as it is to imagine – I'm decrepit and old [he laughs sanguinely], but not *that* old – the London literary scene of my teenage years was a pretty modest thing. Small, small bookshops... you couldn't swing a cat in them... Then Tim Waterstone started up his chain, and things got a bit bigger, and even my own shops. But they're *recent*. If you just take the tiny little example of my own shops, we now do one or two events a week, which are particular – you pay your £8, we fit 160 odd people in… we started doing that, probably only 15 years ago, relatively recently. No-one else was really doing it then. We had fantastic authors because they were our customers as well, like Michael Palin – big, big names – and it slowly, slowly built. And I remember when we'd do one a month, and even that was quite a struggle… Now you put it online, 150 people snap up your tickets, and bang: you're done'.

'Why did you first want to start doing events?', I ask. 'I'm an incredibly selfish bookseller', he says, smiling mischievously. 'I simply do my own bookshop purely for myself… and we **booksellers love meeting authors**! And it's about giving our **customers access to the authors** too. If you're an average reader, you read an author's books… and you're quite *intimately involved* every night with this person, and you might only read about six books a year, so these are people you're deeply *connected* with, and that's why I'm talking about this evolving maturity. I don't know when you first came to Hay, but it wasn't this big and expensive! [laughs] It was a little field. It's a bit like the way that the Daunt Books events have gone from 20 people to 150; Hay has become this extraordinary thing. Now festivals are everywhere you turn'.

Are people's connections with the books much deeper after encountering the author at a live event?, I ask, and are they much more likely to buy the book? He tells me there is an **impact on book buying**—but that he was surprised to find, when he began running events, that the impact extended long beyond the book being presented. 'As a retailer, when we started running these events… we found we would sell a lot of copies of that book. And then we would sell the *next* book, when we hadn't done an event about it at all, and go way beyond the number of people that came to the initial event. So that was a strange thing'. It is also about **authors** 'learning to put the effort in', he feels. 'Authors who work *hard* do *better*. I think that. Of course you can be an absolute swine, and either be very bad or obnoxious or terribly shy, and succeed – but nevertheless if you do work hard people seem to latch onto that and there is clear correlation between that and book buying'.

I ask how, in his opinion, hearing an author read from their book affects the ways readers then read them, and think about the author. 'I think there are lots of things going on. There is definitely the celebrity thing going on. But for the *thinking reader*, I think, to be able to put a face to that author, also to be able to **pigeonhole** them – as you know, we can pigeonhole everybody very precisely by their social group, and that does give you a little bit of a background. You know, I would read Rachel [Cusk]'s book rather differently having met her... You *do* want to *know* who the author is [definite]. A Russian book I read recently, I thought it was a very, very masculine book, but halfway through I realised it was written by a woman, and that did slightly *change* it [reflective]...'.

'But it's... it's also **the ability to share and *talk* with others**', he continues. 'In Daunt Books we run an absolutely batty thing called the walking book club... 40-80 people go for a walk for a couple of hours on the Heath and discuss a book. The walking bit of it works because people can split up and move around.... I think what's going on there – and we're selling lots of those books, way beyond the number of people going on a walk... so I think it's giving people an *arena* in which to discuss and discover. I think that's the thing with a literary festival – there's so much going on – so much you can discover, and we find things we would never normally do'. He is talking about **curation** now, I reflect—and it is revealing that Hay's curation clearly serves to influence booksellers' ensuing curatorial practices in their shops,[79] as well as reader-audiences who are participating in the Festival.

When I ask what effect he thinks live readings have on audiences, as opposed to conversations and Q&As, he frowns in thought. 'I'd person-ally be very curious about this', he says, frowning in concentration. '**We don't do signings** [at Daunt Books], which I regard as – I don't know, I'm very purist about it... If you meet an author, and have the conver-sation, that's what you do – but without the talk, I don't get it. Signing queue, signed, gone, boom. But obviously other bookshops... they do it everywhere, and claim successful "events", but to my mind that's not an event; there's *nothing engaging* about it, it's simply a signing... Events are about getting people *involved*... So I was coming onto saying that **I will *never* do a fiction reading**'. I raise my eyebrows; I had not expected this. 'I figure all my customers can read', he explains. 'I know people can do poetry enormously successfully but we *never* do fiction. If we can get two or three serious authors in to discuss ideas, we do that, but we *always* try to stop them reading'. I ask whether this is because he thinks writers tend to read badly—but he shakes his head. 'Again, because I'm so *purist* about this… even the great readers – like Julian Barnes reads beautifully – but I don't *get* that. I don't *want* to hear him read his novels. I'd like to get him into talk about it, but just… this interminable reading that goes on, I don't get it'. I ask whether he feels attached to the practice of silent reading as being the heart of literary culture, and perhaps protective of it. 'I *do* think that. And I'm arrogant enough to say that, with my own bookshops, I do my shops for me!'.

I ask what he thinks about the more performative author readings. 'Well there are exceptions for whom I would have a reading. Will Self is one – I know I'd be getting something extraordinary. But that's a *performance*. It's also about his style of writing. But… I've sat through things that just *reek* with boredom. And I always want to save myself from that'.

Given his views on live readings, I am curious to hear how he views audience questions. 'You have to be very disciplined', he says, diplomatically. 'The 20 min long question which is really all about themselves, how do you turn that off? We all have our own strategies… But when you get a *good* question, and the **conversation** *ignites*, I think for the audience, it adds a huge amount to the evening. And there's something about just connecting authors directly to readers that's very – it should be what bookshops aspire to do'.

One of the most striking things about this conversation, for me, was Daunt's vehement personal distaste for live readings by authors, even those whom he reveres, based on his admittedly-purist sense that the essence of reading is a private pleasure to be experienced silently; and yet his sense that there is a profound impact and value to the experience of encountering an author in person, including for interpreting and valuing their texts. On the part of audiences, he allots value to the visual 'pigeonholing' of authors through live events—a form of socio-cultural evaluation of their personas—but he does not seem to allot value to the role of their vocal qualities, or the sound and rhythm in the interpretation of a text through their performed readings. Like Jo Glanville, he is clear about his preference for silent reading as the foremost mode of experiencing literary texts.

First on my event, itinerary for the day is a **Waterstones**-sponsored panel on **fiction debuts**, chaired by the chain's fiction buyer, **Chris White**, and featuring **Kevin Maher**, **Taiye Selasi** and **Gavin Extence**. White explains the three authors had been selected by a panel of Waterstones staff as part of the 'Waterstones 11': a list of debut novelists they rate, and commit to promoting in their stores for 11 months of the year, leaving December for Jamie Oliver and the Christmas crew. The books are all quite different; according to the programme, 'Maher's lyrical and funny *The Fields* tells of an interrupted adolescence in 1984 Dublin'; Selasi's *Ghana Must Go* is 'the story of the simple, devastating ways in which families tear themselves apart'; and Extence's *The Universe Versus Alex Woods* is 'a funny and heart-breaking tale of an unexpected friendship, an unlikely hero and an improbable journey'. White begins by linking the three novels in terms of the theme of family, and inviting them each to introduce their book with that angle. The author-performers are then prompted in turn to answer questions about their characters and how they were conceived; how they began writing their novels; and whether character or concept came first.

Extence, speaking somewhat hesitantly, with tense-looking shoulders, says that his novel started with the character of Alex, specifically his voice. He describes how he had already been writing a different novel for 18 months, realised it was bad, abandoned it and started this one having learned valuable lessons about writing. He also reveals, with a quick look out to the audience, that his wife supported them financially during all this, then grins shyly.

During the audience Q&A, a middle-aged woman tells Extence she 'wanted to adopt Alex', and asks whether there will be a sequel; he answers that he's very honoured, but 'frankly' he thinks that 'if any more weird things were to happen to Alex' it 'wouldn't be credible'—and he imagines him in future as a very boring particle physicist, which prompts appreciative audience laughter. Another woman starts asking a question of Extence, and then remembers that she had actually been referring to Kevin Maher's novel, and then realises that she'd misheard the place name that she was trying to ask about anyway, stutters and apologises for wasting everyone's time. She clearly hadn't given any advance thought to the question, despite it being asked so publicly, and had just felt moved to speak her thoughts aloud. Kevin Maher kindly jumps in with a related comedy anecdote to make her feel better.

I am surprised that, again, like the Ishiguro event, there are **no readings** from the novels during this event. I suppose that, with a panel of three, this would eat into the hour-long time slot, but it still feels like an absence.

I find the three authors afterwards. Two have to dash off, but **Gavin Extence** is keen to have a chat about his experience. I'm interested to hear his perspective; while he spoke very well, engaged the audience and made them laugh, he didn't come across as a natural public speaker, at ease with a big stage. He tells me he's done a few small events so far, but this is the first that 'feels like a festival with a site and tents and stuff'. I ask how he's found presenting his novel at live events and whether it has changed the way he thinks about it. 'It hasn't changed the way I think about the novel, I don't *think*,' he says, but 'it's a part of being a writer that I just hadn't thought about *at all* and it's come as a bit of a surprise, how much there's been of doing bits of public speaking… it's a really, really *nice* part of the experience actually, because writing's a very solitary experience, obviously, so having that interaction, having someone actually *talk* to you about your book, is just a very, very nice thing when you've spent so long doing it'.

I ask how he finds the **audience questions**. He grins. 'The oddest one I had was in an event at Waterstones in Covent Garden, and it was the usual thing of a ten-minute reading and then questions, and this guy's hand shot up immediately at the front, and there were about 15 people there, and he said: I notice from your blurb that you're from Sheffield. I used to live in Sheffield; have you ever been to Chubby's kebab house? That was a random one! The questions tend to cluster around the same things, but… it doesn't actually feel that repetitive. It feels quite new every time'.

The whole process of doing events, he says, has made him '**more conscious of the people who are actually reading and buying the book**, which is nice – it's slightly daunting as well, especially while you're writing the second book, that there's this expectation... you're not in a void any more. But these are the people who liked the book, and if they *really* like the book, it's wonderful, but also, like: I've got someone who I've got to *please* [laughs]. So it does make me think slightly differently about the writing, but it's something that can be switched off, and **needs to be switched off**'.

I wonder how he's found **reading** excerpts of his novel **aloud**, at this and other events. At first, he says, it was '**the hardest thing**', and felt 'like a really strange thing to do, especially to an audience – but I really got thrown in at the deep end. I did a thing in London – it's called 'The Book Stops Here' and it's a sort of, um, literary night that's in a jazz club, and essentially they bring in authors... it's in a little bar called the Alley Cat, and it's really good [enthusiastic grin] – they have authors up on stage reading for ten minutes, and that's all it is, there are no questions or anything, and that was the first time I had to read aloud from the book, and I was just put on the stage with a light on my face so I couldn't see the audience [swallows, a little nervously at the memory], and it was quite helpful in a way, because it was just being thrown in the deep end, and after that it felt very normal'.

He smiles at something he's just thought of. 'There was actually an audiobook as well, and that really helped, because I listened to the audiobook, a couple of times before reading for the first time, and that – it gave me the rhythm of how to read it [reflective]. It's strange, because when you're writing you don't necessarily know *how to speak it*, in a way that works.' I had not previously imagined this as a dimension of live literature: an author learning how to perform their text, for an event, from an actor's recording. 'So, the **actor** Joe Thomas **read the audiobook** – from *The In-Betweeners* and a few other things – and he's just got the most *fantastic* comic timing. And your impulse is to read very, very *quickly*, and you have to fight against that, and really, *really* slow it down so people aren't lost. And, you know, if you're doing dialogue, there's separation, and things like that'.

I suggest, gently, that he doesn't sound like he feels naturally inclined towards performing. He agrees with this vigorously. 'No I'm not inclined to it, in the sense that – I don't naturally like being the centre of attention, I don't like being on a stage... I don't *particularly* like public speaking – er, but it, it feels slightly different in this context, because… it probably goes without saying that the events tend to be very *friendly*, and informal in a sense, and there isn't this expectation that you're going to perform something seamlessly, that there'll be a certain amount of hesitation and bumbling and everything else – and I think people actually *respond* to that, because it's… it's just a *human* thing. And I think once I was aware of that it became much easier. And it helps as well that… I like talking about books and I don't find the experience of talking about my book dramatically different to that. It's like a discussion you'd have with a friend about a book; that's how it feels, really'.

He confesses, then, that **he had been to 'zero literary events' before appearing in one as an author**. 'I was very **superstitious** about them', he says. 'Lots of people, aspiring writers, go to a lot of events, trying to find out about the business, hearing authors they love and everything like that, but I was *really*, sort of, dead set against it… I'm not superstitious in any way, but it felt like the sort of thing that I was doing in the privacy of my own home, and until I'd got something that I was really happy with, I didn't want to think too much about the actual publishing side of it'. Now that he's been to some events, while at festivals, he's found them '*really*, really interesting… It is just interesting hearing other writers *speak*! [revelation] I hadn't had any particular exposure to just *talking* to people *about writing* before. And finding about what people do, how things differ and what's the same – those things are really useful. And writers talking about their own insecurities – that's lovely as well [smiling] – because you get this, like, feeling that I'm not the only one who feels like I'm just winging it…. So yeah, having interactions with readers and writers are what festivals are all about. It's a very… *fulfilling* experience'.

After a coffee and a walk around the increasingly-busy site, I head over the book tent to browse the books on offer: all works by author-performers at the Festival. There are plenty to stock up a giant tent. It is quite busy with other browsers and is bifurcated by a long queue of people waiting in a queue in front of a table where **A. C. Grayling**, the renowned philosopher, is **signing his new book**, *The God Argument*. A lot of the queuers have short conversations with him when signs their book—asking him to make their copy out to someone, who might be them, and perhaps telling him that they enjoyed the event, and perhaps that they have read his previous books. I mull over Daunt's comment about being befuddled about reader-audiences' desire to get books signed. I have always felt similarly about this before—but being here at Hay, and seeing so many people engaged in the practice of signing, which takes place after every single event, I reflect on it anthropologically. The signing process is a **ritual** at literary festivals and most other live literature events—a ritual that forms part of the event; it not only happens immediately after the staged event, but it is also common for the chairperson or host to invite reader-audiences to go and buy the books and get them signed before the staged event finishes. The ritual is clearly intended to induce more people to buy copies of the new book—usually a hardback. It requires a significant commitment of time as well as money when the queues are long. In return for that commitment, the ritual enables the reader-audience member to take away a physical book that acts as a memento of the event, with a bespoke signature on it from the author-performer that acts as a testament to the reality of the experience, and to the connection that the event has forged between them. The ritual also enables reader-audience members to engage in an **intimate one-to-one conversational encounter** with the author-performer, in close quarters, elevating them from being simply an anonymous member of the audience to being an individual, who is named and directly addressed by the author-performer; to somebody whose words—be they a form of thank you or explanation about a connection with the work—might resonate personally with the author-performer, and be remembered by them, and vice versa. Back at the reader-audience member's home afterwards, the signed book will sit on their bookshelf as a material reminder of that ritual as well as the main event.

The book signing ritual was explored in a smart autofictional novel, *How to Be a Public Author* (2014) by **Francis Plug**: a pseudonym for Paul Ewan, in which Plug—the not-yet-published-author protagonist, desperate to break into the literary scene—tracks a list of Booker-winning authors around multiple literary events, not to attend the events themselves, but for the sole purpose of getting the authors to sign his copy of their book afterwards—which he never purchased on site—and to force them, in the process, to respond to his off-beat, often drunken description of his own authorial persona. The novel ably conveys the oddness of this quasi-celebrity-stalking pursuit, while also revealing the depth of meaning it has to Plug, by functioning as a tangible link between a distant-seeming writerly ambition and its 'real' manifestation in established literary culture.

I move a little closer to A. C. Grayling, whose signing queue is almost over now. A few thank him for the event, and one woman tells me she has enjoyed all his books. The last woman in the queue comes up to him and says: 'I just want to ask you, how can you be so sure about what's come before the big bang?' He begins to reply, but she cuts in: 'Ah, but we can't really know can we, so isn't it really just about a step of belief either way? And if so, don't you wonder how your life might have new meaning with faith in God?' He explains his contrary point of view further, and gamely allows her to continue with a back and forth for several minutes, smiling all the while. She has clearly waited to go last in the queue so that she can have this out with him without being time-pressured by the person behind. So intent is she that it appears that she genuinely believes that, in this moment, right after Grayling's big event, she might cause him to hold up his hands, in a gesture of revelation, and tell her that yes: she's absolutely right, he hadn't thought of that, there might well be a God after all, and so he must home, rewrite the book he has just sold to everybody and refund their money. After several minutes, as it becomes clear that she won't desist in her efforts, he thanks her repeatedly for her interest and her questions, and gets up from the table, not turning away from her, but backing away slowly, still smiling, as she keeps on going, before finally accepting that the exchange is finished.

I speak to Grayling about this incident, briefly, outside the tent, and he appears utterly unfazed by it, remaining wholly genial. He **likes to see that people feel engaged enough by his work to want to debate** these things, he tells me. I reflect that such a discursive approach to the signing ritual is less likely to be directed at an author-performer who has just presented a book of fiction, since fiction doesn't work as an 'argument' in this way—but still, the encounter highlights for me the potential impact and power of the signing ritual felt by reader-audiences.

On my way back to the green room, I spot **Gaby Wood**, *The Telegraph's* **Books Editor**, and chairperson for multiple events this festival,[80] eating a bite of tapas for lunch at the corner of the Spanish bar on site. She kindly invites me to join her and begins by explaining the background to *The Telegraph's* sponsorship arrangement with Hay. She has a good relationship with Florence, she says, but they are quite careful in terms of programming and respect a '**Chinese wall**'—though he does ask her to chair a few things. I ask **how Hay alters the Books section** of the paper. 'It's nice to have **focus**!', she says. 'A kind of *celebration*. I really like putting together that supplement for the first Hay weekend because it's – a *celebration* of who's at Hay, but for the whole country'. Supporting Hay, she says, sends a '**signal**, not just about books, but about culture generally, and ideas… it's a way of saying to the world, we really *care* about this stuff. And it's worth giving some money to, in a world where money for culture is diminishing…'.

She goes on to admit that it was also about the paper getting a **competitive advantage in books coverage**: 'what I found when I first arrived, say a book was coming out in April and you wanted an interview with the author. The author had committed to giving his first interview to *The Guardian* because he was coming to Hay, and this was all tied up. So the publishers will delay publication to coincide with Hay, so you can have serial rights, you can have an interview, you can have a live appearance, you can do it all together… The paper that sponsors will get the whole lot. I realised, well, this is a kind of *power!!* [pause] They're able to, what's the word – *skulk* the presentation of a book before it arrives in the world'. I too am surprised now by the degree of behind-the-scenes triangulation between the press, publishing and the Festival, well in advance of books' release into the public domain.

I ask what Wood thinks about Hay's diversification from literature to ideas and the perceived focus on **celebrity**. 'I don't agree about the celebrity thing', she says, decisively. 'The only celebrities here really are the people entertaining in the evening… The definition of celebrity is basically someone who's on TV. If we're saying Salman Rushdie or whoever is a celebrity then it's kind of a pointless phrase. Because no one would say that they are ineligible to attend a literary festival!'.

She mulls over the link between fiction and non-fiction events. 'But I have to say, in terms of **fiction vs non-fiction**, fiction is *incredibly hard…* to represent *live*. Very hard to *talk* about'. I recall Alex Clark outlining a similar perspective on chairing. 'Novelists are on the whole quite *bad* at talking about their work. And on the whole there aren't *that* many questions about it – how did you write this novel, why did you write this novel?, *oh well it just came to me* – you know… – and I've chaired millions of them, and Peter often puts novelists together for the simple reason that, usually, it's likely to be more interesting having novelists talking together rather than a conversation between you and **a novelist, who doesn't necessarily *want* to talk about their novel because they just want to *write* them**. And also you don't get the audience numbers… **People are *more* interested in hearing a story told live about non-fiction** than they are about fiction. There *may be* masses of people reading fiction, but they just want to *read it*! You know? … In books pages it's the same… non-fiction is easier to review, because you can talk about the subject matter, and it's very easy to illustrate, and fiction is almost impossible… and on the whole, readers want to know: should I read this book or not? If it's fiction. Whereas with non-fiction they'll be perfectly happy just to read the review because it's an interesting story. Someone stands up and tells you the story of, you know, a great escape, that's interesting regardless'.

She eats a couple of *patatas bravas*, and I feel guilty about intruding on her meal and causing it to get cold; I apologise for interrupting, but she kindly shakes her head: 'This is going to sound contradictory to the whole idea of a literary festival', she says, 'but it is fundamentally *unfair* **on a writer to expect them to be able to present their work**. I think. You know, they're not the same practice. At all. And the person who's best at writing is not necessarily going to be the best at presenting.… Now, most writers do know that they're expected to do that, so they practice, but they don't necessarily do it all that well… but those things are really *changing…* It's really significant, the specific moment we're in now: if people want to have books published and sold they have to enter a completely different game. It's **a different *job***'. She reflects further. 'I've actually been surprised *here* though at how *good* people are at reading their own words. But I – don't think it's a skill everyone has. And I don't think it's necessarily reflective of the way they *hear* it, either; it's not always what they're hearing when they're writing'. I'm intrigued by this apparent shift of perspective during the conversation. Isn't a pre-existing assumption that writers are inherently likely to perform readings badly contradicted by an observation that, in fact, at Hay, they haven't? Or is this just a consequence of Hay's status and ability to select the best-known writers, who are generally well-practised at performing at live literature events by the time they arrive?

'Do you think the popularity of live literature is connected to the rise of the **digital**?', I ask, and she frowns a little, thinking. 'It's hard to tell... It seems to make sense that people want some sort of *real* human contact, the more *vicarious* things feel through digital media.... But I don't *think* that, the more digitally people read, the more deprived they are. And it's not as if seeing a writer in person is that great; it depends who they are!' She finishes her food, reflects some more. 'But I do think that, if you go to a **really great live event... you *don't* know what's going to happen**. [Definite tone.] And you have the *feeling* you don't know what's going to happen. And that's the reason very few of these things are *just* readings... One of the *most* exciting things I've *ever* seen here was two years ago, a debate between Rowan Williams and Simon Russell Beale, about faith in Shakespeare. And there they were, two people, from two completely different backgrounds, with different experiences of Shakespeare...that conversation couldn't have happened any other way, and it was happening *there*, in front of you, *live*! So, you know. That can be really exciting'. I'm intrigued by this view of the value of liveness— echoing Hahn's suggestion that the conversational element enhances a literary event because of its unpredictability, and because it derives from interpersonal chemistry as well as ideas.

My mention of the **audience Q&A** sessions at festivals makes Wood grin wryly. 'You do always worry you're picking on the wrong person, and if you'd asked the person next door you'd have got a much better question', she says. 'And if you're chairing an event with more than one writer, people will only ask questions to one of them and you'll have to try to find someone interested in asking something to the other one... **People**

**like to have their** *say* [cautious], and they're entitled to! [laughs]... Usually they're very nice, like: *I love your work or I really enjoyed that.* But the whole point of leaving so much time for that, you know, fifteen minutes – a good quarter of the event – is that they continue the discussion'. In terms of fiction, she continues, reader-audiences tend to be **interested in process**: 'people genuinely want to know how this magical thing got produced. And the questions that will lead to that are inevitably quite limited. And the answers are almost quite inevitably unobtainable [laughs]'. Once again, I note how similar her views on this are to Clark's; how both chairpeople consider the fiction events that they present to be inherently problematic.

I ask whether any of the events she's been involved in have changed her relationships with particular books, and she puts her head on one side. 'That's interesting. I don't know. Maybe... [musing, reflective] Maybe only when it's *bad*! The only reason I'd say it *hasn't* changed my view is that I usually enter the events I chair very well-disposed towards the books. So, if it were a positive reaction, that wouldn't actually be a shift. But sometimes people can be very pompous. I mostly put middle-aged men in that category. For me, seeing them live doesn't help me. **I would rather not** *know* **that they are self-absorbed, pompous old farts, narcissistic writers** – and writers *are* narcissistic because they have to spend a lot of time on their own... I just mean, if their work is really good, it shouldn't matter'. I nod, slowly. This goes to the issue of authenticity again and the role of the authorial persona in the interpretation of fiction. In literary cultural terms, is it better for the pompous narcissist who is widely considered a 'great writer' to be judged on the basis of his fictional texts and not his personality—or might an embodied insight into that personality, as Daunt suggested, add something meaningful to the interpretation of his fiction? Or, as Coetzee might have it, should all fiction be best judged on its 'own terms', via individuals' silent, private engagements with the text on the page?

Going back to Wood's earlier point that live events have become an increasingly core part of the role of the writer now, I ask: does she see a risk that the most confident or pompous writers get more stage time, which could be damaging for the best writers? 'I *do*! I do think so!', she says. 'I think the truth of the matter, the *secret* truth of the matter, **is if**

**you're really really *really* good at this, you're probably not spending enough time on your own in a room**. You know? And the really good writers are probably too screwed up – I mean, you *hope* they're too screwed up – to stand up and explain to everyone how great they are! You know, we can't be on the side of that view, because we're supporting this. But the truth is, if you're really *really* good at this, at writing, then send someone in your stead. The French writer **Romain Gary**, do you know about him? He had a double. He wrote a book which won the Prix Goncourt, and you can't win the Prix Goncourt twice, so he wrote a whole load of other books under someone else's name, he won it *again*, and no one knew until quite the end that he was both people. And when the second person was sent to do the tour, he sent them material to perform. And I think, if we're going to do more events like this, we should treat it like theatre! I mean, there's absolutely no reason why you shouldn't have a double who's better at performing!'.

Intrigued by this—and recalling Stan and Kira's view about Toni Morrison vs an actor reading her audiobook—I check whether she means that it makes **no difference whether the author is performing, or an actor**, as long as the performance is good. 'Well', she says, mulling this over. 'I like writers, lots of my friends are writers, and I spend a lot of time with writers… *But*. I don't think the *authenticity* is in their *person*. You know. **The *authenticity is on the page*** [revelation]…. But it's not usually *about* a reading – it's about what they've got to say for themselves. If it was just a reading, then of *course* an actor would be better'.

Next on my menu is an event featuring novelist **Andrew O'Hagan**: a Scottish writer in his late 40s, who is lined up to be in conversation with veteran journalist **Rosie Boycott**, in the big BBC Arts tent, about his new novel, *The Illuminations*. It explores ideas of love and memory in the context of the war in Afghanistan, and it is a novel I've read recently and admired. The tent is packed, mostly with grey heads but a significant number of younger people too. I remember that Elsa had never heard of O'Hagan, but had bought a ticket for this, and look around for her, but don't spot her. As they kick off, O'Hagan's body language on stage is alert but relaxed, and he seems entirely comfortable in the spotlight.

Among other things, they talk about how the women from his child-hood informed one of his characters, Maureen. 'Anne is your heroine' Boycott says, in conversational but clearly performative mode—intro-ducing the character to the audience yet addressing O'Hagan directly. 'And she's an extraordinary character: a photographer slipping into dementia, next to her neighbour, Maureen…' O'Hagan cuts in. 'It surprised me that Maureen was the first character to speak in the book, actually…'—and Boycott cuts back: 'It surprised me too! So why was she?' 'Growing up in Scotland', O'Hagan replies, 'I was conscious that in every aspect of life there growing up in those council estates there was *always a Maureen*, though she was usually called Isa – the Scottish short form for Isabel – or Barbara [he grins at the audience, who burble laughter] And even to this day, my mother will say 'Barbara said that people who listen to Radio 4 have got too much time on their hands' [audience laughs more loudly, in a knowing way] And she said when my book came out: "By the way, that Maureen [long pause]… Who was she *based* on?" [Audience giggles. Another pause.] "Imagination, you know!" [He adopts a tremulous, high-pitched tone for imitating his own response, which prompts more laughs] But she was based on many women I grew up with, including my mother – the kind of madams of the street who knew more than you could ever know about matters of the human heart and weren't slow to tell you where you were going wrong, which was all the time… That kind of person has always interested me… there's always a kind of Maureen [audience hmms, intrigued.] Muriel Spark is famous for her own Maureens: the slightly bitter, knowing too much, but having their own back story that is revealed…'.

'Now let's come to *Anne*', Boycott proposes. 'Is she based on someone? Because my father had dementia, and it was heart-breaking, being reminded of those details. O'Hagan nods, seriously: 'That took years, Rosie. **Readers are very sharp**. [He glances out at the reader-audience, as if to say: *I'm talking about you.*] I take four to five years to write a novel, because **you've got to respect the readers' imagination**. You hand them the arithmetic when you're writing a book. If you're trying to write well, you're trying to give them what they need to *create the book in their heads*. That's where the reward comes from reading a good book – you're involved in the *doing* of it. For me the first year was spent with people with dementia, just noticing things change every day, and over the period of months and years, how they're able to speak, how they're able to express themselves – and I had to have that mapped so carefully, so that, every time you come back to Anne, she is slightly different on her journey through this illness'.

This conversation already reveals an author who **knows exactly what the audience wants** in this kind of literary performance: he's cracked jokey imitations that make them laugh; he's set the scene of his own childhood on a Glasgow council estate that gives insight into his experience of working-class characters such as the one being discussed, for those who want to know more about who he 'really' is and his autobiography; he's also put those characters into perspective within literary fiction, while giving the audience a reference to a great Scottish writer, Muriel Spark, whose work has similar tonal elements and characters to his own, giving the event a broader scope and revealing his literary influences and knowledge; he's talked about the craft of writing, in particular the judicious omission of certain details to make a book more rewarding for readers; and he's made the case for the quality of his own new novel, which he's promoting, by illustrating how extended research and reflection shaped the characterisation and 'authenticity' of the story—all in the space of a couple of minutes, and in an easy, conversational tone, making regular eye contact with the audience, who remain rapt.

For a reading from the novel, O'Hagan chooses a tense scene featuring the character of Luke, Anne's grandson, when he's out fighting in Afghanistan: an apparently separate storyline that becomes interlinked during the novel when Luke returns and tries hard to forget his memories, just as he's helping Anne to rekindle hers. It's a provocative scene to have chosen, not least because of the density of swear words. 'This is during a firefight, an unexpected firefight, just on a ridge in the middle of Helmand', O'Hagan explains by way of an introduction. He then leaves long pause to indicate the start of a reading.

'Docherty at some point came up behind Luke and told him he thought the major was pretending to be asleep. He was inside one of the vehicles crouched down.

- "What? Are you messing with me?" [Here O'Hagan sharply changes tone to a fast-paced, intense, panicked anger, marking the start of Luke's part in the dialogue.]
- "He's in the vector." [In contrast, this Docherty character's voice is performed in a much more muted tone, still fast and urgent-sounding, but quieter, lower, even a little timid – the tone of somebody attempting to sound reasonable, but conscious of the hierarchy and the other man's anger and dominance.]
- "What? What are you talking about? Get him in here, he needs to support this shit and support the boys."
- "He threw up."
- "Are you fucking having me on, leper?"
- "No sir. He's not well. In seconds the boys would notice."
- Luke knew they would notice and he feared their bottle might collapse if they knew the major was hanging back in the van during the fire-fight. Yet he knew something was wrong with Scullion and he'd felt it since they left Bastion.
- "Holy fu… Jesus, am I the medicine man for this whole platoon?", Luke said.
- "Let's cover for him, boss", Docherty said. "It's been a bad week for him and – we can easily cover it…"
- "What is it, his fucking *period*?" [He barks this word, prompting uncomfortable audience titters]
- "It's gonna be fine, do you just…"
- "It's gonna be fine? It's gonna be fine? *Is* it? I don't know what binoculars *you're* looking for Docherty, but mine tell me there's Terry fuckin Taliban crawling up our fuckin arses right in here." [Again, the pitch, speed and volume increase.]
- "It's fine sir, we're covered."
- "No we're *not*!" [The pitch of Luke's narration has risen to its peak here. O'Hagan leaves a dramatic pause, then drops the pitch but increases the pace.] "Scullion's losing it, I'm telling you leper, he's out the fucking game… Fucking Jesus Christ, he's supposed to be up here, commanding his soldiers, he's the CO, he has to be out here – he could be back in the headquarters eating Pot Noodle with the rest of them, like a normal… but he wanted to be involved with my section and

he's here, fucking erupting with crap…you're seriously telling me he's sweating his bollocks off in the vector to help with the turbine? It's about the boys!". Luke got on the radio… "… we're out in the open here… we reque… yeah we're out on the open, we reque… we request ur… urgent air listen listen…requesting urgent air fire…'

O'Hagan's pace of **delivery** gets faster and faster during Luke's radio attempt, each syllable staccato, conveying his utter panic in the situation, causing his language to fracture, in speech, as it is illustrated in the text. He performs this reading in the most **performative** sense of that word—giving it maximum intensity, reflecting the substance, emotions and drama of the text. He reads with a pace, stress and intensity that are represented in the text and the dialogue; and he has obviously chosen a dialogue-heavy section to perform, so as to create a **dramatic experience** for this reader-audience. He performs the text as if it were a **screenplay**, not going so far as to vary the accents but giving each person's lines a distinct tone and energy. The swear words take on a new meaning when they're performed here; they seem almost excessive in the text on the page, but here they sound appropriate and vital to the text, particularly when matched by the intense frown on O'Hagan's flushing face. They convey the intensity of the war situation, and the panic of the young soldiers, who in that context would be likely to let swear words fly when under fire. And their furious, dense articulation feels deliciously subversive, somehow, in the context of the clean, ordered aesthetic of the Hay format and the BBC branding.

Afterwards, I spot **O'Hagan** in the green room, talking to the author **Colm *Tóibín*** on a sofa over a cup of tea. *Tóibín* is at Hay to promote a new documentary about his work, following the publication of his novel, *Nora Webster*. I am loath to interrupt, but too curious about their perspectives not to, so I tentatively go over to them and mention that I am researching live literature. O'Hagan is intrigued; *Tóibín* **sceptical**: 'I don't have anything much to say about *that*', he says. 'It is very interesting, the rise of live literature events', O'Hagan says, kindly. I mention how performative I found his reading, and how much he got into his characters. He smiles in acknowledgement. 'He does that too', he says, jerking his thumb towards *Tóibín* with a sly grin.

'What?' *Tóibín* asks, as if mildly put out.

'You create the characters when you're doing a performance, right?'.

'Yeahhh….' *Tóibín* responds, musing. 'You don't want to *bore* people'. He speaks with a dry and lugubrious dead-pan tone, extending his vowels and emphasising key words in a way that is compelling to listen to. 'And if you mumble, you *bore* people, and they come up and say they couldn't hear you and you say – well that's *awful*. You want people to hear you, so you've got to try and speak properly. And if you want people not to be really *bored* and want it to be *over* soon, **you've got to try and pick a section that *works*. On its own, dramatically**. And if it doesn't, explain the context. And then, yes, if you can use your *voice* dramatically… but, it's **dangerous**! Because if you start when you're writing, thinking, *oh yes this will sound great when I'm reading it*, then I think it would ruin whatever you were doing, there and then, in writing'. He's echoing Armitage, here, in proposing that the writing process might be negatively affected by the active anticipation of performing at literary events—but with a heightened articulation of the impact, in characterising it as 'dangerous'.

'Yes', O'Hagan agrees, nodding vigorously—'it's going from the interior into this open space where it's *echoey*, and it's ***performative***, and – I think Colm's right – **you've got to *modulate* that** very carefully. I remember when I was just starting out, watching ***musicians*** and how they treated the score, and thinking actually, *that's* probably a more intelligent way to use a piece of fiction that you've written, is to have it there, almost as a score – of course you're reading from it, but you're not really *just* reading from it; you're *lifting* from it – and the analogy rings true for me, that each time it will be *different*, and these marks on the page will give rise to something fresh each time'. This idea, of the literary text functioning as a musical score, reminds me of David Almond's emphasis on sound and musicality, albeit his focus had been on rhythm—and also of Le Guin's ideas about the fundamental relationship between sound, rhythm and text.

'The thing is that the work comes from ***emotion***', *Tóibín interjects*. 'It's quite an odd process because there's only one poet I can think of, that's Ian Hamilton, who said that he *couldn't* read his own work, because it had come from raw emotion, and it would *release* raw emotion if he read it out loud, especially for him, because it was all too close to him. It was **too** *much* for him. And I know the feeling [raised voice, reflective], not the *too much* part of the feeling, but the feeling of – something you write comes from something that has *mattered* to you. And reading that out loud to an audience, then, is not merely a *performance* of something abstract and distant; it's actually quite *raw* and *close*, and reading it out loud you're – **revisiting** it. Or at least **rel*eas*ing** it. And afterwards you feel that something funny has happened. If the audience *gets* it, you feel you've actually shared it, or evoked it, or communicated it or done *something* to it that allowed it to affect them'.

'I'm with Colm on that – **against the notion of** *recitation*', O'Hagan says. 'People can parrot material, but … if a reading's gone well it's because I've discovered something *new* about the piece while being on stage… there's a **discovery** in it for me. You know that moment in Hamlet, the advice to the actors to *coin* the thought as you're having it. You know, you don't just – *read* – out loud… that seems to me a missed opportunity'.

I am intrigued by their shared emphasis on finding new qualities in their texts through the act of reading them aloud at live events, and transforming the texts for both themselves and reader-audiences; yet how they approach the idea of performance differently. *Tóibín is clear that the transformation lies in the conduction of emotion that produced the text; whereas* O'Hagan thinks of the process in terms of theatrical **performance**—an approach that is reflected in his delivery style as I observed it.

Do they have a sense that readers are interpreting the fictional texts they're performing more autobiographically in a festival context, when the readings are performed alongside on-stage conversations about their lives and work? *Tóibín* nods, reluctantly, at this question. 'Yeah', he says, in a dismal tone. 'But I remember hearing **John Banville**, who reads very well – he reads in a sort of dry, distant tone, but whatever he does with the rhythm, he brings the *emotion* in. But he read an account of someone recovering from injuries, as a result of a fire, someone who'd been burned, whose skin had been burned, and described the pain and the days, and we all just realised this has *never happened* to *this* man, *he* has not been burned – but whatever he was using, it sounded real and *true.* Sometimes writers can do it simply by having felt the *emotion* to write the scene: the emotion revisits when you read it out loud. It doesn't have to be directly autobiographical to actually *matter* to you'. This gets back to the idea of authenticity—but authenticity residing principally in emotion, rather than in authorial biography or identity.

I recall Simon Armitage's idea about the ideal degree of performativity in a live reading being one that allows the words need to speak for themselves: this seems to contrast with O'Hagan's more dramatic approach. So I ask whether, in their view, a **flatter style of reading** might feel for a reader more **akin to the experience of reading on the page** than a more actorly performance would do. *Tóibín nods, thoughtfully.* 'There are very few prose writers who throw the work *away* when reading', *he says.* 'There are some poets who do it… But I don't know any prose writers in particular – I can't think of anyone [musing] – who deliberately *sets about - not -* giving the audience something from the reading that is *emotional…*'.

O'Hagan cuts in. 'I think there is an example, and it's **Margaret Atwood.** I'm not sure if it's a decision or the way it is, but it [her delivery style] has a particular effect on your understanding of the prose. She always kind of **pulls all the music *out*** of it – for *me*'. I reflect on this; I have witnessed Atwood reading aloud from her work a couple of times, and she is very wry and dry—but I had 'read' that tone that as reflective of a key characteristic of her prose style and humour, rather than something that sucked energy or music from the text. *Tóibín laughs appreciatively, and nods his agreement. With Atwood,* 'you feel sort of: if anyone thinks *I'm* going to get you all to *emote?* – we've been *through* that, girls we've *had* emotion', he mimics, somehow mocking but with an affectionate reverence. O'Hagan takes this implied political angle a step further, returning to the text. 'I always think it's a political act in that way: that I'm not *doing entertainment.* Bringing you back to the *bare concrete experience* of these words, in this order… it's just a technique; it's as much stylistic effect, I think, as you would be able to distinguish in the work'.

Pursuing this line, I ask whether, in their view, literary readings performed by authors are fundamentally different to theatrical monologues performed by actors. 'Yeah', *Tóibín says, reflectively, adding:* 'There are times, when some writers do it, that it's more **hamming** than acting. And *actors* listening to *writers*, it's like – "oh my God, if you had any idea how *bad* you sound from *our* point of view – technically it's all over the place; you should stick to your day job, sonny". Because of the whole way of using your breath, or…' O'Hagan laughs, nodding, and chips in: 'You never feel that *actors* think, like, oh my god, *the soul speaks!*' *Tóibín grins and raises an eyebrow:* 'They *really don't* think that'. He sighs. 'I think that, with a writer reading, you *do* get something *pure* and *interesting*'.

*Tóibín sits forward, remembering something.* 'I did a reading last night, and it's the only funny bit in the book – at least *I* think it's funny – but someone came up and said to me afterwards: "**that doesn't read funny on the page**, but the way you read it, you give dialogue such a dry sound that it sounds funny out loud, in a way that if you read it, it doesn't". I didn't know that! I thought it was *always* funny'. I'm taken by this revelation that, as an author-performer, *Tóibín* has discovered something genuinely new about how his work is being interpreted on the page, through performing at a live literature event. 'I think that's really important', O'Hagan joins in. 'And one of the reasons for doing these events, apart from the obvious reasons that authors come and publicise their books, and all the rest of it, is that there is an **enjoyment** in it for a certain kind of author – in *reinhabiting* **the work**. Because you don't, as a rule, walk up and down your hall, er, *giving voice* to your work…. Or do you? [to *Tóibín*] Walk up and down the hall reading your own work?' 'Oooh, imagine if that started!', he replies, and they both laugh. 'So this is a nice opportunity to actually go back inside, and you *do* do it differently each time – I think', O'Hagan concludes.

'So, do either of you **read out loud when you write**, as part of the writing process?', I ask. 'I do, definitely', O'Hagan says. 'I *have* to *hear* it'. *Tóibín* jerks his head to look at him closely, with an incredulous expression. 'You read it *out loud?*' **Yeah!**', O'Hagan laughs back, as if it were obvious. 'Oh I *never* do that', *Tóibín says, shaking his head.* 'Oh my god, if I started to do that… I don't know what would happen!' [We all laugh.] 'Do other people do it?', *Tóibín asks O'Hagan, genuinely curious.* 'I don't know, do they?', O'Hagan asks, turning to me. 'Well, I've come across a lot of authors so far who say they do', I offer. O'Hagan nods, as if he fully expects this answer. 'I *need* to hear it', O'Hagan reiterates, 'because you can… sometimes you get too much into a *screen*. Yes, it's to do with screens… When I was working as an editor at the London Review, some pieces you used to get in and you'd think, oh, the screen wrote that. It was too *enmeshed* in the screen'.

I'm intrigued by this idea that screens might have transformed the writing process for authors, making reading aloud more important than it was before. And I am fascinated by how opposed O'Hagan and *Tóibín are when it comes to reading aloud while writing. Their divergence on this issue, I note, reflects their respective views about performed readings at events.* 'So you've *never* read your work aloud as you've written, or as a form of editing?' I ask *Tóibín, just to clarify.* He leaves a dramatic pause before answering me. '*What*? No! I'm too old. And I don't like my own voice! I don't – like – my own voice'.

I can't quite tell to what extent this is a joke. I conclude that it's not. 'But you read very lyrically', I say, having heard him read at an event in the past—and it's true; he is even speaking lyrically in conversation, now, with a very distinct, lilting rhythm, which isn't just about his Irish accent. His prose on the page is notable for being spare yet remarkably lyrical. 'I know. I know!' he agrees. 'It's an ***inner* voice**'.

It seems, from the author-performers I have spoken to at Hay so far, that there is a marked split between those who read their work aloud as part of the writing process and those who don't. I wonder how many of the latter, like *Tóibín,* nonetheless link their writing to an 'inner voice'—the phenomenon that the poet **Denise Riley** has interrogated so thoughtfully (see Chapter 2). *I am amused and pleased by the way in which Tóibín, despite his initial reticence to engage in a conversation about live literature, became even more involved in it than O'Hagan. And I am interested in the sense I got, rightly or wrongly, that Tóibín had only just thought about these issues seriously for the first time during the conversation, and was genuinely surprised to discover that his own practices and approach differed to O'Hagan and others.* I begin to suspect that this is the case for many authors of fiction, since live literature seems to be so rarely discussed in its relationship to their craft, and is so often characterised as a 'mere' publicity exercise.

I head outside and chat to a couple of festivalgoers who are wandering down an aisle: Janet and Tim—both about fifty, white, one a lecturer and one an IT consultant. They've attended several events so far—including Lucy Worsley's, which had the room 'gripped' and led them to buy her latest history book; Sandi Toksvig's lecture on reading which was 'very engaging' as 'she's a good wordsmith'; and Michael Palin's event about his new book on Brazil, which was 'disappointing' because they'd wanted more 'stories from the past, about Monty Python', and instead 'just' heard about the book. When I ask whether they enjoyed hearing authors read from their books, Janet says: 'I think it's very personal to them... it depends how much *emotion* is put into it. If it's something very personal, very funny, I think it really transcends – having somebody reading it themselves, they were there, relating something *they* experienced...' I note the automatic connection made here between a sense of **authentic emotion** and **autobiography**: a connection that *Tóibín* might take issue with.

'You might have read the book in advance', Tim adds, 'but you might not get ... there's a lot *behind* the words that they're trying to get across'. In contrast, Tim's comment is more focused on **authenticity of interpretation** and comprehension.

I ask whether they go to other literary events and festivals. 'Oh, we'd definitely choose a festival like Hay over going to stand-alone literary or book events', Janet says. 'There's so much going on here, and so much choice, it's nice to *be* here, to meet people, and.... I like books! I haven't got a kindle and I don't want one – **I like the *touch and feel* of books and I like *people* with books** – I like that this festival is *promoting that*. I feel like we're all quite similar minds, and it's nice, you know, to be part of a literary crowd'. This links back to Almond's emphasis on the materiality of books, and I am intrigued by how Janet links that to the experiential quality of being in the physical, embodied space of Hay. This echoes other reader-audiences' expressed feelings about the sense of being part of the physical environment at this festival—which fits with Victor Turner's ideas about festival density and the role of liminality in the way in which participants value the experience (see Chapter 2).

Back in the Green Room, I spot **Simon Garfield**. His new non-fiction book is *My Dear Bessie*, which is based on a collection of wartime love letters that he found in the Mass Observation Archive, between a serving soldier and his fiancée back in England. Selected letters from it are going to be performed at the Festival by the actors **Jude Law** and **Louise Brealey**, as part of an event produced by *Letters Live!*: a successful performance enterprise set up by the publisher **Canongate**. 'Now it's on stage for the first time!', Garfield fizzes. 'It's just an extraordinary thing… The letters *did* work really well *on the page*, there's no question. But the minute you get actors to read… an actor takes it up *seven notches*, and people are in their *thrall*, and you think, this is actually happening live! You'll see – it's just **magical**'.

I ask him whether he thinks letters, as a form, as opposed to fiction, work particularly well in performance—because the narrator is likely to be giving voice to their thoughts in a similar register to the way they would speak to the other person. It's a leading question, but I feel sure he will have an independent view—and he nods, emphatically. 'Yes. Especially *these* letters. Because they're **not written by *famous* people**. With an Oscar Wilde letter, he has in the back of his mind that someone may print this, or collect it… But these people weren't famous; the letters were collected by their sons, so they are *absolute **raw honesty**. That's* why they work *so well*. Because you know there's no angle… there's nothing but truth and total commitment to the words as they are there'.

Is an audience likely to get something different from an author reading their own words than an actor, in a fiction context?, I ask. 'Yes – if you're Alan Bennett', he replies. 'But if you're some novelist who's a brilliant writer but not a performer, then less so… I would have thought. It's interesting, because in the last ten years there's been an ***enormous* transformation I think in the way writers *appear* at events**. [pause] I mean, you could say they've become **less literary and more performance-based**. So you know, with Simon Armitage and so on are great performers and funny… but it used to often be the case that a famous writer would turn up and read from a novel and not give anything other than what was in the text, and read it in a very flat, monotonous tone… it's kind of a *dead* event, you know [musing]. And you couldn't get away with that now. *Now* it's about being *involved* with the audience – everything, the Q&A, and maybe having a chair ask questions first, then putting it out there, choosing the choice bits, you know - *engaging*. All that kind of stuff'.

What do you think is driving this desire for more liveness?, I ask. 'I think there must be an element of... for want of a better word, *fandom* about it', he says. 'And then I think there's just this thing which is – true of live performance in general, beyond literature – which is, because of the internet, now, I think you kind of get the feeling *everyone is seeing exactly the same thing at the same **time*** on a screen. But a live event is a ***unique*** event... The thing with *Letters Live!*, and we've done about ten or twelve now, is that you know you will *only* get, on that *one* evening, the likes of Stephen Fry, and Sarah Lancashire, and Jude Law, and everyone else, reading *that* particular letter at *that* particular time. And it'll *never* be repeated. And it's great! You know, you're there, you want to see what happens. There is **a *uniqueness* about *being there***... and also, there's a ***participant*** thing that we were talking about, that *you* are actually *part of* the event'.

I go to *Letters Live!* that evening, and the performance is sold-out, packed—and as electrifying as Garfield had assured me it would be. Jude Law and Louise Brealey perform the love letters with verve, vulnerability and emotion.

Afterwards, I go back to the Green Room, queue up for a cup of tea, and find myself standing next to none other than **Jamie Byng**, Director of Canongate, who tells me to come over and meet Jude Law. 'Oh great!', I squeak. **Law** smiles like a friendly Cheshire cat as I tell him how much I enjoyed the event. I ask him how he finds performing letters compared to, say, a play script. 'A play's written to be *played*, to an audience', he says, 'and what *this* proves is that *anything* – well, not *anything*, but the *written word*, performed with an audience... suddenly some alchemy happens, and it can be potent stuff. It's *really* interesting'. I ask whether he thinks there's something special about the letters, compared to other forms of writing. 'Yes, and *these* ones, they are – it's life and death! Bombs are dropping on them... they're writing, and churning up absolute, guttural... like, *I've got to say this now!*... It's mainlining fucking content, like, *mainlining*, like – no *play* has quite *this* material. It's raw'. I nod. 'There's so much fragility, as well as humour in them...', I suggest. 'Humour's the interesting thing', he cuts in. 'Because we all read stuff, and have a chuckle or whatever... But in a *shared reading*, when people really *laugh* – and once you get a bit of a laugh [he postures now as if he's on a stage, cracking a joke, and everyone around us laughs]... shared humour is a really *magical* thing'. It is a strong reminder of **how important laughter is** in any verbal, embodied performance: it is the clearest possible sign, for a performer, of the audience's **collective engagement**. Coming from Jude Law, who doesn't exactly need reminding that audiences enjoy watching him perform, I am struck by quite how empowering it must be, as an actor, to feel assured of being able to summon up such responses. After a bit more chat, they head off for a party at Revel Guest's house. I chicken out of asking for a selfie.

## Day Four

On my final day in Hay, I head to a headline act in the main tent: **John Le Carré** (the pen name for David Cornwell), now in his eighties, being interviewed by Philippe Sands—'his first time at Hay!' Philippe informs the audience—again, a full house, for an event that has long been sold out. Sands pauses for the predicted, vociferous applause, before adding, ' – and he *says* it's the last' [more laughter]. 'I try to avoid the **toils of publicity**', Le Carré explains, wryly but gently, in a pristine RP [received pronunciation] accent, his voice soft with age, and yet very clearly enunciated, his tone immediately endearing himself to the audience. 'I do believe **I'm better read than heard**', he adds, reflectively, alluding to a philosophical critique of the literary festival—and, indirectly, encouraging the reader-audience to buy his books.

Nonetheless, he goes on to deliver a **riveting conversation-performance**, which does not involve a reading from his new novel, but mostly describes his own life story and the points at which it intersects with various of his novels. This includes anecdotes about his time as a spy, and times when researching his books took him to dangerous places. He has an uncanny **ability to craft a verbal story**, apparently impromptu, that keeps the entire audience captivated. His language is simple and conversational, yet evocative and tonally varied; each scene he narrates has a well-paced story arc; and his delivery is quietly confident and easy, and rhythmically and tonally varied, including extended monologues in response to questions, and mingling humour with seriousness.

The **understated** quality of his delivery reminds me of the way Colm *Tóibín* described John Banville; but rather than conveying an *emotional power*—the quality *Tóibín* valued about Banville's performance—the power Le Carré conveys is, to me, more about an *energy*: a kinetic quality of language and content, delivered with a constant wit, or threat of it, and a tendency to effect a sudden turn of phrase. These elements of delivery, fused with the characters he's describing—including himself, while negotiating astounding scenarios—make you feel certain he is about to come out with something else extraordinary any minute, as if it were an everyday occurrence; and that you need to keep your attention fully switched on so as not to miss something.

Le Carré seems to be the **personification of literary craft**, in a way. His oral narrative has a pace and 'readability' as well as an intelligence and complexity that mirror his novels. I feel curious to read his autobiography on the page, now, but that is something he says he will never write.[81] He makes clear that he is, at heart, a fiction writer and wants to be read as such. So this event, I reflect, is the closest thing I'll get to reading his autobiography[82]—and it seems preferable, in fact, since now I have had the chance to witness him speak, and to 'read' his body language and delivery style. The experience will, I'm sure, enable me to vividly remember his stage persona and his way with words, via the embodied experience, when I next come to his fiction. And the event has worked on the level of publicity too, since it has made me want to read his newest novel, even though the thriller is not a genre I turn to often.

As I wheel my case out of the Festival site and begin the long journey back to the city, I smile inwardly at the recollection of my initial Blytonesque woodland fantasy of the perfect literary festival. I have had a fulfilling and fascinating experience at Hay—even though it was much more formally organised and commercially-oriented than I'd expected, or than the word 'festival' in its oldest sense might suggest to the uninitiated. The experience of being there did not feel liberating as various music and cross-arts festivals I'd been to: events that featured more spacious, scattered site design and un-ticketed, unsynchronised events, allowing for more spontaneity and a sense of creative disorder, transcending the routine of everyday life. But it did feel unusually 'dense', in the sense of being jam-packed with interesting author-performers and texts and perspectives and ideas and possibilities, and as such it was richly satisfying—though it is impossible to tell whether I would have quite the same way had I not been there as a researcher as well as a reader-audience member.

My conversation with Gaby Wood revealed the **tight triangulation of Hay with the publishing industry and the media**, and illuminated the ways in which the economies of publishing shape the Festival's design and feed its growth. Book sales at the big festivals, Hay and Edinburgh, particularly through '**conversion**' sales directly after events, have become so significant to the publishing industry that Nielsen BookScan has now begun tracking them independently[83]—a fact that is indicative of the impact of these festivals have on the publishing industry, and on literary culture, which can only increase the motivation on the part of publishers to lobby for their big titles to be featured. I came away with a sense that economics significantly shaped, not just Hay's curation and programming, but the hyper-efficient design and layout of the space, the precise event synchronisation, the impeccable organisation and standardised event format. Every single event I witnessed was impeccably run, precisely to schedule. In combination, all these factors can make Hay seem like a giant **mechanism of industry** control over consumers.

But **reader-audiences** I observed and spoke to did not *experience* Hay that way. They rarely betrayed any concern about the industry influence on Hay, or even awareness of it. Most of them were simply enjoying being present there, with some, like Elsa, euphorically relishing it. And there are experiential advantages to Hay's precise organisation and layout: they allow the meta-event to flow remarkably smoothly, despite the huge numbers of people present, and a remarkable density of concurrent events. This enables the experience to feel simultaneously animated, collective and peaceful, and—once tickets are bought—allows for a focus on the content of events, rather than on logistics.

Despite the Festival's internal **orderedness**, its rural setting, in tents among rolling hills, does create a sense of **liminality**—perhaps particularly so for somebody like me, or Elsa, who has travelled there from an urban environment. The programme, while being curated princi-pally around household names and commercially-promoted writers, was packed with varied and interesting events.

And the standard event format, while being **predictable**, worked reli-ably well; individual sessions rarely lagged or felt baggy, and were almost always engaging in themselves. The **quality** of the events I witnessed was uniformly high—even if, after a while, the standard formula grew repeti-tive, and even though I often wished there had been longer readings and more performative experimentation.

But I mull over whether this broad-brush overview of the reader-audience experience of Hay amounts to a grand **deception**, which I, and other reader-audience members, had fallen for. Had we all been lured to this famous festival as part of a giant book publicity and sales exercise, in which we had been led to *believe* we were playing an **audiencing** role; but were actually functioning as **customers**? Were we like fish emptied into a pond, successfully lured towards the hook of book-buying by a tempting selection of bait? My suitcase is certainly four books heavier than when I came. This is true to an extent, perhaps—but there was also much more of value in the experience than that.

One of the main things that strikes me, in reflecting on how I valued my experience of Hay, is how engaged I felt, during the course of each event, with the process of acquiring an **evaluative sense of each author-performer** through a combination of factors like **voice, body language, prosody and attitude**, as well as what **was said and what was read**—and how this evaluative process felt like a valid way of determining how I would probably **evaluate their fiction**, even if I had only heard that person read from a fraction of their book.

I don't feel wholly comfortable about this. Like reader-audience members Sarah and Katherine, I almost always wanted to hear **read-ings** from the texts, as well as a staged conversation, in order to get a definite sense that I could make a meaningful evaluative judgement about the literary work being presented. Even so, isn't it fundamentally flawed and irrational, and even anti-literary, to be making such a natural linkage between an evaluation of an author-performer's **'authentic' self**, observed partly through performed conversation, and evaluating their fiction? As Jo Glanville and James Daunt felt: isn't the only genuinely valuable literary experience the act of reading a book, silently?

In part, as neuroscientists have shown, and as Will Storr has recounted in his book, *The Science of Storytelling*, this is just how we are wired as humans:

> We're wired to be fascinated by others and get valuable information from their faces. This fascination begins almost immediately. Whereas ape and monkey parents spend almost no time looking at their babies' faces, we're helplessly drawn to them. Newborns are attracted to human faces more than any other object and, one hour from birth, begin imitating them. By the time they're adults, they've become so adept at reading people that they're making calculations about status and character almost immediately, in one tenth of a second.[84]

This is all part of the same '**theory of mind**' process in the brain—an active form of empathy—that is proven to be so actively engaged while reading fiction.[85] So there is a direct link. As neuroscientist Tali Sharot has explained, our brains also wire us to retain and value information received from other humans, in person, particularly when the emotions are engaged, priming us to respond with even more emotional engagement as part of an embodied audience.[86]

While gazing out of the window as the bus swerves and rattles on its way to the station, I ponder on how often the idea of *authenticity*[87] had recurred during my conversations with participants, both explicitly and implicitly, in reference to what they valued about the literary festival experience—the various meanings they seemed to ascribe to the concept, and the different ways in which they seemed to value it. The word 'authentic' was used frequently but inconsistently and was applied phenomena and elements of the festival experience ranging from their interpretations of the text to their authors and to the festival itself. If the concept of '**authenticity**' is a **golden thread** running through multiple aspects of Hay, based on my conversations with participants, then how meaningful is it, and what can it reveal about the value of experiencing the Festival?

It is worth unpicking how authenticity has been theorised as a contemporary concept, and how it relates to notions of value. 'Authenticity' has been held up as a **key theme of the twenty-first century**, and a 'pervasive trope' of twenty-first-century fiction, literary culture, the wider culture and even human subjectivity,[88] and is the subject of a raft of theorising.[89] Whereas in the Romantic era, authenticity was seen as a way of connecting with the true feelings of the self[90]; in the twenty-first century, authenticity is seen as more **multifaceted**,[91] mutable[92] and constantly contested.[93]

The widespread desire for authenticity is often seen a direct **counter-response to digitalisation**, in two key ways.[94] One is the way in which the mediatisation of people's communications has given people a sense the world is becoming 'deeply inauthentic'.[95] The second is the 'inexorable flood' of information available online, which makes individuals feel an anxious sense of 'too-muchness',[96] and a desire to connect more directly with other humans and with tangible, organic planetary life—which (as I discussed in Chapter 2) partly explains the increased emphasis on liveness across contemporary arts and culture. It explains why reader-audiences' sense of being able to 'read' author-performers through their embodied presence, at a live literature event, in conjunction with the content of their communications, is experienced as being 'authentic' and therefore as valuable.

Authenticity is usually linked to a sense of 'realness', but most contemporary scholars who have theorised it agree on one paradox: that its meaning can never fully be pinned down. Authenticity is understood to extend to both personal and collective experiences, products, performances,[97] and affective and aesthetic responses. It is integral to heated debates around identity and cultural appropriation.[98] In terms of aesthetic evaluation, authenticity has been linked with a 'sense of connectedness'[99] to the world, a feeling of 'ecstatic flow' and a feeling of 'fusion with one's community'.[100] It has been attributed to the 'appetite, especially among the middle classes, for the genuine and unvarnished', for instance in 'organic consumerism'.[101] Performance studies scholars have named it as a key element of audience experiences.[102] Does this make it too broad a concept to be useful?

**Phillip Vannini** and **Sarah Burgess**, in writing about authenticity, have argued that, despite its multifacetedness, enough people 'believe it matters' to make it a powerful cultural force worth exploring.[103]

In relation to live literature, and its cultural value, I am particularly interested in the idea of authenticity, as articulated by Vannini and Patrick J. Williams, as an '*interpretive process of evaluation*, engaged in by individuals and groups – and process that is entirely dependent on the particular social or cultural context in which those individuals and groups are interacting' [emphasis added].[104] Applying this idea to Hay, I reflect on the extent to which the idea of authenticity shapes the ways in which participants—including me—evaluate their overall experience of the festival, and of events, author-performers and texts that they encounter within it.

My sense of uncertainty about whether my evaluations of author-performers' 'authentic' identities should legitimately affect my judgements about their fiction was reflected in several of my conversations with author-performers. Colm *Tóibín*, in particular, expressed strong resistance to the idea that reader-audiences should be led to draw any links between his fiction and his own autobiography, or anyone else's. And yet the conversation-based event format that characterises Hay and other literary festivals inevitably invites such links to be made. As such, the literary festival forms part of a wider 'resurrection of the author' in contemporary literary culture.[105] And there is now neuroscientific evidence to support the idea that readers of fiction are very susceptible to the framing of fiction in their interpretation of it.[106] Consequently, the foregrounding of autobiographical links to fiction at live literature events is likely to have a significant effect on how the text is read.

How significant is this **preoccupation with authenticity** for literary culture? Arguably, it is **impacting on literary writing**—even to the point that it could lead to the '**end of fiction**'. This sounds like an overstated hypothesis, but there is a logic to it. The widespread contemporary preoccupation with authenticity, and the linked notion of **identity**, which connects to a concern across publishing with how authors' 'authentic' autobiographical identity relates to their publications. That in turn leads to an expectation that autobiographical links will be present in their fiction. And the current trend for autofiction has been said to point to the 'end of fiction'—according to renowned literary critics, including Alex Clark and Anthony Cummins.[107]

Persistent diversity deficits across culture, including in publishing and fiction, and the important quest to rectify these deficits by increasing the presence of authors who identify as belonging to marginalised minority groups have had the effect of leading authors who identify as being part of minority groups to feel they should write fiction about their own experiences, in their #ownvoices. The same preoccupation links to a concern with identifying cultural appropriation on the part of authors who write fiction about the experiences of characters from minority groups of which they are not themselves a part; this leads authors who do not identify as being part of a minority group to feel that they would be safer in writing about characters with cultural experiences similar to their own.

The expectation that fiction will reflect authors' authentic identities is not simply attributable to diversity problems, though the preoccupation with authenticity goes deeper than that. It is also linked to **social media** and the expectation it has created of having **access to public figures' 'real' lives and views**—even though social media is clearly a forum for the publication of personas which are often hard to distinguish from 'reality'. The consequences of this, for sought-after authors, can be as dramatic as the hounding of **Elena Ferrante** by a male journalist, for having published novels under a pen name and being 'audacious' enough to resist the clamour and decline to engage in public discussion about their 'real' identity, or discuss the extent to which their fiction may in fact be read as **autofiction**.[108]

The **triangulated issues of authenticity, identity and cultural appropriation** in fiction came to a head on a literary festival stage in 'Shrivergate': an event at the Brisbane Writers Festival in 2016, when **Lionel Shriver** used her keynote speech to attack the notion of 'authenticity' in literary culture. In her view, the notion is entirely rooted in identity politics and has mutated into cultural appropriation that has infected the health of fiction. She expressed her views on this in uncompromising terms, with a clear focus on its impact on white writers like herself, arguing that they are no longer 'allowed' to write outside their experience, and 'any tradition, any experience... any way of doing and saying things that is associated with a minority or disadvantaged group is ring-fenced'. This, she argued, was threatening the entire concept of fiction, which, to her, made no sense. '**Fiction is inherently inauthentic**', she proposed. 'It's fake. It's self-confessedly fake; that is the nature of the form, which is about people who don't exist and events that didn't happen'. It is a form 'born of a desperation to break free of the claustrophobia of our own experience'.[109]

Her speech prompted furious responses, including from author **Yassmin Abdel-Magied**, who wrote an article about walking out of Shriver's speech, calling her position 'arrogant' and making the point that: 'it's not always ok if a white guy writes the story of a Nigerian woman because the actual Nigerian woman can't get published or reviewed to begin with'.[110]

Shriver had indeed failed to acknowledge the **very real diversity problems in publishing**, and paid no regard to their **impact** on people who identify as belonging to marginalised minority groups. She presented her case in a way that was utterly insensitive to the importance of these underlying diversity problems. Her main point, about the fundamental characteristic of fiction being invention, and the value of imagining oneself into another's shoes through both writing and reading, is, to me, valid and important. But the effect of her speech was **divisive**—and the divisiveness was heightened by, not only her omission of diversity problems and her choice of language, but also her delivery, which was fiery and uncompromising.

On a Hay Festival stage—not in Wales, but in Cartagena—**Zadie Smith** was asked about authenticity and cultural appropriation in fiction, and responded incisively: 'If someone says to me: 'A black girl would never say that', I'm saying: 'How can you possibly know?' The problem with that argument is it assumes the possibility of total knowledge of humans. The only thing that identifies people in their entirety is their name: 'I'm a Zadie'. Collective identity, she added, was sometimes necessary to invoke in order to 'demand rights'; but she quoted her husband, the author Nick Laird, as complaining to her in dismay: 'I used to be myself and I'm now white guy, white guy'. She replied to him, at the time: 'Finally, you understand'. 'But the lesson of that', she told the Hay audience, 'is that identity is a huge pain in the arse. The strange thing to me is the assumption [of white people] that their identity is the right to freedom'.[111]

It may be that having more conversations on festival stages along these lines, engaging with questions about diversity in publishing, the role of 'authentic' authorial identity and the significance of the idea of cultural appropriation in fiction will cause festival events themselves to shift in how they foreground and approach authorial identity.

As J. M. Coetzee might argue, though any conversation-based live literature event format will almost inevitably foreground a conversation with an author about elements of their autobiography—and also about their views about culture, society and the world in generally, rendering them a kind of sage figure. This, in Coetzee's view, effectively diminishes the cultural value of the literature that is supposedly being featured, reducing the significance of the literary forms that have been carefully crafted in order to be read on the page.[112] The only true form of literary 'authenticity' on this view lies in the experience of turning the pages of a book.

But my research at Hay suggests that **literary authenticity is multi-layered**—or, at least, that it means different things to different people—and it does not necessarily turn on the experience of silently-reading the printed word. David Almond, for instance, is an author-performer who explicitly links literature, at its core, to sound, the voice, rhythm and the ancient practices of storytelling, echoing the views of **Ursula K. Le Guin**[113] that I discussed at the beginning of this book. For Almond, that is where literary authenticity lies, and he pays attention to this in his performed readings, which audiences—like Liz and Laura—rave about.

The idea that true literary authenticity is rooted in orality challenges **Walter J. Ong**'s theory that contemporary literature, based on writing, is fundamentally different in nature from ancient oral literary traditions (see discussion in Chapter 2). It accords the view of anthropologists of communication, like **Ruth Finnegan**, who challenge any meaningful divide between oral and written literature, in any cultural context, once it is performed. My live literature research suggests that many author-performers, such as Andrew O'Hagan, regularly read aloud during their writing process, revealing that **orality** is a fundamental part of their **literary craft**. Even Colm *Tóibín*, who insisted that he never read aloud during his writing process—though he also admitted to disliking the sound of his own voice—talked about an 'inner voice'.[114]

Could it be that the rise of live literature—in conjunction with the rise of audiobooks—is bringing literary culture 'back' to a point where literary value is more closely linked to orality?

It was very clear from my conversations with reader-audiences at Hay that many of them hugely valued the **embodied, oral elements** of events, particularly the performed readings, often linking this to a sense of an **'authentic' experience** of the literary work, as much as to the author-performers themselves. They often responded sensitively and deeply to qualities such as tone, accent and rhythm, as well as body language, and this often led them to evaluate both the performance and the work in what were felt to be meaningful and 'authentic' ways, aided by the staged conversations. Examples are Stan and Kira's descriptions of how valuable it was for them to hear Toni Morrison's rhythm to get an 'authentic' sense of her work, and Liz and Laura's descriptions of their emotional responses to Simon Armitage's vocal qualities, which resonated with their own sense of connection with an 'authentic' northern identity. Katherine and Sarah felt short-changed when there was no performed reading in Ishiguro's event because they felt that they had been denied something that, for them, would have been of real value by giving them an authentic insight into the text—from an author-performer they were already familiar with, and had already seen and heard live at Hay. In contrast, they described the impact of witnessing Hanif Kureishi read from a novel of his at a previous Hay Festival, which they described as being delivered in an 'angry man' style: an affective evaluation that had enhanced their understanding of his work and their own subsequent reading of it. Many reader-audience members talked about **'hearing' the voice** of the author-performer **'in their head'** while they read their books after events.

While *Tóibín* was resistant to the idea of live literature events leading reader-audiences to make autobiographical links with his fiction, he did acknowledge that his performed readings could enable them to interpret them more 'authentically' on the page, and gave an example of an encounter with a reader-audience member that had made him realise that.

Crucially, my research revealed that reader-audiences **valued** the sense of experiencing an **'authentic' performance** by an author-performer more highly than what might be viewed as an overtly **'good' performance** in actorly, theatrical terms.

Event chairpeople and producers did not seem to take this into account when worrying about the inclusion of performed readings and assuming that reader-audiences would be bored by them. That worry, in turn, was partly founded on a common—flawed—**stereotype** that authors were inherently **introverted** hermits and uncomfortable with performing, in comparison with actors and presenters. But reader-audiences did not necessarily value a theatrical style of delivery by an author-performer—unless, that is, the delivery was interpreted as 'authentic': in other words, unless it chimed with the assessments they were concurrently making about that author-performer's persona, in conjunction with their faces, vocal characteristics and body language.

An example of a **theatrical** performance style is **Andrew O'Hagan**'s. In talking about his approach, he felt that performing a reading should involve '**reinhabiting**' the work, interpreting it like a musical score and thus experiencing it anew each time—suggesting an 'authenticity' that relates to present, embodied engagement with the text and the audience. This approach is much more akin to the work done by an actor in performing a script. It suited the scene from his novel that he chose to perform: a highly dramatic battle scene. It also seemed to resonate with O'Hagan's dynamic personality in conversation.

A contrary approach to performed readings is that such readings should primarily 'serve the words'. On this view, an '**authentic**' performance of literature is one that enables the words to be at the forefront, or, at least, allows the inherent qualities of the **text** to shine. This fits with the general advice given to the earliest talking book narrators on what makes a good performed reading of a novel.[115] Notably, Simon Armitage is an example of an author-performer whose performed readings generated an equally if not more effusive response from reader-audiences, even though his delivery style is very different to O'Hagan's; it is, in comparison, more subtle and understated in its performativity. Again, this is reflected in Armitage's conversational demeanour, including his dead-pan humour, as well as in his lyrical literary style.

Gavin Extence, a debut novelist just getting used to performing at events, spoke of his initial worry about **how to perform dialogue** from his own text, fearing that, off the page, he might spoil the experience of the words on the page for reader-audiences; this prompted him to **'learn' his delivery from an actor** instead. But, as Stan and Kira suggested, in talking about Toni Morrison: while they highly valued witnessing her 'authentic' performance in person, they ultimately wanted something different from an entire audiobook narration.

*Tóibín* and O'Hagan pointed to examples of performed readings where emotion was ostensibly devoid from another author-performer's reading due to a **'flat' delivery style**. *Tóibín* cited John Banville, whose reading was very quiet and apparently flat—*but*, he added, you could tell that **emotion was bubbling beneath** the surface. The implication was that this discernible emotional quality made the reading **authentic** and therefore valuable. O'Hagan cited Atwood, who, they both agreed, was deliberately flat in her delivery—and yet agreed that her particular flatness was imbued with a wry dryness that they attributed, possibly, to political motives, linked with her wider public persona, her feminist credentials and the aesthetics of her literary style; or perhaps to her 'real' self and sense of humour; or to her literary aesthetic, which is often dry and witty. In Ishiguro's event, which did *not* involve a performed reading, he responded to a similar characterisation made of his writing style by literary critics early on in his career; he talked about how the literary aesthetic of his writing was described by initial reviewers in terms that he didn't necessarily see, but had come to embrace over time—and which, to me, reflected his delivery style in performance.

**'Authenticity'**, in literary performance, clearly involves many potential **layers of interpretation**. The *process* **of determining what is authentic** about a performed reading or conversation, and why— including through references to the text—seems to be a fundamental part of the way in which literary festival events are appreciated and valued by reader-audiences.

There were other ways in which the experience of Hay was valued in terms of authenticity. One is a sense of **liveness**: a notion that was frequently linked to the dynamics of impromptu conversation. As Hahn and Wood suggested, the more **improvisatory** the conversation seemed, the more alive and 'authentic' the experience felt. While the standardised format of Hay events can manifest as a form of artifice; it means that every event involves an unpredictable element of conversation and audience participation that seems to heighten the sense of liveness. And, to me at least, a refreshing layer of 'authenticity' was added when performers offered **ironic meta-commentary** about the event format, as Hahn did, since this highlighted the fact that every participant present had an awareness of the expected form of the live performance that all participants were experiencing.

The idea of authenticity at Hay also lay in the way it enabled reader-audiences access to the imperfect, human process of *making* **literature**: a point emphasised by David Almond, who pointed out how the product of literature is most often presented, at Hay and elsewhere, in the form of a perfect, shiny hardback, available for sale only for those who can afford it. Consequently, in his events, Almond emphasises his **'authentic' process** of making literature by showing his **messy notebooks**.

Hay was also valued in terms of authenticity on the basis that it provided participants with a **live, embodied experience** in **contrast to the digitalisation** of their daily lives and communications. Several reader-audience members I spoke to, like Dave, emphasised how important it was to them to **retreat** from the constant digital bombardment of everyday life to a space where they would be able to immerse themselves in embodied events where they could really focus on and connect with an author-performer—while also experiencing a sense of connecting with their families and friends too, and other festival-goers. This seemed to give them an 'authentic' sense of being part of a **humanised ritual** and an embodied **community**.[116]

Similarly, the Festival's rural **setting**, and its tent-based construction were valued by many participants experientially and as a form of authenticity. This is manifested very clearly in the experience that Elsa described, of the relief of escaping from her busy, city-based life to a remote field, oriented around human conversations and ideas: a form of secular **pilgrimage** that takes on a liminal quality.[117]

Authenticity, then, can be usefully understood an important **interpretive process** that illuminates the multifaceted, overlapping, sometimes contradictory ways in which the Hay Festival experience is valuable for participants. The interpretive process of deciphering authenticity seems to be a core part of participants' evaluations. While the role of the publishing industry and the media in Hay might appear to make it seem inherently 'inauthentic' and commercialised to some[118]—it reveals the very real ways in which literature is intertwined with the cultural world in which it is produced.

I get off the train in London and lug my case out onto the thickly-fumigated air of the Euston Road, already feeling reminiscent about Hay's clean greenness, and the contained vitality of the festival site. Life feels so simple and stimulating when all you are expected to do with your day (aside from research) is wander around some tents with a bunch of other people and soak up new ideas and stories.

# 4

# Polari Salon: A Literary Cabaret with an Activist Twist

Behind a low stage illuminated in flamingo pink, still empty but for a small wooden podium at the centre, ceiling-high windows display a spectacular backdrop of the Millennium Wheel, mere metres away. It's glowing emerald—though, as I watch, it begins to shift to a brilliant orange like a giant reverse traffic light installation. Behind the wheel is a sparkling black ribbon: the Thames, underlining the Houses of Parliament. The view could almost be computer-generated, but this is really what London looks like from the fifth-floor function room at the South Bank Centre.

Screens on either side of the stage, however, show a 'real' computer-generated image of the same Millennium Wheel backdrop, but with a larger-than-life man lounging in the foreground, sporting a top hat garnished with a feather and a purple sparkly tie reminiscent of Willy Wonka, and holding a paperback which he is regarding with an exaggerated expression of gleeful shock, half looking at the camera. Several other books float and flit around him like butterflies amidst sparkles of magic dust.

A full-house of about 150 people has gathered here on this chilly January evening, to a soundtrack of feel-good funk, and the chatter

© The Author(s), under exclusive license to Springer Nature
Switzerland AG 2021
E. Wiles, *Live Literature*, Palgrave Studies in Literary Anthropology,
https://doi.org/10.1007/978-3-030-50385-7_4

is noisy and ebullient. Some are queuing for drinks at the little bar, exclaiming at how good it is to see each other, hugging, jostling, joking and chatting. The majority seem to know several others and act like regulars. Seats are quickly filling up. I'd say there is a mix of men and women here, ranging in age from twenties to sixties.

As the music volume ramps up a notch, the man from the screens takes to the stage in the flesh, wearing a flamboyant combination of white sunglasses, a silver top hat—which turns out to be the same hat in which he once posed nude for a gay magazine cover[1]—a candy-floss suit jacket and a boldly-patterned tie. 'Welcome!' he grins. 'I'm Paul Burston and I'm your host for this evening. Now, are there are any Polari virgins in the house?'

A scattering of hands cautiously ascend as members of the audience 'come out' as Polari virgins—I estimate about a third. Burston regards them for a moment, before slyly semi-reassuring them: 'we'll try to be gentle with you'. He explains to us that his tan is thanks to his trip to Rio last week—assuming a general familiarity with his normal appearance, I note, which further suggests the presence of a regular community of audience members. 'I was lying there on the beach, imagining you all in budgie smugglers', he adds with a lewd grin—a comment that I presume applies only to the men in the room, so probably about two-thirds of the audience.

\* \* \*

For any 'Polari virgins' reading this, who have never previously considered themselves as such: Polari is a literary salon with a particular orientation: namely towards **LGBTQ+** writing, and LGBTQ+-identifying authors and audiences.

I'll hover here over the term 'LGBTQ+'. When I was researching the Polari Salon for this ethnography, host Paul Burston was using the term 'LGBT' to refer to Polari's identity,[2] despite regularly inviting authors who self-identified as queer or who had other sexual or gender identities to perform. When I asked Burston about his choice of acronym and its implications, during one post-show conversation, he shrugged cheerfully, and told me that anything beyond LGBT just sounded 'too

complicated' to him, so he usually used that term for Polari communications—but he didn't really mind what other people wanted to use; 'queer'
is fine as far as he was concerned, or 'whatever'. However, the Polari
website reveals that, in the past year, he has shifted to using LGBTQ+:
now by far the most widely-used acronym to encompass people who
identify as Lesbian, Gay, Bisexual, Transgender, Queer; any combination of the above; or who have other gender or sexual identities such as
intersex, pansexual or asexual—ultimately, anybody who does not identify as heterosexual or cisgender. This seems to represent a cultural shift
in the public conversation and perception of gender and sexual identity
towards overt inclusivity.[3]

'**Polari**', though, is a term that originated squarely in the 'G' category:
it is the name of a **coded language** that was taken up by the gay community in London, in an era when homosexuality was illegal, as a means
of disguising their activities.[4] It became a core element of London's
burgeoning gay scene after World War II, centred in the gay bars of
Soho. Deriving from the Italian *parlare* (to talk), the language dates
as far back as the sixteenth century, when it was used among circuses
and show travellers, then developed and spread in the merchant navy
as sailor slang, evolving along the way to include elements of London
slang, Romani slang and Yiddish. After peaking in the gay community
in London in the first sixty years of the twentieth century, it began to
decline after the decriminalisation of homosexuality in 1967—notably
when the term 'gay' became common parlance.[5] It is still around today,
though, and has undergone something of a renaissance[6]; it made up the
entire script of a 2015 short film by Brian Fairbairn and Karl Eccle-
ston called *Putting on the Dish*.[7] Its longstanding role and significance in
the context of London's gay scene is vividly depicted by journalist **Peter
Burton** in his memoir, *Parallel Lives*, as he recalls going out in Soho in
the 1960s:

> As *feely hommes* (young men), when we launched ourselves onto the gay
> scene, Polari was all the rage.
>
> We would *zoosh* (style) our *riahs* (hair), powder our *eeks* (faces), climb
> into our *bona* (fabulous) new *drag* (clothes) and *troll* (go, walk) off to

some bona *bijou* (little) bar. / In the bar we would stand around polarying with our *sisters, varda* (look at) the bona *cartes* (male genitals) on the *butch homme* (man, pronounced 'o-me') *ajax* (nearby) who, if we fluttered our *ogle riahs* (eyelashes) at him sweetly, might just troll over to offer a light for the *vogue* (cigarette) clenched between our teeth.[8]

The **Polari language was 'never meant to be written'**, Burton points out. In those days, he explains, the gay community 'flaunted' their homosexuality, and were proud to broadcast their difference to the world—but *'only when we were in a crowd;'*[9] they were all conscious that Polari, while enjoyable as a mode of communication, was ultimately a 'secret language born out of repression'. He goes on to expand upon the distinctive way in which it was spoken, its tonality and its resonances. It had a **double edge** even when spoken in the 'safe', collective context of a gay bar— Burton describes its tone as having a 'particularly brittle, knife-edged feel', especially when brandished by 'some acid-tongued bitch whose tongue was likely to *cut your throat*'; 'queens with the savage wit of the self-protective'.[10] Nevertheless, he reflects, 'there was something deeply reassuring about Polari'; its 'bizarre' and 'secret' nature gave those of us who used it an additional sense of corporate identity. We were **part of a group** – and that knowledge was both a comfort and a curious protection'.[11] There was, simultaneously, a ***protectiveness*** of the Polari language on the part of the gay community, perhaps exemplified by the reaction against its usage by Morrissey in 1990 in a song called 'Piccadilly Palare', on the basis that the singer-songwriter was not openly gay— although he had publicly stated that he was attracted to both sexes the previous year.[12]

The **Polari Salon** was **founded** in the heartland of its namesake language; Burston started it in 2007 as a pop-up initiative in a **Soho gay bar**, *The Green Carnation*, where he was then DJing to supplement his writing income. The idea was borne out of 'frustration'; by that point, Burston had published three novels and a number of nonfiction books, but claims he had not once received an invitation to read at a literary event. Identifying a widespread reluctance to promote gay authors, and a concurrent demand among gay authors for opportunities to air their work,[13] he pitched the idea to other bar owners, and it expanded. In 2009 Polari was headhunted by the **Southbank Centre**'s literary manager, plucked out of Soho, and relocated across the river, whereupon its audience numbers and public profile quickly expanded.

Following its success, and its recognition as a platform for emerging LGBTQ+ writers, Burston founded the **Polari First Book Prize** as a way of further promoting emerging LGBTQ+ literature and writers, and the Salon was subsequently funded by Arts Council England to go on a **national tour** to festivals, libraries and theatres, expanding its reach to towns and cities beyond the capital. It is **ticketed**, but at a relatively **low price** of £5, which—in live event terms—makes it accessible to people with diverse incomes.

It is a marked contrast to the elite character of the **historical literary salon phenomenon**—a phenomenon that had been thought to have faded out forever in the **nineteenth century**, after its peak in the eighteenth century in Paris, London and beyond. The former salon format usually involved **high society** hostesses, or salonnières—often women—inviting groups from high society to the salons of their grand domestic houses in order to discuss books, ideas and tastes, often through performed readings to the assembled company.[14]

The historical salon phenomenon has been the subject of much academic attention since **Habermas** cited it as a core part of his well-known theory of the emerging public sphere in eighteenth-century Europe, on the basis that salons provided a unique new opportunity for interpersonal communication and exchange in urban centres, nurturing rational and critical debate.[15] Pierre **Bourdieu**, in 1996, went on to examine the literary salon's role in the formation of cultural tastes and class distinctions and as a location for 'genuine articulation between the fields' of literature, the press and politics.[16] More recently, Susanna **Schmid** has explored the role of **women** in British salons, considering groups such as the Bluestockings, and these salons' unique role as intellectual and cultural hubs,[17] and Maria **Popova** has written about the impact of women's salons in America.[18]

It is only in the last decade that there has been a marked revival of the salon in the contemporary British literary scene, alongside the growth of festivals and other forms of live literature event. The best-known literary salon is **Damian Barr**'s—which started life as the Shoreditch Literary Salon, but changed identity alongside the ascending star of the event profile and its host's. Sparklingly entertaining, and yet with an ability to discuss literature in depth on stage, Barr drew in the best-known authors, and the salon soon migrated from a packed-out back room of the Shoreditch House club to the grand surroundings of the 5* Mondrian Hotel.

The Word Factory's 'Short Story Salon' takes place in the event space in Waterstones Piccadilly, a large bookshop in central London, and is primarily aimed at new writer development; it features a panel of three writers reading from their work, followed by a discussion and audience questions, and is often programmed in conjunction with creative writing 'masterclasses'. More recently, **publisher-run salons** have emerged, like that founded by the literary imprint of Harper Collins, 4th Estate. Perhaps most akin to historical iterations of the literary salon is that run by Mieke Vogel, founder publisher of Peirene Press, who hosts gatherings in her London home. Unlike the historical salons, though, all these contemporary salons are more publicly-available events, ticketed at a price, and not limited to select bourgeois invitees.

The **literary salon revival** is undoubtedly linked with a growth of other regular live literary events with similarly-intimate audience sizes, all of which have a more performative, less overtly commercial orientation than the literary festival format tends to have.

Right from the outset, at Polari tonight—even from the projected image—it clearly displays a **distinctive aesthetic** among literary events, which Burston has described as 'a **literary showcase** with a **cabaret feel**'.[19] In the light of what I have been reading about the Polari language, I reflect on the ways in which both the salon and the language started out as performative manifestations of London's gay sub-culture. Not only is there an obvious resonance between the spoken nature of Polari as a language and the spoken nature of its namesake salon, but the 'sharp' texture and 'cutting' effect of the language that Burton describes, in tandem with the 'queendom', camp and sexualised humour that still remain so characteristic of the London gay scene, are already clearly mirrored in Burston's on-stage persona and his aesthetic framing of the event.

To what extent, I wonder, does Polari salon—along with other comparable cultural events—now operate as a contemporary source of collective LGBTQ+ identity in the city, in lieu of the fading Polari language? How do the 'L', 'B' and 'T' categories relate to the 'G' now that Polari salon has moved beyond the gay scene? And what about 'Q' and '+'?

Scholar **Jennifer Reed** interrogated the issue of sexuality labelling in cultural performance in an article about the cultural impact of the US-based *Ellen* sitcom, from which **Ellen DeGeneres** was famously dropped after she came out as a lesbian. When Ellen returned to screens a few years later with her own talk show, she generally referred to herself as 'gay' rather than as a lesbian—but, according to Reed, performed that identity in a '**postgay** kind of way. That is, in a way that said: "I'm gay, but it doesn't matter"'.[20] Reed argues that the approach taken by Ellen's producers 'allows the show to sidestep the challenge that lesbian subjectivity makes to the heterosexual contract',[21] and allows liberal straight audiences not to be 'bothered with any of the real differences that lesbian identity can present or with their own homophobia'.[22]

Reed does not underpin this with any evidence of liberal straight audiences' views, or consideration of how far what Ellen's 'postgay' approach, as she calls it, has positively impacted upon discriminatory attitudes towards performers identifying themselves with any sexuality or gender label other than straight. Nor does she consider how large and diverse Ellen's audience would have been had the show producers chosen to foreground the 'lesbian' label. Perhaps most crucially of all, she does not acknowledge the agency that Ellen DeGeneres herself must have had in her show's approach to her own re-labelling, given that she is one of its Executive Producers. But she makes a wider argument that 'the use of any label grounds the politics in a particular place. That is, each term (gay, lesbian, queer, homosexual) carries with it the histories and politics of meanings'.[23]

In Burston's case, there is a clear attempt not to get ground down in the **politics**. I note the parallels between The Ellen Show and Polari, in terms of their presenter's deliberate flexibility and lack of emphasis on identity labels—albeit, in Polari's case, the situation is complicated by virtue of the salon's self-identification, initially as a gay literary salon, and later as an 'LGBT' and then 'LGBTQ+' salon. This deliberately distinguishes it from other, more mainstream live literature events.

Burston summons the first '**performer**' up to the stage—his choice of term, which I note immediately, as it differs from almost all other literary events I have been to previously, in which people who speak about and read from their books on stage are more commonly referred to as 'speakers', 'authors', 'writers' or 'readers'. '**Persia West** has worked as a bar girl, financial journalist, model… English teacher, garden designer, activist on human rights with a special focus on trans rights, and has just published her *first novel – I Am Alessia!*', Burston tells us all in proud tones, and applause bursts forth.

West is a tall and elegant woman, who appears to be in late middle age—she wears her hair in a long, gingery bob, and her neck is sheathed in a sheer, flowing scarf. At the podium, she greets us, and tells us, in low, breathy and seductive tones, that her novel was inspired by Lorca's *Blood Wedding*. She pauses for a long moment to look around at the audience, apparently meeting several pairs of eyes, and then begins reading aloud from the opening.

The scene describes, in the first person, the narrator's experience of walking down the aisle with her father at her wedding to marry a man when she is in fact in love with her cousin Alexandra, who is standing in the congregation, watching. '*We stood at the back of the cathedral, my father and me… I was electrically alive and full of expectancy…*' West drawls out her vowels and glances up at us suggestively every so often. It occurs to me, some way in, that she probably identifies as a trans woman.

'*My stage the church, my audience the congregation… we walked slowly down the aisle… My eyes locked on hers… Sweet and strong… Time stood still for an eternal moment… I'd been caught in the iron grip of my father…but now a note within me shrilled with the thrill of the wild unexpected*'. The writing might bulge with clichés, but it is delivered with a sincerity, passion and poise. West doesn't shy away from hand gestures to accompany significant changes of pitch, and is clearly revelling in this performance, in an **overtly theatrical** way that is rare in a literary festival context. Some people in the audience look rapt, while others glance at each other with expressive uncertainty, but an intent and respectful atmosphere is sustained throughout the reading.

It turns out that West has a lot of experience of public speaking, though not of publicly reading aloud from her fiction; this novel, her debut, has only just come out. Her website reveals that she does indeed identify as a trans lesbian woman and is an activist in relation to gender. She defines herself as a 'storyteller' and 'speaker' as well as a 'writer', and states that she gives regular talks about 'gender, spirituality and consciousness', and has also given a lot of thought to the subject of reading aloud in general.[24]

For West, her voice has an integral relationship with her writing. 'I feel that the written word is frozen speech… I write like I speak, the voice inside me, but with more colour, so in some ways it goes deeper to speak it out loud', she writes.[25] She goes on to compare the written and spoken word with visual media, juxtaposing them via the metaphor of heat, based on their impact on imagination: 'Such channels of perception as TV and movies are *cold* media; this is because they leave nothing to the imagination… Reading or radio or storytelling are *hot* media; we create our own movies of the mind within ourselves with the stimulus of words alone, each to our own imagination'. She distinguishes the written and spoken word in theatrical terms: 'I just love **the *theatre* of spoken words** [emphasis added], because they have their own power and resonance, and when I speak to a group, an audience, I feel some 'fluence rising in me and projecting out to the listeners, who become charmed, entranced and taken to another world'. This combination of overtly romantic and fantastical language, and the notion of '**entrancement**' in reference to audiences, clearly informs the distinct performativity of her reading. I wonder to what extent West's fascination with voice and performance in relation to her fiction links to the way in which she has had to learn to perform her voice socially in a culturally-feminine way, focusing on its timbre, tonality, affect and effect in the process; there is an inherent performativity in being trans.

In life beyond the salon, West's twitter feed reveals that she is passionate about the public presence and perception of **trans lesbian** identity in performed contexts, and angry about its **marginalisation**—including by the gay and lesbian community—and is unafraid to say so in strong terms. This was exemplified in the context of London Pride when a group of lesbians protested against trans participation, on the basis, as one of them put it, that 'a man cannot be a lesbian, a person with a penis cannot be a lesbian'.[26] In response, West took to Twitter and posted: 'For my many lesbian friends who support the reality and goodness of we trans people #LwiththeT After the hideous lunatics being able to lead Pride in London with their hatred… some bizarre delusion'.[27] But she does not discuss such events or views tonight at Polari.

I note that, although lesbian sexuality is foregrounded in her fiction, as evidenced by the extract she reads aloud, this particular text engages with lesbianism between women who do *not* identify as transsexual. West has been public about her anger at trans identity being 'used' in fiction by authors who do not adopt that identity themselves, as a form of cultural appropriation. In another tweet, she stated: 'Radio 4, the Today programme this morning, interview with @SalmanRushdie, writer, selling his new book, all about gender identity it seems, having the knowledge of knowing 2 trans people a bit. Drives me up the fucking wall, writing the usual shit to make a buck out of us all grr'.[28] In the light of this, I can't help wondering about West's choice to write fiction from a non-trans lesbian point of view, and feeling curious about how she might write about a lesbian relationship involving a trans woman, in a way that wasn't—as she implied in that tweet—exploitative and inauthentic.

The most public debates over recent years around cultural appropriation in fiction, and linked ideas of morality and authenticity, have been in relation to race. Debates have aired on literary festival stages and continued in the media (as I discussed in Chapter 2).[29] I note that the format of the Polari salon, being readings-focused, does not leave space for questions that might prompt such ideas to be aired and debated as part of the event—and I wonder now whether Burston's **decision to foreground readings** is a *deliberate* means of **avoiding such debates,** so as to forge **connection** rather than fuel **division** between members of LGBTQ+ communities in this context.

Clearly the socio-political implications of **gender identities** are **central to Polari's raison d'être.** While it manifestly retains a camp, quintessentially **gay aesthetic,** that links to its Polari roots; its physical migration to the Southbank Centre coincided with its expansion from a gay to an LGBT (and later LGBTQ+) 'identity' as an event. West was chosen as tonight's first author-performer, and three out of the five performers for this evening identify as female, it seems clear that there is no intentional bias towards gay authors, and that Burston has genuinely sought to make the event **inclusive.**

As the applause for West subsides, Burston bounces back onto the stage to introduce the next writer, **John R. Gordon**: a novelist, playwright and screenwriter, and the founder of a publishing company called **Team Angelica.** Team Angelica aims to **celebrate queer writing,** as part of a mission to 'bring out books that are **provocative,** original and inspirational', to 'present and **represent the un- and under-represented,** and to enable and encourage new and diverse voices, especially voices that are gay, queer, black and of colour', and 'to put out work that is transformative, and that celebrates difference and diversity and the maverick spirit'.[30]

Gordon looks the part of a maverick spirit; his head is closely shaved at the sides with a long, styled central top section, and he wears angular glasses and a beaded shoestring necklace. I would guess he's in his late 40s. He holds up a paperback copy of his novel, *Souljah*—published by his very own Team Angelica. 'It's about a mother and son, Poppy and Stanlake, who are refugees from a civil war in West Africa', he tells us. 'Stanlake is a seventeen-year-old boy, who's very effeminate with long dreds. They come over here and then are relocated to a grim house down the Old Kent Road, where they encounter petty drug dealers who don't realize that Stanlake might be very effeminate but he has been a child soldier and has done terrible, terrible things… and eventually the lead gang member becomes erotically fascinated by him'.

He begins reading aloud from the book with a scene in which Poppy has just got back from the housing office and is making tea for Stanlake, whom she notices is wearing eye shadow and lipstick; this is the moment that the narrative begins to reveal the erotic power Stanlake will prove to have over the drug dealers who have been persecuting them. His reading voice is soft and level, making me lean forward fractionally to be sure I hear every word, yet it is assured and compelling, in a very different way to Persia's more performative **reading style**—and it turns out to be in stark **juxtaposition** to the **shock value** of the **text**.

A couple of minutes in, we are introduced to Stanlake's inner erotic thoughts with a description of how his cock hardens at the sight of the men's underwear catalogue at a bus stop, and this is quickly followed by gruesome flashbacks of Stanlake's time as a tiara-wearing child soldier, when a rebel soldier '*put the raw flesh on the end of the bayonet... then placed it on his tongue... mucus membrane... was sticking in his throat and he began to gag and retch.. then he threw up the slimy hunk of muscle...*' Audience members near me wince and grimace at this, and one woman, who looks physically ill, whispers not-so-quietly to her neighbour: 'ohhh god!'

Not only is Gordon's performance style very different to West's, the novel extract he has selected—and indeed the tone, style and content of the novel as a whole as he outlines it—could hardly be more different from either, save for the common theme of non-heteronormativity. This text sheds light on a rare manifestation of trans-sexualisation in the context of certain refugee communities with traumatic roots that is rarely aired or discussed in British publishing in any form.

I wonder about the degree of expectation there is, at Polari, to include reference to sex and sexuality explicitly in the texts performed. Jennifer Reed, critiquing Ellen DeGeneres's decision to evade talking about sex and sexuality directly, argued that it was essentially damaging to the lesbian community's cause; in Reed's view, by representing herself as 'a lesbian without being lesbian, or a postgay lesbian', the impact of Ellen's presence diminished the potential force of the important challenge that needed to be posed to the 'heterosexual social contract'—because, 'without lesbian desire, there is no lesbian. Under the all-encompassing force of the heterosexual contract, the lesbian is lost'.[31] The problem with Reed's argument here seems to me to be: what about the agency of the individual performer or artist? What if they want to be recognised for their talent in a way that does not directly involve sex and sexuality; and do not want to feel compelled to shape their work in order to function as part of a community-based challenge to heteronormative dominance?

The next author-performer, **Catherine Hall,** is a slim woman in her early thirties with a blunt fringe and long bob. She is introduced by Burston as 'born and raised in a remote sheep farm in the Lake District', which is the geographical setting for her first novel, *The Proof of Love*, which won the Green Carnation Prize—an 'LGBTQ+' award. She tells us in a light, soft voice that she now 'lives in London with her two small sons, their father, and their father's boyfriend, which sometimes feels like a lot of disaster for one small lesbian to live with', immediately making people laugh, and also making her own gender identity clear at the outset.

She is going to read, she says, from her latest book, *The Repercussions*, which is about a war photographer just back from Afghanistan. Before beginning, she briefly introduces the book and its main characters. 'Jo, the war photographer, has just moved into a flat inherited from her grandfather, and finds there a diary of a lady called Elizabeth who looked after soldiers who fought for Britain in WWI. This causes Jo to come to terms with what happened to her in Afghanistan but also what's happening now with her husband and her female lover'. The chapters alternate between Jo's letters to her ex-girlfriend Susie, and Elizabeth's account of nursing Indian soldiers at the Brighton Pavilion in 1915.

Hall begins the performed reading with a scene where Jo is writing a letter to Susie, describing her current situation, sitting on a balcony of her Brighton flat. '*I feel strange as I always do when I get back, caught between different worlds…*' She reads at a **fast, nervous pace**, which is hard, at first at least, to latch onto. She moves onto a World War I diary extract by Elizabeth and then reads from a travelogue from her time in Afghanistan after the Taliban emerged, which comes to life with evocative descriptions—'*balconies hung cracked over gracious houses*', and '*human bones on the street, dug up by children from graves which were shaken by bombs*'. While the content, style and setting of her chosen extracts are varied, Hall's reading tone does not vary much, and nor does she settle into a slower reading pace, making it difficult to remain engaged in the text. She is clearly nervous, but I find myself sympathetic to her nerves—partly as I was endeared to her by her initial self-deprecating and funny introduction—but also, as I am drawn to her story, language and literary style, I find myself actively wanting to absorb it properly, so I concentrate hard, and find myself adjusting to the reading and appreciating the writing and the performed reading more as it proceeds. I note that, in Hall's performance, there is no explicit reference to sex, sexual desire or sexuality.

During the **interval**, I ask a woman sitting near me if she'd mind speaking with me for my research, and she immediately replies: 'of course!'—an attitude that will be reflected in almost all my Polari participant conversations, and seems to match the relaxed, enthused vibe of the event. Robin is a petite 52-year-old South Londoner with a short blond bob, dressed in a check shirt and jeans, and is here for the fourth time with a group of friends. The venue, she tells me, was her initial attraction: 'I've been coming to the **Southbank** since I was a child. As a **venue**, it's really one of a kind'—but Polari also appealed because 'you hear new stuff and get to chat to other people', and because it's 'pretty much the **only event of** its type in London which is just… gay and lesbian'. This is fascinating; while I had been aware of divisions within the LBGTQ+ community, I had not realised how far that translated into the existence of **shared arts and cultural spaces**, and how **rare** Polari was perceived to be by those who attended it.

I ask Robin if she is here at Polari more for the **community and social side or the literature**. 'The literature first', she says, 'but *obviously* because it's gay and lesbian – and the social aspect to it probably second'. The **queer perspective** of the writing by the featured authors is **important** to her, she explains, and more so than their individual identities as authors—but the two do interrelate. 'Most of the writing at Polari touches on gay and lesbian issues', she says, and even if that's sometimes 'quite indirect… that's fine. Really it's just interesting to hear whatever the subject matter might be about, from a lesbian or gay perspective. Even if it's fictional'.

The **quality** of writing at Polari is 'pretty **mixed**' in her view, but she praises its range and diversity. Coming here has prompted her to read books she wouldn't otherwise have read, including poetry by Stella Duffy (who is performing later tonight) and it has caused her to put lots of other writers on her to-read list—though she can't recall any names off the bat. The kind of writing that works best in performance, she thinks, is '**observational humour**'. She grins as she says this. 'People always like to laugh don't they? – so I think any writer that can choose something from their work that can make people laugh and is about observation and human nature, that can cut across all sorts of things – that's going to work really well'. She finds the **standard of performances** at Polari **mixed**, as well the writing, but, immediately after making this point, clarifies to me that she doesn't necessarily *expect* writers to be good performers: 'that's not their forte; they might be writers but that's a very different thing'. This echoes my conversations with reader-audiences at Hay: the idea that a **'good' performance, in a live literature context**, won't necessarily be theatrical or dramatic, and that a sense of authenticity in performance is more valuable.

Clara, a tall, slim, quiet woman in her late forties with cropped hair and glasses, tells me she's here by herself, and for the first time. She's just finished a literary PhD and is currently working as a university administrator. Her sexuality isn't obvious from her dress style or presentation, and she doesn't make any allusions to it in our conversation. 'I heard of the salon because my cousin is John Gordon who's one of the writers here tonight', she says. 'I've also read Diriye Osman's *Fairytales for Lost Children*' (another book published by Team Angelica, which will be featured at the next Polari; Osman's first book won the Polari First Book Prize).

'So far I've found it brilliant. **Fantastic**! I love literature – but I'm used to reading, so I tend to find it **difficult to *listen***, because my mind wanders – but with the three readings tonight, my mind hasn't wandered! I've been **riveted**, so far. I've loved it'. I ask why she thinks her mind usually wanders while listening to literature being read aloud. 'I think it's to do with the way my brain works', she muses. 'I'm a creature of the mind, and I'm a very reserved person, and when a narrative enters through my eyes very privately and then I think about it, I like that, whereas if I hear it… I just tend to be aware of other things more'. She mulls this over for a moment, then adds: 'I suppose I've felt like **listening** to narrative is a more *childish* thing – which is not to say that it's *bad,* but… I find it difficult to reclaim it'.

I'm intrigued by this explicit link between reading aloud and childhood. How far is that changing with the rise of podcasts and audiobooks—that I discussed in Chapter 2—and how does attending literary events like this cause you to *practise* listening, as an audience member, and attune your ear and concentration? I reflect that I have already found myself working on my own listening concentration tonight, during Hall's performance; and, over the last few years that I have been listening to more and more audiobooks, I have found myself better able to concentrate on the literary narrative that I'm listening to.

I ask Clara whether she thinks she was absorbed this evening more by the **performances or** by the **content**. 'The content', she replies, decisively. 'The first one [Persia West's reading] I thought was completely brilliant. I would like to read it'. She also found West to be the best performer, intends to buy her book from the Foyles bookstall in the corner after the event, and feels sure that having heard West read it will affect her own subsequent reading. 'I would **remember** what she said, *absolutely* **differently**, now that I've seen her read, and I would really look forward to the scene around the fish pond'. She doesn't think she hears voices in her head when she reads books normally, not having heard the author read aloud from them. 'I… think I *feel* **the voices** in a different way. I don't hear them, exactly'. I'm reminded of Denise Riley's work on the 'inner voice', and the new neuroscience around that concept (see discussion in Chapter 2).

The only live literary events that Clara has previously been to are book launches in bookshops, which she says she has '*quite* enjoyed', in a tentative tone—but proposes that: 'because the readings here [at Polari] are longer, you can get your teeth into more, and have a real sense of what is being read from'. That said, she feels that the authors' short **introductions** to their texts so far this evening have been **key to her enjoyment** of the readings. 'I would have struggled otherwise', she admits—then adds, a little darkly: 'particularly with the *last* one'.

'I **don't feel a Q&A is necessary**', she adds, firmly. 'Nor would I feel the need to ask questions if there was one… though I'd possibly be interested to listen to others' questions. But so far, tonight, I thought the format was *perfect* – three readings, then an interval'.

Has she ever been to a **literary festival**, I wonder? '*No!*', is the emphatic answer. 'I feel as though it wouldn't be my cup of tea', she explains. 'I think I'd find it **too middle-class and right-on**. I mean, *I* am middle-class but I'm not very right-on. I just don't think I'd fit in. But this is fine!' She sounds surprised about that, on reflection. 'Here, it's friendly but…. it's… leaving me alone? I don't feel *alarmed* that it's going to ask any more of me than I want to give. Which I like'. In contrast, she imagines the type of crowd at a literary festival to be: 'middle-class people with their children who don't let their children watch television because they think they ought to read instead… it's just *disgusting*'. I am a little taken aback by this sudden vehemence and can't help grinning. Conversely, she proposes: 'You wouldn't look at the **people** *here* and imagine they are **literary**, right? This could be anything!' I look around and nod slowly, trying to see the scene through her eyes. I am reminded of my conversation with Jo Glanville at Hay, whose sentiments about literary festival audiences were similar (see Chapter 3). And I am struck by the apparent contradiction that Clara described herself to me, at the start of our conversation, as a lover of literature with a PhD in the field; and yet she has this passionate wish not to be among others who look as if they might be quintessentially 'literary'—which she clearly equates with whiteness.

Clara tells me she that would definitely come back and go to more events like Polari—but stresses her point about festivals further, expanding on her vision of them: 'I still wouldn't want to go to a literary festival with *grass* and *marquees* and *falafels* on sale'—each item listed as if it were a mosquito she wanted to slap.

A lesbian couple in their forties called Sal and Jo tell me enthusiastically that they are regulars and come to Polari about five times a year. Sal is a student in counselling and psychotherapy, and Jo a social worker. 'One of our friends is an author', Sal tells me, 'and she's quite a regular on stage here… so we came first to see her, but then we made lots of friends and came back. It's quite a **community**'. I ask which is the bigger draw: the community or the literature. 'It's both…', she says, 'but I wouldn't go to just any literature event. The fact that it was a **queer event** drew me…. And the fact also that it's really **cheap**, it's five pounds! Brilliant. South Bank is a brilliant **location** too'. They say they haven't been to many other live literary events, except 'friends doing launches', a Jeanette Winterson reading, a reading by Judith Kerr at the Southbank where they took their nine-year-old daughter, and the lesbian arts festival, L Fest.

They enthuse about how L Fest includes lots of **interactive** sessions with author readings and audience questions. 'That's the stuff we like, where it's very interactive', Sal says. 'Here at Polari, while there's no Q&A with the author, it's still great because you can always go up and approach them – like, if you see someone you really like, you can go up to them in the break and say hi and they'll be really happy'. They both tell me they don't hesitate to talk to the authors personally, and do this often. 'I love the fact that **you can get to them if you want to**. And trust me, we do', Sal says. They both laugh. They say they often **buy books** here and get them **signed**, either for themselves or as presents for friends.

I ask what they think they gain from hearing the author read aloud from their books, as opposed to just reading the books on the page. 'Well, there are books here that I wouldn't normally buy…' Sal says—'but for me it's also that I can then hear their voice inside my head as I read it. It **brings it to** *life!* Especially if it's funny… I love seeing people read from their own stuff. I think it's really *interesting*'. I ask if that, for her, is partly to do with being part of a responsive audience, as she's described. She agrees, but not entirely—'it's also that I just like to hear their voice, the way they're **phrasing** things… Some guys who come on even act stuff out as well'.

While Sal 'definitely' prefers authors who add more **drama** to their readings, Jo chips into say that she thinks it's always better to see an author than an actor doing a reading, even if the author's reading is less dramatic. 'You're getting their interpretation of the whole theme and characters and ideas… and what we really want is the ***authenticity*** of the original authors' (see last section of Chapter 3 for an extended discussion of authenticity). 'So even if they aren't so eloquent, and fluff a few lines, hearing their *spirit* through their words and through their characters is really interesting. And also recognising how, although their characters might be quite diverse, each one is a small snippet of their personality'. Sal adds that listening to the writer read their work aloud always enhances the way she then reads their books, beyond the sound of the voice. 'Some stuff, I've read and I haven't really enjoyed that much, and then I've seen the author read it and I've read it *differently*. It's better'.

However, when I ask them both if they've ever experienced a badly performed reading, which made them conclude that they might have liked the book better if they *hadn't* heard it read, they laugh knowingly. 'Couldn't possibly comment!', Jo giggles. 'There are definitely better readings than others', Sal adds, diplomatically.

What makes a *good* reading, then?, I wonder. Sal puts her head on one side. 'If someone's **nervous** it makes *me* feel nervous, so I'm a bit funny about that', she offers. 'If someone's mumbling and fumbling and tripping over stuff… I struggle to connect with it. I just think: be relaxed! The pace shouldn't be too fast, unless it's appropriate – and just that bit of character brought to it'.

I ask them to expand a bit on what they each mean by authenticity in this context. Jo nods vigorously: 'It's about **genuineness**, rather than trying to act it out', she explains. 'Just being comfortable with their own words really'. She uses the last reader, Catherine Hall, as an example: 'some of it was quite fast, but she relaxed a little more into being comfort-able with what she was saying and you could feel that coming through. So although it wasn't as *lyrical*, as if an actor was reading it, but you still get more meaning from the words because you can hear what she *intended*'.

Neither has a preference for either **comic or serious** writing; they like the **variety** that tends to be represented at Polari. 'We've been here in tears before, literally *crying*', Sal says. 'It's something about …the author's connection to the work. If they feel really connected to it and there's the connection there and the confidence there – you really *feel* it'. When pressed, she couldn't recall exactly which authors or texts moved her to tears, but Jo tells me: 'There's often a lot of stuff about **loss** that people are prepared to share through their writing, and that's something that everyone can connect with in different ways…if you can hear that in that writer, and then that touches you, and it's very moving'. Sal agrees and **links** this to the **LGBTQ+ identity** of the event: 'With the gay community, and how we can be treated, there's something about that **shared experience of rejection and prejudice**… when someone comes up and speaks to that it really *resonates* throughout the whole room. And you really feel like a community, together, understanding that'.

This value placed on a sense of '**emotional community**'—a term coined by **Max Weber** in the 1950s[32] and adopted by **Michael Maffesoli** in the 1990s to refer to urban sub-cultural groupings[33]—has been echoed this century by researchers exploring gay culture in contexts such as tourism. Many propose 'emotional community' as an important means for participants to gain 'competency in performing gay identities' and enable them to 'cope with issues associated with homophobia'.[34]

Of tonight's readings so far, Sal says the first one was 'a little bit Mills and Boon!', but they were both fascinated by Gordon's reading. 'He was giving me a view into something I don't know much about and it felt very real', she explains. Jo agrees and says she was particularly interested in the way that Gordon approached gay identity. 'The thing he was focused on, about child soldiers, was that loss of self and how they were expressing themselves with wigs, dresses, make up, nail varnish, which changed them in some way physically but with no recognition of their former selves, and they needed that to move forward… I think that was something really refreshing and *new* in terms of a take on that situation'. Sal nods. 'It took a queer identity into a context I had no knowledge of'. They concur that most of the writing performed at Polari has a queer identity theme. 'Or, if they've been straight people they've usually been really camp', Sal adds. 'Like Celia Imrie – she's straight, I think, but she's camp and has a big gay following'. As for the material: 'it doesn't have to be gay and lesbian issues, but it's really nice to be able to come here and know you'll relate really closely'.

Compared to other LGBTQ+ arts events, Sal says Polari is '**special**'. 'There's something about this setting, the fact that it's live and that there's an interval where people chat and we get to know one another… There is a real sense of *community* here'. There's also 'something **immediate**' about a live literary reading, she says, which is not present in other contexts. 'At another art thing, if you were just walking about looking at stuff, you wouldn't necessarily *react* in the same way'. Jo adds that Polari's **informality** contributes to its audience appeal and makes it more **intimate**. 'When the authors are reading... it's less of a formal performance – just like it's their turn to speak in a **conversation** or something – it's so much *closer*... whereas there is that fourth wall, when you're performing as an actor, or musician'. Sal pays tribute to the host for cultivating this atmosphere: 'It's the way **Paul** does it, too [I note the use of his first name here, as if he's a pal] – he encourages people to sort of like clap or cheer or – get *involved*, you know?'

Paul Burston takes to the stage for the second half. 'Hello everyone! Did you have a nice interval? Are you nicely *lubricated*? [He pauses for an audience titter.] You'll need to be for our next performer. **James Maker** is a former rock singer, spoken word performer, and world expert on the New York Dolls. In June 2011 he won the inaugural Polari First Book prize for his memoir, *Autofellatio*'. Burston lingers on each syllable of this title, then grins wickedly. 'After 10 years living in Spain he returned to London, his home town. He can't work out how Oyster cards work, but he can produce a *sensational* omelette'.

A small, bald man, dressed in a black velvet floral shirt, Maker thanks Burston and tells us he's going to read an extract of a chapter which is a **work in progress**, from a book which is a **mixed genre**—some travelogue, some autobiography.

He begins his performed reading in a deadpan, northern voice—and by the end of the first sentence he has got the audience cracking up loudly, immediately transforming the tone and atmosphere of the event. He lightly, yet relentlessly, mocks the British expat characters featured in the piece, two of whom silently judge him and his young gay local companion from across a Spanish restaurant. '*I was shown to a table with a clear view of a British couple from the East Midlands. I'd met them before. The husband was an electrician who was proud of having fitted a villa with British three pin sockets, which was akin to erecting a Gone with the Wind staircase in Northumbria. And his wife was a martyr to menopausal hot flushes... someone had suggested to her that, as we lived in a climate where al fresco dining was common, she should rent herself out as a heater*'. I wince a little at this, and wonder what the menopausal women in the room make of it.

In prose liberally sprinkled with **double entendres**, Maker adds lashes of gesticulation for suggestive actions such as dipping bread in seasoned oil as he goads his judgmental onlookers. His performance grows increasingly bold and camp, and he makes plenty of eye contact with the audience, regularly shifting his reading glasses up and down to adjust from page to people.

For the finale of the night, another experienced performer takes the level of theatricality up yet another notch. '**Stella Duffy** has written 13 novels, 50 short stories and 10 plays', Burston informs us. '*The Room of Lost Things* and *State of Happiness* were both longlisted for the Orange Prize, and she's twice won Stonewall Writer of the Year. Her latest book is a collection of short stories, *Everything is Moving, Everything is Joined*'. As well as a writer, Duffy is a co-director of Fun Palaces: an organisation that seeks to engage people from all communities in the arts.

Duffy mounts to the stage to the tune of loud **whoops**: she has been here many times before and is obviously highly popular. 'Yeah, twice longlisted for the Orange, I reckon that adds up to a shortlisting' she says. She is in her mid-fifties but looks younger. She wears a tight floral dress printed in black, white and teal. She introduces the story she's about to read by telling us that it's part of a collection that was published after she tweeted a fan's request to Salt, a small indie publisher, and they agreed to it. 'I love Twitter!', she exclaims, jubilantly. She explains her decision to perform this particular story on this particular night: 'it's because of where we are [she gestures to the window] – that's a *fuck off* view, right?!' The story, 'From the River's Mouth', is set around the Thames, and was commissioned for Radio 4, so 'written to be read aloud'. Duffy tells us that, for the broadcast, the actor Samantha Bond performed it from inside the Greenwich tunnel, on her request. 'I'm sorry I'm not Samantha Bond', she says—'but she does kiss me at parties now which is great. And people liked her performance so it's been repeated a lot. And actors get bigger repeat fees than writers do'.

I note that Duffy is deliberately emphasising, in this introduction, her **presence, popularity and status** in the arts and literary world **beyond**

**the LGBTQ+ community**, for those who are not already aware of it, indirectly underlining her status as a headliner for this event with plenty of humour.

Duffy's performance, when she begins, is **actorly** compared to most performed fiction readings I've seen at live literature events—but doesn't convey the camp, mannered mode of theatricality employed by West or even Maker. She starts reading at a deliberately fast pace, delivering a dialogue section in a strong Cockney **accent**, which many author-performers hesitate to brave. '*Sorry luv, don't do south… need a passport don't you?… Not me, can't go south, don't go south, won't go south*'. Then the pace slows suddenly: '*Enough.* [Long pause]. *I have heard enough.* [Another pause]. *There is time and there is tide and theeeere - is the Thames* – [her voice drops to a whisper.] *Here is the Thames. Old Father Thames they used to say because they don't know any better.* [A poetic rhythm starts to build]. *I am no more father than I am mother* [declaratory]. *But I do have my children, my tributary babies, running to me, clinging to me…I am tired by these people who are frightened by water, worried by the south… I twist and I have turned… yet you are too scared to cross me don't cross me then* [a snappy, angry tone]'. Having managed to traverse what seems to be the majority of human moods in under a minute, Stella proceeds to read the rest of the story in a comparably dramatic, lyrical style, making frequent eye contact with the audience, and employing occasional gestures like beckoning and flicking away. The story itself does not have a direct LGBTQ+ theme or content, I note.

Looking around, I can see that the **audience is captivated**. A palpable sense of collective engagement is maintained right until the end, when Duffy is rewarded with rapturous applause and more whoops. I'm reminded of O'Hagan's performed reading at Hay—though the audience dynamic there was far more muted. Also, he wasn't reading a **complete story**, which affected the perceived sense of his reading as a performance.

Duffy has a background in theatre—she usually describes herself in bios as a '**writer and theatremaker**'. Consequently, she has given a lot of thought to the **performance** element of her literary events. On her blog, she refers to them as 'rehearsed readings', and issues the following instruction to other authors: '***authors, rehearse your readings!*** *edit them, make them work for reading aloud not just on the page – it makes SO* *much difference. I always rehearse, even for gigs like this, so I have readings ready if audiences want them*.[35] This, from my now-plentiful experience of speaking to authors about live literature events, is a rarely-articulated perspective. Those authors who do edit texts for performed readings tend to do so at the last minute, with pencil scratchings-out on their personal copies. 'To rehearse' is a little-used verb by fiction writers. The practice really can pay off, though, judging by tonight's performance.

Duffy's blog reveals that she has also given thought to the quality of live-ness in other live literature event formats, notably literary festival events that incorporate audience questions, and she links that element to the notion of authenticity that so many reader-audience members, like Sal and Robin, say they value. 'Instead of second-guessing what people want to hear/know about', she writes, 'I now prefer (if the festival will let me) to v quickly tell the audience the kinds of things I do and care about and then ask them what they're interested in, responding to that, and finding a narrative in their suggestions. It means they get something that is more like a show, but it's also led by them, and it also means they get a more *authentic* me,[36] because I'm choosing to respond to them, live, rather than just give them a rehearsed reading and a bit of Q&A... Not surprisingly, audiences are far more interested in something they have input into, and I'm far more interesting when I'm being **genuinely *live***. We all win'.[37]

Duffy does not directly address her sexuality tonight at Polari; but she writes prolifically in her blog about her lesbian identity, and her ideas, emotions, anger and activist motivations relating to gender identity and equality—revealing that she still experiences these issues as central to her sense of self, that they are inextricable from her authorial identity, and that they affect her sense of performative authenticity.

> even now, I can't really hold Shelley [her wife]'s hand in public without feeling like it's a 'thing' – a statement, a gesture – even now, after 25 years together. How for so long – at only 53 – my sexuality (and my gender) have been a thing outside the mainstream, outside the welcomed and accepted norm, that it became part of me too, that being other became

part of me….now, most of the time in my moderately liberal, generous, London life, people are open and kind. But those many many years of feeling othered don't just go away. They live inside me. Othered as a woman. Othered as a gay women. Othered as a woman from a working class background. And it doesn't disappear because things are (often) nicer now, (sometimes) easier now I'm older (ageism and my breaking body aside, obv), certainly easier now I'm more established in my work – that feeling outside, that feeling apart, that feeling [of being] not welcome. Not really, not fully, *not as my whole self* … I realise why I still feel so other. / Because our gains are so newly won, because they are not the norm (for the whole world), because it takes so little to put the clock back, to put our lives back. It's really really not fixed yet.[38]

When I see **Duffy** perform at Polari again, **two years later**, she will strike a very **different tone**, ratcheting up the anger expressed on her blog to another level. After briefly promoting two of her recent books, she performs an autobiographical non-fiction piece, which was published in *Granta*—'I've never been in it before – it's a proper literary magazine and everything', she'll proclaim proudly, while waving her copy aloft for a crowd—who, she clearly assumes, are unlikely to be *Granta* readers. This piece confronts and describes, in frank, direct and angry tones, the **sexual abuse** that Duffy was subjected to as a child and the impact it has had on her as an adult. It goes on to argue passionately that lesbians' experiences have been neglected in all the mainstream **#metoo** conversations.

'Fuck off with your pussy grab. My cunt is – *not – kitten-cute*', she reads, glaring at the audience like a spitting cobra, before wilting a little. 'I am washed out… But this is true. This is mine. This is my story. Me'.

This performance seems to fly a defiant flag for the LBGTQ+ community—by making the point that, as queer culture scholar **Thomas Peele** has put it: 'proliferating **queer representations** in popular culture' have 'not eliminated the problem of heteronormativity or antiqueer violence'[39]; and also by announcing that these kinds of experiences have now entered the 'literary' mainstream, in part thanks to Duffy herself. It is a performance that acknowledges how well the Polari reader-audience community has got to know Duffy, both as an author-persona and through her writing—certainly well enough not to be abashed by extremely hard-hitting autobiographical material. Conversely, Duffy will appear entirely confident that they will want to hear the piece in all its rawness, and to be left with it ringing in their ears at the end of a Saturday night.

During the slightly stunned silence before the applause, I will reflect on how much in common this performance has with *Nanette*, the Netflix show of a live stand-up performance by **Hannah Gadsby** in which she tackles abuse and discrimination against lesbians, and announces her own performance as the end of comedy. The show became a viral phenomenon when it was released on screen, and was marked out by critics as a piece of work that would change the whole landscape of comedy writing in relation to sexuality post-#MeToo, operating as a 'dividing line'.[40]

Back to the present. Burston energetically invites all writers back to the stage for a final bow, tells us the names of the author-performers he has lined up for the next salon, and bids everyone goodbye. The music is ratcheted up in volume again as the audience starts to chat, to get up, put on coats, or head to buy books or drinks.

I ask Sal and Jo what they thought of the second half. 'Well, we know Stella', Sal says, proudly. 'But Robin's seen James [Maker] before but I hadn't, and he was fantastic. Considering it wasn't a finished piece as well! So brave'. She particularly likes hearing new work-in-progress tested out like this, she says. 'We all **get together to hear something that *no one else* is hearing**, simply because we're part of a community! It's cool'.

The idea of **being the *first*** to hear a piece of writing in public, before it has even been published, constitutes a heightening of the **temporal** quality of a live experience, that I will see rewarded by particularly enthusiastic audience applause at future Polari salons. The presentation of new work to salon reader-audiences is something that traces back to the **Enlightenment**; as Habermas put it, in relation to seventeenth-century France, 'the salon held the monopoly of first publication: a new work… had to legitimate itself first in this forum'.[41] While the notion of 'newness' is promulgated by other live literature events too, it is more often in relation to 'first' live readings from newly published novels; this is a core element of Damian Barr's literary salon, for instance. It is also true of the bigger festivals like Hay, where there are negotiations with agents and publishers behind the scenes to stage first presentations of novels by the most critically-acclaimed and bestselling authors (see Chapter 3)—though festivals, being large, annual productions, cannot be as time-sensitive to publication as regular salons. This fetishisation of the experience of being the *first* to discover new artworks appears across other forms too, such as music, film and theatre, often through the terminology of a world or country 'premiere'. But it is arguably heightened in the context of performing a new short story to an audience, before it has even been through the initial filters of editing and publication for a live audience. It heightens the feeling among participants that they are unique, in an unrepeatable moment, in being the first to receive that story in any form.

Sal's reference, once again, to the notion of '**community**' at Polari, when describing her experience of hearing new work in this way, suggests that the regularity of this event heightens that experience still further: the impact of the live performance '**feedback loop**' is increased through a sense of collective experience among a familiar group.[42]

She reiterates how great it is to hear people who are well-known, like Duffy, who's 'managed to **bridge** the **gay-straight**-kind-of-thing', as she puts it, as well as 'people who are just starting out'. The inexperienced ones are not always great performers; 'sometimes you're like urrrooooohuurrrr…', she says—but ultimately 'there's still the *love*. The love is always there'.

This idea of '*the love*' underlines the unusually positive and encouraging atmosphere here at Polari. There is a tangible sense here that, not only are the most successful 'headline' performers still battling against the dominant system in an attempt to 'bridge the gay-straight-kind-of-thing' and therefore need backing; but also that the newcomers are *expected* to be poor performers—and therefore the audience takes an active, valued role in supporting them to develop and succeed.

Put this way, the Polari community appears akin to a **nurturing literary microclimate**, consciously aware of its fragility in relation to the broader ecosystem, but carefully cultivating its new shoots as well as its established flowers.

I get chatting to another audience member, Dom, who is forty years old, lives in East London and works as an interpreter. He's come to Polari before, a few times, he says. 'I like reading – I read a lot. And I write myself. So I like hearing writing – particularly LGBTQ+ stuff. I like the way **Polari feels quite spontaneous**, and you get to see a range of authors from relatively big names to people who aren't published'. The **quality** of the performers, in his view, 'really **varies**. *Massively*. The quality of what they read and the performance…'

That variety does not put him off coming, but it does affect what he decides to read on the page after the events. He was very struck by Stella Duffy tonight, he says, and plans to buy some of her work, either here now, or at some point soon. 'She's a very good reader and performer, but it was also the text. It was very creative, and quite poetic. **I liked that it was a self-contained piece**, and I think she said she wrote it with reading aloud in mind… I think **authors need to choose well**, what they read. Duffy's piece really *worked* – it wasn't just that it is self-contained… another thing is that it was about the Thames, so there is a connection between the place we're sitting, here, and the writing – I like that. London writing, also LGBT stuff – both of those subjects would make me listen more carefully'.

I ask him what he feels about the audience at Polari, as a regular member. He looks uncertain, and a bit sheepish. 'It probably feels a bit more **intimate** than other events', he says—'but it does feel a bit *cliquey*. I come on my own, because I don't have any friends who are into this kind of thing, so I kind of observe others socialising here. It's not *unfriendly*, but… yeah, *maybe* cliquey. There are quite a few people here I've seen before but not talked to'. He has been to literary festivals before, he tells me—he even went to an event earlier today that was part of the LSE Literary Festival, which he says was 'good because it was free', and he also told me he had enjoyed a little literary festival at Laugharne in Wales, where Dylan Thomas lived, which is 'a bit leftfield, leftie – more than the Hay Festival now is, which I've been to too, which started off small but is now more corporate'. He mulls for a moment, then adds:

'while it might be cliquey here, but it's still also a bit like *family* – I don't mean a nuclear family – but you get a real sense here that lots of people know each other. And at other [literary] events, even small ones, it feels like the speakers are… distant, somehow, but here it feels like they're more part of the audience. That's a big positive. I think it's more **relaxed** than *any* literary festival. Probably also because there's alcohol and it's in the evening'.

Emma, a woman in her early forties who works at a sixth form college, tells me that she has never been to any kind of literary event before—she came to Polari tonight with a friend. 'I like reading, and I'm part of a **book club**, but this was like finding a **whole new *side to reading* for me**', she said. 'It's even *more* engaging than reading on the page, I think, to hear the pieces being read aloud… you see the *facial expressions* too, which really helps bring it to life. I'm *definitely* going to go to more now'.

Burston is happy to make time to talk to me, even amidst the thanks and goodbyes. He talks about Polari's move from Soho to the Southbank, a few years back. 'It just snowballed here', he says. 'There turned out to be a really big, **untapped audience**, who were just saying, *give us some stuff*!' Now, he says, it has come to expand both in terms of numbers and profile but also in terms of significance for the LGBTQ+ community, because of the supportive Polari community, or sub-sub-culture, that has emerged. 'Whether it's a first time or self-published writer who's never performed in front of an audience, they're just so *welcoming*', he says, fondly, as if talking about a beloved brood of grandchildren.

He compares the Polari audience to the audiences for readings he's done as an author in other contexts. 'I've done tonnes of readings in bookshops and libraries and stuff like that, and *there* they're like: *Impress Me*'. He gives a cynical eyebrow raise, imitating a hard-to-please audience member. 'It's very hard. Whereas this is nurturing. It's a family environment. I didn't create that – *they* created it. I don't take credit for that. It's lovely'.

That said, he talks about how he actively cultivates the atmosphere through his programming. 'I don't programme it as if it's **a "*literary event*"** [he pauses here to waggle two fingers, miming inverted commas.]

I programme it as if it's **a *cabaret show***. That's the way I think about it. You need to ***entertain*** people'. This doesn't mean it's all about humour, though; Burston prioritises variety. 'My own novels have been comic novels, so far, and that's easy to present to an audience because you know you're going to get a laugh. But you can't present a literary night on that basis because that's basically a comedy night… There *has* to be a mixture of genres and styles'.

I ask Burston to expand on the **readings-focused format** of Polari, in comparison with a standard literary festival event format involving discussion and **audience Q&A**. He raises his eyebrows. 'I'm sorry, I'm a journalist, and *even I* find that [Q&A] boring. I mean, obviously if someone's a cult author and everyone just wants to ask a question, that's a different thing. But for most authors, the audience would really rather hear the work, I think…. **For *me* it's about the work. Polari** is a ***showcase***… And people seem to like it'.

But he's equally passionate about the **community function** of Polari as an event, which he contrasts to literary festivals. 'Whether you're gay or gay friendly, people come here because it's a ***social space*** where they can meet their mates, listen to some writers, have a drink - it's a *social* thing. It's not a *we're-going-to-be-worthy* thing'. He gestures, almost regally, around the room. 'Half this audience is regulars. Literally. I mean – this bunch over here come every night [pointing to one group], this bunch over here come every night [pointing to another]'.

Putting this in the context of the wider LGBTQ+ community, Burston tells me that he is using Polari to pursue an **extra-literary mission** to bring the LGBTQ+ scene back to 'how it used to be. Over the last twenty years', he explains, 'I saw the London gay scene become a *shadow* of itself – it got bigger, but far less hospitable, far less friendly, far less **inclusive**, more body fascist, gender divisions… women not being with men, men hating women… *horrible*. All the things I hate… there's so few places to go now where there's a nice mix of people! I love the fact that this thing started, and it's so varied and ***diverse***'. The mixture of men and women is something you 'never see on the gay scene these days – never', he says, emphatically. 'And all **different ages and backgrounds**, you know, 18 to 80. And that's amazing, to have that social space that's so *inclusive*. It's *partly* the force of my will to make it happen, because I'm determined to make things better!'

Polari, he adds, has proved it can draw similarly diverse audiences **outside London**. 'We just did the first Polari tour towards the end of last year – it was Arts Council funded, and we went around the country – and it was exactly the same there. I was amazed!'

I ask what he thinks it is about *live literature*, specifically, that contributes to this effect on the LGBTQ+ community—as opposed to any other form of live or community event. 'I really think **LGBT people are still** *starved* **of these** *stories*', he says. 'They *need* them'.

During our conversation, several different people come up to Burston before heading off, saying things like: 'Thank you Paul! See you next month!'—and in return he ladles out affectionate compliments like: 'You're looking very fruity tonight, Jan!', and: 'Alright gorgeous, take care!'

Burston returns to the subject of how Polari fits into the wider gay cultural scene, and the role he wants the Prize to play. 'We have gay soap operas now, which we didn't have when I was growing up, and we have gay drama which can be quite dramatic and a bit stereotypical. There are books now, but very *few* books. **Publishing is actually** *worse* now than it was twenty years ago, **for gay books**. There's not a single gay publishing house – not one. [I think about Team Angelica, but don't mention it.] Publishing houses now, since the financial meltdown, are so *nervous* of publishing queer stuff. So when we started the Polari Prize in 2011, we made the decision to make it open to **self-published work**. A lot of self-published work is shit, obviously, but a lot of it isn't shit; it's self-published because they couldn't get anyone to buy it. The winner last year, **Diriye Osman** – his is an *extraordinary* book. If he wasn't queer, that book would be in Waterstones. It's ridiculous. It's an amazing amazing *amazing* piece of work. For a debut'.

I saw Osman at Polari, before he won this prize, and he was a highlight among the author-performances I have witnessed there over several years, certainly in theatrical terms. A gay, transgender Somali writer with a bleached hair top, big statement glasses, and a huge, confident and mischievous smile, he thanked the audience for 'coming and jamming, as we call it', introduced the extracts from his quasi-autobiographical story collection, *Fairytales for Lost Children*, with a snapshot of his autobiography, describing, with a light touch, his traumatic move from Kenya to Somalia as a child, and how, at age 17, he 'specialised in only two things: weed and sex'. During his intense, dramatic, impassioned reading, delivered with a strong sense of poetic rhythm, akin to spoken word, he made plentiful eye contact and at one point looked at the audience with a glint in his eye, divulging: 'I'm getting into this!', tacitly encouraging them to do the same. He told me afterwards how he had written his stories specifically for performance, and loved to perform them with the accompaniment of hip hop beats which he had done in other venues.

Tonight, when we chat after the event, Burston emphasises to me just how important **Polari** is as a **platform for emerging LGBTQ+ writers**, whether they are published, self-published or unpublished. 'In an ideal world there shouldn't be a need for this. But there *is* still a need. Stella Duffy would probably get a gig somewhere else. But no-one else on this bill would get a gig anywhere else, which is ridiculous because they're fucking talented writers'.

The situation has evolved just this year, however, after the submissions opened for the Polari First Book Prize 2018. In a recent blog post,[43] Burston wrote:

> The prize has grown enormously. The number of submissions this year was four times the number we received [last year]… But it would be naive to think that LGBT content is no longer an issue in publishing. Earlier this year, author Matt Cain crowd-funded his novel 'The Madonna of Bolton' through Unbound after it was turned down by many major UK publishers for being "too gay". It became the fastest-funded novel in the history of Unbound.

He added a warning about future threats to LGBT[Q +] publishing:

> This week a writing competition caused a stir on Twitter. Based in America, The Creative Writing Institute have a flash fiction competition that rules out submissions containing "sex, graphic violence and LGBT content." As if our lives and our stories are somehow pornographic by

nature and on a par with graphic violence. I had to remind myself that this is 2018. Not 1958. For as long as attitudes like this exist, and many publishers remain risk averse to books with LGBT content, there will still be a need for prizes like ours.[44]

For the moment, though, Burston tells me that he is proud of the audience numbers that Polari regularly pulls in which, he points out, are rare for literary events, even those in the mainstream. 'I've done author tours for the last ten years, and a lot of the time you just get a few people. A handful. But here we get a *huge* audience, and it's so *lovely* to have that. To say to the authors: *okay, come on – I can guarantee you a really good audience and a bookseller.* And they're like: *Okay!!'*

I ask why he thinks live literature events have proliferated, despite the issue of audience numbers, at least at the other events beyond Polari that he's alluded to. The '**packaging and presentation**' are more **important** than many live literature producers assume, he opines. 'A lot of people think: an author reading – boring. But if you repackage it and present it as a *salon, festival,* blah blah, whatever – it's an *event.* An event is fun. A cultural event'.

He muses on the importance of the **venue** to the dynamic of an event. 'On our tour… we did a mixture of ten touring events, a mixture of existing book festivals, theatre events and libraries. For the theatre ones – every one I hired, we *sold out.* So I think it's about the presentation. The *New York Times* has said Polari is the most *theatrical* salon of all. And that's why I dress up so much and am a bit silly on stage. It just makes it – approachable'.

Is it a problem for him that some writers are better at performing than others? 'Yes, yes, yes, *yes*', he says. 'Many times I don't know what they're going to be like. But what I do know is that **in this space this audience is very receptive**'. The added risk of novices being poor performers is built into his programming, as I had come to suspect: 'Often the first few people on the bill at Polari have never been on stage. That's a *deliberate* thing that I've done. Showcasing new talent in a safe environment. This audience will not boo and heckle them, because if they do they know I'll come and slap them. I'm joking! But they *know* it's going to be **supportive**. So even if they stumble a bit, and they're not the best performer in the world, it's okay, because the audience are really here for the headliners anyway'. I am fascinated by the idea that Burston has almost **trained** his **regular reader-audiences** to behave supportively, therefore cultivating a deeper sense of community among them and *with*, as well as for, debut authors, priming them to expect and accept the worst performances alongside the best.

'Having created something so successful, which I created out of pure *vanity* for myself, I'll be honest…I absolutely feel a **moral duty to use that to support the next generation** of people', Burston continues. 'Not just in terms of their age, but where they are in their careers. Whether they're writing their first novel at 17 or 70 is irrelevant to me. Because they're *new writers*. For me, Polari, without the new writers thing, would not be the same. It's *really* important to me. At every event there's someone new. The first person or two people on the bill. Tonight is a Friday in January, so we stacked it more heavily because it's a difficult night to fill. But most nights here are on a Tuesday or Wednesday – and then there will often be more people in the first half who are untried and untested'.

Do events like this change the way that he responds to the books presented as a reader? He ponders this question for a moment. 'I don't like **audiobooks**', he says, somewhat evasively. 'It's a silly thing but I just don't like them… **to me reading a book is a very *private* interaction**, and listening to something is a bit more like television or radio. And I do too much of that. Reading for me is quite precious. **But… it *does* make a difference to me if I read the book after hearing the author reading it. I *hear the voice*'**. He's warming to this idea now. 'Yes: Stella is a good example. Stella's work is quite challenging for the reader, and yet she's such an amazing performer that it makes the work more accessible. And that to me is a really important thing. That's part of what Polari delivers to the audience'. I'm intrigued by the apparent paradox here: the privacy that Burston attributes to his own practice of reading; and the performativity of this readings-focused event.

I leave wondering how much impact the author-performers have on each other at Polari, whether the 'headliners' inspire the novices, and what impact it has on the novices to be sharing a stage with them.

*

I get a new insight into this at the next month's Polari, when talking to **Christopher Fowler**, the '**headliner**' for the night. Like Duffy, the previous month, Fowler performs a stand-alone **short piece written with the intention of being read aloud** at Polari. While Fowler is a prolific novelist and short story writer in his early sixties, the piece he performs is not fiction but a travelogue-come-personal essay, composed in a conversational tone. It evokes a walk he takes around London while reflecting on subjects ranging from the city's widening wealth gap and its impact on the arts to its special character as one of the few European cities without a single old centre. In it, he mulls over how London is, to him, a spiritual state as much as a place, and how it is reflected in writing, from Dickens to gay London writers. He expounds upon how gay fashion is now mainstream, and gayness is accepted and even depicted on TV in programmes like *Cucumber*—but 'we're still outsiders'; to how gay writers can rebuild London using original, 'outsider thinking' in their work. On stage, he delivers the piece with commitment and panache, and it receives thunderous appreciation from the audience. More than one person sitting near me comments to their neighbour that it was '*brilliant*'.

Afterwards, talking to Fowler, I am intrigued to hear that he decided to **write** the piece, in this **form and style**, *directly* because of his experience of performing at a previous **Polari**. 'I was programmed to read from my novel directly after this new author whose background was in slam poetry', he tells me. 'He was *so amazing*'. Fowler shakes his head slowly and dreamily at the memory. 'He was talking about his father and his peers, his life… things I just don't know about. I live in Kings Cross, so I'm in the heart of London where things are happening, and I like that – but still, as you get older, you end up largely with your own peers, largely because the young don't want to hang out with you!… and so I felt like the older statesman, coming after him and just reading from my novel, so I thought, right: next time *I* should write something new!'

Fowler's prediction—that a new, autobiographical piece related to the city in which he and the audience were situated in the present moment of the performance would resonate more deeply when performed aloud than pre-published work—was manifestly realised. It chimes with observations I have previously made at Hay and other live literature events:

that reader-audiences value authenticity, which can partly be defined by an active sense that, through the performance, they are able to connect the texts being performed with the author-performer's 'real' self. This links, to some extent, with the contemporary expectation of access to public figures' 'real' life narratives via social media, and with the rapid growth of autofiction, and literary debates around identity.[45] By offering something spontaneous and 'new' that the reader-audience would not be able to access elsewhere, it also enhances the sense of liveness.

Fowler also reveals that he had already been giving serious thought to the way in which **focusing on reading aloud** has compelled him to **adjust his writing style** in such a way as to increase the '**immediacy**' of the text. 'I wrote a novel called *Paper Boy* a couple of years ago', he tells me, 'which came out of several pieces I'd written to read aloud – so it's different to look at it book form: it doesn't look like a normal book – and I got great reviews from readers saying it was very *immediate*. And I thought, *yes*, it *is* immediate! I think you cut out the tongue twisters, but also the long-windedness, when you focus on reading aloud. [He grins, wryly.] You know, I've come out of some readings thinking: what was I *doing*?! [an expression of anguish crosses his face] So I think it really does make writing better, to write to read aloud'. He's echoing the author Michael Hughes here, I reflect, when speaking of the painful experience of narrating his own audiobook, and how he later adjusted his writing (see Chapter 3).

'I used to run a reading group in Kentish Town called Big Words', Fowler tells me. 'We had a young, 24-year-old, blind American there once. He said: "ask me anything you ever wanted to ask a blind man but were too afraid to ask" – and it turns out what he talked about that night was exactly in his book, and it was amazing to read it, hearing his voice in your ear, and that's partly because he writes exactly how he speaks. Of course, if the person is *boring*, though, it's like being *stuck*. And you've still got to be original in your language. I was reading Margery Allingham today, who nobody reads any more, and the language is bonkers – someone said, "are you going senile?", and he replied: "I've yet to take my plate into public"... We need more of *that*: more unexpected turns of phrase!'

It is not just the immediacy of the writing that affects the success of a performed reading though, for Fowler; he points out that '**audiences can be tricky**' for authors to deal with. 'Once or twice here [at Polari] in the past there have been tricky crowds... once there was a bunch of drunks! Oh, and there's a club called The Garage by Highbury corner, and there used to be a literary night there – and drunks would always pour up after the live music act and find themselves walking through and say "what the fuck's goin' on in ere?" It could be like a baptism of fire if you were new, I can tell you'.

I ask for examples of **standout live literary events** that he's been part of, either good or bad. 'Well, Polari is really interesting', he muses. 'It's very varied. I was amazed once by... what's her name... an author who performed from her novel, *In Search of the Missing Eyelash*. She came on after an astoundingly *boring* Canadian lesbian who read a laundry list of her life [he rolls his eyes]... and then she was just *brilliant*! She really *performed*'. I know exactly who he is talking about, as it happens: **Karen McLeod**, whom I saw at a small underground venue in Hackney in her comedy guise as *Barbara Brownskirt*, in which she 'self'-defines as 'the worst living lesbian poet performing today'. When her name was announced, I remembered, there was an awkward silence, and it was made to seem as if she hadn't turned up—but then she scampered up from the back of the audience panting loudly, wearing a raincoat with the hood up, thick brown plastic glasses and a long brown tweed skirt, which turned out to be part of the act, proceeded to read her comic poetry aloud with buckets of charisma, triggering a lot of laughter.

'**Actors' readings *can* be more successful** than authors'', Fowler adds, thoughtfully. 'If you get an actor who *understands* what they're reading. **Audiobooks *can* be great**. The series I've got going on with elderly detectives is read on audio by a guy who *really* gets it – he understands the intonation, and brings it to life – in a way that I just can't. They can make a line *work* that doesn't on the page – an unfunny line funny. It's a talent. **An art**'.

Fowler thinks that there has been a change in **the live literature scene over** the **decades** since he has been involved in it as an author—but overall, in his view, while the volume of events has grown, the **quality** and value has diminished: an opinion that contrasts with those of many people I've spoken to about this, including John Crace and Simon Garfield at Hay. 'I think it's died on its feet', he says, grimly and firmly. 'I used to do a lot – small literary events all over the country. Now I do a *fraction* of what I used to do'. I propose that this is interesting, since in some respects live literature has burgeoned—certainly in terms of the number of literary festivals around. 'The *format* has definitely changed', he agrees. 'But the **big festivals now are like being shipped into a *chicken farm*.** I did Cheltenham last year and it was like that… Harrogate is good, the audiences are really *engaged*, and you get good questions that are on the nose… I've never been to Hay though, never been invited – I'm not on their radar… don't have a TV series. [He grins and raises one eyebrow.] Cheltenham is different. It's grander. And it can give people grand ideas. One author there behaved like a total *cow*. I was doing an event with her, and she came on stage, and we were sitting down about to discuss how to write murder mysteries – and then she stood up and said "for all my *fans*, I'm sorry I missed you last night – but I'm *here now*" – and I thought: Who made *you* queen?!'

'But this year… [he leans forward now, with both eyebrows raised] I was part of a **literary festival in Whitstable**, run by a young woman with a background in PR, trying her hand for the first time – and she *aced* it. Everything ran perfectly: the booking, the planning, the thought that went into it, theming of the days – *everything* **worked**. It's obviously going to be a fixture now. The first author she featured was someone local… the whole thing sold out… her dad picked authors up from the station… and you thought: *you go girl*! So the festivals *can* be good'.

He shakes his head slowly with a wry smile. 'But a lot of literary events are **what you most *fear* you will get from a reading**. I used to live in Barcelona, and I remember the time I came over to London to do an event at this private members' club, and it was just the *worst*. Everyone was being very worthy, and not engaging. It felt like the worst waste of time. In my head every creative work forms **a *triangle*: the creative writer, the piece they create, and the audience**'.

Polari, in his view, is a rare example of a live literature event that genuinely caters for its audiences. '**The live literature scene** needs pepping up, like *this* – it needs beefing up – it **needs to entertain *and***

**inform** *and* **excite.** And I think you have to do something else with the format now, **something** *different*... At Polari there have sometimes been performances of staged excerpts – there was once a pole dancer, and *that* was popular!'

*

**Polari's aesthetic character** continues to reflect its Polari language **origins** in the gay bars of Soho, and it is key to its current, distinctive identity and its experiential quality. Upbeat music, coloured lighting, cabaret-style table seating at the front and the presence of a bar render the atmosphere informally theatrical and entertainment-oriented, and this is corroborated and enhanced the host's extravagantly camp outfits, short, jocular introductions to each 'performer', and emphasis on their readings, with no conversation or Q&A.

Importantly, though, the **programming at Polari** is *not* just focused on entertainment; it **emphasises literary variety**, in terms of form, tone, style, voice and aesthetics as well as content. The majority of texts performed come from newly-published novels featuring LGBTQ+ characters, but they include both published fiction and work-in-progress, short stories, poetry, memoir and non-fiction. This ranges from observational comedy about awkward sexual situations to moving confessional memoirs about the discovery and exploration of gay identity.

A standout performance in this vein that I witnessed was by **Mansell Stimpson**, who recounted from his memoir about the experience of not discovering he was gay until he was forty, and the subsequent recasting of his past life that entailed, as well as his need to imagine a different future. There have also been histories of gay culture, including a very entertaining reading from a new non-fiction book about The Gateways, London's first lesbian venue.

Reflecting on the variety of literature performed within the LGBTQ+ frame now, I am reminded of Peter Burton's comment in *Parallel Lives* that, from a gay publishing perspective, when editing *The Gay Times*, he found it perpetually 'fascinating, trying to produce a specialist publication for a group of people who have only their sexuality in common'.[46] Burton decided upon the following curation objectives: that 'the magazine should have the broadest basis of appeal; that it should not become over-intellectual; that the contents should reflect the widest possible range of gay life; that the magazine should promote a completely positive view of gay life; and that our freelance contributors should feel a part of the magazine'. All these objectives, expanded beyond the remit of 'gay life' to 'LGBTQ+Q+ life', seem to be manifest in the programming approach at Polari.

The majority of author-performers at Polari identify as falling within the **LGBTQ+** category, and/or one of its sub-categories, and perform texts that touch on themes relevant to their sexual and/or gender identity—but this is **not a prescribed rule**. Straight writers sometimes perform, and the subject matter of the writing by author-performers identifying as LGBTQ+ in their personal lives might only engage with those themes indirectly. However, most of the texts performed do engage in some way with issues of gender identity and sexuality—and they do so in a marked variety of ways. The consequence at the end of a Polari event—and even more so after being part of a number of Polari events— is **an impression of diversity and multiplicity within the LGBTQ+ experience**, which challenges not only external stereotypes, but also reductionist perceptions that fuel divisions between sub-categories of LGBTQ+.

While almost all the author-performers I have seen at Polari have either expressly defined themselves as trans, gay or lesbian, or implied this through their readings, having fiction as the dominant literary form performed means that the authors' personal sexual and gender identities never necessarily need to be revealed or discussed, and also dissuades audiences from focusing-in on associated personal judgements.

Almost every Polari author-performer I have spoken to has told me, with apparently genuine enthusiasm, how much they have enjoyed and appreciated the salon, and many have commented on how unique it is. Few have expressed a sense that there is an expectation to argue for or represent a particular iteration of gender or sexual identity.

**One author-performer**, though, who **identifies as a lesbian**, told me that she was glad to have been invited to Polari but felt **she didn't fit in**; that **the aesthetic was too camp to represent her**, and it was still, at heart, an event designed for gay men. This rings true to me: the origins of Polari, in the gay bars of Soho, are still manifest in its tone and aesthetic, and the tone of the host reflects that, despite his evident and genuine intentions to be entirely inclusive.

Polari audiences tend to appear unusually enthused and conscious of their collectivity in comparison with those at other live literature events. **Many** reader-audience members are **regulars**, and even those who are not regulars have a strong sense that they have participated in a close-knit, familial community, and regard the salon as a social as well as a literary event. Even the person who admitted to regarding the regular audience as somewhat 'cliquey' did not feel excluded, and referred to the feeling of being part of a family. There is a sense of warmth, informality and openness at Polari, which extends to a strong foundation of support and affection for all the writers performing, whatever the quality of the writing *or* the performance; it could be described as part of the social 'contract' of this particular audience that they are there, in part, to help provide that support. As Sal put it: 'The love is always there'.

The **diversity** of Polari audiences, in terms of age, gender and class— less so race and ethnicity, since reader-audiences and author-performers I have observed have been predominantly, though never exclusively, white—is remarkably **rare** in London's contemporary LGBTQ+ scene, as many reader-audience members commented in conversations.; and it is also rare in the 'mainstream' literary scene. Burston admits to a personal **mission** for Polari that goes beyond the literary, to **champion diverse social spaces**, and this mission appeared to be succeeding based on observations and conversations I had with audience members. Most of those I spoke to were part of gay and lesbian couples and friend-ship groups, from a mix of ages, though the majority were in their forties. Several had come to Polari alone, several were connected to the performers, and a handful were aspiring writers themselves. There was a strong feeling among Polari audiences that the salon was an important and effective forum for exploring and sharing issues of LGBTQ+ iden-tity, particularly in relation to experiences and structures of prejudice and exclusion.

Most **reader-audience** members at Polari told me that they **came for the writing and LGBTQ+ community aspect equally**, but that, while the writing was centrally important to their decision to attend, they would not define themselves as particularly 'literary'—and some, like Clare, saw **literary festivals**, in **contradistinction** to Polari, as places where 'literariness' was **expected and performed** inextricably with other manifestations of middle-class social conformity.

As many of the regular reader-audience members acknowledged, there is a real **variation in the quality of literary texts** performed at Polari. On one occasion I witnessed the performance of a frankly terribly-written self-published text that the performer admitted Burston had, at first, been reluctant to accept, until giving way after repeated pleas. But, importantly, the potential for quality variation is not perceived, by most reader-audience members, or indeed author-performers, to diminish the value of the event. In fact, the opposite is true. Naturally, Polari does not market itself on the basis of variations of literary quality; and yet the expectation of some such variety is implied to some extent by its **showcasing of emerging writers**.

Burston seeks to make programming decisions, however, to ensure (usually) a base level of quality, and that texts of high literary quality are always featured during each event. The established event format and structure—whereby each event begins with someone new and 'untested', and ends with an established 'headliner' who is pretty much guaranteed to be good—creates a clear expectation of a wide spectrum of literary quality on the part of the reader-audience.

Moreover, the **tight time limits** imposed on individual performances not only make the event run smoothly but mean that, if there is a particularly bad performance in the early stages of the evening, it will not need to be endured for too long. Finally, and perhaps most importantly, Burston has cultivated an '**emotional community**' in which it is clearly understood by all participants—both reader-audiences and author-performers—that Polari functions as a platform for emerging new writers who wouldn't otherwise have an opportunity to perform their work, particularly given their niche categorisation as LGBTQ+ writers, and that they need and deserve support. This, to me, seems integral to its literary-cultural value.

The creative impact upon author-performers of witnessing their peers on stage at Polari is not only 'bottom-up', for the benefit of novice writers; the impact goes both ways, as Christopher Fowler's experience demonstrates.

The salon clearly affects reader-audience members' **reading practices** beyond the event itself. Many told me that they regularly bought books by author-performers whom they saw, heard and liked at Polari, and got them signed; others said they planned to read books by author-performers they liked at a later date; and most said that the performances led them to read more and different books than they would otherwise have done.

The performances also affected the quality and nature of reader-audiences' **silent reading** experiences. The vast majority felt that having heard the author-performers read aloud enhanced their subsequent experience of reading their book, often by allowing them to 'hear the voice' of the author in their head, and also by enabling them to retain a visual image of the author-performer, and their facial expressions and mannerisms. It also affected their interpretation of the texts themselves: their humour and their significance for their individual and collective identity. Reader-audiences often said they valued a sense of 'authenticity' during the performed readings, which seems to be key to both the event experience and the subsequent reading experience.

*

Fast forward a couple of years, and Burston invites me to read from **my own novel**, *The Invisible Crowd*, at Polari. I don't identify as LGBTQ+, and neither does the protagonist of my novel, Yonas, who is an asylum seeker from Eritrea; but it is a polyphonic novel, in which two of the central characters are gay, and sexual identity does become a critical issue in the story. Burston apologises that he can't **pay** authors to perform, but offers two comp tickets and reminds me that there is a bookseller present. I accept the invitation gladly, especially after having experienced Polari as a reader-audience member, and ponder over which parts of the novel to perform. I choose a scene with comedy in it, and a poignant and dramatic scene that I think will provide a good counterpoint, both of which touch on the way in which the characters' gay identities impact on their lives. I bring a couple of gay friends along to the event who haven't been before and are curious. The performance, happily, seems to go well—at least, the reader-audience is as supportive as it had seemed while I was a part of it at previous events. They laugh at the right places, seem attentive, and clap energetically. A few buy a copy at the bookstall. In retrospect, I wish I'd been a bit less restrained and more performative on stage in comparison with others.

A couple of days later, I receive an email via my website from a comedian and author who had seen me listed on the Polari bill, asking if I would like to come on her **radio show** to talk about my book. I said yes, and she promised to send me details. A few days later, she got back in touch to say that she'd worked out that I didn't identify as LBGT myself and so wouldn't be suitable. I felt a momentary flash of disappointment—but then guilt for having that response. The incident illustrated to me how much Polari is contributing, beyond the realm of literature, to a wider cultural environment in which both LGBTQ+ voices and themes are shared, noticed and valued. Through my research and experiences at Polari, I now have a deeper understanding of how important it still is to many people identifying as LGBTQ+ to have spaces, like that radio show, that are reserved solely for sharing other LGBTQ+-identifying voices and in order to ensure that they have a **platform** within a supportive sub-cultural community. The experience has also revealed to me how exceedingly rare it is to have spaces, like Polari, that are dedicated to supporting, celebrating and exploring LGBTQ+ identities through literary and artistic work, and yet do *not* limit the gender identity of participating author-performers and artists.

In the **Andrew Sean Greer**'s Pulitzer Prize-winning novel, *Less,* the protagonist is a mid-list gay author called Arthur Less, who is perplexed when he notices that his fiction seemed to be being ignored by the gay community, while also being of only marginal interest to the mainstream literary community. Finally, at a party, he is told by a well-meaning friend that he is widely seen as a 'bad gay', because he doesn't engage with gay characters and issues enough in his writing: a label that floors him, temporarily, because he had not previously considered his authorial identity as being aligned with his sexuality. The narrative alludes to the **risks** inherent of **identity-based literary communities** which can start out as ways to support writers who are otherwise marginalised because of their identity, and their perceived membership of a group, but can risk entrenching divisions over time. It illustrates how identity judgements, both 'inside' and beyond communities, can distort the ways in which audiences respond to fiction. To me, Polari treads this line deftly, by being overtly supportive of a marginalised identity-based group, and yet being inclusive in its scope, and foregrounding the fiction more than the authorial persona through its performed reading-based event format.

Researching Polari has convinced me that, when well-curated, with awareness of their audiences' needs and characteristics, **live literature events** can serve as a **uniquely valuable forum** for **airing, sharing and forging identities**, for **nurturing, supporting and strengthening communities**, and **for furthering equality and understanding in society**, for both reader-audiences and author-performers.

In relation to LGBTQ+ identities and community, the act of performing of fictional texts at an embodied live event like Polari clearly has the ability to **communicate in-depth experiences, emotions and perspectives in varied, complex, multifaceted ways**—crucially without that author-performer necessarily having to articulate or represent a personal position on the issues or experiences raised in the text, or to make embarrassing personal, autobiographical admissions. The **absence of Q&A** or staged conversation at Polari means that **no participant is pressured or required to enter into tense, politicised debates** about identity as a consequence of the publication of their writing, when that writing was not necessarily intended to fuel or prompt such debates. The salon works as a nuanced, positive forum for activism: a distinctly literary form of activism.

The act of sharing such texts, within an embodied reader-audience community that is largely LGBTQ+, creates a particularly **strong and palpable sense of shared emotion and bonds**—particularly in relation to loss and pain, as Sal so clearly articulated—but also through laughter, and other physical responses that communicate emotional and aesthetic reactions, including attention-focused silences and noisy moments of applause. The literature acts as a **super-'glue'** holding together the 'emotional community' of this 'metropolitan tribe', as Maffesoli would conceive of it:[47] a tribe, or 'affinity grouping', that 'revalues the ancient anthropological structure of the 'extended family'.[48] The 'proxemics' of being part of a regular, embodied, 'tribal' event means that participants acquire an 'embodied knowledge rooted in a corpus of customs',[49] forge 'collective memories', and are able to 'provide warm social spaces in the heart of the cold, inhuman metropolis'.[50] As **John Dewey** wrote, back in 1916: 'There is more than a verbal tie between the words common, community, and communication'[51]—and the verbal performance of fiction, at Polari, seems to tighten the knot.

The value of Polari is not, however, solely about using literature in such a way as to forge socio-cultural connections and emotional solidarity through an aesthetically-, textually- and spatially-linked community. Vitally, on the other side of the coin, Polari appears to be making a valuable **contribution to** the **creation, composition, production and publication** of more diverse, interesting and socially-representative new writing that engages with LGBTQ+ experiences, and that is welcoming to new voices and audiences.

The relatively small-scale, community-based, and performed-reading-focused characteristics of Polari—and other, comparable contemporary literary salons—are key to understanding their role and phenomenological impact for participants, and within literary culture. Their impact, and their cultural value, is distinct from that of larger, more commercially-oriented libel literature events such as festivals—neither less, nor more, but different.

The 'literary salon' has **metamorphosed** in its revival from its Enlightenment-era form into something new, relevant and meaningful—and the success of the salon revival is testament to the potential power of embodied intimacy and community in a live literature event. In comparison with the literary festival model, the Polari model of foregrounding performed readings, and foregoing Q&A, has a **particular value** for its primarily-LGBTQ+ participants as a way to forge a deeper sense of 'emotional community'. It illustrates the experiential variety that is possible within the live literature scene.

# 5

# Experiential Literary Ethnography: A Creative Approach to Revealing Cultural Value

This is the chapter where I dive into the pool of theory and craft on which this book floats. I discuss how I composed the ethnographies, why creative writing techniques were integral to the process, and what this allowed me to reveal about live literature and its cultural value.

Experiential literary ethnography emerged out of the work of a long line of other anthropologists and writers over the years—particularly the powerhouse that was Zora Neale Hurston: a black woman working in a privileged white male enclave in 1930s New York. I reflect on how I developed this approach, and explain why it offers a particularly fruitful approach to researching and writing about live literature today—and how it makes this book materially different to other publications that have looked at comparable subjects relating to literary culture and live performance.

Experiential literary ethnography has significant potential for practical application in various cultural contexts. In this chapter I discuss how others can use it, and its limitations and benefits, and I make a case for its use by scholars, producers, funders and anyone seeking to prove or understand the cultural value of a particular live arts-based experience in these impact-driven, economically-unstable times.

© The Author(s), under exclusive license to Springer Nature
Switzerland AG 2021
E. Wiles, *Live Literature*, Palgrave Studies in Literary Anthropology,
https://doi.org/10.1007/978-3-030-50385-7_5

# Experiential Literary Ethnography: A Summary

Experiential literary ethnography is an approach to writing about experience that uses creative writing techniques to *evoke and examine* that experience, in order to reveal its cultural value.

One element of crafting the experiential literary ethnographies in this book entailed carefully populating each one with 'thick descriptions'[1]—a common ethnographic term for granular, multisensory details of embodied experience which are based on the writer's own observations, such as sounds, smells, settings, gestures, utterances and emotions. In crafting my live literature ethnographies, it was important to include specific details about elements such as the performance space, for instance, whether that was a tent in a field, or a room in a concrete urban arts centre, since those elements are a key part of the experience, and distinguish it from any other.

Thick descriptions are woven together with extracts from conversations with a variety of participants. In the ethnographies in this book, participants included reader-audiences and author-performers. I aimed to have conversations that were informal and unstructured, allowing the participants to express their own ideas and perspectives over time, if they wished. Consequently, my ethnographies include numerous extended passages of conversation. These passages illustrate the texture, rhythm, and distinctive, nuanced perspectives of the participants. They also feature multiple points of view—in this case from a range of author-performers and reader-audiences—and I did my best to ensure that each ethnography contained a representative diversity of points of view. Some of the most surprising and revealing responses came through during long, unstructured conversations, and many of them illuminate, and illustrate, the complex dynamics of situated experience at live literature events.

I ensured that my ethnographies of live literature events included extracts of literary texts performed, alongside description that indicated how these performances were delivered—for instance, accompanying body language, pauses and audience responses. This seemed to me to be a vital way to show how the event was connected to the text, and how participants' interpretations and responses to that text were shaped by the experience.

In between these elements of description, conversation and quotation, I threaded through wide-lens reflections about the context and the wider culture—in this case, patterns and dynamics in literary culture, such as genre trends, audiobook listening or authors' incomes, and other cultural shifts and debates.

I also populated the ethnographies with selected quotes from media and social media commentaries; references to trends, structures and practices in the publishing industry and literary culture; and reflections on linked social, cultural and theoretical contexts and concepts.

Experiential literary ethnography might seem to some readers, who are looking for clear, rational answers, to make for loose, even rambling narratives—narratives that might seem to be riven with all kinds of details and minutiae that don't answer the fundamental questions they have in a straightforward way, or that don't contain measurable data that legitimately justifies the conclusions drawn. My main response to this critique is that experiential literary ethnographies seek to evoke *experience*, including embodied, aesthetic experience—and that experience does not take the form of concise, rationalised points of argument or quantifiable, measurable data. To present event experience as if it did so, in a piece of evaluative writing, would be reductive and distorting—even untruthful. As Maggie Nelson put it in *The Argonauts*: 'How to explain, in a culture frantic for resolution, that sometimes the shit stays messy?'[2]

## Crafting Evocation: A Lesson from Dewey

I call experiential literary ethnography an 'approach' to writing, rather than a 'method', because the word 'method' implies a scientific, standardised process; whereas the word 'approach' alludes to the creative ways in which experiential literary ethnography is crafted.

The craft of creative writing is integral to the objective: it enables the dynamic complexity of experience to be evoked and communicated. When the goal of a piece of research or writing is to communicate the

value of an arts-based event, it becomes *particularly* important to cultivate a form of writing that can evoke experience of participating in that
event, including its aesthetic qualities.

As John Dewey put it, way back in 1934, while writing about art and
experience:

> To perceive, a beholder must *create* his own experience. And his creation
> must include relations comparable to those which the original producer
> underwent… Without an act of recreation the object is not perceived as
> a work of art.[3]

Clearly, no form of worded narrative about an arts-based experience can
replicate the experience itself. But Dewey's idea of re*creation* suggests that
an actively *creative* approach is needed to evoke an experience, retro-
spectively, in order to value it in a meaningful way. Literary writing is
well-equipped for this. As Deleuze put it, literary writing is 'inseparable
from becoming'.[4]

## Ethnographic Ancestry: Wrangles Over Writing Culture

'Experiential literary ethnography' is a new term that I've come up with,[5]
but it emerges out of the evolution of humanistic anthropology over
decades towards more literary and evocative forms of writing.

That journey has not been a smooth one. The whole notion of using
a literary style of writing in anthropology been hotly contested. In the
1980s, what is now known as the 'Writing Culture' debate was triggered by a book of that title, edited by anthropologists George Clifford
and James Marcus: it made a case for use of poetic literary techniques
in ethnography, and it stirred up fury among many other anthropologists who disagreed vehemently that such techniques were legitimate.[6]
In 1988, Clifford Geertz weighed in with a book arguing for anthropologists to see themselves as authors, and offering literary-critical readings
of four classic anthropology texts by the disciplines founders.[7] Decades
of argument followed between the more science-oriented contingent of

anthropologists and the more writing-oriented contingent. This tension still rumbles on.

In a nutshell: the science-oriented contingent of anthropologists broadly feel that paying attention to literary technique in ethnography is frivolous, a distraction from the core, factual subject matter, and ultimately an egotistical exercise. They think that ethnographers should be focused on documenting fact and using objective language do to it, not on producing fancy prose.

The writing-oriented contingent, on the other hand, believe that pure objectivity is never really possible, and that, as feminist and decolonial scholarship has revealed, purporting to be entirely objective can be a form of deception. They think that using nuanced language in their ethnographies, and attending to literary craft, enables them to engage with their subjects more honestly, deeply, affectively and effectively.[8] Some of them recognise that, in order to communicate the meaning of their research into distinct lifeworlds,[9] it can help to compose their narratives in a way that evokes the *experience* of those lifeworlds—including the ways in which people actually speak.[10]

A pioneer of literary ethnographic writing was already crafting both fiction *and* literary anthropology fifty years before this debate flared up. She is Zora Neale Hurston: a woman who was well-used to being 'othered' as the only non-white and non-male person in a room, and well-used to privileged white men purporting to be producing the only legitimate and 'objective' form of anthropology. As early as the 1930s, Hurston cultivated a vivid, performative approach to her ethnographic writing—which was about, among other things, the cultural significance of patterns of speech and language, and the interlinked experience of slavery and blackness in America.[11] Hurston's work was a visionary forerunner for a host of creative anthropological writing that emerged decades later.[12]

Since Hurston,[13] several prominent contemporary anthropologists have pursued a literary writing practice that crosses conventional divides into the realm of fiction, literary memoir and poetry, including Michael D. Jackson,[14] Ruth Behar, Ruth Finnegan, Kirin Narayan and Paul Stoller.[15] All of their work has inspired elements of this book.

In some corners of ethnography, experiential and literary modes of writing ethnography are now flowering.[16] Intriguingly, though, they are quite rarely applied to research in contemporary Western arts contexts. Other, newer methods of research and communication—notably visual, arts-based forms, like video and photography—are more popular.[17] These visual forms have distinct strengths: they can depict cultural practices in immediately arresting ways, and they are very well-suited to making an impact through social media. But researchers who are focused on these forms sometimes assume that prose is rather old-fashioned in comparison—or that it has done the best it could, and now is the time for the new. I wholeheartedly celebrate creative and multimodal diversity in ethnography, including video and other multimodal forms. But in this book I want to make a case for the creative and critical practice of word*ing* ethnography as a still-vital form of research and communication.

The potential for ethnographic writing to communicate the value of contemporary 'Western' arts-based events in a meaningful way was foreseen a decade ago by the literary and cultural theorist Steven Connor. He wrote an article arguing for a new 'cultural phenomenology', which he envisaged as an evolution of cultural studies, involving evocative, embodied and reflexive writing about experience.[18] Inspired by Geertz's anthropological work,[19] he identified ethnography as the single form of writing that has come closest to this vision.[20] I see experiential literary ethnography as one way to make it materialise.[21]

## Literary-Cultural Research: A Sketch of Its Evolution

To explain how experiential literary ethnography offers a new way of thinking about live literature, and about literary culture in general, I will sketch out the ways in which literary-cultural research has evolved over the last century, primarily through the discipline of literary studies.

Firstly, as I mentioned in Chapter 2, literary studies has historically been focused on text and has distanced itself both from orality and from the lives of authors. This text-focused orientation arguably began in the

1920s, with the 'practical criticism' movement founded by I. A. Richards at Cambridge. Richards began setting his students literary texts to read without any information about who wrote them or when they were written, and then wrote an influential book about his findings.[22] Roland Barthes' notorious 'Death of the Author' treatise followed in the 1960s,[23] in which he argued that readers should never rely upon aspects of an author's identity for interpreting their work. Putting the emphasis on the individual reader, Barthes proposed that it is their task to determine the multiple possible meanings of any given text—the tacit assumption being that this process will be achieved through silent reading.[24]

Barthes' theory took hold, but was modified by Stanley Fish in 1980 when he introduced the idea of 'interpretive communities' of readers.[25] As Fish saw it: while any individual reader does interpret a text subjectively, they do so as part of an interpretive community, and so the meaning they ultimately take from the text is shaped by cultural assumptions made by that community.[26]

In the 1990s, Gerard Genette encouraged literary studies scholars to take another step back from their focus on literary texts: in practice, he argued, 'paratexts' inevitably affect the way in which a literary text is read,[27] and so they should not be artificially excluded from consideration. By paratexts, Genette meant features of physical books, like the blurbs and cover design,[28] and also other elements that are not part of the physical book, like publishers' press releases.[29] Based on this definition, live literature events would count as a paratext—but Genette, in the same ways as many other literary scholars, did not consider events as being relevant.

Juliet Gardiner pushed still further in this direction. In an article published in 2000 titled 'Recuperating the Author' (posing a direct challenge to Barthes), she argued that, while Genette might be right to take account of paratexts, his view of paratexts is problematic. Among other things, he elides the roles and intentions and motivations of the author and the publisher in deciding on the packaging of a book, when in reality they might have quite different points of view.[30] Ultimately, Gardiner argued, Genette presented paratexts as 'vulgarizing commercial add-ons'[31]; -whereas, in reality, the contemporary idea of the author has become increasingly foregrounded in literary culture for multiple reasons, and scholars should acknowledge that. Factors like the growth of consumer choice, and the rise of identity politics, have 'undoubtedly' recuperated the role of authorial biography in readers' minds,[32] and can legitimately affect the interpretation of any given text.[33]

The rise of live literature in the twenty-first century can clearly be seen as another leap towards 'author foregrounding' in literary culture. Yet it has continued to be neglected when considering the reception of literary texts.

# Existing Live Literature Research

The majority of the niche collection of studies of live literature events so far have come from the publishing studies field, with a sociological focus. Within those, by far the dominant focus has been on literary festivals.

As I mentioned in Chapter 2, the early studies of literary festivals were mostly dismissive of their cultural value. In 2004, Caroline Lurie wrote an article painting them as examples of mass cultural production that served to dumb-down literary culture by replacing the currency of texts with the shallow façade of literary celebrity.[34] A year later, Michael Meehan published an article on the literary festival in which he opined that it was a positive force in its 'early days', when it functioned as a 'kind of de-industrialisation ritual',[35] but it had already become too commodified, along with its popularity. He went so far as to diagnose it as being infected with a 'deep cultural putrescence'.[36]

Scholars over the last decade have gradually began to consider contemporary festivals with more focus and nuance. Liana Giorgi suggested in 2011 that they were contemporary manifestations of the Habermasian public sphere, and functioned as a rare space where ideas can be freely and democratically discussed between people from diverse social groups.[37] A year later, Katya Johanson and Robin Freeman considered audience experiences at festivals in an article, based on a day of qualitative interviews conducted at the tiny Eye of the Storm Writers' Festival in Australia (where there were only about 100 audience members, making it an unusually small and remote event in literary festival terms).[38] They noted a common desire among audience members for an authenticity of experience, gained by 'the medieval experience of being read aloud to'—these, it would seem, being the scholars' words, rather than their interviewees'.[39] Audience members, they said, also appreciated 'time to reflect' while at the festival, and felt a sense of 'artistic community' there.[40]

Breaking out from the festival focus, in 2013, Danielle Fuller and DeNel Rehberg Sedo co-authored a new book exploring 'mass reading events'[41]—that is, events broadcast through media channels, including 'televised book clubs and community-wide reading initiatives', engaged in by groups of 'leisure readers'. This involved several case studies including the Oprah Winfrey's Book Club and Canadian Broadcast Corporation's 'Canada Reads' project. They critiqued dismissive attitudes expressed among literary scholars about such 'popularizing' projects for 'mass' audiences as 'dumbing-down' and 'vulgarizing'[42] interpretations of fiction—and argued that such events in fact have important economic and ideological implications: they create social connections and forge intimacy, and as such they 'hold out the promise of belonging' and 'affective community' within a globalised economy.[43]

With a similarly open mind towards popular elements of literary culture, Beth Driscoll's book, *The New Literary Middlebrow: Tastemakers and Reading in the Twenty-First Century*, published the following year in 2014, sought to reclaim and interrogate the value of literary festivals, among other popular literary practices that she characterises as being 'middlebrow'. One chapter focuses on the 'middlebrow pleasures of literary festivals' through a case study of the Melbourne Writers Festival, based on extensive survey data. Driscoll concludes that literary festivals have 'value and meaning' for audiences and 'provide intellectual stimulation, a sense of intimate community, and opportunities for social and ethical reflection. They add a layer of personal meaning to books and offer the entertainment pleasures of large-scale performances'.[44]

Millicent Weber's book on literary festivals (2018) is the first devoted to the subject.[45] She critiques Driscoll's characterisation of literary festival attendance as a 'middlebrow' activity, since this discounts the individuality and variety of audiences' engagement[46]—albeit Driscoll describes her own tastes as encompassing the middlebrow.[47] However, building on all other aspects of Driscoll's approach to festivals, she too challenges earlier studies that painted derisive pictures of them as sites of mass cultural production that served to dumb-down literary culture.[48] She argues that this is a symptom of a wider 'false opposition between commercial and cultural spaces'.[49] One of her central points is that literary festivals, like literary prizes,[50] operate as microcosms of the 'literary field', as characterised by Pierre Bourdieu[51]: they are spaces where authors, readers and other stakeholders in the literary industry 'compete for legitimacy through the acquisition of cultural, social and economic capital'.[52] Like Driscoll, Weber used surveys to research audiences. Her surveys addressed motivations for attending festivals,[53] and from the results she suggests that audiences generally value literary festivals as 'accessible and social forms of cultural consumption',[54] with 'aesthetic, cognitive, affective and social dimensions'.[55] These categories have clearly been worded and presented by the author, rather than the participants themselves.

Although Weber, like Driscoll, foregrounds survey data as her key form of evidence, she also used structured qualitative interviews with audiences, extracts of which make it into her text—and she makes clear that she did this in order to avoid the 'homogenising tendencies'[56] of other sociological studies. Including such qualitative data, she argues, is 'fundamental to understanding the way in which literary festivals are experienced' and their 'value'.[57] The individual accounts form a fairly small fraction of text in this book, but when they appear they enliven the prose.

Weber also considered the relationship between festivals and social media, observing the complex relationship that has evolved between digital culture and communities, and live and print-based literary spaces.[58] She notes that the 'live' and 'unique' quality of the events often functioned as a 'pull' for audiences, in comparison with digital alternatives,[59] and comments that it is 'worth noting the pertinence of this impact of "liveness" to further discussions of literary festival experience'.[60] My research picks up where hers leaves off in this respect.

There has been a rather 'singular focus' on literary festivals among people researching and writing about live literature: a fact that has recently been pointed out by David Finkelstein and Claire Squires in a short study of 'book events' and 'book environments' in the second half of the twentieth century.[61] Festivals, they argue, really need to be considered within a 'broader view' of events and environments encompassing a 'range of activities and spaces',[62] including 'literary award ceremonies, mediatised book spaces and sites of literary tourism'.[63] They point out how productive studies of such events can be for understanding the relationship between the publishing industry and the literature contained in books, notably by shining a 'particular spotlight on the author as the promoter of his or her books' and the 'ways in which readers have encountered both books and authors'.[64]

Driscoll and Squires have since collaborated to take the scholarship of literary and book culture in new, playful directions. In 2018, they co-authored 'Serious Fun: Gaming the Book Festival'[65]: an article making a case for a new conceptual framework of 'game-inspired thinking' to contribute to the study of book festivals, by using board games as an arts-informed method,[66] involving 'metaphors that concentrate and exaggerate aspects of book festivals in order to produce new knowledge about their operations'.[67]

This represents a creative turn toward considerations of affect, experience in literary and publishing scholarship. It highlights the fact that, until now, studies of contemporary literary culture, including literary events, have focused quite narrowly on power structures, often relating to economics, and generalised patterns of behaviour. They have also tended to be communicated through traditional forms of scholarly writing. And they have been ignored by many scholars working within the castle walls of literary studies.

Overall, most of the existing literary festival research that attends to participant experience, ethnographic or otherwise, is sociological in nature and focuses exclusively on audiences rather than author-performers. Within that, audience research tends to focus on audiences' social and cultural roles and their instrumental motivations for attending events. It rarely evokes audiences' lived experience, or explores how that lived experience connects with author-performers' experiences—or how the two diverge.

My ethnographies aim to bridge that gap. They interrogate the *dynamic* way in which, as Le Guin brilliantly put it, words are events that 'do things, change things. They transform both the speaker and the hearer; they feed energy back and forth and amplify it. They feed understanding or emotion back and forth and amplify it'.[68]

## Ethnography and Contemporary Literary Culture

Has anthropology shaped thinking on 'Western' literary culture? I would say it has—but less than might be expected so far; and it has, as yet, barely touched on live literature.

An early adopter of this branch of 'literary anthropology', the exploration of literary-cultural practices, was the scholar Q. D. Leavis—though she did not see herself as an anthropologist.[69] Her 1932 book, *Fiction and the Reading Public*, was the first of its kind to explore how the literary industry and public taste in the UK shaped popular novels and vice versa. She conducted her research by composing surveys and posting them out to authors, and her conclusion, in a nutshell, was that literary culture was disintegrating as 'lowbrow pulp' took over.[70]

It was not until the mid-1980s that a notable ethnographic book about literary culture was published that took readers' perspectives more seriously. Janice Radway's book, *Reading the Romance: Women, Patriarchy, and Popular Literature*, is an innovative ethnographic exploration of the culture around reading romance fiction in America.[71] It interwove individual readers' accounts of their reading from the anonymised town of 'Smithton', with Radway's own criticism, and offered multiple viewpoints in order to reveal the 'complex social interaction between people and texts known as reading'. This way, Radway was able to make a case for the richness and 'ideological density' of romance as a genre, and its relationship to the 'culture that ha[d] given rise to it'[72]—contrary to dismissive establishment perceptions of the genre and its readers.

In the late 1990s, Radway went on to publish a more autobiographically-oriented study of a subscription book club, of which she was once a member: *A Feeling for Books: The Book-of-the-Month Club, Literary Taste and Middle-Class Desire*. This was an even more radical experiment in the way it incorporated autoethnography into a structural sociological inquiry to better explore questions of emotion, aesthetics, taste and sociality.

Despite the manifest influence of her books, Radway has lately expressed surprise that ethnography has not been more widely taken up within literary studies in the subsequent decades.[73]

A rare anthropological exploration of a corner of 'Western' literary culture is Adam Reed's *Literature and Agency in English Fiction Reading: A Study of the Henry Williamson Society* (2011). This book investigates the impact of a readers' society on members' engagement with their favourite author's work. Reed explores how readers themselves 'create meaning'[74] from their participation in the society, rather than 'trying to locate the source of agency' himself in a top-down fashion. As he admits, his study becomes an ethnography of a 'certain stratum of British society' as much as a readership—but it does reveal the 'vivid' ways in which 'Henry', the author, captured members' imaginations and impacted on their lives beyond their reading and society activities.[75] Reed, like Radway, has flagged the absence of comparable anthropological work on literary culture, stating that 'a body of important ethnographic work [remains] undone'.[76]

My own first book, *Saffron Shadows and Salvaged Scripts: Literary Life in Myanmar Under Censorship and in Transition* (2015),[77] which I mentioned in Chapter 2, is another contribution to this very small branch of literary anthropology—but it is now growing.

Helena Wulff is one of its main pioneers. In her book, *Rhythms of Writing: An Anthropology of Irish Literature* (2017), she asks: 'How come the Irish are such great writers?', and goes on to explore the social world of contemporary Irish writers, tracing a path from training and creativity to seeking recognition, while operating as a public intellectual, writing journalism alongside fiction, 'selling stories' in the publishing market, all of which is 'built on the rhythms of writing', including 'long hours at the desk, alternating with periods of promotion'.[78] Wulff's research is based on a combination of observation, in-depth interviews, journalism and analysis of literary texts.[79]

Of all the literary-anthropological studies of contemporary literary culture, Wulff has also authored the only one I have come across that explores live literature events as a performative and social experience for participants: an article titled 'Literary Readings as Performance: On the Career of Contemporary Writers in the New Ireland' (2008). Wulff reflects on the 'multisensorial embodied experience' of live performances of fiction at events, distinguishing that from the experiences of recorded performances that are 'mediated' through a camera. She highlights some apparent paradoxes—for instance, she points to the 'unpredictability' and 'risk' of live performance; yet notes that all the writers in her study denied preparing for readings in any way. She suggests that Irish writers seem inherently disposed towards public performance, yet notes that 'some writers' in her study were 'shy and introverted'. She alludes to the multi-faceted role of the performing author who has to act as both the 'narrator in the text' and 'their public persona'.[80]

This book echoes and expands upon all those themes and explores how they play out in practice through situated ethnographies, in order to interrogate their cultural value.

# Now, Talking of…: Communication Studies, Orality, the Ethnography of Speaking

Although, as I have shown, there has been very little research to date on contemporary live literature events, there is a trove of anthropological scholarship on performance traditions in oral literary cultures, which have influenced my thinking in this book, and have contributed to the shape and content of my ethnographies.

As early as 1923, Malinowski emphasised the importance of communication for understanding social dynamics in a culture, including phatic communication—that is, speech that is apparently trivial or purposeless in any given situation.[81] Communication burgeoned as a sub-field of anthropology in the 1970s, largely in the wake of Ruth Finnegan's work on Limba storytelling in Sierra Leone,[82] in which she pointed out the fundamental role of orality in literature outside the bounds of Western culture. Soon after, Raymond Williams offered a class-based critique of 'scriptocentrism' in Western literary and cultural scholarship[83]—though, as I have already implied, this did not go on to have a very significant effect on literary studies at the time; literary scholars remained focused on text.

Finnegan's emphasis on the importance of paralanguage in spoken performances—that is, factors like the rate of speech, length, pause duration, pitch contour, tone of voice, volume and stress—led other linguistic anthropologists[84] to think up ways to incorporate those features in their ethnographies. In Richard Bauman's book, *Verbal Art as Performance* (1975), he argued that anthropology had neglected the 'social use of speaking' and that more 'ethnographies of speaking'[85] should explore 'speech communities', and the 'socioexpressive dimension of speaking'.[86] He discussed the Japanese *rakugo* tradition, in which professional storytellers have to undergo years of special training before they are culturally permitted to perform,[87] as an extreme example of how 'performance as a mode of spoken verbal communication' 'rests on the knowledge and ability to speak in socially appropriate ways' relative to the cultural context'.[88] He linked this to the new 'performative turn' in scholarship, which emphasised the power of the 'emergent quality of performance'[89] to bind participants through a 'special enhancement of experience, bringing with it a heightened intensity of communicative interaction'.[90]

Finnegan took this idea further in her book *Oral Poetry: Its Nature, Significance, and Social Context* (1977), in which she looked at poetic live literature as performance through a postcolonial lens. In a similar vein to Raymond Williams, but with a wider multicultural perspective, Finnegan critiqued the Western literary establishment's devaluation of orality, and its tendency to sneer at oral literary cultures as 'primitive'[91] in literary terms. 'If a piece is orally performed', Finnegan proposed, 'it *must* be regarded as in that sense an "oral poem"', even if it is by a Western poet, since the concept of 'oral-ness' must be relative, and 'oral poetry' is constantly overlapping into 'written poetry'.[92] The 'circumstances of the performance' are 'integral to the identity of the poem as actually realised', she argued; 'if a poem is differently performed, or performed at a different time or to a different audience or by a different singer, it is a different poem'.[93] Material factors in any Western literary performance, just as in any Sierra Leonean performance, can include the 'context and setting', the performers' 'mode of delivery', 'the audience's actions' and the atmosphere of 'play' rather than 'reality' in the course of an event that is set apart from 'real life'.[94] Ngũgĩ Wa Thiong'o went on to develop a linked critique of Western literary scholars' tendency to devalue orality, and the inherent ethnocentrism of this stance.[95]

Walter J. Ong looked at orality and literature from a slightly different perspective, casting his gaze way back to the advent of writing and literacy.[96] This moment, he argued, fundamentally changed literature and culture, partly by causing a transition from a world of sound to a world of sight. In 'primarily oral cultures' that do not use writing, he explained, 'the phenomenology of sound enters deeply into human beings' feel for existence, 'as processed by the spoken word', and this helps to 'form close-knit groups',[97] through a form of communication that is not only verbal, but is embodied, being formed around the process of audience feedback in real, 'evanescent' time.[98] Not having writing, such cultures *need* to use spoken language in such a way as to preserve information, so rely on stylised techniques such as proverbs, which writing renders unnecessary—and they also tend to think about history cyclically. Writing, on the other hand, causes cultural thinking to change from being cyclical to being linear and evolutionary, resulting in more climactic linear plots, rather than episodic narratives,[99] and it also causes literature to shift towards interiority and individuality. Ong saw the role of twentieth-century media and communications as a different kind of orality: a 'secondary orality' that coexists with writing and relies upon it.

Ong's perspective was radical in the 1980s. But his theory—like so many other literary theories—fails to account properly for the continued role of embodied orality in multiple core elements of literary practice and culture, from writing to reading,[100] over the ages.

## The Performative Turn: Ritual, Liminality, Communitas, Evocative Writing

In Finnegan's wake (the anthropologist, that is; not Joyce's novel), the 1980s saw anthropologists' concern with communication and orality evolve into a more widespread preoccupation with performance. Vital to this development was the work of Victor Turner. Turner drew from his early research on rituals in Zambia to develop broader concepts about the effects of ritualised performances. One key concept was 'liminality': a state of being 'betwixt and between'[101] while participating in a ritual event, that is characterised by a mood of 'maybe, might-be, as-if, hypothesis, fantasy, conjecture, desire'.[102] Another key concept he put forward was 'communitas': the feeling of camaraderie associated among a group experiencing the same liminal experience or rite.[103]

Turner applied these ideas to Western performance contexts, and into practice.[104] He collaborated with theatre director and scholar, Richard Schechner,[105] who in turn forged the new (inter)discipline of performance studies.[106] Turner's ideas have continued to be applied by anthropologists in contemporary Western cultural performance contexts as diverse as sports events and the Burning Man Festival.[107]

As performance studies spread its wings, scholars like Della Pollock developed evocative, performative modes of writing about performance as a way of engaging more meaningfully with its impact and value.[108] Performance studies approaches have recently been seeping into literary studies in relation to poetry,[109] spurring new interpretations of traditional canons,[110] as well as the new studies of contemporary practices.

But there is, as yet, little comparable, performance-focused scholarship that deals with the embodied performance of fiction. Again: these ethnographies are a way of filling that gap.

# Beyond 'Tasteless Theories': The Bodily and Sensory Turns

The performative turn in scholarship was followed by 'sensory' and 'bodily' turns in scholarship in the 1990s. These emerged from a growing awareness, linked with developments in neuroscience, that conventional assumptions about the mind-body dualism were fundamentally flawed. Adrienne Rich emphasised the role of the body in understanding the world through feminist scholarship,[111] and many scholars gravitated back to the work of Merleau-Ponty, who emphasised the central role of the body and senses as sites for knowing and understanding the world as early as 1945.[112] Anthropologist Thomas Csordas applied these ideas to audience 'attention', in the context of performances: he argued that attention involves a 'more bodily and multisensory engagement than we usually allow for'.[113]

Two books by Paul Stoller explored the translation of these ideas into ethnographic writing. To me, Stoller's work offered an energising vision of how an ethnography of a live arts-based event might be composed so as to incorporate these elements of embodied experience. In *The Taste of Ethnographic Things: The Senses in Ethnography* (1989) Stoller argued that, for most anthropologists, 'tasteless theories' had become more important than the 'savoury sauces' of ethnographic life; that ethnographies have lost the smells, sounds and tastes of the places they study. He describes 'coming to his senses' about this issue through his long-term research into the lives of the Songhay of Niger, while actively observing and participating in their cultural productions.

In *Sensuous Scholarship* (1997), which opened with an evocative conversation about Sufi storytelling and French toast, Stoller developed his thinking further about how to write scholarly texts.[114] He critiqued the ways in which the 'fixed standards of science' are too often applied to lived experience,[115] and argued for 'a fully sensuous scholarship in which experience and reality, imagination and reason, difference and commonality are fused and celebrated in both rigorous and imaginative practices as well as in expository and evocative expression'.[116] While I prefer the term 'sensory' to 'sensuous',[117] Stoller's argument and literary style manifested many elements of what I felt the need to capture in writing ethnographically about live literature experiences. It also resonated with what I had practised and reflected upon as a creative writer about the narrative power of involving all the senses in evocative modes of writing.

Stoller's work was followed by a flowering of scholarship attending to the senses in other disciplines, some of which was ethnographic.[118] Inspired by both Stoller and Turner, sociologists Phillip Vannini, Denis Waskul and Simon Gottschalk co-authored a book called *The Senses in Self, Society and Culture: A Sociology of the Senses* (2012),[119] in which they emphasised the importance of somatic experience for understanding culture, and argued that sociology 'badly needs to catch up with anthropology' in this respect.[120] Their illustrative ethnographic narratives include an experience of a wine festival, described as a Turner-esque 'ritual', in which participants' performed descriptions of taste and their evaluations of the wines are portrayed as a form of transformative artistic meaning-making. Like Stoller, they proposed that scholars not only need to engage with the 'deep significance of sensations', but they 'need to present sensations in evocative, passionate, carnal and imaginative ways'. They not only pointed out that this may require experimenting with writing,[121] but they also offered useful writing guidelines for social scientists to help them break out of their traditional academic strictures. These include abandoning traditional forms and structures; beginning with a descriptive scene to draw in the reader; abandoning disembodied voices, mingling description and analysis; being reflexive in relation to encounters and experiences, and to how one's own biography shapes one's experience; using an embodied style of writing; and conveying a sense of situatedness and emergence when describing experiences.[122] They emphasised that writing in this way to evoke 'lifeworlds' is an acquired *'skill'* and a *'creative act'*.[123]

This emphasis on evocation through writing was developed by scholars working in autoethnography, notably Carolyn Ellis and Art Bochner. Ellis and Bochner have made a case for 'evocative autoethnography', arguing for the legitimacy of creative and reflexive modes of storytelling that focus on the author's subjectivity and internal 'lived experience', often by using poetic and performative forms and styles.[124]

In literary-cultural scholarship, scholars working on the history of reading began to incorporate ideas about embodiment and literary evocation. Michel de Certeau has proposed that 'readers are travellers; they move across lands belonging to someone else, like nomads poaching their way across fields they did not write'[125]—and that scholars should 'try to rediscover the movements of this reading within the body itself, which seems to stay docile and silent, but mines the reading in its own way. From the nooks of all sorts of "reading rooms" (including lavatories) emerge subconscious gestures, grumblings, stretchings, rustlings, unexpected noises, in short a wild orchestration of the body'.[126]

Experiential literary ethnography seeks to bring the body to the forefront of live literature research, drawing on that rich vein of scholarship.

# Liveness, Time, Attention, Experientialism

Liveness, and the interlinked concept of time, are key considerations when writing about the experience of a live performance event. As I mentioned in Chapter 2, liveness has long been a focus for scholars working in performance studies, several of whom have considered the relationship between embodied liveness and 'mediatized' liveness, i.e. live events relayed via a screen, and opinions have been passionately divided—though neuroscience seems to have come down squarely on the side of those who argue that live, embodied performance is qualitatively, significantly different to live, digital performance.

Liveness had largely been neglected by social scientists until Les Back and Nirmal Pawar addressed it in their book, *Live Methods* (2012).[127] They made a case for sociological writing that not only puts the senses at the centre, but also pays due 'attention to time', including 'the multiple shapes duration assumes during lived moment',[128] and the 'unpredictable attentiveness' of perception.[129] This, they propose, needs to be reflected in scholarly writing, through a 'liveliness of words', and by 'incorporating a vivid imagination' into the research design.[130]

David Wiles, in his book *Theatre and Time* (2014),[131] explores the linked issues of time, duration and rhythm in performance.[132] He points out that, in writing about live events, all these temporal factors have to be linked to *memory* in order for any theory of liveness 'to have real meaning'. Memory, David Wiles points out, is therefore 'vital to any discussion about the importance of a performer's 'presence', or the experience of a spectator relishing that presence.[133] He quotes Peter Brook as saying: 'When a performance is over... the event scorches into the memory an outline, a taste, a trace, a smell – a picture'.[134] This speaks to my own concern with exploring, not just participants' experience of live literature events as they were taking place, but the nature of the lasting *impact* of the experiences, beyond the site and duration of the events themselves: questions of how participants' memories of experiencing an event affect the valuations of it, and affect their daily lives and cultural practices accordingly.

As well as leaving a subjective impression on an individual memory, David Wiles argues, the memory of a live performance has a 'collective element'; the experience of being part of an audience in a shared time and space creates 'mnemonic communities'—that is, 'people bound together by possessing a shared system of memories that are shaped over time'.[135] This idea links in with Fish's idea of 'interpretive communities', and Benedict Anderson's notion of 'imagined communities'[136] that shape culture and society.

Drawing upon these ideas, my multivocal ethnographies involve conversations with live literature event participants about their long-past and future-projected memories, as well as more immediate, 'present' experiences, and memories of events in the immediate past. They are based on the idea that memory is vital to value—and it is also, always, a creative act.

## Emotional Brains: The Revolutionary Neuroscience of Emotion; Implications for Impact and Value

Intimately bound up with these intertwining notions of the performance, the senses, embodiment, memory, attention and value is another key element of live event experiences, and that is *emotion*. As I discussed in Chapter 2, the revolutionary twenty-first-century neuroscience of emotion has revealed what a fundamental role emotion plays in human decision-making and evaluation, in contexts such a politics—and literature—that were previously assumed to be driven by rational and intellectual thought.[137]

Emotion and affect have long been themes in scholarship relating to the arts, but usually in the context of aesthetics. They have been thought of primarily in terms of audiences' subjective responses to works or events: responses that do not necessarily contribute to their cognitive, aesthetic or cultural value.

Raymond Williams shook up thinking on this back in the 1970s with his theory that 'structures of feeling' produce a 'collective sense of a generation or period',[138] rather than being simply individualistic or subjective. This echoed his view that 'style' and aesthetics are formed, not by individual artists' impulses, but out of a myriad of idiosyncratic qualities that make up any social group. In a similar vein, within anthropology, Ruth Behar pioneered a feminist case for incorporating emotion into ethnography, to render it more empathetic and socially-engaged.[139]

Neuroscience and other scientific research has increasingly shown how live, embodied events, featuring verbal performances, can create resonant connections between people,[140] harnessing emotions and the senses—and can consequently have a significant impact on audience's collective memories. Crucially, this can affect their judgements of value in profound ways—including literary and aesthetic value: an important form of impact.

There has been a resurgence of interest among scholars in the power of collective, embodied, live experiences and ideas like 'structures of feeling'.[141] A related theory that has regained prominence is Michael Maffesoli's idea of 'emotional communities'. These can exist among groups of people assembling in contemporary, urban 'tribal' groupings—live literature events, for instance—and the communities are characterised by an empathetic 'sociality' that is formed and 'expressed by a succession of ambiences, feelings and emotions'.[142]

In the context of musicology, Georgina Born has recently proposed the idea of 'affective publics' as a comparable way to understand how music generates social relations—and argues that, in order to understand the impact of this, scholars need to study the 'microsocialities of musical practice'.[143] Here Born echoes Radway, who has advocated for more 'microsocial' research into literary practices (see earlier discussion). Both Born and Radway hold up ethnography as the best way to achieve this goal.

The emotions 'revolution' in scholarship has prompted many scholars to suggest that wider structures of academia and modes of writing need to change. As Billy Ehn and Orvar Lofgren have put it, scholars need to stop 'camouflaging' the real role of emotion in their writing,[144] and academia needs to change from being a 'world in which feelings are either denied or denigrated'—it needs to move away from the a traditional 'mode of producing knowledge' in which emphasis tends to be put on 'rationality, scientific objectivity and a constant rhetoric about keeping "person and thing" separate'.[145] In his book, *Language and Emotion* (2009), linguistic anthropologist James Wilce argues that the 'fusion of language and feeling' is the 'very stuff of culture',[146] and so not only do cultural stories about this fusion 'need telling',[147] but the *mode of telling* really matters. He points out that 'all speaking and writing is inherently emotional to a greater or lesser extent', and 'objective, distant coolness *is* an emotional stance'.[148] Wilce, in a similar vein to Born and Radway, recommends that 'ethnographies of local linguistic-emotional practices' should 'attend to the microinteractional engagement of bodies', as well as to matters of 'language, feeling, and embodiment'.[149]

These ideas have now started seeping into the field of literary studies—even if this is still mostly in relation to ideas about silent reading. In a special edition of *Textual Practice: 'Affect, Text and Performativity'* (2011), Alex Houen points out that, while aesthetics and literature 'both thrive on feeling', that fact has rarely been discussed explicitly within literary studies[150]—but it is now clear that 'how a text functions as a literary form or genre is contingent upon social performativity', as well as upon the 'forces of affect', and that emotion actively affects the way in which a text is received and valued.[151] In the same volume, Derek Attridge proposes that a literary work should be seen as 'less an object than an *event or encounter* for its readers'.[152] He identifies a 'paucity' of vocabulary within literary studies for 'dealing with affective experience', which he sees as a reflection of the poverty of our understanding of this domain of our lives', and argues that our new knowledge about affective experience better reveals 'the capacity of literature to engage powerfully and subtly' with this complexity.[153]

As Gilles Deleuze proposed: literary writing has a unique capacity to translate, or 'catapult', lived processes—processes of becoming—into affects and precepts, to combine them into 'blocks of sensation' by their conjunction in composition,[154] and thereby evaluate a work of art in terms of its 'vitality' or its 'tenor of life'.[155]

Experiential literary ethnographies of live literature events have the capacity to encompass these ideas, and to contribute to new understandings of literary culture that take emotion and affect into account.

# Aesthetics, Experience, Sociality, Transformation

I have already referred to 'aesthetics' several times. But since it is so central to the idea of 'cultural value' in arts contexts, and so controversial as a term, I will take a moment here to explain how I approach it in this book, and why I see it as being central to my approach in writing ethnographies of live literature events.

The word 'aesthetic' is commonly used to refer to 'the perception, appreciation, or criticism of that which is beautiful', or relating to artistic taste.[156] But it has been a contested concept ever since Plato and Aristotle's disagreement—and, no doubt, before that and across cultures. As philosopher Berys Gaut points out, there have been several historical threads of aesthetic thought, in which aesthetic value has variously been seen as having a primarily moral dimension; being about beauty and form; and moving us emotionally. Gaut's own view is that it involves all these threads—though he substitutes morality for ethics.[157] He does not clarify, though, how this perspective might translate into practice to inform aesthetic evaluations in specific socio-cultural contexts.

Bourdieu's formative work on literary culture and cultural capital has influenced many scholars working on the sociology of the arts and literature—but it has been criticised for marginalising questions of aesthetics, including value and judgement, notably by Georgina Born.[158] Born, who is both a sociologist and an anthropologist, specialises in music and the arts, and her research is informed by her background as a practising musician as well as a scholar. She makes a counter-case for the 'social aesthetics'[159] of arts participation.[160] In her extended ethnographies of arts and cultural institutions—a Paris music institute (in 1995)[161] and the BBC (in 2006)[162]—aesthetic questions are seriously considered, alongside structural and political ones.

Born, Eric Lewis and Will Straw have highlighted the socio-cultural dimension of aesthetics in their book, *Improvisation and Social Aesthetics* (2017). They argue that aesthetics should not be viewed in terms of abstract concepts, because they end up being 'barren of nuance' and 'blind to how such social relations as those pertaining to class, race, ethnicity, religion, gender, sexuality, or nationality…. inflect aesthetic experience'.[163] Instead, aesthetics must be seen as 'immanently social' in nature:[164] they are affected by social relations, and they have the capacity to affect social relations in return. Any aesthetic inquiries, the authors argue, therefore need to explore the role of 'social and cultural processes' and how they influence 'individual aesthetic judgments'.[165] The inquiries need to engage with 'situational' elements of experience, including the 'sensory, perceptual and embodied'[166] elements by looking at the 'microsocialities' of practice.[167]

Twenty-first-century neuroscience has also delved into aesthetics, to the point that a new field of 'neuroaesthetics' has emerged, pioneered by Anjan Chatterjee. So far it has mostly been applied to visual art.[168] As Chatterjee explains, brain imagery has revealed that the appreciation of art involves multiple different areas of the brain, across both hemispheres, which interact in a 'flexible ensemble', including through the work of mirror neurons and reward circuitry. This means that any evaluation of art must involve both the senses and the emotions.[169] Chatterjee acknowledges the limits of a neuroscientific approach, though, pointing out that understanding the *historical and cultural context* behind an artwork can enhance aesthetic appreciation, and add to its 'richly textured meaning'.[170]

G. Gabrielle Starr has considered the neuroaesthetics of poetry and music in her book, *Feeling Beauty: The Neuroscience of Aesthetic Experience* (2013). Along similar lines to Chatterjee, she sees aesthetics as being formed of a powerful 'web of value', emphasising that aesthetic pleasures tend to be *mixed*, and include 'multiple positive and negative emotional factors',[171] as well as senses, ideas, events and perceptions, which exist in a '*valenced* relation' to each other.[172] Together, they 'have a neural value, a reward value, that helps produce the structure of aesthetic experience'.[173] Starr also describes how this affects audiences' memories and retrospective formations of value: after a particular event is over, the '*durable* potential of complex aesthetic experience' lies in how it 'allows us to integrate unexpected or evolving knowledge in new ways', as part of a 'dynamic form of learning'.[174] Like Chatterjee, Starr acknowledges that there is much in neuroaesthetics still 'to be discovered', including the impact of 'the broader somatic context of aesthetic experience'.[175]

In a live literature context, the overtly 'aesthetic' quality of events—in terms of their artistic content—is variable. In a conversation-based literary festival event, like those that are typical at the Hay Festival, the element of performed reading from literary texts often represents a small proportion of the whole event. Even so, as recent neuroaesthetic insights reveal, the context from which any artwork was created is integral to any aesthetic valuations of it. Elements of any literary performance events that may affect audiences' overall evaluations of the text featured will therefore include not only the performed reading of the text, and aspects of delivery, but also the design of the space, the architecture of the staging, and even appreciation of a performer's facial features. Even if the performed reading element of such events is short, it may still be an important element to consider in terms of questions about the literary reception and value of a text, as well as its wider cultural value.

My experiential literary ethnographic approach to writing about live literature events is informed by the evolutions in aesthetic ideas that I have described here. It aims to reveal the complex nature and value of aesthetics as an element of participant experiences, and in doing so, it incorporates nuanced, individual participant responses and details that are specific to each event.

## Practical Application: Proving Cultural Value

I hope that I have demonstrated in the last two chapters how experiential literary ethnography can work as a fruitful way of revealing the cultural value of live literature experiences.

I also want to advocate here for its potential for wider application as a flexible, practical approach for producers, funders or anyone seeking to better understand or communicate the cultural value of a live arts-based experience.

As I mentioned in the introduction, the problem of how to prove cultural value of any given project, event or experience has already been stirring up research among those concerned with making, producing and funding live arts-based events. Plenty of researchers, funders and funding applicants have turned their minds to it. The standard approach to evaluating participant experience at arts and culture events is through demographically-oriented data analysis, and audience surveys, in which participant audience members are invited to award marks out of five for enjoyment. In addition to an expansion of quantitative audience research in recent years, there has also been a growth in qualitative research, which often references comments from members of an audience made in response to set questionnaires or structured interviews. The results of all these kinds of research can be highly useful and informative, in a host of different ways. But these research exercises almost always seem to miss the essence of the experience—in all its variety and complexity—and consequently its true cultural value.

## Currents in Audience Research; Modes of Measurement; Cultural Value Assessments

I have already emphasised the urgency there currently is, among practitioners and scholars, to demonstrate impact and cultural value in the arts. Consequently, over the last decade, funders and scholars have been focusing on new ways to understand audiences. Notably, most have done this in ways that do *not* directly engage with the thorny concept of aesthetics, but seek to highlight other aspects of impact.

'Audience studies' has emerged as a lively field spanning several disciplines, particularly in the context of theatre performance. The verb 'audiencing', initially coined by John Fiske,[176] is sometimes used to describe the activity of being an audience member, in contrast to the passivity that had previously been assumed.

This has coincided with new, exciting neuroscientific research into the physiological impacts of live, embodied performance events on audiences that I discussed in Chapter 2.

However, none of these forms of audience research, by themselves, can fully reflect the complexity and multifaceted ways in which participants experience and evaluate such events.[177]

In the realm of performance studies, scholars have been investigating 'audience experience' in ways that aim to address this complexity with an increased focus on subjectivity. This has included a variety of ethnographic and other qualitative research, involving interviews with audiences at events that seek to engage critically with their experiences, including, sometimes, their emotions.[178] An interview-dominated method, though, will inevitably be limited in its capacity to explore the nature and dynamics of experience during the live event itself.

In England, Arts Council England (ACE) has become increasingly focused on communicating the value of the arts and culture. On their website, they make a 'case' for their value, stating that: the arts and culture 'bring us joy, they help us to make sense of our own experiences and to empathise with others', and 'benefit us economically, socially, and educationally'.[179] In 2014, they published a report on an 'evidence review' they had conducted on the issue,[180] which highlighted multiple 'instrumental' benefits of the arts, including 'promoting social and economic goals through regeneration', 'attracting tourists' and 'contributing to the delivery of public services'.[181] But the report admitted that there were evidence gaps, including this rather significant one: 'we cannot demonstrate why the arts are unique in what they do'.[182] It concluded that a larger evidence base was needed.[183]

Criticising ACE's choice of wording, cultural value scholar Eleonore Belfiore published an article after the report's release, pointing out that even using the phrase 'making the case', in the context of the arts' value, pointed to an economically-focused notion of 'impact' that is linked in turn to the prevailing power structures that continue to shape public funding. She sought to debunk the way in which the term 'impact', when understood instrumentally, and particularly economically, is too often used as a 'proxy for value'.[184] The following year (2015), a group of scholars at Warwick, including Belfiore, published a report on the 'future of cultural value', entitled 'Enriching Britain: Culture, Creativity and Growth'. This report focused on pragmatic recommendations to government, including ensuring more diverse access to arts and culture, and more investment for research aimed at exploring audience engagement and cultural value.[185]

The year after that (2016), the UK's Arts and Humanities Research Council (AHRC) published their report on a Cultural Value Project, which was based on seventy commissioned studies conducted over three years. In their conclusions, the authors, Geoffrey Crossick and

Patrycja Kaszynska, did not critique the notion of impact per se, but argued that there is a need to 'transcend' old debates between the 'intrinsic and instrumental camps' when it comes to the arts, and to put the 'experience of individuals back at the heart of cultural value'.[186] They suggested doing this in various ways, including through case studies[187]—notably by prioritising 'phenomenological approaches',[188] which they said had previously been 'neglected'[189]—in part due to the 'politics' of evaluation. They pointed out that 'measurement' and 'value' need to be disentangled,[190] and argued that trends in evaluation suggest that 'evaluation models' must be 'more sensitive to what they evaluate'.[191] Helpful phenomenological approaches, they suggested, might include 'first-person perspectives',[192] and ways to capture 'feeling and experience',[193] including forms of 'empathy' and self-reflection,[194] community relationships,[195] connections to place,[196] and ways in which affective and cognitive dimensions of experience interact.[197] Phenomenological approaches to audience research have been explored in more depth by one of the report's contributing scholars, Matthew Reason, in relation to performance studies.[198]

The AHRC report considered ethnography and arts-based research as potential methods. Intriguingly, they viewed these two categories as being separate—which suggests a flawed assumption that ethnography cannot be arts-based. They gave cautious support for ethnography as a valuable method to 'supplement' others,[199] but suggested that it was 'resource-intensive'.[200] It is far from clear from this that they were aware of the breadth of approaches to contemporary ethnographic research.

As for arts-based research methods: they proposed that these were useful on the basis that they could enable 'access to forms of knowledge and awareness that are difficult, but not impossible, to articulate in words'.[201] Again, this statement is problematic as it assumes that arts-based methods are never themselves worded. Encouragingly, they suggested that the potential value of arts-based methods lay in their ability to create an 'imaginative re-visiting of the original experience'[202]: a core principle underpinning my approach to experiential literary ethnography. But, ultimately, this report did not reckon with the imaginative possibilities of wording ethnographies experientially, or using literary techniques to achieve this.

Ben Walmsley, one of the researchers on the AHRC project, sought to develop some of these ideas by using anthropological tools. In 2018, he published an substantial article reflecting on his experience, titled: 'Deep hanging out in the arts: an anthropological approach to capturing cultural value'.[203] He argued—as I have done here—that any approach to evaluation needs to engage with participant experience and feeling, in the course of the researcher's own immersion in the experience, and not focus on 'rationalising' value.[204] For me, though, several of his key conclusions omit the potential power and scope of language. For instance, Walmsley suggested that, because the language used by their team's interviewee audience members (of which there were only five) in answering questions at an arts festival proved to be 'limited' in terms of revealing the event's cultural value, the role of language in ethnography itself is limited.[205] But, anthropological writing traditions—notably those inspired by Zora Neale Hurston and her evocative approach to writing ethnography—suggest that participant conversations can in fact be conducted, transcribed and described with much more nuance, if careful attention is paid to language and literary technique.

On the recommendation of its 2016 report, the ARHC has created a new collaborative Centre for Cultural Value for ongoing research, led by Walmsley.[206] As a result, research on this subject is continuing to expand.[207]

The experiential literary ethnographies in this book seek to contribute to that ongoing project, in part by showing that responsive and open-ended conversations with participants can lead participants to use language in more interesting ways than a brief or more structured conversation might indicate, and also that nuances or omissions in participant responses during conversations can be explored through the ethnographer's own use of language in the surrounding narrative. They incorporate multivocal material including extracts of conversations with participants, and weave this in among my own experiential description, and reflections on wider critical and socio-cultural dynamics and patterns.

Through its emphasis on lively, evocative writing, I suggest experiential literary ethnography offers an accessible and engaging way to communicate the value of participation in live literature, and other arts events, for the benefit of a diverse audience of readers. In the context of funding pressures in the arts, the impact agenda and linked concerns with demonstrating cultural value, this goal has become ever-more important.[208] The dramatic impacts of the Coronavirus upon the arts, particularly the performing arts, are likely to make the stakes even higher.

## Experiential Literary Ethnography: Limitations and Qualifications

All that being said, I want to acknowledge the limitations of experiential literary ethnography as an approach to revealing cultural value.

I would like to be clear that I am in no way dismissing the value of alternative approaches to researching cultural value. Each method or approach has its own strengths. When it comes to participant experience, no single method or approach on its own can ever be comprehensive in capturing the impact or value of an experience for even one single person—the author—never mind multiple participants. Different approaches to research and writing have different strengths and weaknesses.

In considering the issue of cultural value, data and statistics can be vital for revealing patterns of behaviour and response, often on a large scale: patterns that more qualitatively-focused researchers might well miss. Statistics revealing gender or ethnic diversity in any given cultural context—or, more likely, the lack of it—can be powerful instruments for catalysing much-needed change, although they can of course be manipulated with distorting effects.

However, in order to make a communicative impact, all data and statistics need to be conveyed through narrative and in ways that resonate. The most effective narratives involve engaging storytelling that seeks to illuminate insights, rather than simply to inform about facts. As Susan Sontag memorably put it: 'Information will never replace illumination'.[209]

This perspective is increasingly important as data increasingly dominates the operation of all human action, and as it has become increasingly clear how easy it can be to deploy quantitative data in ways that distort meaningful reality.[210] Similarly, data-driven narratives that are purportedly objective fact-based, and that are narrated in an omniscient third-person, are always composed of material that has been selected and shaped by one or more writers, on the basis of their own subjective perspectives, experiences and interests—and so they are not necessarily as representative of reality as they are often made to seem. Experiential literary ethnography is a necessarily reflexive approach, focused on evocation as much as fact, and there is an honesty in that.

One final pragmatic limitation of experiential literary ethnography that I would like to note here is its difficulty. Creative approaches to academic writing are often characterised by scholars who distrust them as soft or insufficiently rigorous, implying simplicity or ease. But the process of composing these experiential literary ethnographies has not been easy, just as literary craft in general is not easy. Still, if others feel moved to try it, or something similar, having read this book, I hope that the effort proves worthwhile, or at least enjoyable.

# 6

# Summing up the Story: Patterns, Divergences, Insights, Ideas

To illustrate the contemporary live literature scene, and live literature as a practice, I have crafted ethnographies that delve into two very different events: a large, mainstream literary festival and a small, performative LGBTQ+ salon. By evoking participant experience at these events through experiential literary ethnography, I have revealed and examined the cultural value and impact of these events.

After reflecting on the inspirations and merits of experiential literary ethnography as an approach to researching and writing about live literature, and made a case for why it can offer genuinely new insights and ways of thinking, and its potential to untangle the cultural value and impact of other live arts-based events.

In this concluding chapter, I draw out some key insights about live literature.

## Narrative Ethnographies vs Distilled Insights

Looking back on the Hay and Polari ethnographies, there are many common themes and also some stark differences that deserve to be

© The Author(s), under exclusive license to Springer Nature
Switzerland AG 2021
E. Wiles, *Live Literature*, Palgrave Studies in Literary Anthropology,
https://doi.org/10.1007/978-3-030-50385-7_6

extracted and considered. Although I argue, in this book, that extended ethnographic narratives are vital in order to evoke the complexity of experience and thus to reveal key aspects of an event's cultural value; distilled sets of insights can also be extremely useful in conjunction with such narratives, particularly for those readers who are interested in applying some of the ideas and practices discussed.

The insights that follow have varied implications for live literature participation, which can be read as both positive and negative. Some, for instance, suggest that live literature enhances participants' engagement with literary texts and culture, while others point to persistent problems with live literature's role in contemporary literary culture. Ultimately, context and detail are key. For that reason, I am not seeking to make generalised claims in what follows—but I do want to highlight a range of interesting themes and patterns that have emerged in this book and that offer new ways of thinking about, and valuing, live literature.

I have divided my key insights into three main sections. The first focuses on reader-audiences; the second on author-performers; and the third on experiential literary ethnography.

## Key Insights: Reader-Audiences

### Reader-Audiences: An Overview

Participating as a reader-audience member in a live literature event is clearly a popular activity; the growth of live literature makes this obvious. But, as my ethnographies show, reader-audiences' experiences at live literature events, and their evaluations, are as diverse, complex, and multi-faceted as the individuals themselves—contrary to prevalent stereotypes.[1] This book delves deeply into the nature and quality of those experiences. It offers insights into *how* and *why* they are valued, what the consequences are for participants' ongoing literary practices, tastes and values—and, more broadly, for literary culture.

## Reader-Audiences: Curation, Conversion, Evaluation

One central function of live literature events is as a form of curation. The digitalised twenty-first century, has seen the value and importance of curation increase across culture, including literary culture, in conjunction with the new 'attention ecology'.[2] My ethnographies suggest that the popularity of live literature events, and their curatorial value for reader-audiences, is linked to this phenomenon. Live literature events help people to navigate the otherwise-overwhelming sea of choices—not only which books to read, by which authors; but how to spend leisure and family time.

Live literature's increased curatorial value this century corresponds with the emergence of 'experientialism'.[3] In a digital age characterised by an abundance of clickable entertainment and information choices, live and embodied event experiences that capture participants' attention away from the screen, and induce them to spend 'quality time' on something memorable, are increasingly highly-valued.[4] Reader-audiences I spoke to at Hay and Polari clearly valued live literature's function as a form of experiential curation for these reasons. Participation in live literature often seems to have a significant impact on their reader-audiences' individual literary judgements, choices and practices, and also for wider patterns of value, choice and behaviour across literary culture.

The most obvious and immediate evidence of live literature events' curatorial impact upon participants' reading practices is the effect known as 'conversion', whereby reader-audience members buy the book presented at an event afterwards.[5] This is facilitated at many live literature events where there are bookstalls or bookshops in place for the purpose. It is interrogated in my ethnographies through various conversations, including those with Daniel Hahn and James Daunt. The term 'conversion' speaks to a core objective behind the event on the part of publishers and, author-performers: namely to convert their investment of time and money in the event into profit from book sales—particularly sales of publishers' key titles.

Beyond that: with its religious connotation, the term 'conversion' also suggests an objective of causing reader-audience members to make a longer-term *commitment* to the literary work of the author-performer in question. As my conversation with Daunt made clear, embodied events involving readers meeting an author in person—even just book signing events that are minimally performative—can affect sales of that author's future work for years to come. Reader-audiences I spoke to often suggested that, even if they do not 'convert' at an event, by buying a physical copy of a book on site immediately afterwards, there is still an increased likelihood that, after having a positive experience at the event, they will go on to buy or read a book by that author-performer at a later date.

Book sale statistics from the big festivals, Hay and Edinburgh, now reveal how significant the immediate purchase conversions, and overall book sales, are to publishers today. The stakes have increased in recent years, to the point that these two Festivals' sales are now tracked by Nielsen BookScan.[6] As my conversation with Gaby Wood at Hay alludes to, the curatorial decisions of the big festival producers are significantly shaped by lobbying from the publishing industry to promote key titles, usually the titles in which they have invested the most money. Increasing book sales at festivals will only increase publishers' motivation to lobby festival producers still harder in favour of their lead titles.

The impact of live literature curation also extends beyond the effects it has on individual reader-audience members: it affects other forums for literary curation too. The big festivals like Hay directly affect bookshop curation, since booksellers come to festivals, or simply peruse festivals' programmes, in order to gain inspiration and knowledge about titles to promote and display in their shops[7]—and this in turn impacts on the reading choices of many more people.

At live literature events that focus on presenting newly-published titles—particularly the big literary festivals—the books offered on sale are generally in hardback, and consequently cost reader-audiences much more to buy than they would do after the later paperback release. This makes the financial cost of immediate conversion relatively high, and that is on top of ticket costs. So why do so many reader-audience members 'convert'?

Part of it seems to come down to their in-depth exposure to the books and authors featured during the event. The temporal hype of access to the new is also a factor: Hay's curatorial focus on presenting the latest books written by the most high-profile or critically-acclaimed author-performers—with events often billed as the 'first ever' event to feature a given text—endows reader-audiences with a heightened sense that their participation is a unique and ultra-present experience: an experience that will bring them up to date with the latest ideas, literary trends and public figures. An experience that will put them ahead of their peers. While reader-audience members I spoke to did not talk about cultural capital per se (unsurprisingly), many were very well-aware that they were discovering the newest work produced by significant authors, who were often widely-known names, and they valued this.

However, it was not at all clear that a sense of cultural capital or of 'newness', or the ability to talk about their access these 'new' literary phenomena after the event, tended to be the sole or even major factor causing reader-audience members to 'convert'. More impactful was the *experience* they had at the event, and their wish to deepen that experience by reading the book that lay at the heart of that experience. My conversation with Stan and Kira at Hay reflects this: at the end of our conversation, they told me they were heading to the bookshop to look at 'other books' by the author-performer, Philip Gross—not necessarily to buy the new collection he had just been presenting and reading from at the event.

The earliest scholarly research on literary festivals first decade of this century, and the journalism of that time, tended for foreground and denigrate the commercial aspect of festivals' impact, and the emphasis placed by producers on big names.[8] Festival audiences were simplistically painted as shallow cynics who only attended in order to take a shortcut to the prestige associated with having been in the same space as celebrity authors, and being familiar with the most popular new books, without bothering to read them—just so that they brag about them at dinner parties afterwards. This skewed stereotype has already been soundly critiqued in more recent research,[9] and my ethnographies lead me to expand upon that critique in this book.

I have shown how smaller live literature events, like Polari, tend to be far less influenced by publishers in making their curatorial selections than the big literary festivals that have, until now, been the dominant focus of live literature research. At Polari, the curation of books to be featured is determined far more by their relevance to the LGBTQ+ community, in conjunction with the host's assessment of their literary quality, than either their acclaim within the established literary-critical forums, or their publicity profile generated by their publishers' expenditure. This goes to the heart of Polari's identity as an event. I saw many author-performers at Polari performing from books that have barely had any other publicity, including self-published titles, and even new works-in-progress. Reader-audiences I spoke to valued Polari's curatorial role immensely in presenting a selection of author-performers, and their literary work, that would otherwise be neglected in the mainstream literary industry, including the mainstream literary festivals, possibly because of its LGBTQ+ orientation.

Conversion is rarely a primary aim or concern for reader-audiences when choosing to attend live literature events—even the mainstream literary festivals. While many do in fact end up buying a book immediately after experiencing a live literature event, that purchase is rarely intended or planned. This is even the case at Hay, where the book-buying element of the Festival is foregrounded as much as possible for the attention of reader-audiences, and in multiple ways—including by a standard invitation to reader-audiences at the end of each event to go to buy a book and get it signed, and through the design of the festival site, with its continually-expanding bookshop. It was clear to me from conversations with reader-audiences, across multiple live literature events, that the vast majority would not attend if they did not expect the events to be rewarding experiences on their own terms, regardless of whether or not resulted in a book purchase.

Even at the big literary festivals, reader-audiences tend not to be conscious of, or at least focused on, the influence of publishers' commercial interests on the curation and dynamics of the events—including the extent to which publishers feature their key titles, which are linked to financial investments made in the form of author advances. Even if reader-audiences are aware of events' relationship to the publishing industry, they rarely accord weight or significance to this in relation to their own experience, or in making judgements of aesthetic value about the books presented. On one view, this amounts to a successful deception of reader-audiences by live literature producers on behalf of publishers—particularly at the big festivals—in that they do not see themselves as publishers' 'customers', and are not consciously aware of the degree to which their choices are being skewed by the selective presentation of key titles; and yet they go on to behave as such.

But to take that characterisation as the whole story would be a distortion. It would miss the way in which live literature events give reader-audiences a sense of real *agency* in relation to their evaluations of both texts and author-performers. The experience of participation in an event enables reader-audiences to reach aesthetic judgements of quality and value that they would not necessarily make after being introduced to those texts or authors in other ways—for instance through the blurb on a cover, or through other forms of literary curation such as book shop tables or blogs. My ethnographies reveal more about how and why live literature events are valued so highly as evaluation tools by reader-audiences: how they work, not just as fulsome introductions to certain books, but as meaningful communicative and aesthetic performance experiences in their own right.

When participating in live literature events, and experiencing them as performances, reader-audiences enter into a *multi-layered experiential process*: a process that helps them to shape not only their future literary practices, judgements and values, but also their perspectives on their own identities, relationships, communities, and the culture and society in which they are situated. These multiple dimensions combine to contribute to live literature's cultural value.

## Reader-Audiences: Embodied Liveness vs Digitalisation

A key facet of live literature's cultural value is its 'liveness'. The rise of live literature is part of a rise of liveness across art forms and culture in the twenty-first century, and the economic and social value of live experiences has risen accordingly—particularly live embodied experiences that are not solely digital. My ethnographies reveal more about what embodied liveness means to reader-audiences at live literature events.

My conversations with reader-audience members suggested that they often accorded a high value to liveness in multiple respects, including temporal, spatial, geographical and physical elements of events. They often mentioned the fact that their experience of the event they were attending could *never be replicated* or repeated, even if a particular event were to be recorded and broadcast online later—as Hay Festival events are via the Hay Player.

On the subject of the Hay Player: this is just one example of many online sources for videos of live literature events. It serves as a rich source of retrospective access to individual events within the Hay Festival for the benefit of anybody in the world—from reader-audiences who, perhaps for health reasons or financial reasons, were unable to get to the Festival in person; to scholars who, like me, are interested in viewing past events. The videos can not only offer viewers the full content presented on stage at individual events, but can also give them a good sense of the author-performers, enabling them to engage to some extent with elements like their vocal qualities and delivery style.

Live streaming technology has allowed digital reader-audiences around the world to access some live literature events in real time, as they are physically taking place: a form of 'digital liveness', in contrast to the 'embodied liveness' of events I have focused on in this book. Watching a live stream of an event can give digital reader-audiences a sense that they are temporally, if not physically, sharing the experience with the participants who are present in person. There is much to celebrate in these developments, particularly in terms of access to more diverse audiences, in terms of class and race, who may not be able to afford to attend in person, and digital reader-audiences can clearly glean a vast amount from such live streams, videos and also audio recordings of literary events. The value of live digital participation in live literature has been demonstrated in 2020 when COVID-19 has forced a number of live literature events to 'go digital', including the Hay Festival. Hay Festival Digital events were watched by nearly half a million people[10] and prompted a barrage of requests by reader-audiences in online comments for more live digital streaming in future years. Clearly, digital streaming can have a huge impact on the accessibility of live literature.

I welcome this development entirely. But my ethnographies in this book reveal what is distinctly valuable for participants about the *embodied experience* of in-person participation. Reader-audiences often spoke of the way in which they valued the fact that participation in embodied live literature events *required them to disconnect* from the electronic devices, and screen-based communications, define so much of everyday twenty-first-century life. This was manifested particularly clearly at Hay: many reader-audience members I spoke to on site specifically linked the quality of their experience at the Festival with their digital disconnection. Dave, for instance, spoke about how rare it was for him not to be checking email, and how much he was enjoying being cut off from phone reception, after an initial phase of anxiety. Interestingly, this seemed to link another comment of Dave's: that Hay was the only time in the year when he would actually make time to sit down to read a book of fiction.

In comparison with digital screenings, participation in embodied live literature events seems to have a highly resonant communicative impact on reader-audiences, and affects their judgements of literary value. Recent neuroscience has revealed the profound extent to which live, embodied events generally, particularly talks and events that involve verbal storytelling, affect reader-audiences decisions and value judgements, in part by harnessing their emotions[11]; and my ethnographies have illuminated ways in which these ideas translate into specific experiences and contexts.

The activity of witnessing author-performers in the flesh performing from their literary texts triggers a mesh of concurrent evaluations of various elements of their performance—from gesture, body language, demeanour, facial expressions and dress, to vocal qualities, characteristics of delivery, accent, rhythm, phrasing and timing. Reader-audiences often revealed in conversation with me that they pay close attention to such details, which are experienced as being inextricably intertwined. Such descriptions are often framed around the idea of discovering the author-performer's authentic voice and story,[12] which remains in the memory, and shapes their evaluations of the texts presented.[13]

Again, this ties in with the idea of experientialism in the digital twenty-first century.[14] Neuroscience has proved that the impact of embodied performances upon audiences is *enhanced* in a digitalised culture, in part because embodied experiences resonate more deeply in the context of a bombardment of digitally-accessible information. My ethnographies illustrate this in practice—and suggest that the extent of the communicative impact of live literature experiences is often underestimated, even by those involved in its production.

The *proxemics* of live literature events, including spatial characteristics and geography, are also more significant to reader-audiences than they are often assumed to be. Live literature events such as festivals that are situated away from urban centres, so that participation often requires a substantial physical journey away from reader-audiences' everyday lives, often do seem to provide an enhanced sense of liminality that intensifies participant experience—particularly if festivals also offer a density of events.

Reader-audiences I spoke to often value this sense of escape from everyday spaces and link it with accessing an authentic experience. Many I spoke to at Hay commented on the pleasure they felt in 'getting away from it all' in order to experience the festival—by taking themselves to a rural, usually-distant place that contained none of the distractions and stresses of home, particularly for those who live in urban environments. My conversation with Elsa at Hay emphasises this, and her characterisation of Hay as a form of pilgrimage was notable. For her, Hay has become an annual ritual in which she travels physically far away from her work and family commitments in the city order to immerse herself, on her own, in the event experience and all the ideas and stimulation that the festival has to offer. Her expressive language revealed how much emotional value she attaches to this. Several other reader-audience members also explicitly referred to the experience of travelling to Hay in pilgrimage terms.

But a live literature event in an urban context can have a comparable impact. Polari usually takes place at the Southbank Centre, in the centre of a busy capital city, to which many reader-audience members travel only a short distance on a bus; but still, most reader-audience members I spoke to indicated that participating in that space had a significant impact and value for them: it allowed them to be physically present as part of a collective group in a performance space that felt immersive and removed from everyday life.[15] Hilary, for instance, a reader-audience member at Polari, talked about why the South Bank Centre location is important to her as an iconic cultural space that she has been conscious of since her childhood in South London, and expressed what it means to her emotionally for Polari now to be based there, and to offer a regular physical space within this particular building that is dedicated to LGBTQ+ literary cultural appreciation and community. The visual and design aesthetics of Polari—including the use of cabaret-inspired lighting, the projected pink-and-purple magic-realist promotional image, and Burston's overtly camp dress for the performances—work together to enhance the sense of performativity, and to generate a dynamic atmosphere, in which participants feel kinetically involved.

The embodied presence of an audience member in any shared physical space is central to the value of its liveness. We now know, from neuroscience and from performance research, that embodied live performance experiences are experienced as being qualitatively different from digital experiences due to the nature of the feedback loop process between audiences and performers.[16] The neuroscientific revelation that audiences' heartbeats synchronise at emotional moments in live performances proves what an unconscious and yet profound experience embodied audiencing can be.[17] My ethnographies bear out these ideas: while I was unable to prove heart beat synchrony and did not seek to, I did observe, feel and often extract, through conversations, a visceral sense of connectedness during live events. This was often manifested as a heightened atmosphere in a shared space. Some reader-audience responses during events, ranging from rippling laughter to palpable stillness, are observable, and are described in my ethnographies—and they speak to the meaning and value of that collective experience.

Another core element of liveness is the sense of *risk* and even potential failure involved: a factor that pertains to the value of all live performance events, and adds a sense of high stakes and intensity to the experience. This has a particular resonance within the realm of twenty-first-century digitalisation. On the one hand, failures or defects in live performance cannot be rectified as they could be, through editing, in video versions of the event published later. This creates a sense among embodied reader-audiences that they are experiencing a more authentically 'human' performance, with all its flaws, wrinkles and rough edges, than they would be likely to access online. On the other hand, the quick-response mode of social media, particularly Twitter, means that any failures in an embodied live performance can be shared with audiences outside the event at high speed, and then exaggerated or taken out of context. My ethnographies illuminate how a background awareness of the potential for failure has an impact for reader-audiences. There were no spectacular 'failures' in any of the events I observed and depicted in the ethnographies—though these do exist. An example might be when several people walked out of Lionel Shriver's infamous event at the Brisbane Writers Festival[18]—though it is quite likely that Shriver intended to trigger such a reaction, or at least foresaw it.

Even though manifest 'failures' on a grand scale seem to be rare in a live literature context, feeling underwhelmed by the experience is a more common form of failure. Reader-audiences often say that performed readings at events can be dull. They occasionally mention apparent flaws in individual performances, like facial or speech 'tics', as Stan and Kira observed in Philip Gross.

Notably, though, observations of personal flaws like this were often ultimately characterised *positively* by reader-audiences, as being evidence of the author-performer's '*authentic*' persona. In a post-event conversation, though, small, momentary flaws in performances are unlikely to be picked out by reader-audiences as worthy of mention—either because they are not remembered precisely, or because it might seem petty to mention them. Tiny flaws are present in almost every live literature event I have attended—and by this I mean things like an author-performer hesitating a bit awkwardly in an answer to a question, or fluffing part of a reading, or the chairperson almost forgetting to say something they meant to. I have described several of these moments in my ethnographies. To me, and I suspect to most reader-audiences, a scattering of small 'failures' of this nature is not only inevitable—it contributes to and *enhances* the sense of liveness and presence at a live literature events. If such flaws were to be perceived as dominant, or significant enough to interfere with a narrative or the presentation of the event, then that value might be diminished.

Participation in embodied live literature events clearly impacts on memory in resonant ways. Neuroscientific research has proved that embodied, live experiences enable reader-audiences not only to focus their attention but also to *retain* conveyed information better than other sources; and that this memory value has been enhanced by widespread digitalisation[19]—and my ethnographies corroborate this in a live literature context, suggesting that reader-audiences' memories of events are strong, and have real impacts on their future relationships with the books and author-performers presented, and on their broader literary and cultural practices, choices and values.

Reader-audience members often talk about how they experience a somatic or bodily, sensory memory of the live event when they go on to read the books presented silently, in their own time. The process acts as a conduit for re-accessing a memory of the author-performer's voice, pace and tone: many talked about hearing the authors' voice 'in their heads' while reading. This also shapes their judgements and evaluations of the texts.

None of this means that contemporary reader-audiences are consequently snubbing digital sources of literature *en masse* in favour of embodied experiences; or that they are abandoning digital modes of communication, information, culture or entertainment. It does not mean that reader-audiences are ceasing to use e-readers, to read literary reviews, to participate in social media literary groups, or even to watch videos of literary events. Far from it. Reader-audiences are constantly reacting to live events through digital devices and social media—posting pictures of literary festivals on Instagram, for example. It is not *despite* this integral role of digital communications in everyday life and literary culture, but *because* of it, that many feel that the experience of embodied live literature events is qualitatively different in terms of value: that its impact goes deeper, and extends for longer.

## Reader-Audiences: Conversation-Based Fiction Events: Dominance, Appeal, Inherent Issues

If you ask most people to describe a typical live literature event involving fiction, most will describe a conversation-based event: the typical event format at literary festival. In essence, as I discussed back in the prologue, this type of event usually involves at least two author-performers and a chairperson, who have a staged conversation about their recent books, probably each give a very short reading from those books, and then take audience questions. On the face of it, conversation-based live literature events appear to be based on the broad principle of informative introduction to literature—that is, both informing reader-audiences about the books being presented, and about author-performers' point of view and background. From a publisher's perspective, a key objective behind live literature events is to achieve a purchase 'conversion'.

And yet conversation-based events are not marketed as publicity presentations by event producers. Neither are they marketed as being solely informative events. From a reader-audience perspective, there is an ontological uncertainty around them; it is unclear whether they are supposed to be valued primarily as sources of education and information, or as entertainments or arts-based performances with their own aesthetic value. Notably, the performance element of these events is rarely emphasised, even though these events often include performed readings as well as performed conversations.

In my ethnographies, this uncertainty is reflected in terminology reader-audiences use when speaking with me about them. Many flitted between using the terms 'author', 'speaker' or even 'talker', and sometimes expressed uncertainty about which was right. They also veered between referring to the events themselves as 'talks' or 'events', and between referring to the text-based element as a 'reading' or a 'reading-aloud bit'. Few actually used the terms 'performer' or 'performance', even though many speak of their experiences in what are essentially performance terms, and manifested a clear consciousness of their audiencing role.

The notion of conversation-based fiction events as primarily *informative*, or educative, seems to contribute to an aversion of them on the part of some prolific and passionate fiction readers. For instance, Jo Glanville, at Hay, had difficulty with whole concept of live literature for this reason, suggesting that a focus on explication of literary writing in an event is a distraction from the core literary experience, which lies in the experience of silently reading the book in question. And many author-performers indicated that they would not themselves attend live literature events, as reader-audiences—unless those events formed part of a meta-event, like a festival, in which they were performing.

My ethnographic research reveals that there can be much more to reader-audience experience of conversation-based events than just being informed or educated, and that reader-audiences often want to have a more performative experience. Conversation-based events are always performances of a kind, even if they are not presented particularly performatively, which is often the case at literary events. For instance, at Hay, the quality of event presentation is generally extremely high, even though the format is undramatic and predictable.

There is a quality of liveness that is specific to the conversation elements of live literature events, and it hinges on a sense of unpredictability that is linked to *risk*. As Daniel Hahn emphasised, when an unscripted conversation is staged between two author-performers, who may never have met before, who may or may not get on with each other or have chemistry on stage, and who could be asked anything, and who might come out with anything—perhaps something unexpectedly controversial, or illuminating, or funny—this contributes to a *heightened sense of liveness*.

Conversation-based live literature events also function for some reader-audiences as a unique forum, within contemporary culture, to access trusted, inspirational and '*authentic*' insights on life and the worlds. This function bears many similarities to the ritual gathering involved in attending a religious ceremony, where a priest or guru imparts wisdom on life by speaking about or around the ideas contained in religious texts (also forms of literary narrative). Religion has a vastly diminished role in public life in the UK, and other Western countries, in the twenty-first century, and the increasing practice of attending a live literature event can be seen as a contemporary substitute.

The importance allotted to Q&A sessions, where author-performers are asked to present their views on multiple subjects, suggests that reader-audiences increasingly value live literature events as forums for *enlightenment* in the context of a widespread sense of distrust of politicians and other traditional sources of authority in the 'post-truth era'; and also in the digitalised era, where traditional sources of opinion, formerly trusted as being authoritative, are now challenged by a myriad alternative sources. The sense of being able to evaluate an author-performer's perceived authenticity, through embodied observation and evaluation of their presentation, in person, is a means of determining *trust*. When viewed in this way, it seems particularly ironic that the sharp decline in authors' incomes and the financial valuation of their work, which is linked to the devaluation of literary and other artistic work through digital piracy and the mass availability of alternatives online,[20] has been concurrent with an increase in authors' moral or 'truth-telling' currency.

There are some inherent difficulties with the conversation-based format for fiction events that come through my ethnographies—though these difficulties are more often articulated by chairpeople and event producers than by reader-audiences. One difficulty lies in the fact that the conversation-based format links to a perceived function of live literature events as forums for acquiring new knowledge about literature, as opposed to a means of *experiencing* literary work. This works well for non-fiction events, which tend to naturally facilitate wide-ranging conversations about the core subject matter of the book; but fiction rarely has such a clearly defined core subject matter. It is more fundamentally about the imagined characters and events that befall them, and its value turns on language and form of the writing in which the narrative is composed—that is, aesthetic qualities of the prose.

Event chairpeople tend to see it as a much steeper *challenge* to engage reader-audiences in fiction events, and to introduce them to new fictional worlds—particularly where there is a perceived risk of plot-spoiling by summarising the narrative. They are also often wary of being too esoteric for reader-audiences by going into detail in conversations about matters such as language and style. It is perceived as being easier for reader-audiences to talk about 'themes'—Daniel Hahn's bugbear—which consequently often dominate lines of questioning, even if the fiction being featured does not obviously address any particular theme.

Yet my research suggests another disjunction between perception and experience here: that reader-audiences rarely described the content of conversation-based fiction events as being too esoteric—even in the case of events in which questions of form, style and language were addressed in some depth. It may be that some of the perceived difficulties in this respect are, to an extent, caused by an underestimation of reader-audiences' capabilities or interests.

It is clearly easier to demonstrate the aesthetic literary qualities of a work of fiction via the inclusion of a performed reading in an event, rather than seeking to discuss those qualities solely through conversation, and yet my ethnographies show that the inclusion of performed readings is often perceived by chairpeople and event producers at literary festivals to be problematic and even risky.

There is a structural issue at play here: the fact that *the novel*—the dominant form of fiction in publishing and presented at live literature events—is generally far too long for anything longer than a fraction of it to be performed aloud in a single event. The *performed reading* is thus inevitably an *incomplete* rendering of the text as a whole, and yet it needs to function as a representative experience of encountering the novel. Performed readings from novels at conversation-based literary festival events often last under five minutes, which allows for approximately 750 spoken words, or 0.75% of a 100,000-word novel. There appears to be a common assumption among chairpeople and event producers, from my research, that the performed reading element does not add a great deal of value for reader-audiences, even though it is usually included as a gestural sample. My ethnographies lead me to challenge that assumption.

Having said that, the practical issue of being able to feature only a fraction of a novel in a performed reading, especially in the context of a conversation-based event, does pose the real problem of making the readings feel more like *token samples* than satisfying performances with aesthetic value in their own right. It was for this reason that, when conceiving of my own live literature project, I decided to feature short stories, in order to be able to stage fictional narratives with a complete story arc, as part of a quest to create a kind of event that was more inherently performative.

Another risk that chairpeople perceived in including performed readings in conversation-based events is that the readings will be dull, and will *bore* reader-audiences. Sometimes they are boring, and many reader-audiences testified to experiencing boredom on occasion. But, as I will expand upon below, there is a common misapprehension about *what makes a performed reading interesting and valuable*, from a reader-audience point of view—and it is not necessarily linked to a charismatic, theatrical delivery. Anxiety about the potential dullness of readings in events appears to be linked to the common, broad-brush *stereotype of authors* as introverts and poor performers of their work, who would far rather be sitting at home at their desk than performing—a stereotype that my research reveals is flawed. It also links to a perception of reader-audiences as having short attention spans, and little patience with being asked to step quickly into a brand-new fictional world through a performed reading, preferring 'easy', informal conversation—again, a perception that is often distorted.

Reader-audiences I spoke to tend to value the inclusion of performed readings in conversation-based events, even if the readings are short and only represent a fraction of the novel being presented—and even if they are not judged to be performed particularly 'well'. My conversation with Sarah and Katherine after Ishiguro's event at Hay is revealing in this respect: they expressed their disappointment that the event omitted a performed reading, and spoke warmly about readings they had experienced at past Hay events—citing one by Hanif Kureishi. They described how much that his performed reading added to their subsequent experience of reading his work silently, and to how they *felt* about his work, and his presence and persona as an author.

The dominance of conversation-based fiction events within the contemporary culture of live literature—and the minor, peripheral or absent role of performed readings within those events—means that many reader-audiences are led to assume that this is the default format; and that any performed reading element is only ever likely to be short and of minor importance. This is part of a wider under-appreciation of the role of performance generally in live literature. It risks having the catch-22 effect of causing author-performers to put less effort into their performed readings and conversations than they otherwise might.

There is also a gender dimension to the dominance of conversation-based events at literary festivals, and a linked sales dimension. Within literary festivals, non-fiction events tend to command larger audiences and are much more popular with male reader-audiences—which is unsurprising, as men are much less likely to read fiction.[21] Several men I spoke to among reader-audiences at literary festivals expressed their preference for non-fiction events in firm and absolute terms, often explaining it by stating that they liked *learning* from presentation-style events, as well as by making clear that they did not read fiction. Women reader-audience members, in contrast, tended both to be open to attending both fiction and non-fiction events, whether or not they came out with a clearly definable learning outcome. As such, it clearly makes financial sense for festival organisers to pay attention to providing non-fiction events; and it makes logistical sense to apply a standard event format to non-fiction and fiction books. But this does not necessarily cause fiction to receive its optimal presentation in performance.

## Reader-Audiences: The Role of the Q&A; Reader-Audiences as Performers

Q&A sessions with reader-audiences, a standard element of conversation-based live literature events, have also yielded some interesting insights.

The Q&A is often caricatured and mocked by literary commentators, on the basis that reader-audiences often either ask bizarre or apparently tangential questions, or even fail to ask a question at all, instead beginning with the familiar refrain: 'It's more of a comment than a question…' This phenomenon was satirised in an article for McSweeney's by Evan Williams, titled 'The art of asking a question to a literary festival panel'[22]:

> The key to asking a successful question to a literary festival panel is preparation. You'll want to have every detail of the preface to your question prepared, such as your name, age, and entire medical history. Don't worry about the actual question; you can make that up as you go along.
>
> Once you finally find the microphone after several doomed attempts to follow the clear directions of the host, you're going to want to cut short your unprompted analysis of how your eczema has influenced your approach to creative nonfiction to ask an important question:
>
> Can the sound guy give you some more foldback, please? You really need some more foldback for when you ask your actual question.

There is clearly an element of literary-cultural snobbery here: an expectation that, just because the event has involved a discussion framed as being about a literary text, the question should therefore be expressed intelligently and concisely, and should engage with a novel aspect or the text presented, or the conversation that has been performed around that text; and a judgement that most questions fail to reach that hurdle.

My ethnographies, though, suggest that Q&As do not often conform to the usual caricature. At Hay, reader-audience questioning tended to be fairly closely engaged with the preceding staged conversation or reading. And the majority of Q&A sessions I have witnessed at other conversation-based live literature events also frequently involve reader-audience members asking pertinent questions that arise from the conversation or performed text, or that seek to explore other matters that are in some way literary.

Often, my research shows, reader-audience members' questions imply that the questioner is an aspiring author; there are frequently questions about methods of editing and routes to publication, as well as daily writing routines. Some of these same questions, of course, can be attributed to a generalised curiosity about creative processes, rather than as a quest for personal writing advice. Sources of inspiration is another very common subject; the question 'Where do you get your ideas from?' was discussed by Ursula K. Le Guin in an essay titled: 'The question I get asked most often'.[23]

Having said that, the Q&A sessions can certainly result in bizarre questions, and commentaries that do not contain any obvious question at all. The question Gavin Extence was asked about a kebab house in Sheffield is one example mentioned in this book. It was initially surprising to me that people would fairly regularly begin to ask a question, even as part of a huge audience, at an event that is being filmed for public broadcast, when they clearly had not yet worked out what it is they really wanted to say.

Also, as the stereotype suggests, Q&A sessions do occasionally encourage certain people to speak out who do not appear to be closely engaged with the texts, or with any literary elements of the staged conversation, but who feel a need to publicly air their opinion or even their voice publicly, and want to take the Q&A opportunity to do so. Notable in my ethnographies—perhaps to an exceptional degree—was Diana, at Hay, who told me that the *sole reason* she had attended a certain event (non-fiction, I note) was in order to have the opportunity to ask 'her' question. She was furious when someone else got in there first.

Whatever is asked, or said, at a Q&A session, the session inevitably adds a significant table-turning dimension to a live literature event, effectively reversing the established power relations. Reader-audience members who do take up the opportunity to speak are effectively transformed into reader-performers themselves, for a short time, transforming the author-performer into a member of the audience in turn. This gestures towards democracy, making the event in some way comparable to a Habermasian public sphere.[24] As an embodied, participatory event, this is a rare phenomenon in contemporary digitalised society, where communities are increasingly fractured. This arguably makes the Q&A element of live literature events even more valuable for reader-audiences. It gives questioners a sense that they have a public voice that deserves to be heard.

The Q&A session is valued by many reader-audience members even if they do *not* ultimately choose to ask a question themselves, because it offers the sense that they have the *opportunity* to engage directly in the event—and this potential agency intensifies their engagement. Recent neuroscientific research confirms the reward value for audiences of having the opportunity to interact directly in an event[25]; and, again, this was borne out in my live literature research. I found that even those reader-audience members who do not usually like to ask questions themselves were rarely opposed to the practice of Q&As. Conversely, most felt that Q&As were an important element of those events.

Even contributions to Q&A sessions that are perceived as bizarre or rambling can therefore be considered valuable: they are an active form of collective, democratised participation. They illustrate the diversity of the reader-audience, and the sheer *unpredictability* of what any single member might contribute. They not only create a sense of risk that is linked to an enhanced sense of liveness; but they give the reader-audience a more concrete sense of themselves as a collective, living entity. Regardless of the *content* of the contributions made, *vocal qualities* of audience contributions, like accent and tone of voice—qualities that are so important in reader-audiences' evaluations of author-performers—are manifested in the multivocal diversity of questions asked. This too creates a tangible sense of community.

Polari is an example of a live literature event that deliberately eschews Q&A. In Polari's case, this appears to have two main purposes—beyond host Paul Burston's personal dislike of them, that is. The first purpose is to make the whole event more performative through its structure, by focusing on the performed readings, and eschewing discussion. The second purpose, in Polari's case, seems to be to avoid the kinds of direct, often political and tense, emotive debates around LGBTQ+ issues deriving from broader social marginalisation of LGBTQ+ -identifying people, and divisions within LGBTQ+ communities. The focus on performed fiction readings successfully operates, at Polari, to make the reader-audience feel like a diverse-yet-united community: a collective of people who have come together for a shared experience of literary narratives in performance—narratives that have power precisely because, to the extent that they approach those political issues, they do so 'sideways' through literature, in a way that is less likely to trigger divisive debate, and more likely to trigger feelings of empathy.

## Reader-Audiences: Performed Readings: Theatricality, Boredom, Authenticity, Interpretation

As I have suggested: reader-audiences are likely to value performed reading readings at live literature events highly—much more highly than is often assumed. Despite this, most of the event chairpeople I spoke to during my research were wary of including performed readings in conversation-based events unless they are extremely short. Specifically, they worried that reader-audiences were likely to find the readings *boring*. Throughout my research, and not just at Hay, this perceived risk of boredom was often given as a reason by event producers and chairpeople for minimising or cutting performed readings from live literature events.

This wariness of inviting performed readings was often linked to a common stereotype of authors as being inherently unlikely to be good performers. Many expressed this empathetically, by making clear that they did not *expect* authors to be good performers, since that role had essentially been thrust upon them with the rise of live literature. Ultimately—so the line goes—authors are happiest as hermit figures, and prefer retreating into a solitary place to write to being on stage, and so live literature events are simply not their natural habitat. My research suggests that the hermit personality stereotype is usually, though not always, inaccurate—and that even author-performers who consider themselves introverts usually enjoy performing at live literature events.

The Polari salon, an event that is structured primarily around performed readings, and contains no performed conversation or Q&A, works extremely well for reader-audiences. Polari reader-audience members only occasionally complain of dullness, even though performed readings at Polari are far longer than they almost ever are in conversation-based events.

It seems that some chairpeople and producers are ware of performed readings based on assumptions about what defines a 'good' performance: assumptions aligned to what they would expect from an actor in a theatrical production. But reader-audiences' do not necessarily evaluate performed readings in this way. Unsurprisingly, a monotonous, mumbling or error-ridden reading is likely to be evaluated negatively by reader-audiences. But this does not mean that its opposite—a slick, energetic and theatrical performance of fiction—is always the kind of performance that will be deemed successful, valuable or meaningful.

Sometimes it is; many performed readings I observed to be on the theatrical end of the delivery spectrum were effusively received. During many post-event conversations, reader-audiences expressed glowing praise of readings they had witnessed, occasionally expressing a wish that the reading had lasted longer. At Hay, for instance, Andrew O'Hagan's blazing, performative rendering of a scene from his novel was relished by the reader-audience seemed to relish; the same is true of Stella Duffy's performance at Polari.

In contrast, Simon Armitage is an example of an author-performer whose performed readings generated an equally if not more effusive response—and yet his delivery style is very different to O'Hagan's; it is far more understated in its performativity. To me, neither one was *better* than the other—but Armitage's delivery style in his performed reading reflected his general demeanour and dead-pan humour, as well as his lyrical literary style; whereas O'Hagan's dynamic, fast-paced style was both appropriate to the scene and to his energetically witty self-presentation. In line with this, my ethnographies reveal that a vital factor for reader-audiences in evaluating whether a performed reading is successful, valuable and meaningful is whether they perceive it to be *authentic*. By that I mean, in part, an authentic rendering of the text—but, more importantly, an authentic version of the text as it is imagined by the author-performer, and that reveals something of the author-performer's personality, as well as the intention behind the text. 'Authentic' performance, in a live literature context, appears to trump an overtly skilled or confident performance.

Reader-audiences are subtle judges of verbal communication and paralanguage when evaluating performed speech, and this includes readings. They 'read' performed readings at live events, combing them for authenticity, among other qualities—whether or not they are able to articulate this in detail in subsequent conversations. Even an author-performer who is perceived by reader-audiences as being relatively vulnerable or uncomfortable with being on stage—who may, for instance, struggle to generate laughter responses so successfully as other author-performers—may still be evaluated positively by reader-audiences after a performed reading, so long as reader-audiences interpret their disposition as being authentic. A slightly halting performance might be characterised as endearing, or as 'human', and the author-performer and book in question, and the event as a whole, may be evaluated positively—perhaps even more highly.

Reader-audience members tend to feel that experiencing an 'authentic' performed reading enhances and *aids their interpretation* of the literary text—even if they cannot put their finger on exactly how. Performed readings are experienced by many as a kind of channel that enables them to gain a sense that they have accessed *authorial intention* in a meaningful way, as well as other elements of the author-performer's 'true' voice and character, all of which are felt to inform a fuller understanding and evaluation of their work.

I was struck by how often reader-audiences referred to *sound and rhythm* in describing why performed readings mattered to them. Many spoke about being affected by a combination of elements beyond the text as it would be encountered on the page, including prosodic qualities like tone of voice, accent, pitch and speech, as well as timing and sense of humour. Finding the humour in a text was frequently cited as a benefit of hearing the author-performer read it aloud at a live event: when collective audience laughter is experienced, this contributes to an sense of being able to 'correctly' identify the humour in the text, alongside others who are 'reading' it the same way. This can lead to a greater sense of authenticity in relation to the author-performer's intentions and can shift evaluations of quality too. Similarly, several reader-audience members commented that performed readings helped with their more straightforward quest to *comprehend* the texts.

Reader-audience members often commented on how the experience of performed readings affected their experiences of reading books silently to themselves after the event—notably, often through an experience of hearing the sound of an author-performer's voice in their heads: a version of Denise Riley's 'inner voice'.[26] This is often felt to be a meaningful and significant impact of a performed reading; the memory of the voice is often described viscerally, and seems to be experienced almost as if the ghost of the author-performer has accompanied the reader-audience member from the event to their chosen reading spot.

Collectively, these effects and impacts of performed readings are significant.

But not all performed readings are deemed to be successful and valuable by reader-audiences, even if they *are* interpreted as providing a sense of authenticity. I have witnessed plenty of performed readings that I would characterise as awkward and stumbling, usually because they were clearly unpractised, and appeared to have been approached with a lack of care—to the point where, as a reader-audience member, I became disengaged with the performance, and consequently with related reflections on its interpretation. Many reader-audience members have mentioned to me in conversation that, from their experience, performed readings do not 'always' work well, 'can' be boring—and can serve to put them off reading the book. I note that I did not encounter any reader-audience member at Hay, or at Polari, who dismissed a reading they had just witnessed as being boring—or, at least, who felt comfortable naming names.

Despite perceiving a very limited risk of outright boredom from performed readings, I found reader-audiences to be highly likely to be positive about the *potential* value of the experience of a performed reading. They tend to be open to the risk of being disappointed by a performed reading, without necessarily judging the event itself negatively—so long as the *evaluation process* that that the experience provided was engaging.

There is clearly another disjunction here between what is often assumed about reader-audience experiences, and what they actually experience—and, importantly, what they value about that experience. There may be many reasons for reader-audiences to judge a performed reading as being less engaging than another, including the quality of the text and the clarity of delivery—but a root cause is quite likely to be cultural. The *act of performing readings* is so often *under-valued*—not just by author-performers, but producers and publishers too—the author-performer in question is quite likely not to have practised in advance, or to have given the performance any careful thought. This is arguably a symptom of a wider perception of live literature as a form of publicity, education and information; rather than as a form of performance and reader-audience experience.

It is illuminating to compare what reader-audiences value in experiencing performed readings by author-performer at live literature events and in listening to performed audiobook readings by actors. The history of the early 'talking books' reveals that there was extensive debate in their early days over what made a good reading of a novel, as opposed to a play script.[27] The broad consensus was that the best readings 'serve the text' and should *not* be approached in the same way as a theatrical performance; the delivery should be less heightened, allowing the language and narrative to speak more for itself. This sentiment is echoed in my ethnographies, articulated by Simon Armitage and others. At live literature events, actors are almost *never* invited to perform extracts of an author's book.

When I suggested to reader-audiences the hypothetical prospect of an actor performing readings at the event instead of an author-performer, they invariably looked surprised. However, many also stated that they listened to audiobooks regularly, and that these are often narrated by actors. When I offered these people a hypothetical choice between an author and an actor performing a recorded version of the text for an audiobook, many felt that an actor would probably be likely to do a better job—but that this would depend on who the author/actor in question was and how he or she read. This suggests that the visual, embodied connection with the author-performer at a live literature event is often material to the way in which their performed readings are evaluated.

My conversation at Hay with Stan and Kira about Toni Morrison provides an illuminating example of how audiobooks are valued differently to live literature events. Both had witnessed Morrison perform a reading from her novel at a Hay event, years before, during which Morrison had critiqued a version of her audiobook recorded by an actor, telling the audience that it had been 'done all wrong'. They had subsequently listened to her reading her own audiobook. They both concluded, with certainty, that witnessing Morrison perform at the live event was vitally important experience for their future readings of her work, and how they *valued* her work, particularly because the sense it gave them of her *rhythm*. But they also felt that, over the length of an entire audiobook, Morrison's performance lacked clarity, and an actor's narration may have been preferable.

More performative events like Polari, which tend to emphasise performed readings, seem to be on the rise. As I outlined at the start of the book, there are many different forms of live literature now springing up, some of which experiment with performance in new ways. My own live literature project, Ark, is one example; but there are now many more, ranging from literary entertainment nights to theatre shows to live art performances. However, reader-audiences at the more mainstream literary festivals are often unaware that such 'other' forms of live literature exist. With the exception of performed poetry, live literature is rarely considered on its own terms as a genre.

But some influential author-performers may be starting to shift this perspective. Neil Gaiman's work, including the curation of events such as *The Truth is a Cave in the Black Mountains,* a short story he wrote and performed with a live string quartet and large-scale animation, represents an outstanding example of this creative approach to the practice of live literature. Notably, Gaiman explicitly defines himself, not as a novelist, or even as a writer or author, but as a storyteller.[28] This enables him to deliberately straddle multiple genres and artforms, and to challenge normative assumptions about the scope of literary-cultural practices. Reader-audiences clearly relish this.

## Reader-Audiences: Meanings of the Book-Signing Ritual

The practice of book-signing after live literature events is central to many forms of live literature. It certainly takes place at all literary festivals I have attended, and also at other literary events, including Polari, usually after a purchase 'conversion' at the event bookstall or bookshop.

While the practice of book signing might appear trivial, and is certainly assumed to be so by some in the literary industry—notably James Daunt, who admitted that he still doesn't 'get it'—and while it is certainly directly linked to the commercial objectives of selling books at events—my research suggests that the book signing process is important to many reader-audience members, and is often experienced as a meaningful form of ritual. A great many participate in it, despite the cost of buying a book to be inscribed—usually a hardback—on top of an event ticket.

I had never had an interest in obtaining signed copies of books before beginning this research, but I have since had several new books signed at the end of events. My experience chimes to some extent with what reader-audiences have told me in conversation, and what I have observed at book-signing sessions. The purchased book serves as a personalised memento of the event that effectively materialises the text presented in the event. It will be read silently at some point after the event, and trigger ongoing associations with the event including, perhaps, 'hearing' the author-performer's voice while reading. The process of signing involves a direct, one-to-one encounter with the author-performer at close proximity, which is likely to involve the reader-audience member sharing their name and a snippet of their personal experience with the author-performer, which might touch upon their relationship to the author-performer's work and how they enjoyed the event. Witnessing their own name being written down in the author-performer's own handwriting, perhaps with a personalised message reflecting and documenting the brief conversation, is akin to a witnessing process at a wedding ceremony. As a ritualistic process, it can strengthen the sense of connection that the reader-audience member has with the author-performer, deepen their memory of the event, and impact on their reading experience and affect their evaluation process.

## Reader-Audiences: Community and Diversity: Emotional, Social and Interpersonal Experience at Live Literature Events

Experiencing a live literature event can generate in reader-audiences a significant sense of interpersonal connection and emotional community.

Many of my conversations reveal the ways in which the experience of live literature events worked to deepen reader-audiences' relationships with friends and family. For instance, at Hay, Dave and Clive each talked to me about coming with their family to the festival every year, and valuing it as a unique place for them to bond by sharing a collective experience. They would go off and see their own individual events if they wanted to, according to their respective interest, and would then reconvene between events to share accounts. Similarly, Sal and Jo attended Polari regularly together as a way of both celebrating and deepening their relationship through a shared literary-cultural experience at an event which, through its LGBTQ+ emphasis, explicitly values and supports same sex relationships like theirs.

Reader-audiences often value the *community* element of being part of an audience at a live literature event, even if they do go with friends or know anyone else there personally. It is easy to observe a sense of collective connection at live literature events, from the ways in which people react and behave during performances—leaning forward, smiling, laughing, for instance—to ways in which they speak and interact after the events, both between themselves and in conversations with me. Simply being part of an embodied reader-audience gives many people a sense of being actively included in a form of community, whether or not they actually interact with each other directly or verbally. The intangible sensation of this experience has also been evidenced in neuroscientific research through the synchrony of audience responses at live events.[29]

At both at Hay and Polari, many reader-audience members emphasised how the experience of participating felt like being part of a group of like-minded people, through a shared interest in reading—even if, as at Hay, they confessed that they might not actually meet or talk to anybody they didn't already know. As such, live literature events create a sense of a physical 'interpretive community' that affects each participant's ongoing interpretations and evaluations of the text and author-performer, via shared memories—thus creating a sense of an ongoing 'mnemonic community', or a community of memory.[30]

An annual festival like Hay leads many repeat visitors to experience a ritualistic repetition of participation over decades. This can lead them to feel part of a deeper, longer-term community than they might at other festivals—even though many would not recognise other repeat visitors given the scale of the festival.

The significance of the community element of participation was distinctly heightened at Polari. This is not just because Polari is a far smaller and more regular event than Hay, so that reader-audiences are more likely to recognise each other visually; it is also because the sense of a community defines the founding principles and continuing identity of the salon, in the context of wider LGBTQ+ marginalisation in society. This was clearly manifested through the interactions I observed between regular reader-audience members, many of whom recognised each other and chatted to each other during the interval, and before and after the performance, and it emerged through conversations too. Polari's clear sense of community is attributable not only to a shared interest in LGBTQ+ literature, and shared identity concerns; but also to the way in which the event is hosted and produced by Burston, which actively fosters a sense of camaraderie. Most participants in Polari experience a strong sense of 'emotional community'.[31]

That said, this has the converse effect making participants who may be newer or less regular, feel excluded. At Polari, the obvious familiarity between people who were long-term regulars made some individuals, like

Dom, feel slightly left out from what was perceived to be a 'clique'. But despite feeling that way, Dom still perceived the event to be generally friendly and welcoming. Notably, for some at Polari, like Clara, a strong sense of a diverse community was in direct comparison to their perception of how they anticipated that they would feel at a literary festival: while Clara was delighted by her experience of Polari, she would still '*never* want to go to a literary festival' because it would be 'too white and middle-class': a dominant category of community that she did not want to identify with.

Diversity is a key issue in contemporary literary culture—as in culture generally—and affects any notion of community. Literary festivals, as the most dominant form of live literature, are widely perceived to be insufficiently diverse, not only in terms of race, but also in terms of other minority categories. In contrast, part of the way in which Polari is valued by reader-audiences is in its role as a forum that *contests* the deficit in LGBTQ+ representation in mainstream publishing and literary culture. This links back to Burston's original motivation in founding Polari.

Diversity has been the subject of much discussion in the media in relation to literary festivals, including in relation to Hay. It has also become a major issue within the publishing industry generally. Increasing campaigns and initiatives in the publishing industry over the years that have sought to increase diversity, particularly in relation to race, but also in relation to class. However, as important recent research by Ramdarshan Bold, Saha and others shows, the diversity deficit in publishing continues to be marked and significant, with neither enough authors or fictional characters of colour being represented in any genre.[32] This causes literary culture to be perceived by many as alienating and excluding, and damages its cultural relevance and value.

My Hay ethnography reveals how closely the big literary festivals are connected to the publishing industry. Because of this, the lack of diversity on festival stages is interconnected with that wider publishing industry problem. However, it is clearly not the reason for it. Each event director, producer or curator is ultimately responsible for the structure, characterisation and publicity of their own event, and for ensuring its diversity.[33] Inadequate diversity affects not only perceptions of live literature and literary culture, but substance, too. It does not only manifest itself in which authors get exposure, but which literary texts get published, and which get written in the first place. It also affects the subject matter and characters in the texts, and the language and form in which they are addressed. It affects which readers gain access to those texts, and how much cultural impact literary texts and their authors are likely to have. Hay has not historically been sufficiently diverse to reflect the population,[34] and the same applies to most other literary festivals.

Fortunately, now, Hay and all literary festivals I know of are actively seeking to improve their diversity, in part by attending to the curation of their programmes to include more ethnically diverse author-performers. There is clearly a long way still to go. Some festivals are leading the way in terms of diversity. In the UK, the Bradford Literature Festival[35] explicitly foregrounds ethnic diversity, and is an example of curation which has energetically and adeptly responded to the wider diversity challenge. A relatively young festival, Bradford has sought to be more representative of its local community, and in particular its large population with an Asian heritage. While doing so, it has also shown itself willing to confront themes that may not be immediately seem likely to be popular with large audience numbers.

This live literature research process has reinforced my sense that, if literary culture is going to thrive, particularly in a digital age with so many competing forms of entertainment, aesthetic engagement and information, it is imperative that it diversifies more, to be more representative of the wider population—and live literature is a vital element of that project.

## Reader-Audiences: Identity, Authenticity and Cultural Appropriation; the Role/Problem of Live Literature

The issue of diversity is linked to issues of identity and cultural appropriation in fiction: all issues that raise complex questions and cause tensions that swirl through contemporary literary culture.[36] How do they affect the cultural value of literature, and of live literature events? What implications do they have for fiction events, specifically?

Fiction inherently entails imaginative invention. It necessarily allows for narrators and characters to be 'made up' in ways that do not necessarily correspond with an author's own autobiography or background. The idea of cultural appropriation limits the extent to which authors of fiction should legitimately do that, thus. The current debates around cultural appropriation highlight the role of the author and their biography in relation to their fiction, and points to a broader 'resurrection of the author' in literary culture.[37]

Live literature—particularly conversation-based forms such as most festival events—serves to 'resurrect the author' still further, since conversations inevitably interrogate the inspiration for the fictional text, and its connection to, or divergence from, the author-performer's 'real' biography. The questions, and the answers, clearly impact on how reader-audiences interpret and value the work. Not only do conversation-based live literature events provide for such questions to be discussed, but they also provide additional 'clues' to the relationship between the author and their text, for instance in their vocal qualities such as accent, rhythm and timing. These are elements of communication that are not necessarily manifest in the text on the page, but are inevitably manifest in a live event. My ethnographies show that these elements do affect reader-audiences, including in their determinations of 'authenticity' and their evaluations of the texts presented. Reader-audiences tend to assume, uncritically, that it is always legitimate to explore links between an author-performer and their fictional characters and texts.

If taken to an extreme, an emphasis on identity-based authenticity, based on links between the author and their fiction, would throw into doubt the future legitimacy and cultural role of fiction altogether—in the sense of an author being able to freely invent voices other than their own, and to have their work positively valued. Lionel Shriver made this point in her controversial and deliberately provocative speech at the Brisbane Writers Festival—but her failure to acknowledge the real diversity deficits in the publishing industry that lie behind identity representation issues, and her ridiculing of concerns about diversity, distorted the reality, and unsurprisingly prompted a furious backlash.[38]

The issue of cultural appropriation has arguably changed the whole direction of fiction, even pointing towards a negation of its value. As critic Anthony Cummins has put it, the rise of autofiction can be seen as a means for authors to 'sidestep an increased nervousness about cultural appropriation as well as imagining the lives of others, something novelists – not least those of the state-of-the-nation variety – once took for granted'.[39] Author-performers who opt not to participate in conversation-based live literature events, or to otherwise discuss the relationship between their fiction and their 'real' identities publicly, like Elena Ferrante, can be hounded for it.[40]

Polari is a rare example of a live literature event with a specific mission to engage with diversity deficits in literary culture relating to LGBTQ+ issues, and yet it is also an event that comprehensively avoids *compelling* reader-audiences to draw links between authorial biography and fiction, by keeping the event open to author-performers who write about LGBTQ+ issues as well as those who identify as LGBTQ+, and also by omitting conversation and Q&A as part of the event format.

Of course literary festivals and comparable conversation-based events are not solely to blame for incidents like Elena Ferrante's hounding by journalists seeking to reveal her 'real' identity; this is the result of a much wider cultural shift. It can be seen as both a consequence of global digital media, and the way in which social media, in particular, has raised expectations of how much audiences should get to know about the personal lives and opinions of artists and other public figures and celebrities—and also the way in which globalisation has led to a heightened awareness of identity, diversity and representation across culture. In literary culture, this has manifested itself in the increasingly heated debate over cultural appropriation and an increasing preoccupation with authorial voice and identity.

But the dominance of the literary festival and of conversation-based literary events based on the literary festival model contribute in a real way to a literary-cultural shift towards *identity-based authenticity* as a factor in determining literary value. The impact ripples out—it shapes these ongoing literary-cultural debates, and it affects the ways in which fiction is experienced, perceived and valued by its reader-audiences. It

even shapes the ways in which literature is composed and published—
which leads me onto the next set of key insights: those relating to
author-performers.

# Key Insights: Author-Performers

## Author-Performers: An Overview

Author-performers are at the heart of live literature events. Yet they are
often not paid for their performances.[41] And they often don't think
much about them, or prepare for them in terms of performance—
because of the culture and the narratives around live literature events.

Not much has been written about what literary authors think and feel
about contemporary literary culture, or how they feel about performing
at live events. I felt it was vital, in my ethnographies, to incorporate
author-performer's perspectives and experiences, as an element of participation, and to relate and compare them to reader-audiences' perspectives
and experiences. This yielded an array of interesting insights.

As an author of fiction myself, and as part of various author networks,
I know that authors often have a variety of vulnerabilities and insecurities
around their public personas and live literature performances that are
unlikely to be divulged in the context of a conversation at an event. But
one of the key insights from my research is that most author-performers
enjoy the experience of literary events, or at least find them rewarding,
regardless of those insecurities—certainly more than is often assumed by
publishers and journalists who frequently caricature authors as introverts.

## Author-Performers: Live Literature and Career
## Impact: Pressures and Tensions; Payment and Value;
## Author Networks

Many author-performers see live literature events as a duty that forms
part of their contemporary role as an author of written texts: a duty
that many veterans—by which I mean people who were publishing

their work before the twenty-first-century live literature boom—say has fundamentally changed the shape of their writing careers. Even more recently-published authors sometimes admit to an initial degree of surprise about the extent to which participation in live literature is expected of them by their publishers after their book comes out.

Having said that, very few debut novelists, as Gavin Extence was when I spoke to him, are championed enough by big publishers to enable them to get onto the Hay stage. It is important to note that, at Hay, the picture of author-performer experience in this respect is distorted relative to the experience of the majority of author-performers. Those who are selected to appear on Hay stages are likely to be those at the top of their publishers' promotion agenda: a position that is likely to be linked to the size of their advance payments, and they are consequently likely to be scheduled to perform at a great many other, smaller-scale live literature events in the year of their book's release. In contrast, authors who are lower down the priority list for their publishers, or who are published by smaller presses with smaller advance payments linked to smaller marketing and publicity budgets, will need to seek out more events for themselves.

This does not mean that those authors feel any less expectation or duty to perform; quite the opposite, in fact. There is a general understanding among contemporary authors that they are *required* to be author-performers alongside their writing, at least to some extent, in order to succeed, and that the more events they manage to appear in, the more copies of their books are likely to be sold, which will improve their chances of having future books published, and generally, enhance their books' reception and their career prospects.

Consequently, author-performers feel under increasing pressure to sell their books through live literature events, particularly festivals. They experience pressure to be *invited* to appear at them, and they have feelings of inadequacy and disappointment if they are not invited—especially by the bigger literary festivals. Such invitations are clearly experienced as markers of cultural capital within the literary industry—as reflected in my conversation with Colm *Tóibín*, who admitted that he was only glad to be invited to perform at events because otherwise he would feel he were *not* being invited—the implication being that this would signify that his work had been devalued. Conversely, Paul Burston started the Polari salon partly in frustration that he had published several novels but had *not* been invited to perform at a literary event: something he felt was linked to his LGBTQ+ identity; consequently, he feels he has a moral duty to give a platform to new and unsung LGBTQ+ writers.

Authors often cite a tension between the expectation of self-publicity through live events, the time this effort takes, and the outward-facing perspective it demands on the one hand; and, on the other hand, their need to focus on writing the next book. Many of the most successful authors, in sales terms, who are the most in demand for events and embark on lengthy international book tours, tend to feel an exacerbation of that tension and a burden upon their personal lives—though they do it regardless, aware of the benefit in book sales and career terms. Ali Smith navigates the balance by writing each book in four months of a year and doing events only outside that time[42]—but then Ali Smith's writing has well-established popular and critical acclaim for her writing, which, in my view, is very well-deserved on its own terms. Few authors I have spoken to are—or feel able to be—quite so rigorous about organising their time (or so capable of writing a brilliant novel in four months).

The tension relating to time-management and attention is compounded by the concurrent pressure of expectation upon authors to perform their authorial personas digitally, online and through social media. As author Lan Samantha Chang put, it in an article about how difficult it is for writers to protect their 'inner lives': 'new authors… are threatened that their book will fail unless they keep tweeting, giving readings (if they are lucky), reading reviews (if they are lucky) and writing dozens of small articles and Q&As that will stay online forever'[43]—revealing the psychological impact of this combined publicity expectation. 'Book publication is more public than it has ever been', Chang continues. 'It is public information that one's book has or has not been touted as a book to watch out for on certain websites, or has/has not made certain favourite lists or sales lists, or a hundred end of the year lists. This is not to mention the prize season, which can make the writer lucky enough to be a finalist feel like a runner-up in a beauty pageant'.[44]

To add to the impact of all this pressure, authors have faced a steep income decline over recent years, and consequently, even the most successful author-performers often genuinely need the money that live literature events can provide through appearance fees. And yet many events do not offer fees. Not getting paid for appearing at the big literary festivals, where ticket costs are high, diminishes author-performers' sense of self-worth and value, even if the cultural capital gained is high— hence the British Society of Authors' campaign, and Phillip Pullman's act of protest, against festivals that invite authors to participate without payment.[45]

Most authors expect to be asked to perform without payment in small venues, particularly bookshops, which are notoriously cash-strapped in the era of Amazon, as a form of both self-publicity and book sales and support to the shops. In return, it is hoped that the shops will put more effort into promoting the author's books. Some bookshops, despite the difficulty of making bookselling pay, still find ways to pay authors for their time in doing events that does not involve cash—as I was grateful to find when I was invited to perform by Daunt Books, Hampstead, and was presented with a generous credit voucher in the form of a postcard. But the majority do not. Nor do many live literature events beyond festivals. Polari does not pay author-performers for its Southbank events—though Burston was apologetic about this, and pointed out that there is a bookstall to sell copies. Author-performers are now paid for Polari's on-tour events outside London, which are funded by ACE.

There is clearly a balance to be struck between keeping the ticket price down and supporting author-performers. To many authors, the balance feels unfair when it results in no payment. But most will, as I did, agree to perform at live literature events for free, encouraged by the knowledge that a book stall will be present, and acutely aware of the importance of their sales figures for any future book deals—even though, financially, they are likely to get negligible royalties from book sales at any single event.

Author-performers also participate in live literature because of its function as a network opportunity: a forum where they can connect with each other and cultivate a wider and more meaningful literary community. As my ethnographies show, this is manifest most obviously in green rooms, which are often greenhouses for literary gossip. I have stayed in touch with several author-performers whom I met through shared events, including events in bookshops without green rooms—and have valued that connection hugely. It creates a sense of solidarity and even teamwork in what is otherwise a generally-solitary line of work, marked by pressures relating to income, publicity and sales.

There is now a multitude of online author networks, on Facebook and through other forms of social media, that offer a similar support and solidarity function for authors, even if they do not get the opportunity to meet in person at live events. In my experience, many authors value these networks highly, as respite for the constant pressure to sell books and get good reviews, and to be publicly present, both in the media, and live at events.

## Author-Performers: Connecting with Reader-Audiences and the Authorial Persona: Persona vs. Personality; Social Media vs. Live; Community vs. Diversity

Participation often causes author-performers to gain a deeper sense of connection with their reader-audiences. As my conversation with Gavin Extence illustrates, this connection is usually experienced as being rewarding for writers at any level or fame, even if they do not consider themselves to be natural performers with a committed readership.

The embodied presence of a reader-audience creates a tangible sense of a readership that is otherwise invisible, and that can appear distant or even non-existent during the low or anxious moments in most authors' lives and careers, when they feel under pressure in relation to book sales and reviews, at a point when the content of the book is unalterable and the reception is varied or uncertain. It is like witnessing an interpretive community materialise.

As I illustrated in the prologue, describing my own experience of performing from my novel among an audience and seeing, sensing and hearing their feedback, this experience can make a book's impact on the world feel far more tangible and meaningful for author-performers. There is a sense of empowerment bound up with this experience, which can be rare in a post-publication phase that is often characterised by behind-the-scenes vulnerability and anxiety.

Social media has added a new dimension to the post-publication experience, in terms of reader-audience connection—and its impact is double-edged for many authors. Reader responses are far easier to access than they used to be, in the form of online reviews, including reviews from readers who are geographically distant to the author. Positive reader responses can be heart-warming and gratifying for authors, as another route to accessing a sense of the value and impact of their work, and a tangible insight into the distinct ways in which the book has moved or otherwise resonated with individual readers. Soon after the hardback publication of my own novel, I was contacted through my website by a man who had long been resident in Singapore who had just picked up my novel randomly in a bookshop and loved it, even though it was not the kind of book he would usually read, and felt sufficiently moved to get in touch—I had been unaware that the book was even being sold in Singapore, and the sense of gratitude I felt at his message has stayed with me.

However, as with so many social media narrative patterns, online reader responses can be negative, nonsensical, wildly insulting, vindictive, peculiar, misguided or all of the above—in ways that not only upset authors, and do not offer constructive criticisms, but are experienced by authors as actively destructive to their self-esteem and to their future careers. Online reviewers often appear to feel more liberated about being strongly critical through digital anonymity, or simply in view of the likelihood they will never have to meet the author in person and be confronted about their comments. A tweet by the novelist Celeste Ng illustrates this:

> Hi, quick PSA [public service announcement]: you have every right to not like a book, and every right to say whatever you want about it. But please don't tag the author if you didn't like it. It serves no purpose other than to be rude. We are humans with feelings too. Thanks! [46]

She was responding to a tweet by a reader (whose identity she blacked out) which read:

> Did NOT like "Little Fires Everywhere" by @prounounced_ing.
> Well-written and an interesting story – but it infuriated me when it came to adoption, a mother's love and interracial
> family dynamics. However, it made me appreciate
> my upbringing even more: 0 stars #books #family[47]

After Ng's tweet got over 5,000 likes and a lot of engagement, she posted a follow-up:

> Aw, thank you all for the kind words. My ego is fine, honestly— putting this out there because I know this stuff happens a lot, to a LOT of writers, and I figure a reminder to be kind to each other never hurts.[48]♥

It has become clear to me through my own author networks that many authors frequently experience strong emotions of upset and self-doubt after reading strongly negative or personally-insulting online reader reviews; yet, understandably, rarely publicise such feelings.

Notably, in contrast to this social media realm, I found that live literature events are far more likely to result in positive responses from reader-audiences, or at least in more sensitively and constructively-expressed criticisms. This is partly because they have usually invested more in their attendance of an event, in terms of both time and money, so are more likely to be positively inclined towards the book or author in question. But it is also because those responses are modified by the fact of being face-to-face with the author-performer in person, and, concurrently, by being observed and judged, by other reader-audience members, which inhibits vituperative responses.

In general, live literature events tend to have a friendly and supportive atmosphere. Just as neuroscience has shown that live experiences have more impact in a digitalised culture,[49] it seems that the experience of receiving positive, embodied responses in a live literature context is valued more highly by contemporary author-performers in the context of the negative experiences that many have though social media and online reviews.

## Author-Performers: Reading Aloud and the Practice of Writing: The Role of Orality and Voice

Some of the most fascinating insights from my ethnographies speak to the ways in which author-performers negotiate the relationship between writing practice and their live literature practice through the role of the *voice*.

This can be traced back to the writing process, and the question of whether or not authors read aloud as they write. This question has been neglected in literary research, as John Mullan pointed out at Hay. My ethnographies reveal that many author-performers *do* read aloud as part of their writing and editing process. Andrew O'Hagan is an example of an author who regards that practice as a necessity. This points to a connection between literature and orality that is rarely acknowledged, in a culture of scholarship and publishing that focuses on the printed text. For an author-performer, the process of reading aloud inevitably ceases for a period, once the book is in the process of publication—but it is then returned to, once the book comes out, in the forum of live literature events.

I was intrigued to find out, during my research, that some authors claim *never* to read aloud while writing their fiction. Colm *Tóibín* is an example—although he spoke, instead, about writing through his 'inner' voice. It seems likely to me that writers such as O'Hagan who tend to write more performatively in terms of dialogue and scenes are more likely to rely on reading aloud as part of their process; in contrast to writers, like *Tóibín*, who may focus more on descriptive prose.

Author-performers prepare in different ways for live literature events. Only a few admit to practising their planned readings at home in advance. Of these, a few, like Stella Duffy, are very vocal about the *duty* upon author-performers to practice, for the benefit of their audiences and the reading public—and Duffy has a background in theatre. Other author-performers admit to not practising at all before their readings—occasionally, as *Tóibín did*, expressing surprise even at the suggestion that they might. This response reflects a wider perception of live literature events as being primarily publicity appearances, rather than performances, and neglects their experiential value for reader-audiences.

As live literature becomes a more significant part of authors' careers in the twenty-first century, it seems that more and more of them are now beginning to see themselves as author-performers—albeit they do not use that term. Consequently, practice before events is perhaps becoming more common—or, at least, authors seem to be attending more carefully to the practice of reading their work aloud, with an increased awareness that this is a form of performance.

The scope for performance of literary texts at live literature events, particularly the standard, conversation-based event format, is often very limited, because readings are usually required to be short. This presents author-performers with a challenge: how to select a single passage for an event, when it will be received by reader-audiences as representative of the entire book? The task can be particularly difficult where a novel has multiple narrators, or in cases where the author-performer does not want to give away any 'spoilers' by reading a passage that is too far in.

The opening of a novel seems to be chosen the most frequently as a sample to perform at an event. Alternatively, the choice of passage is often made on the basis that it is funny or dramatic, and is therefore likely to make a swift impact, and produce an audible or visible reaction in reader-audiences that creates a sense of engagement, such as laughter—thus stimulating a 'feedback loop' that creates dynamism in the performance.[50]

By incorporating audience responses, like laughter and murmuring, my ethnographies illustrate how these the literary passages chosen by authors actually work in performance. They show that a wide variety of texts, in terms of tone and content, can be successful—and that the perceived authenticity of the performance is important, in conjunction with the text performed.

Many author-performers admit to thinking about *the prospect of performing* their fiction at live events while writing; but most—notably Simon Armitage and Colm *Tóibín*—say that they actively try to quell that thought. They do this for fear that it will impact on their writing, either in ways that it 'shouldn't'—based on an idea that their creative integrity will be compromised by a desire to please an embodied audience; or that it will make them too self-conscious, hindering the flow of the writing process.

Some author-performers—notably David Almond—place a high value on the sonic qualities and musicality of their prose fiction texts while composing them, in a way that is *not* directly linked to anticipating the prospect of live literature events; but is, instead, part of a deeper conviction that literature should be connected to orality, and more than that, to sound and rhythm. This aesthetic and philosophical view of literature as a musical, sonic thing, is more commonly associated with poetry, but applies to fiction too—as lucidly argued by Ursula K. Le Guin.[51]

During my research, several author-performers I spoke to, including Almond and Armitage, explicitly connected their live literature practice with ancient storytelling traditions, and to a core idea they have of their basic function as storytellers. From this perspective, literature akin to a contemporary architecture that has grown up around live storytelling traditions: print publishing is the 'addendum' phenomenon here; not live literature events.

Even for those author-performers who are less focused on rhythm, orality and storytelling as an element of their role and the core of their writing practice than others, the act of reading aloud from their books at live events is often experienced as a 're-inhabiting' of a text that they had once been consumed by, during the writing process; but had subsequently become distant from during the pre-publication phase, and before the cycle of literary events around the book began. Andrew O'Hagan spoke passionately about his sense of reinhabiting his texts through performance, and also admitted to finding new and surprising qualities about his text during each subsequent reinhabitation.

The reinhabiting process can be an emotional one for some author-performers, though—in fact 'too emotional' for some.[52] This serves as a reminder that many authors choose to express thoughts and feelings through fictional narratives on a page, precisely *because* they would not otherwise have felt able or willing to share these stories through oral performance. The growing prevalence of live literature may now be affecting how those authors approach their writing.

That said, the more sensitive passages in any given novel can usually be avoided in performance. I was once asked by a chairperson at a live literature event to read from the most harrowing scene in my novel, which I had previously avoided doing, as I felt it would give a distorted sense of the book as a whole—and affect the tone of the event—but on the spur of the moment I decided to try it anyway, keen to oblige and curious to find out how well it would work. I felt awkward during the reading, and glad that I had the opportunity to read a couple of other short passages after it too, so that this would not seem like the sole representative part of the book. Several reader-audience members did 'convert' by buying a book afterwards; but it was impossible to tell whether any had been put off by the harrowing passage, or assumed that it was more representative of the overall tone of the text than it is.

Some author-performers feel conflicted about their oral, performed voice vs their 'inner voice' in a live literature context, even after years of doing performed readings and conversation-based live literature events. *Tóibín's striking,* self-deprecating declaration: 'I don't like the sound of my voice', was a striking example.

Others seek to render, through performed readings, the variety of fictional voices that they have created in the text, by adjusting their voices for different narrators or characters, and adopting varying tonalities that suit those characters—but only a few go so far as to brave different accents. This approach to performed reading necessitates confidence and some advance practice—which, as I have discussed, is not always done. Most authors lack confidence to attempt different characters' voices, even after practice, and many admit to some anxiety about how performative to be in relation to characterisation, dialogue and multiple narrating voices. I have occasionally found myself perplexed about the best approach to take with my own novel, which has a multi-voice structure, when faced with performing some of the first-person sections narrated by characters who vary considerably in terms of gender, nationality, region and class: all factors that can affect delivery.

These varying approaches link back to the historical debates relating to 'talking books' about how far it is 'appropriate' to dramatise a literary text when reading it aloud, and how far to allow the reader-listener room for interpretation, or to allow the text to speak for itself. My conversations with *Tóibín* and Armitage are representative of a widespread sense among author-performance that an actorly 'hamming-up' of a text does not necessarily do their text the best service—and that there is some compromise into be struck by the author-performer between dramatisation and textual integrity. I was struck by Gavin Extence's admission that he 'learned' how to perform his own novel aloud by listening to the actor's renditions on the audiobook edition. This possibility is increasingly available to author-performers as audiobooks grow. But reader-audiences' frequent reference to the importance of authenticity in a performed reading problematises that idea. Stan and Kira's commentary on Toni Morrison was striking: that it felt vital to hear her 'authentic' rhythm in live performance at an event; but that, when listening to the text in its entirety as an audiobook, the actor's rendition was preferable.

Many authors keep their reading-aloud style flat or dry. Sometimes this is borne out of such a view about the primacy of the text, but often it appears to be indicative of the author-performer's personality and usual speaking style. Margaret Atwood an example, as debated by O'Hagan and *Tóibín*: she has a fairly flat, dry reading-aloud tone that they speculated was political, as a kind of feminist statement; but that also clearly matches her writing style, which is notoriously witty and packed with dead-pan humour as well as acute human insights and sharp descriptions. Her performed reading style is similar to her performed conversation style, which suggests that both are simply manifestations of her personality. Audiences have a tendency to draw links between an author's perceived personality and their literary style, a phenomenon that Ishiguro discussed, self-deprecatingly, in relation to his own work—and the same seems to be true of delivery style during performed readings. Reader-audiences embark on an interpretive process of evaluation of an author-performer's 'authenticity' while experiencing a performed reading.

## Author-Performers: Responding to Questions: Explaining Invention; the Role of the 'Sage'; Authorial Persona vs. Autobiographical Identity

Conversation-based live literature events often involve discussion of themes and intentions behind an author-performer's composition of their fiction. This often entails an attempt to summarise key elements of a text which, often, has taken them years to craft, and which is, almost by definition, incapable of accurate summary. As L. Samantha Chang put it: 'We make art about what we cannot understand by any other method'.[53] Similarly, Lorrie Moore has pointed out that: 'No one who has ever looked back upon a book she or he has written, only to find the thing foreign and alienating, unrecallable, would ever deny its mysteriousness'.[54] And yet conversation-based events require such analytical exercises to be undertaken—and require the author-performer to provide explanations for reader-audiences that are both clear and engaging. As Armitage put it: author-performers are required to learn a 'patter' for each book. This can become wearing over time.

Author-performers are frequently expected to offer opinions, during conversation-based events, on matters beyond their autobiography and their writing, such as politics or other moral or societal issues. This links to a widespread idea of the author as a 'sage': an idea that Coetzee has notably positioned himself against, on the basis that the literature itself should take priority, and that literature's distinct mode of expressing ideas needs protecting and valuing.[55] Ishiguro's performance at Hay represented a wry embracing of the 'sage' role, and this seems to be a more common attitude among author-performers than a Coetzeean reticence.

Neuroscientific evidence shows that the act of sharing advice triggers reward mechanisms in the brain.[56] Many author-performers admit to finding the opining aspect of events rewarding—even if they find the prospect stressful, and even if they ultimately consider it to be only distantly connected to the literary work that they are supposed to be presenting.

For my part, I have been happy to answer questions at events about relevant issues in my novel—such as immigration policy; to me, this has made the book feel useful and resonant for readers, and that it is playing into relevant conversations in the wider culture, however small and isolated. But I am always glad when questions reveal an emotional engagement with the text, too.

Author-performers tend to critically evaluate the reading styles of fellow/competitor author-performers when they witness them in performance at live literature events, even if they do not readily admit to this, as O'Hagan and *Tóibín*'s conversation demonstrates. However, few published fiction authors regularly attend live literature events in which they are not performing professionally. In part, this is due to a perception of conversation-based events being primarily targeted at publicity for others' books, and introducing readers to those books, combined with their educational function. Familiar reader-audience questions along the lines of how to get published are unlikely to be relevant to published authors. Author-performers are more likely to attend more intimate book launches, as reader-audiences, than literary festivals.

Reader-audience Q&A sessions at live literature events generate mixed feelings among author-performers. Frequent questions, like: *Where did you get your ideas from? How long did it take you? How many hours a day did you write for? How did you know when you'd done enough research?*, suggest a desire on the part of the questioner to understand the process of writing better, and/or to work out how get their own book published. Some author-performers betray impatience with such questions; from my ethnographies, Dorthe Nors is an example. A small minority of author-performers, such as Will Self, openly sneer at reader-audience questions in Q&A sessions for being insufficiently literary, unengaged with the detail of the book, trivial and ultimately a waste of time.

Most author-performers are far more empathetic towards their reader-audiences than Self, and more appreciative of their participation in the Q&A process. They tend to value reader-audience questions as a concrete indication of dynamic engagement with, and interest in, their work—and also as a direct way to connect with individual reader-audience members. Q&As are also experienced as a rare forum in which to gain granular glimpses into the divergent ways in which readers have interpreted and responded, emotionally, psychologically, aesthetically and culturally, to the narrative—or at least to an extract or idea of the narrative. The Q&A can act as a form of evaluation that is rare in its directness, and tends to involve welcome positive feedback.

Many authors of fiction feel some degree of anxiety, discomfort or awkwardness about the prospect of divulging autobiographical information to the public in the course of conversation-based events—which inevitably steer towards drawing autobiographical links with fictional texts. Some event chairpeople give author-performers a list of indicative questions in advance, to enable them to prepare their answers—but even then, if the conversation works well, it is likely to evolve away from a pre-prepared set of questions, as both chairperson and author-performer engage dynamically with each other's ideas. By the time it comes to speaking about their books at live literature events, author-performers will already have given some thought to ways in which they are comfortable with making, complicating or ruling out autobiographical links, based on the wider publicity framing of the book. But it can still be difficult to make judgements about what to talk about at live events, particularly when members of their family are involved. When I witnessed Maggie O'Farrell, at Hay, in conversation about her extraordinary literary memoir, *I Am, I Am, I Am: Seventeen Brushes with Death* (2017), which goes into intimate detail about her daughter's severe illness, she spoke, in conversation, about the effort she has to put into planning what she will say at live events, in order to limit what else she reveals about her daughter so as to protect her privacy. Such meta-conversations are common in the context of fiction, too.

The identity debate between Zadie Smith and Nick Laird that I discussed earlier is a microcosmic example of the anxiety and preoccupation that many author-performers now have about the extent to which their autobiography and perceived identity will be used as tools to judge and evaluate their fiction. This anxiety is inevitably increased in the context of an expectation to perform at live events—billed as being about their fiction—in which they will almost inevitably be required to answer questions about the extent to which aspects of their own life, identity, and 'voice' is manifested in their literary work. My ethnographies reveal this line of questioning to be part of a wider quest on the part of readers for a sense of authenticity—which does not necessarily translate to author-performers' understanding of authenticity in relation to their work.

My ethnography of Polari revealed the positive effects of performing fiction as when it is *not* linked to a direct interrogation of an author-performer's autobiography. This is enabled by an event format that focuses on performed readings rather than conversation or Q&A, and that allows the author-performer to frame their performance in their own words through a very short introduction. This approach gives the author-performer more control over the process. It also gives them more of a sense that the event is fundamentally about their fiction, rather than their authorial persona or identity, or as an authority on real-world issues alluded to in their fictional texts. After performing at Polari, I certainly felt liberated by this sense that I was presenting my fiction more prominently than I was presenting my autobiography.

## Author-Performers: Signing Books; Post-event Connections

The book signing ritual that often follows live literature events tends to be experienced positively by author-performers, including as a way to connect even more directly with reader-audiences, and to receive additional feedback that reader-audiences may not have wanted to offer publicly during a Q&A. This, at least, is true so long as a respectable number of people actually do come to buy the book and seek a signature on it; John Banville's account of his humiliation at an event in which he appeared alongside a more famous Pulitzer prize-winner and was essentially ignored by the reader-audience afterwards illustrates how excruciating the ritual can be if this doesn't happen.[57] The signing ritual is also experienced as tangible evidence of 'success' in sales terms, in the form of 'conversion'. The act of signing the physical book—which is not itself the product or property of the author, but the product of the publisher, and now the property of the reader-audience member—nevertheless reinforces a sense of authorship of the text; of its value to the reader-audience member who has bought it; and of the connection being made through the signing process to their future reading experience.

A key difference between an author signing and a celebrity autograph is the common practice of 'making the book out to' someone upon the request of the reader-audience member, by writing a short personal message. This process involves acquiring some information about the person, which gives the author-performer an extra layer of insight into the future life of the book and its reader.

The contents of these messages can cause author-performers anxiety. Signings are, after all, pieces of writing, albeit in micro-form, will be read as 'authored' in the context of the book, and are likely to be given some attention and allocated some weight, by the reader-audience member or their chosen recipient, and yet need to be done at speed, on the spot. *Is Best Wishes too bland?*, I have witnessed author-performers ask each other, and wondered about myself. Once, when I was signing copies of my novels after an event in a library, a middle-aged man told me in depth about his daughter's desire to enter into a law career and the human rights work experience she was now doing, and how my book would be the perfect present for her. Touched, I checked the spelling of her name and began to pen a short message that wished her luck in her career, and, while I was writing this, he commented: 'I didn't expect you to write *all that*!'—in a way that was not phrased critically, quite, yet was intended to make the point that I was doing something beyond what he meant to request—and I felt guilty, as I signed my name, that I had now spoiled his present by making it a little *too* 'bespoke'. She might, of course, have read the message, and the book, very differently. I have no way of knowing.

## Key Insights: Experiential Literary Ethnography and Cultural Value

For the final set of key insights, I'd like to return to experiential literary ethnography—to reflect on how this approach to research and writing enabled me to reveal the cultural value of Hay and Polari, as well as generating a wide variety of insights about live literature in general; and to suggest ways in which it could be applied to demonstrate cultural value in other contexts.

The question of how to demonstrate the cultural value of any arts-based event or experience is a fraught one, and will be even more so after the Coronavirus lockdowns as pressure is piled on arts organisations. It is the subject of ongoing research and debate among producers, funders and scholars.[58] I propose that experiential literary ethnography represents a uniquely fruitful means of understanding and communicating cultural value by *evoking* participant experience using creative writing techniques—encompassing many multifaceted elements of that experience, including aesthetic and emotional elements and diverse participant voices—and also *examining* that experience.

Experiential literary ethnography avoids the common trap of focusing on certain narrow forms of data or pre-determined criteria as evidence of cultural value, presenting a reductive view of participant experience, and consequently draining the meaning out of the event or experience in question.

It has the capacity to reveal how and why multifaceted and complex elements of experience interconnect and interrelate, to each other and to wider cultural structures, patterns and narratives.

A flexible approach to composition, it can both hone in on specific, situated, sensory details that characterise particular events, people, places, texts and activities; and it can zoom out to relate those details to wider cultural patterns, trends and dynamics.

Another key advantage of experiential literary ethnography is that the narratives produced are likely to be more *accessible and engaging* to wider audiences than other, less evocative modes of writing. Consequently they have the potential to make a *greater impact*.

## Key Elements of Experiential Literary Ethnography: A Toolbox

The crafting of each of the ethnographies featured in this book involved a process of interweaving descriptions and multi-textured elements of experience with multiple voices, texts, reflections and analysis, while always maintaining a narrative momentum in order to evoke and recreate the temporal flow and dynamism of the live event experience.

Any experiential literary ethnography will need to be crafted in response to the particular event or experience being considered; there is no set formula. However, I can suggest set of core elements of an experiential literary ethnography that could be applied in any other arts-based event context.

One element is evocative 'thick description',[59] based on the ethnographer's own observations of events and the people participating in them, which might include things like body language, dress, posture, gesture, accent, voice, pitch, pacing, temperature, smell, spatial layout, staging features, audience arrangement, publicity materials, background music, imagery, design, atmosphere.

A second element is participant conversation: extracts of conversational interviews relevant participants—who, in an arts-based event, might include artists/performers and producers as well as audiences. Ideally, these conversations will be themed but fluid and unstructured, allowing the ethnographies to incorporate not only pithy and directly relevant observations, but also to illuminate more tangential elements of speech and commentary—such as speech patterns, wording choices, and trains of thought. This enables an ethnography to illustrate the variety and texture of experience among participants, and the complexities and expressive particularities of individual experiences within a group.

A third element, where an event involves performed text, is quotations from texts performed, or specific descriptions of those texts. This enables the ethnography to effectively evoke the experience of interacting with that text and to reflect on the value of the experience in a sufficiently specific and meaningful way.

A fourth element is the mention of relevant commentaries in the media and on social media where they illustrate the cultural conversation around that experience; this is likely to influence participants' perspectives.

A fifth element is a degree of zoomed-out reflection on wider cultural patterns and tendencies that connect to this particular event. This might involve drawing on the ethnographer's own experience.

A sixth element is theoretical analysis, which might draw from a range of disciplines and sources.

A seventh element is a process of examination of all the other elements, in order to arrive at certain key insights at the end of the ethnography.

All these elements need to be fused together with language that is literary and experiential: the language needs to make the ethnographies as immersive as possible, in order to evoke the experience, and it also needs to be clear, comprehensible, and accessible. This requires paying attention to creative writing techniques—matters such as imagery, form, style, register, metaphor and dialogue.

## Future-Gazing

I cannot predict what the future of live literature will look like—particularly in this strange and uncertain time, as the Coronavirus continues to shake the foundations of culture and society across the world, and live performance events continue to be cancelled, delayed or indefinitely altered.

But my research has convinced me that live literature has already had far more significant impacts on contemporary literary culture than is often assumed, that it will continue to evolve, and that its cultural value is likely to continue to grow along with the digitalisation of culture and communication.

Live literature events are often experienced as authentic and memorable communicative performances that forge meaningful connections between reader-audience members, author-performers and literary texts. They impact significantly both on the ways in which reader-audiences value books and authors, and on the ways in which author-performers relate to their work and their readerships. They can enhance the special capacity of fictional texts to connect people through a process of imaginative empathy.

Live literature can also forge strong and meaningful communities, including close, enduring communities of activism and resistance; and temporary communities of people who might only ever come together for a single event, but still feel themselves to be linked in the moment and in their divergent futures by the memory of the experience.

Certain types of literary events, notably literary festivals and conversation-based events, seem to be exacerbating the tendency across literary culture to evaluate fictional narratives in relation to the biography and identity of their authors. This tendency arises partly out of a widespread socio-cultural preoccupation with identity, in the context of diversity problems and social inequality. It appears to be affecting the substance of fictional texts, by pushing fiction towards autofiction, arguably problematising fiction's validity.

While literary festivals and conversation-based events can be seen as contributing to this trajectory, they also function as a fertile platform for discussing these sorts of issues. In doing so, they reveal the close connection that literature has always had with the culture and society around it, and that it should have in order to continue to be relevant—and they strengthen that connection, making literary culture both more accessible, more relevant to many people, and more meaningful for many people.

Almost all author-performers feel under pressure to appear at festivals and conversation-based events. Most ultimately experience these events positively as a way to sense a concrete connection between their work and readers. But for a few authors—Coetzee and Ferrante, for example—the pressure to be part of conversation-based events, and comparable forms of media and publicity about their books, is experienced as negative, or even damaging to their identities as authors, or to what they see as fiction's cultural value. Part of that resistance is about the distancing effect that these forms of author-promotion are perceived to have upon readers' relationships with literary texts. If performed readings are omitted from live literature events, or are consistently marginalised, the element of live literature's value that derives from direct experiential connections with performed literary texts is diminished.

There are clear indications that live literature is expanding in more diverse, varied, performative, experimental and immersive directions that foreground literary texts. Polari illustrates this trend through its emphasis on performativity—and many more inventive forms have emerged over the last decade. But live literature has potential to enliven and diversify much further, and to evolve an art form in its own right. This, to me, would help to make literary culture as a whole to become even more dynamic, inventive, adaptable, appealing and ultimately sustainable.

The current Oxford Professor of Poetry 2019, Alice Oswald, issued a statement of intent in advance of the voting process which is used to decide between the four nominees, in which she wrote: 'I'd like to stage some Extreme Poetry Events: for example all-night readings of long poems, poetry in the dark or in coloured light, even perhaps a Carnival of Translation, A Memory Palace, a Poem-Circus (like the Music-Circus of John Cage), or an exhibition of mobile poems'.[60] This is a further indication that we are in a pivotal moment for live literature, and I hope that it will lead to more experimentation and immersive performativity.

The Coronavirus has interrupted this trend, temporarily at least. It has forced embodied live literature events, and other embodied live performance events such as theatre and concerts, to be cancelled or to 'go digital' in 2020. While this is causing many producers, and author-performers, to struggle fiercely with funding, Hay Festival Digital 2020 is an example of an event that has adapted to the circumstances and has attracted new, wider audiences through streaming. This may, in future, cause the Festival to be streamed regularly and be accessed online by greater numbers than before. Based on some of the comments made by viewers online this year, the experience of streaming it may attract new reader-audiences to attend in person once it is able to re-open in physical form. I have argued in this book that the experience of digital and embodied participation are materially different—but they can certainly feed into each other and complement each other.

Using ethnography to research both kinds of participant experience can help to understand how the two forms of literary event differ; how they might connect more fruitfully; and how the cultural value of both might be enhanced.

As digitalisation increases across society, it seems inevitable that live, embodied arts and culture experiences, including live literature events, will continue to gain in cultural value—so long as it is possible to take part in them. The more fractured that societies become in the face of pandemics, climate change and other global threats, the more important literature becomes, with its unique capacity to engender empathy and emotion through storytelling. Live literature has the capacity to increase literature's cultural value further. It can make its participants feel more deeply and authentically connected to society, to the cultural communities they imagine, and to each other—as well as to literary texts.

The increasing desire for live, embodied experiences is likely to be matched by an increasing demand for evidence of their cultural value to justify their funding. I hope that experiential literary ethnography proves to be useful approach for those who need it—and for everyone else, I hope that it has made for an enjoyable live literature expedition between the covers of this book.

# 7

## Coda: Inhabiting a Legend

It is a balmy April day in Berkeley, 1998, and you are walking back through Berkeley's familiar green campus where you've been invited to give a talk on sound and the voice in literature. Happy student voices float over the lawns as you make your way to the building where the conference is being held. All literature emerges from a 'wave in the mind', as Virginia Woolf put it in one of her letters to Vita Sackville-West—it begins with emotion, and the desire to communicate through sound. There's far too much reverence around for the printed page, which is only a recent cultural invention after all.

Warm applause begins as soon as you walk through the door, and a hush descends as you begin to speak. You'll be keeping it short, today, but memorable. All your deadpan jokes are rewarded by laughter: yes, they're engaged alright. It's just a shame that the sound of your voice is getting croakier by the day as you age.

You reach the end of the prose part of your talk, but don't let on with your body language. Instead you allow a suspended silence to hang in the air—though of course there's no such thing as silence, as John Cage pointed out, especially in the presence of a room full of beating hearts and itchy scalps. 4 minutes 33 seconds would be overdoing it, but you

© The Author(s), under exclusive license to Springer Nature Switzerland AG 2021
E. Wiles, *Live Literature*, Palgrave Studies in Literary Anthropology,
https://doi.org/10.1007/978-3-030-50385-7_7

wait for a good few, slow breaths to circulate. Enough time for everyone in the room to register the birdsong beyond the open window, a far-off cackle, the creak of a chair, the sniff of a cold-sufferer, the crackle of a page turning in a notebook, the ticking of multiple watches and minds all wondering whether to clap now, or what you're about to say or do next…

'Loud Cows', you announce, followed by another short pause. Then:

> 'It's allowed. It is allowed, we are allowed SILENCE!
> It's allowed. It IS allowed. It IS allowed SILENCE!!
> it *used* to be allowed.
>     SI–EE–LENTSSSSS.
>     I–EE AM THE AWE –THOR.
> REEED MEEE IN SI-EE-LENT AWE.
>         but it's aloud.
>         it *is* aloud.'[1]

# Notes

## Chapter 1

1. Ursula K. Le Guin, *The Language of the Night* (1985), p. 31.

## Chapter 2

1. Le Guin, 'Telling Is Listening', *A Wave in the Mind* (2004), p. 199.
2. See Anthony Gritten, 'Music Before the Literary: Or, The Eventness of Musical Events' (2006) and Willmar Sauter, *Eventness: A Concept of Theatrical Events* (2008).
3. For more commentary on the rise of literary festivals in particular, see Beth Driscoll, *The New Literary Middlebrow* (2014), p. 153, and Millicent Weber, *Literary Festivals and Contemporary Book Culture* (2018). For a historical perspective on other forms of 'book event', see Daniel Finkelstein and Claire Squires, 'Book Events, Book Environments' (2019), p. 6.
4. For more information about Ark, see the website: www.arkshortstories.com.
5. See www.arkshortstories.com and www.ellenwiles.com for more information and detail.

© The Editor(s) (if applicable) and The Author(s), under exclusive license to Springer Nature Switzerland AG 2021
E. Wiles, *Live Literature*, Palgrave Studies in Literary Anthropology,
https://doi.org/10.1007/978-3-030-50385-7

6. *The Invisible Crowd* won a 2018 Victor Turner Prize for ethnographic writing.

7. See Finnegan (2015), EPub, location: 32.4/447. Uncoincidentally, Finnegan's own scholarly prose style is notable for its clarity, and she too has branched into writing fiction.

8. Emphasis added. See Le Guin, 'In Pursuit of the Gorgeous Sound of Language', Ch. 1 of *Steering the Craft* (2015), p. 1. Along the same lines (or sound waves), Joe Moran's definition of a sentence, in any form of writing, is: 'a line of words where logic and lyric meet – a piece of both sense and sound'—see Moran (2018), p. 2. A. L. Kennedy has critiqued scholarly writing tendencies from a similar perspective: in an essay written and performed for radio, she bemoans the fact that academia has long tended to view writing primarily as 'marks on a page', when in fact it is always connected to the voice, just as it is to breath and to music. All writing, she says, 'is a kind of musical notation for the mind… We can choose to work on behalf of one of humanity's deepest expressions: our breath. We can choose *not* to… but where's the fun, the light, the *life* in that?' See A. L. Kennedy, 'The Voice on the Page', *The Essay*, Radio 3, first broadcast 6 February 2019.

9. Beth Driscoll uses the word 'explosion' in her examination of the literary festival, in *The New Literary Middlebrow* (2014), p. 153. Millicent Weber also uses it to describe the growth of literary festivals, in the first line of *Literary Festivals and Contemporary Book Culture* (2018), p. 1. Kevin Parker, founder of the literary festivals website, uses it in his piece, 'The Rise and Rise of Literary Festivals', https://www.literaryfestivals.co.uk/announcements/the-rise-and-rise-of-literary-festivals, 26 February 2015 (accessed 19 February 2019).

10. See Weber (2018).

11. For a historical perspective on other forms of 'book event', see Daniel Finkelstein and Claire Squires, 'Book Events, Book Environments' (2019), p. 6.

12. NB the term 'live literature' does not yet appear in the Oxford English Dictionary and the origins of its common contemporary usage are unclear. However, Arts Council England's Live Literature

specialist, Sarah Sanders, confirms that in her view it emerged in the twenty-first century, and that the Arts Council began using it as a category for funding purposes c.2004, in its previous form as 'London Arts'. Informal conversations with other artists and producers confirmed this view.

13. In the music context, the rise of live events is clearly linked with musicians needing to make money as the rise of streaming has slashed their income from album sales. For a scholarly perspective on the economics of music and liveness in the context of the digital, see, e.g., Fabian Holt, 'The Economy of Live Music in the Digital Age' (2010). Similarly, in literature this century, authors' incomes have nosedived, particularly for authors of literary fiction. For commentary and analysis of literary fiction authors' incomes, see: Arts Council England's report, 'Literature in the 21st Century: Understanding Models of Support for Literary Fiction' (2017). However, unlike musicians at gigs, authors are often not paid a fee for appearing at live literature events, despite their declining incomes. See Finkelstein and Squires (2019), p. 6; and The Society of Authors (eds.), 'Philip Pullman Resigns as Patron of Oxford Literary Festival Over Refusal to Pay Authors' (2016); and Benedicte Page, 'Authors Call for Boycott on Non-paying Festivals', *Bookseller* 15 January 2016.

14. This definition is not explicit in Arts Council documentation, but was outlined to me in an interview with members of the Arts Council's literature team in 2014. Within the literature team, ACE have a live literature specialist who is in charge of all live literature projects—projects that may be categorised under the umbrella of either literature or 'combined arts'. The Scottish Book Trust, in contrast, runs a distinct 'live literature' funding stream which focuses on bringing published authors into community settings; for more details see their website: https://scottishbooktrust.com/live-literature (accessed 12 December 2018).

15. See 'literature, n.', Oxford English Dictionary, online edition, accessed 2 December 2018.

16. See Finnegan (2015), EPub location: 413.1/477.

17. See Giorgi (2011), p. 34.

18. See Hauptfleisch et al. (eds.), *Festivalising!* (2007), pp. 20–23.
19. In her book on the subject, Weber defined it as any 'festival that pertains to literary culture'. She included in her study festivals such as Port Eliot: a festival that used to call itself a 'literary festival' but that, for years now, has just called itself a 'festival' and incorporates literary events as a minority element of a programme featuring music, theatre, comedy and fashion.
20. The choice seems to reflect an emphasis upon a particular aspect of literary culture, with 'book festival', for instance, emphasizing the physical book and therefore the element of commercial exchange; though in reality most of them are very similar in format.
21. I refer here to Bourdieu's notion of cultural capital, as elucidated in *Distinction* (1984), p. 87—and discussed in relation to literary festivals in Weber (2018), p. 33.
22. See the Festival's website: https://www.singaporewritersfestival. com/nacswf/nacswf/about-swf/about-swf0.html (accessed 30 April 2019).
23. See Finkelstein and Squires (2019), for a discussion of 'book events' in the twentieth century that sets out to expand the usual focus on literary festivals.
24. This series was curated by Gemma Seltzer and David Varela. For more information, see the website https://livewritingseries.com (accessed 19 February 2019).
25. The artist/writer here was David Musgrave, and this event was part of Plastic Words at the Raven Row Gallery (2014)—see: https://www.ravenrow.org/exhibition/plastic_words/ (accessed 13 February 2018).
26. This was an Almeida Theatre production in 2015, featuring 66 artists and claiming an audience of over 50,000 across the world, including online. See https://almeida.co.uk/the-Iliad (accessed May 2020) for more information.
27. See Rubery (2016), p. 20.
28. See Susan Somers-Willett, *The Cultural Politics of Slam Poetry* (2009); and Maria Damon, 'Was That "Different", "Dissident", or "Dissonant"? Poetry (n) the Public Spear' (1998).

29. See Rebecca Watts's controversial article published in the PN Review, in place of a review of McNish's work which she refused to write: 'The Cult of the Noble Amateur' (2018). The article prompted heated debate about amateurism vs. elitism in the poetry community and the media, as well as spoken vs. printed forms.

30. See e.g. Alison Flood, 'US Publishing Remains "as White Today As It Was Four Years Ago"', *The Guardian* (2020): https://www.theguardian.com/books/2020/jan/30/us-publishing-american-dirt-survey-diversity-cultural-appropriation.

31. See Melanie Ramdarshan Bold's important studies of diversity in publishing in the UK, revealing a lack of representation persisting despite high-profile diversity campaigns – including 'The Eight Percent Problem' (2018), and *Inclusive Young Adult Fiction* (2019). The 2011 census identified 86% of the UK population as white (Office for National Statistics, 'Ethnicity and National Identity in England and Wales: 2011'; whereas in 2017 the publishing industry was deemed to be 90% white (Alison Flood, *The Guardian*, 6 September 2017). For an interdisciplinary cultural perspective on how race impacts on cultural production more widely, see Anamik Saha, *Race and the Cultural Industries* (2017).

32. See Anamik Saha and Sandra van Lente, 'Rethinking Diversity' (2020): https://www.spreadtheword.org.uk/wp-content/uploads/2020/06/Rethinking_diversity_in-publishing_WEB.pdf.

33. See Speaking Volumes' website, https://www.speaking-volumes.org.uk (accessed 21 February 2019). PEN International is a charity championing the work and lives of imprisoned and persecuted writers internationally, and has national branches in many countries.

34. See 4th Estate's salon page: https://www.4thestate.co.uk/tag/4th-estate-literary-salon/ (accessed 14 February 2019).

35. See LDM's website: https://www.literarydeathmatch.com (accessed 14 February 2019).

36. LDM is currently dormant.

37. See Book Slam's website: https://bookslam.com (accessed 14 February 2019).

38. Faber Social was founded in the late '00s. See Faber Social's website: https://fabersocial.co.uk (accessed 14 February 2019).

39. See The Moth's website: https://themoth.org (accessed 14 February 2019).

40. For an exploration of the growth and impact of The Moth, see Catherine Jo Janssen, 'An Ethnographic Study of The Moth Detroit StorySLAM' (2012).

41. See Elevator Repair Service's website: https://www.elevator.org/shows/gatz/ (accessed 14 February 2019).

42. See Kitson's website: https://www.danielkitson.com (accessed 14 February 2019).

43. See Ryan Gilbey on Sutherland's work: 'The Fresh Prince to the Crystal Maze' (2015).

44. For more on Plastic Words (2014–2015) see Raven Row's website: https://www.ravenrow.org/exhibition/plastic_words/ (accessed 14 February 2019).

45. Homework is currently dormant. An early preview of their work was featured by Rachel Holdsworth in The Londonist (2012).

46. For more about Ark, see the website: www.arkshortstories.com.

47. For more on the Story Machine Project, see their website: https://storymachineproductions.co.uk (accessed 14 February 2019).

48. For more on The Special Relationship, see their website: https://www.thespecialrelationship.net (accessed 14 February 2019).

49. See Jared McGinnis, 'The Event's the Thing' (2016).

50. For more about Neu! Reekie! See their Facebook page: @neureeking (accessed 19 February 2019) and their listing on Edinburgh's City of Literature website: https://www.cityofliterature.com/a-to-z/neu-reekie-2/ (accessed 19 February 2019).

51. This comes from an interview I arranged with Sarah Sanders and Gemma Seltzer from the Arts Council's Literature team in 2014.

52. Richard Bauman, *Story, Performance, and Event* (1986), p. 112.

53. John D. Niles, *Homo Narrans* (1999), pp. 2–3.

54. Richard Jenkyns, *Classical Literature* (2016).

55. Author/teller/performer: Aristides of Miletus. See Steven Moore, *The Novel: An Alternative History* (2010), p. 101.

56. See Derek Collins, *Master of the Game* (2005).

57. See Rosalind Thomas, 'Performance and Written Literature in Classical Greece (2013), p. 34.

58. 'A full understanding of Greek literature', she asserts, should involve 'not simply the written texts, but also how these texts related to their performances', in order to better understand their 'original performative meaning', and the 'social and cultural background to the written texts' which only became 'crystallised as great literature' later. See Thomas (2013), p. 28.

59. *The Economist* (editors), 'From Papyrus to Pixels' (2017).

60. John D. Niles has written, for instance, about the literature produced by the 'people who inhabited lowland Britain in the centuries before the Norman Conquest', as being largely composed of prose poetry 'in narrative form: it consists of stories', and exploring subjects ranging from 'the creation of the world, the fall of Satan and the angels, and the story of Adam and Eve' to tales of 'ancestral kings, queens, and heroes of northern Europe', 'ancient wars and feuds, wonders and betrayals. They heard the imagined voices of people of faraway times of places: voices of singers, of wanderers and pilgrims… all projected upon the mental stage that poetry invited them to contemplate. They sometimes heard stories of newsworthy events: great battles, tragic deaths, and grand heroic gestures. Through versified riddles, one of their more imaginative pastimes, they even heard the mute world speak: they heard beer or a reed pen tell its own life story.' See Niles (1999), pp. 7–8.

61. See Peter Weidhaas, *A History of the Frankfurt Book Fair* (2017).

62. Paul Saenger, *Space Between Words* (1997), p. 1.

63. For more on this practice, see Rosalind Crone, Katherine Halsey, Mary Hammond and Shafquat Towheed, 'The Reading Experience Database 1450–1945 (RED)', in Towheed, Halsey and Crone (eds.) (2010), p. 436.

64. See John Mullan, *What Matters in Jane Austen?* (2012), p. 238.

65. As Mullan has put it: 'there's a telling passage in *Sense and Sensibility* when we hear about this slightly un-expressive, even slightly wooden man, Edward Ferrars, whom Elinor, Marianne's sister, loves, but without being quite sure if that love is returned. He is given some poetry – some William Cowper, who was a great

favourite of Austen's – to read aloud, and Marianne protests after-wards: "he read with so little sensibility", as if the thing you display when you're reading aloud and the thing which is the essential valu-able human quality in the heart or in your soul are the same. As if you know a good person because they're a good reader'. See Abbie Jaggers' interview with John Mullan: On Jane Austen and Reading Aloud', *Listening Books Blog* (2017). For Austen herself, reading aloud from her novels-in-progress to friends and family was an inte-gral part of her composition process; her brother referred to these events as 'gradual performances'; see Lucy Worsley, *Jane Austen at Home* (2017).

66. See JürgenHabermas, *The Structural Transformation of the Public Sphere* [1962] (1991).
67. See p. xii of Thomas McCarthy's introduction to Habermas (1991).
68. See Elizabeth A. Fay, 'Author' (2012).
69. See Amy Prendergast, *Literary Salons Across Britain and Ireland in the Long Eighteenth Century* (2015), EPub: location 46.6/692.
70. See Susanna Schmid, *British Literary Salons of the Late Eighteenth and Early Nineteenth Centuries* (2013).
71. See Fay (2012).
72. See 'Introduction', p. 7, Towheed, Halsey and Crone (eds.) (2010).
73. See Fay (2012).
74. See David Ponting, 'Charles Dickens as Solo Performer' (1983), p. 124.
75. See Ponting (1983), p. 120.
76. See Ponting (1983), p. 126.
77. See Susan Ferguson, 'Dickens's Public Readings and the Victorian Author' (2001), p. 745.
78. Elspeth Jajdelska, Silent Reading and the Birth of the Narrator (2007).
79. See Steven Connor, 'Writing the White Voice' (2009), which includes a critique of Walter J. Ong's *Orality and Literacy* [1982] (2002).
80. See Connor (2009).
81. For a psychologist's neuroscientific take on the prevalence and significance of inner voices, see Charles Fernyhough, *The Voices*

*Within* (2016). For analysis of the psychology and science of 'inner speech', see also Keith Rayner, Alexander Pollatsek, Jane Ashby and Charles Clifton Jr., 'Inner Speech', in *Psychology of Reading* (2013).

82. Denise Riley, '"A Voice Without a Mouth"' (2004).

83. See Fernyhough (2016) and Marcela Perrone-Bertolotti et al., 'How Silent Is Silent Reading? (2012), pp. 1754–1762.

84. See Rubery (2016), p. 6.

85. See Janice Radway, *A Feeling for Books* (1997), for an exploration of the experience of being part of a subscription book club, and its role in wider literary culture and taste formation.

86. This statement is controversial, though; for discussion of it, and a contrary point of view, see Jane Friedman's article, 'Author Income Surveys Are Misleading and Flawed' (2018).

    At the top of it, she quotes Dr. Edward Eggleston, in 1890, as saying: 'Of all the learned professions, literature is the most poorly paid'.

87. For an analysis of the impact of this industry structure, see D. J. Taylor, *The Prose Factory* (2016).

88. For more on this history, see Finkelstein and Squires (2019), and Driscoll (2014), p. 154.

89. An example cited is the 'Bedford Square Book Bang' in 1971 run by the publisher Jonathan Cape, which was an inspiration for the Edinburgh International Book Festival. See Finkelstein and Squires (2019).

90. See Le Guin, 'Off the Page: Loud Cows' (2004), p. 117.

91. See Claire Squires, *Marketing Literature* (2007). See also John B. Thompson, *Merchants of Culture* (2010).

92. See Squires (2007) and Thompson (2010).

93. See Radway (1997), p. 356.

94. See Finkelstein and Squires (2019).

95. For an incisive analysis of the growth, ambitions, publishing impacts and future dangers of Amazon, see, e.g., Guy A. Rub, 'Amazon and the New World of Publishing (2018).

96. For commentary on and analysis of these developments and their implications, see Claire Squires, 'Taste and/or Big Data?' (2017); and Simone Murray, *The Digital Literary Sphere* (2018).

97. See Katherine Cowdrey, 'ALCS Survey Finds 15% Drop in Average Author Earnings Since 2013' (2017).

98. For discussion of these changes, see Padmini Ray Murray and Claire Squires, 'The Digital Publishing Communications Circuit' (2013).

99. For more on the changing roles of publishers as gatekeepers, see Simone Murray (2015), p. 332; and Squires (2017).

100. See Michael Bhaskar, *Curation: The Power of Selection in a World of Excess* (2016).

101. For discussion on the literary-cultural implications of BookTubing, see Kathryn Perkins, 'The Boundaries of BookTube' (2017).

102. See Katherine Cowdrey, 'Nielsen Tracks Sales at Hay and Edinburgh for First Time', *The Bookseller*, 17 May 2016: https://www.thebookseller.com/news/nielsen-breakthrough-hay-and-edinburgh-festivals-329854. Hay stocked 3400 titles and around 55,000 units in 2017, when its sales rose by 17% after an expansion of the bookshop.

103. For commentary on literary fiction authors' incomes, see: Arts Council England's report, 'Literature in the 21st Century: Understanding Models of Support for Literary Fiction' (2017).

104. See Finkelstein and Squires (2019), p. 6; and The Society of Authors (eds.), 'Philip Pullman Resigns as Patron of Oxford Literary Festival Over Refusal to Pay Authors' (2015); and Benedicte Page, 'Authors Call for Boycott on Non-paying Festivals' (2016).

105. See Crawford (2015), p. ix.

106. See David Harvey, *The Condition of Postmodernity* (1990), p. 240.

107. See Crawford (2015), p. ix.

108. Yves Citton, *The Ecology of Attention* (2016).

109. See Crawford (2015).

110. See Tassi (2018), p. 54.

111. Ibid.

112. See Bikerts, *The Gutenberg Elegies*, p. xiv, quoted in Towheeed, Crone and Halsey (eds.), 'Introduction' (2010), p. 4. Several other notable examples of phenomenological scholarship in relation to histories and theories of reading can be found in this volume. These

include Wolfgang Iser, 'The Reading Process: A Phenomenological Approach', pp. 80–92, in which he proposes that the 'activity of reading can be characterized as a sort of kaleidoscope of perspectives, preintentions, recollections' (p. 82); Robert Darnton, 'First Steps Toward a History of Reading', pp. 23–35, where he makes a case for more analysis of reader response in histories of the book and of reading; and Stanley Fish, 'What Makes an Interpretation Acceptable?', pp. 96–108, in which he considers the notion of 'reader-response critics' and the text, not as a 'material object' but as a 'the occasion for a temporal experience' (p. 103).

113. See Brian Glavey, 'Poetry and the Attention Economy' (2017), p. 425.

114. See James Wallman, *Stuffocation* (2015), for a futurologist's treatise on experientialism.

115. For a discussion of Punchdrunk and the evolution of scholarship on immersive theatre, see Josephine Machon, *Immersive Theatres* (2013) and James Frieze (ed.), *Reframing Immersive Theatre* (2017).

116. For an examination of Secret Cinema's immersive design, see Sarah Atkinson and Helen W. Kennedy, 'From Conflict to Revolution: The Secret Aesthetic, Narrative Spatialisation and Audience Experience in Immersive Cinema Design' (2016).

117. See Phelan, 'The Ontology of Performance: Representation Without Production' (1993).

118. Instead, he proposed, liveness was a 'historically contingent concept continually in a state of redefinition'. See Auslander, *Liveness: Performance in a Mediatized Culture* (1999), p. 184.

119. Fischer-Lichte adds that there are 'rules that govern the performance' which 'correspond to the rules of a game, negotiated by all the participants – actors and spectators alike'. See Fischer-Lichte (2008), p. 36.

120. Ibid.

121. See David Comer Kidd and Emanuele Castano, 'Reading Literary Fiction Improves Theory of Mind' (2013). See also Lisa Zunshine, *Why Do We Read Fiction? Theory of Mind and the Novel* (2006), p. 164 for discussion of how readers of fiction gain 'emergent

meaning' from a literary narrative through a process of emotional engagement.

122. See Sharot, 'Does Evidence Change Beliefs?' (2017), pp. 7–8.
123. See Sharot (2017), p. 14.
124. See Sharot (2017), p. 39, my emphasis added.
125. See Iacoboni (2009), p. 659.
126. See Sharot (2017), p. 42.
127. Ibid.
128. See Sharot (2017), p. 41.
129. See Iacoboni (2009), p. 666.
130. See Sharot (2017), p. 41.
131. Biologically, and evolutionarily, 'an emotional reaction is the body's way of saying, "hey, something really important is going on", and it is crucial that you respond accordingly'; so, 'when something emotional happens, your amygdala – the region in your brain important for signalling arousal – is activated. The amygdala then sends an "alert signal" to the rest of the brain, immediately changing the ongoing activity'. See Sharot (2017), p. 40.
132. See Sharot, 'Inside the Brain' (2017), EPub location 289.4/444. Again, Sharot explains that this dates back to humanity's evolution; 'the first humans were social creatures… They had yet to evolve language, but they could communicate fear, excitement, and love with a facial expression, touch and sound. The joy of human interaction could be expressed with laughter, signalling others to move closer'. See Sharot, 'The Future of Influence?' (2017), EPub location 356.0/444. Although language, writing, print then digitalization significantly changed forms and technologies of communication, once again, as Sharot observes that 'the principle organization of the brain has not experienced significant change since written language first appeared', and 'the basic biological principles of how one mind affects another remain.' See Sharot, 'Connecting Humans, Physically?' (2017), EPub location 363.7/444.
133. Experimental psychologists and neuroscientists from the UCL Division of Psychological and Language Sciences (PaLS), for instance, monitored audiences' electro dermal activity at a West

End show and found that watching a live theatre performance can synchronize your heartbeat with other people in audience. See 'Audience Members' Hearts Beat Together at the Theatre', UCL News, 17 November 2017.

134. These include 'psycho-biological measurements based on physical characteristics such as cardiac activity, blood pressure, electro-dermal activity and electroencephalographic activity, measurement based on observation of a motor behaviour such as facial expressions and body movements, and self-reporting via questionnaires. See Tassi, 'Media: From the Contact Economy to the Attention Economy', p. 58.

135. See Le Guin, 'Telling Is Listening' (2004), p. 199.

136. See Le Guin, 'Telling Is Listening' (2004), p. 200.

137. See Le Guin, Telling Is Listening' (2004), p. 196, my emphasis added.

  Vittorio Gallese has also emphasised the sociality of empathetic connectedness through *embodied simulation*: an approach to *intersubjectivity* that helps us to 'share the meaning of actions, intentions, feelings, and emotions with others, thus grounding our identification with and connectedness to others. Social identification, empathy, and "we-ness" are the basic ground of our development and being'. See Gallese (2009), p. 520.

138. See Sharot (2017), EPub location 19.0/444.

139. As Sharot puts it: 'merely sharing is not enough. We need to cause a reaction… Each time we share our opinions and knowledge, it is with the intention of impacting others'. See Sharot, 'Does Evidence Change Beliefs?' (2017), EPub location 19.0/444.

140. See Le Guin (2004).

141. See Chapter 5 for more discussion about this, and the evolution of literary studies as a discipline.

142. See, e.g., Ruth Finnegan, *Oral Literature in Africa* (1970).

143. See, e.g., Ruth Finnegan, *Oral Poetry: Its Nature, Significance, and Social Context* (1977); and more extended discussion on Finnegan and other research in this area in Chapter 5.

144. See, e.g., Caroline Lurie, 'Festival, Inc.' (2004), and more detailed discussion in Chapter 5.

145. See, most notably, Millicent Weber, *Literary Festivals and Contemporary Book Culture* (2018). More detailed discussion in Chapter 5.
146. The key anthology on the history of reading is Towheed, Crone and Halsey (eds.) (2010).
147. See Perrone-Bertolotti (2012) and see discussion of orality earlier in this chapter.
148. See Riley (2004), p. 81.
149. See Riley (2004), p. 95.
150. See Rubery, *The Untold Story of the Talking Book* (2016).
151. See Rubery (2016), p. 25 on the issue of hostility and perceptions of 'reading' and morality
152. See Rubery (2016), p. 86, quoting a letter published in *Dialogue Magazine* in 1976.
153. The American Foundation for the Blind prescribed readings that were 'not overly dramatic or obtrusive', in order to achieve 'complete fidelity to the text'. Quoted in Rubery (2016), pp. 88–89.
154. Quoted in Rubery (2016), p. 95.
155. See Rubery (2016), p. 96.
156. See Rubery (2016), p. 10.
157. See Mladen Dolar, *A Voice Is Nothing More* (2006), p. 22.
158. See Rubery (2016), p. 10.
159. This was part of evidence offered at the Library of Congress, quoted in Rubery (2016), p. 106.
160. See Rubery (2016), p. 209, quote taken from a phone conversation between Rubery and Morrison in 2013.
161. See Rubery (2016), p. 214, referencing a recording made by Dylan Thomas in 1949 on 'reading one's own poems'.
162. See Le Guin, 'Off the Page: Loud Cows' (2004), p. 117.
163. See Rubery (2016), p. 211, quote taken from Le Guin's liner notes for the recording in 1977.
164. My emphasis added. Fowler's article is titled: 'Reading in Public Is Always a Performance' (undated)—accessed on 21 December 2018 on the ILS website at: https://litshowcase.org/content/reading-in-public-is-always-a-performance/.
165. See Banville, in Robertson (ed.) (2003), p. 214.

166. See Lanchester, in Robertson (ed.) (2003), p. 256.
167. See Peter McDonald, p. 496 of 'The Challenge of *Diary of a Bad Year*', *Novel: A Forum on Fiction*, Vol. 43, no. 3, Fall 2010, pp. 483–499.
168. See Coetzee, *Diary of a Bad Year* (2007).
169. Ibid., p. 497.
170. See Armitage, in Robertson (ed.) (2003) and see Barthes (1967).
171. See Alison Flood, Simon Armitage named UK's poet laureate (2019).
    https://www.theguardian.com/books/2019/may/10/simon-armitage-poet-laureate.
172. See 'Will Self's Rules for Reading Aloud', *The Telegraph*, 24 May 2013.
173. This term echoes Juliet Gardiner's term, 'author-promoter'; see Gardiner (2000).
174. The reading/performance distinction is briefly reflected on by Stephen Wade in his introduction to *Reading the Applause*, ed. Munden and Wade (1999), p. 10.
175. This hierarchy is discussed in Rubery (2016).
176. However, as I expand upon in Chapter 5, it builds upon a cluster of related publications over the last few years, including one recent book about literary festivals for example 'Festivals, Literary Tourism and Pilgrimage' in Helen Taylor's *Why Women Read Fiction* (2019), and Weber's *Literary Festivals and Contemporary Book Culture* (2018).

## Chapter 3

1. See Porter Anderson, 'Hay Festival 2018 Sets a Record, Selling 18,000 More Tickets Than in 2017' (2018).
2. See Parker (2015).
3. See Weber (2018), p. 5.
4. I note here that this ethnography is based not just on my first visit to Hay, but on a composite of visits over three different years, lasting a week each; but evokes the experience without a direct reference to the year in question, as if it were my first visit.

The reason for this is to conjure, for the reader, the experience of attending for the first time—when they may well never have been in person. This means that certain details are inaccurate as representative of a recurring event over time; for instance, the sponsorship by the Telegraph, which I mention in my Hay ethnography, only accurately reflects the Festival as I attended it in 2013. While this compromises strict factual accuracy, it enables me to incorporate a greater number and variety of multivocal perspectives and observations that, together, better reflect the Festival's character as I experienced, observed and researched it over time. Other examples of ethnographies that use composite narrative strategies. An example is Alma Gottlieb and Judy DeLoache's book, *A World of Babies: Imagined Childcare Guides for Eight Societies* (2017), in which ethnographic material is shaped into a childcare guide, fictively written by a member of each cultural group being considered.

5. Emile Durkheim first used this influential phrase in *The Elementary Forms of Religious Life* [1912] (1995).
6. See Rosaldo, Narayan and Lavie's discussion of the evolution of Turner's thinking on liminality and the liminoid, at pp. 2–3 of 'Introduction: Creativity in Anthropology' in *Creativity/Anthropology* (1993).
7. See Falassi (1987), p. 4.
8. Key festivalisation studies include Sassatelli et al. (eds.), *Festivals and the Cultural Public Sphere* (2011), Hauptfleisch et al. eds., *Festivalising!* (2007), Taylor et al. (eds.) (2014), Jordan and Newbold (eds.), *Focus on Festivals* (2016).
9. Literary festivals are not included in the 3rd edition of the Oxford English Dictionary, 2011. 'Festival', this edition notes, has since the fourteenth century been used as an adjective, meaning 'befitting a feast-day', 'glad, joyful, merry', and since the Sixteenth Century as a noun meaning 'a time of festive celebration', or alternatively a 'musical performance or series of performances at recurring periods'.
10. See Falassi (1987), p. 2.
11. See Taylor et al. (eds.) (2014), p. 57.

12. See Sassatelli et al. (eds.) (2011), p. 75 and Weber (2018) on literary festivals.
13. See Rebecca Finkel, 'McFestivalisation?' (2004), p. 3; and Meehan (2005).
14. See Taylor et al. (eds.) (2014), p. 69.
15. See Owe Ronström, 'What a Festival "Says" and "Does"' (2011), p. 9.
16. See Ronström (2011). p. 7; see also Tassi on the attention economy (2018) and Citton on the attention ecology (2016).
17. See Rebecca Miles, 'Hay Festival Generates Millions for the Tourism Industry in the Area' (2018).
18. See Wallman (2015). Wallman's argument is not just theoretical but pragmatic; he proposes that we are all fed up of an excess of material things, which are just making us stressed and unhappy, and need to become 'experientialists' who place more value on temporal experiences, shared with others, that create lasting memories.
19. *The Telegraph* was the Hay sponsor in 2013 and 2015, when I was there. 2017 was the first year since 1990 that Hay went without sponsorship from a major broadsheet.
20. See BBC News, 'David Cameron Buys £25,000 Garden Shed "To Write In"', 30 April 2017: https://www.bbc.co.uk/news/uk-pol itics-39761410 (accessed 3 February 2019).
21. For more in-depth scholarly examination of book towns, see Driscoll, 'Local Places and Cultural Distinction: The Booktown Model' (2016). For more on the history of book towns, see Finkelstein and Squires (2019).
22. The plans materialised without Booth's support, who is said to have barked: 'I never met an author who wrote a second-hand book.' See Brenda Maddox, 'Say Hay' (1998).
23. See Aida Edemariam, 'Festival Fever' (2005).
24. See Maddox (1998).
25. See Sam Llewellyn, 'Hay Festival: A Town Set at a Slight Angle' (2011).
26. Victor's clients included Irish Murdoch, David Cameron, Sophie Dahl, John Banville, Nigella Lawson and Eric Clapton.

27. See David Sexton and Rosamund Urwin, 'Goodbye Ed Victor' (2017).
28. See John Freeman, 'Hay Festival: "The Woodstock of the Mind"' (2008).
29. See Moss (2001).
30. 'Making Hay' is also the title of an unofficial blog site about the Festival.
31. See Moss (2001).
32. See Bourdieu (1984), p. 87.
33. See Lurie (2004).
34. See Moss (2001).
35. For instance, Moss quotes Lisa Jardine, who had interviewed Margaret Atwood at Hay in 2001, as saying that Clinton's presence 'really turned the Festival into an event.' See Moss (2001).
36. See Moss (2001).
37. See Finkelstein and Squires (2019).
38. See BBC News, '20 Facts About Hay-on-Wye' (2011).
39. For more on festival density, see Hauptfleisch et al. (eds.) (2007), p. 20.
40. See Turner, 'Betwixt and Between: The Liminal Period in Rites of Passage' (1967).
41. See Ronström (2011), p. 6.
42. See Sassatelli et al. (eds.) (2011), p. 75.
43. See Decca Aitkenhead, 'Confessions of a First-Time Festival-Goer' (2010). See also Lurie's scholarly articulation of this perspective (2004), Driscoll's more nuanced discussion of the 'middlebrow' in a literary festival context (2014), and Weber's debunking of stereotypes (2018).
44. See Helen Taylor, 'Festivals, Literary Tourism, and Pilgrimage' in *Why Women Read Fiction: The Stories of our Lives* (2019), p. 203.
45. When I later asked for survey results, I was told that Hay does survey audiences formally, but does not monitor ethnic diversity, and I was not furnished with the survey data.
46. See Aitkenhead (2010). Notably, the ethnic diversity of authors and speakers featured on Hay stages has markedly increased over the last few years: a development that seems likely to be the result of

an active attempt to redress a negative perception of the festival in terms of diversity.

47. See Ramdarshan Bold (2018 and 2019). The 2011 census identified 86% of the UK population as white (Office for National Statistics, 'Ethnicity and National Identity in England and Wales: 2011'); whereas in 2017 the publishing industry was deemed to be 90% white—see Alison Flood (2017). For an interdisciplinary cultural perspective on how race impacts on cultural production more widely, see Saha (2017).

48. A liminal communitas, even—see Turner ([1961] 1995).

49. For example, a bell tent sleeping up to five people for hire costs £995 for the whole festival for 2019: https://www.pillow.co.uk/hay-festival-pre-pitched-camping-and-glamping/ (accessed 28 February 2019).

50. Port Eliot sadly ceased operating in 2019.

51. For more information on English PEN, see its site: https://www.englishpen.org. Jo Glanville worked in this role back in 2013, when I spoke to her at Hay; see conversation table at the end. The organisation's current Director is Daniel Gorman.

52. Sutherland is the author of *A Little History of Literature* (2013) among many other books.

53. Crace is now even better known as *The Guardian's* political sketch writer.

54. See Angela Bartie, *The Edinburgh Festivals* (2014).

55. I have anonymised all reader-audience participants described in this book. I note that I aimed to speak to a diverse range of participants, in terms of age, gender, class and racial and ethnic background, so far as was possible in the circumstances, but my choices were affected, to some extent, by chance: a material element of any festival experience.

56. The now-late, great Toni Morrison last performed at Hay in 2014.

57. See Society of Authors, 'Where We Stand: Festivals, Teaching, Appearances': https://www.societyofauthors.org/Where-We-Stand/Festivals,-teaching-appearances (accessed 2 February 2019).

58. PFD stands for Peter Fraser Dunlop.

59. See Katherine Cowdrey, 'Nielsen tracks sales at Hay and Edinburgh for first time', *The Bookseller*, 17 May 2016: https://www.thebookseller.com/news/nielsen-breakthrough-hay-and-edinburgh-festivals-329854. Hay stocked 3400 titles and around 55,000 units in 2017, when its sales rose by 17% after an expansion of the bookshop.

60. Anamik Saha has alluded to the awkwardness among white people working in the publishing industry in when discussing race and diversity in 'The Rationalizing/Racializing Logic of Capital in Cultural Production' (2016).

61. Ark, discussed in Chapter 2. See website: www.arkshortstories.com.

62. See Joy Lo Dico, 'Celebrated Literary Feud Ends After Naipaul and Theroux Bury the Hatchet', *The Independent*, 20 May 2011.

63. See Mullan (2012) and Worseley (2018), p. 2 of Chapter 12.

64. BBC Radio 4, Open Book, 16 September 2018 (my own transcription).

65. Ibid.

66. For example, Dionigi Albera and John Eade (eds.), *New Pathways in Pilgrimage Studies: Global Perspectives* (2016) tracks the 'massive increase in the volume of pilgrimage research and publications' (p. 1).

67. Turner, *From Ritual to Theatre: The Human Seriousness of Play* (1982).

68. There are many references to pilgrimage in articles about Hay. See, e.g., the reference to 'secular pilgrims in Jasper Rees, 'The Glastonbury of the Mind: Hay Turns 25', *The Arts Desk*, 31 May 2012: https://theartsdesk.com/comedy/glastonbury-mind-hay-turns-25.

69. See Abantu Book Festival's self-description, 'The Festival': https://www.abantubookfestival.co.za (accessed 8 May 2018).

70. Tourist packages are offered to destinations such as Prince Edward Island, the home of Anne of Green Gables, where 125,000 people visit each year for the purpose of visiting the stone foundations of the house there L. M. Montgomery once lived—25,000 of them, apparently, coming from Japan, from where there are direct flights for this sole reason, as the book has, bizarrely, become a cultural phenomenon. For a scholarly analysis, see Clare Fawcett

and Patrick Cormack, 'Guarding authenticity at literary tourism sites', *Annals of Tourism Research*, Vol. 28, no. 3, 2001, pp. 686–724. See also See Ann (without an 'e') Mah, 'Searching for Anne of Green Gables on Prince Edward Island', *New York Times*, 21 March 2014.

71. This is a transcription of an extract of Armitage's poem, 'From Where I Stand'. For the full text of this beautiful poem, with its published punctuation and formatting, please refer to pp. 116–117 of the book from which it was performed: *Walking Away* (Faber & Faber, 2015).

72. See Rubery (2016), p. 106.

73. See Squires (2007).

74. For one of many examples of this, see Le Guin, 'Lost in Mindspace', *The Guardian*, 21 July 2007: a review of Scarlett Thomas's novel, *The End of Mr Y*, in which Le Guin writes, wryly: 'I hope Scarlett Thomas and her publisher will not take it amiss if I evaluate her book in terms of genre, as to my mind this is to evaluate it as literature.'.

75. CYMERA, for instance, is a new literary festival dedicated to Science Fiction, Fantasy and Horror writing, founded by Ann Landmann, formerly events manager for Blackwell's Edinburgh, who wanted to 'celebrate three often overlooked but hugely popular genres' and 'put genre writing on an equal footing with literary fiction. See CYMERA website, press release dated 23 November 2018, at: https://www.cymerafestival.co.uk/media (accessed 28 April 2019).

76. See Peter McDonald, p.175 of 'On Strong Opinions: Celebrity Authors in the Contemporary Agora', *Celebrity Studies*, Vol. 8, no. 1, 2017, pp.172–175.

77. For more on the economic impact of Hay, see Charlotte Eyre's piece, 'Hay Festival Reports £70m Boost to Local Economy', *The Bookseller*, 12 September 2018.

78. See, for instance, S J Tepper, 'Fiction Reading in America: Explaining the Gender Gap', *Poetics*, Vol. 27, no. 4, 2000, pp. 255–275: https://www.sciencedirect.com/science/article/abs/pii/S03044

22X00000036. See also Driscoll (2014) on the idea of the 'literary middlebrow', including literary festival culture, as being feminized.

79. See Ann Steiner, 'Select, Display, and Sell: Curation Practices in the Bookshop', *Logos*, Vol. 28, no. 4, 2017, pp.18–31.

80. Wood no longer works for a newspaper; she is now Chair of the International Booker Prizes.

81. A few years later, he will publish an episodic memoir: *The Pigeon Tunnel* (London: Viking, 2016).

82. He has since published an episodic autobiography after all: The Pigeon Tunnel: Stories from My Life (2017).

83. See Cowdrey (2016).

84. See Will Storr, *The Science of Storytelling* (2019), p. 35.

85. See discussion of Zunshine's work on theory of mind and fiction in Chapter 2.

86. See discussion of Sharot's work on theory of mind, decision-making and audience influence in Chapter 2.

87. Phillip Vannini and Sarah Burgess have proposed that, in general, 'authenticity refers to the condition or quality of realness'—see Vannini and Burgess, 'Authenticity as Motivation and Aesthetic Experience' (2009), p. 104.

88. See e.g. Daniel Lea, 'The Anxieties of Authenticity in Post-2000 British Fiction' (2012).

89. For articulation of this proposition and discussion of the history and contemporary ideas of authenticity, see Lionel Trilling, *Sincerity and Authenticity* (1972); Charles Taylor, *The Ethics of Authenticity* (1992); Alessandro Ferrara, *Reflective Authenticity* (1998); E. Patrick Johnson, *Appropriating Blackness: Performance and the Politics of Authenticity* (2003); Charles Lindblom, *Culture and Authenticity* (2008); Vannini and Williams (eds.) (2009); and Wolfgang Funk, Florian Groß and Imtraud Huber (eds.), *The Aesthetics of Authenticity* (2012).

90. See Vannini and Williams (2009), p. 6.

91. See Funk et al. (2012), p. 13.

92. See Vannini and Williams (2009), p. 3.

93. See Funk et al. (2012), p. 13.

94. See Vannini and Williams (2009), p. 10, quoting Rebecca Erickson, 'Our Society, Our Selves: Becoming Authentic in an Inauthentic World', *Advanced Development Journal*, Vol. 6, 1994, pp. 27–39.
95. Ibid.
96. See Lea (2012), p. 474.
97. See Vannini and Williams (2009), p. 10.
98. See especially Johnson (2003) for an in-depth exploration of authenticity in relation to 'black' identity, including the idea of cultural appropriation.
99. See Vannini and Burgess (2009), p. 111.
100. See Vannini and Burgess (2009), p. 111, quoting Csikzentmihalyi (1997).
101. See Lea (2012), p. 459. While mulling over this idea as I am writing, I notice a viral tweet by an American electrical engineer for space science, Brad Luyster: 'Me at 19: why would someone with a cool stem degree want to sell kombucha at the farmers market or run a yarn store?/ Me at 30: ohhhhhhh'. Tweet from @zuph, 4 March 2019: https://twitter.com/zuph/status/1102582420900114432.
102. In Radbourne, Johansen, Glow and White's study, 'The Audience Experience: Measuring Quality in the Performing Arts' (2009), they proposed four elements of audience experience: authenticity, knowledge, risk and collective engagement—see pp. 19–20.
103. See Vannini and Burgess (2009), p. 116.
104. Vannini and Williams adopt a similar view, as articulated in their Introduction to Vannini and Williams (2009), p. 14.
105. See discussion of Gardiner's theory of the 'resurrection of the author' in Chapter 2.
106. See Zunshine (2006). Referring to Barthes' 'concept of the 'Death of the Author', Zunshine qualifies the idea that fictional narratives are always stored in a 'metarepresentational format' in our minds, and proposes that: 'We can be very sensitive to any attempt on the part of the writer to pass his or her fantasy as a "true" and not a "meta" representation'.

107. See Anthony Cummins, 'The Struggles of Karl Ove Knausgaard— And Those of His Readers—Are Finally Over' (2018); and Alex Clark, 'Drawn from Life: Why Have Novelists Stopped Making Things Up?' (2018). See also Hywel Dix's edited volume exploring autofiction's history and evolution, *Autofiction in English* (2018); and Marjorie Worthington's examination of autofiction in a post-truth era, 'Fiction in the "Post-truth" Era: The Ironic Effects of Autofiction' (2017).

108. For the notorious 'unmasking' article, see Claudio Gatti, 'Elena Ferrante: An Answer?' (2016) and commentary by Stephanie Kirschgaessner: 'Elena Ferrante: Literary Storm as Italian Reporter "Identifies" Author' (2016), and Orr (2016).

109. Shriver, 'I Hope the Concept of Cultural Appropriation Is a Passing Fad' (2016).

110. Yassmin Abdel-Magied, 'As Lionel Shriver Made Light of Identity, I Had No Choice but to Walk Out on Her' (2016).

111. Claire Armitstead, '"Identity Is a Pain in the Arse": Zadie Smith on Political Correctness' (2019).

112. See discussion in Chapter 2 of Coetzee's approach to the role of his authorial persona, with reference to Peter McDonald's work.

113. See discussion of Le Guin's work in Chapter 2.

114. See discussion of Denise Riley's and Steven Connor's theorisation of on the inner voice in Chapter 2.

115. See discussion of Rubery's work on the history of the talking book in Chapter 2.

116. See discussion of experientialism, stuffocation and the attention economy/ecology in Chapter 2, with reference to the work of Wallman (2015) and others.

117. See discussion of secular pilgrimage and liminality in Chapter 2.

118. See discussion of Lurie (2004), Meehan (2005), Driscoll (2014) and Weber (2018) in Chapter 2.

## Chapter 4

1. See Julie Bindel, 'Paul Burston's Literary Event, Polari' (2012).

2. See www.polarisalon.com (accessed 29 April 2019).

3. For an exploration of the implications of this terminology for librarianship, see Melinda F. Brown and Deborah L. Lilton, 'Finding The "B" in LGBTQ+' (2019).
4. See Paul Baker, *Polari - The Lost Language of Gay Men* (2002), p. 1.
5. See Baker (2002), p. 6.
6. See Baker (2002), p. 8.
7. See J. Bryan Lowder, 'Polari, the Gay Dialect' (2015).
8. See Peter Burton, *Parallel Lives* (1985), p. 38.
9. See Burton (1985), p. 39.
10. See Burton (1985), p. 41.
11. See Burton (1985), p. 42.
12. Piccadilly Palare' was a song, from Morrissey's 1990 *Bona Drag* album, and was about male prostitution around the Piccadilly area of London. The lyrics include: '*So bona to vada...oh you! Your lovely eek and your lovely riah*', which translates as: 'So good to see...oh you! Your lovely face and your lovely hair'. The counter-reaction to the song is referenced in Wikipedia entry on 'Polari', https://en.wik ipedia.org/wiki/Polari, accessed 3 October 2018.
13. See Bindel (2012).
14. See Dana Goodman, *The Republic of Letters* (1994), pp. 101–103.
15. See Habermas (1989), especially pp. 30–36.
16. See Bourdieu (1996), p. 51.
17. See Susanna Schmid, *British Literary Salons of the Late Eighteenth and Early Nineteenth Centuries* (2013).
18. See Maria Popova, *Figuring* (2019).
19. Text taken from the Polari Salon website: www.Polari.co.uk (accessed 29 November 2015).
20. See Jennifer Reed, 'The Three Phases of Ellen: From Queer to Gay to Post-Gay' (2011), p. 19.
21. See Reed (2011), p. 20.
22. See Reed (2011), p. 23.
23. See Reed (2011), p. 12.
24. This was taken from West's website: http://persiawestwords.net (accessed 16 March 2016).
25. Ibid.
26. See Josh Gabattiss, 'London Pride' (2018).

27. See West, Tweet published on 14 July 2018, accessed @persiawest on 8 October 2018.
28. See West, Tweet published on 26 May 2018, accessed @persiawest on 8 October 2018.
29. See Shriver (2016) and Abdel-Magied (2016).
30. Text taken from http://www.teamangelica.com (accessed 29 November 2015).
31. See Reed (2011), pp. 20–21.
32. See Max Weber, *Economy and Society* [1951] (1978).
33. See Maffesoli (1996), p. 12.
34. See Martin Cox, 'The Long-Haul Out of the Closet' (2002), p. 169.
35. See Stella Duffy's blog, 'Talking Books and Writing and Diversity and Stuff' (2018); also 'The Book Event – Thoughts for Authors' (2013), for Duffy's perspective on how few other authors appear to practice readings.
36. Emphasis added.
37. See Duffy (2018). Emphasis added.
38. See Duffy, 'Some Equality Is Not Equality' (2016).
39. See Peele, 'Introduction', p. 5, of Peele ed., *Queer Popular Culture* (2011).
40. See Melena Ryszik, 'The Comedy-Destroying, Soul-Affirming Art of Hannah Gadsby' (2018).
41. Habermas [1962] (1989), p. 34.
42. See Fischer-Lichte (2008), pp. 38–39, and my discussion in Chapter 2.
43. See Paul Burston, 'Polari First Book Prize 2018' (2018).
44. Ibid.
45. See Clark (2018) and Cummins (2018) and discussion of autofiction in Chapter 3.
46. See Burton (1985), p. 118.
47. See Maffesoli (1996), p. 23.
48. See Maffesoli (1996), p. 69.
49. See Maffesoli (1996), p. 25.
50. See Maffesoli (1996), p. 42.
51. See Dewey, *Democracy and Education* [1916] (2001), p. 8.

## Chapter 5

1. See Geertz(1973), pp. 5–6, 9–10.
2. See Moran (2018) EPub location 164.2/446.
3. See Dewey, *Art as Experience* (1939), especially 'Having an Experience', pp. 35–57. See also the epigraph at the beginning of this book by W. S. Piero.
4. Deleuze, 'Literature and Life', *Essays Critical and Clinical* (1997), p. 1.
5. The term '*experiential*' has been used by some anthropologists before, but only to refer to the anthropologist themselves—as a way of emphasising the importance of doing lengthy fieldwork in a place in order to experience living among remote cultural groups before going on to write about them; it has not been used previously to refer to the ways in which ethnographic writing can be crafted to evoke and interrogate the experience of participants in a given event or situation. See, for example, Carol Delany's book, *Investigating Culture: An Experiential Introduction to Anthropology* [2004] (2017).
6. George Clifford and James Marcus, *Writing Culture: The Poetics and Politics of Ethnography* [1986] (2010).
7. *Works and Lives: The Anthropologist as Author*, Cambridge: Polity Press, 1988.
8. For insightful commentary on contemporary genres of anthropological writing, see Helena Wulff (ed.), *The Anthropologist as Writer: Genres and Contexts in the Twenty-First Century*, New York: Berghahn, 2016.
9. 'Lifeworlds' is a lovely term invented by Michael D. Jackson—see *How Lifeworlds Work* (2017). An anthropologist, poet and novelist Jackson prefers the term 'lifeworld' to 'society', explaining: 'When I speak of a lifeworld (rather than a society), I follow Edmund Husserl's claim that we live in a world of intersubjective relationships.... Lifeworlds are open, complex, and never self-contained, and an anthropologist enters a lifeworld as a participant as well as an observer'.

10. See Fiona Copland and Angela Creese, *Linguistic Ethnography* (2015), pp. 9–10.

11. See Hurston, *Mules and Men* [1935] (2009); *Barracoon* [1935] (2018), and *Their Eyes Were Watching God* [1937] (1986). For a reflection on the influence of Hurston's work on the philosophy of language, and specifically 'performism', see Parker English, *What We Say, Who We Are* (2010). See also Dwight Conquergood's discussion of Hurston's legacy for performance studies and ethnography in 'Performance', in Johnson ed. (2013), particularly p. 39. For a discussion of Hurston's neglect in the academy, from the 1950s until she was championed by Alice Walker, see Cynthia Davis and Verner D. Mitchell (eds.), *Zora Neale Hurston* (2013). For a recent historical view of the value of Hurston's work, and the discrimination she faced as a black woman in her time, see Tiffany Ruby Patterson's *Zora Neale Hurston and a History of Southern Life* (2018).

12. See, e.g., Clifford Geertz, *Works and Lives* (1973); Paul Stoller, *Sensuous Scholarship* (1997); Ruth Behar and Deborah Gordon (eds.), *Women Writing Culture* (1996); Alisse Waterson and Maria D. Vesperi (eds.), *Anthropology Off the Shelf* (2011); Helena Wulff (ed.), *The Anthropologist as Writer* (2016); Judith Okely (ed.), *Anthropological Practice* (2013).

13. To an extent, Malinowski's work in the 1920s manifested literary techniques: *Argonauts of the Western Pacific: An Account of Native Enterprise and Adventure in the Archipelagos of Melanesian New Guinea* (1922), includes highly evocative scene setting, often addressing the reader directly—e.g. 'Imagine yourself suddenly set down surrounded by all your gear, alone on a tropical beach close to a native village...' (p. 60). Clifford Geertz has written persuasively about Malinowski's literary influences, and other literary influences in anthropology, in *Works and Lives: The Anthropologist as Author* (1988)—but in that book, and in much anthropological writing until recently, Hurston's influence has been neglected.

14. Different scholars have adopted different labels for their own 'brand' of ethnographic writing which has similar objectives— 'sensuous' (Stoller, 1997); 'evocative' (Ellis and Bochner, 2016);

and 'interpretive' (Ellis and Bochner, 2016). My literary approach to writing experientially is perhaps most closely aligned to Michael D. Jackson's idea of 'radical empiricism' (1989), which he described as a kind of ethnography that focuses on 'lived experience' through an attention to writing. In *Paths Towards a Clearing* (1989), Jackson specifically proposed that this kind of ethnographic writing should involve the use of 'multivocal' forms, the engagement of all five senses, and the inclusion of the ethnographer's own experiences (see p. 8).

15. For examples of scholarly and creative work published by the same author-anthropologist, see: Ruth Finnegan, *Oral Literature in Africa* (1970) and *Black Inked Pearl* (2015); Ruth Behar, *The Vulnerable Observer* (1996) and *Lucky Broken Girl* (2017); Michael D. Jackson, *Paths Toward a Clearing: Radical Empiricism and Ethnographic Inquiry* (1989) and *Dead Reckoning* (2006); Paul Stoller, *Sensuous Scholarship* (1997) and *Jaguar* (1999); Kirin Narayan, *Love, Stars and All That* (1994), and *Alive in the Writing* (2012). See also the work of sociologist Patricia Leavy: *Handbook of Arts-Based Research* (2017) and *Low-Fat Love* (2015). For an overview of contemporary anthropologist-writers, see Wulff (2016), cited above.

16. A great example of experimental literary modes of writing ethnography is Anand Pandian and Stuart Maclean (ed.), *Crumpled Paper Boat* (2017), and also Helena Wulff (ed.), *The Anthropologist as Writer* (2016).

17. See, for example, Patricia Leavy, *Method Meets Art* [2008] (2015); Arnd Schneider and Christopher Wright (eds.), *Anthropology and Art Practice* (2013).

18. 'Cultural phenomenology', Connor suggested, 'would aim to enlarge, diversify and particularise the study of culture. Instead of readings of abstract structures, functions and dynamics, it would be interested in substances, habits, organs, rituals… processes and patterns of feeling. Such interests would be at once philosophical and poetic, explanatory and exploratory, analytic and evocative. Above all, whatever interpreting and explication cultural phenomenology managed to pull off would be achieved by the

manner in which it got *amid* a given subject or problem, not by the degree to which it got on top of it'. This would mean attending to the 'embodiedness of experience', and the 'affective, somatic dimensions of cultural experience', as opposed to the 'out-of-body experiences of cultural studies'. See Connor, 'CP: or, A Few Don'ts By A Cultural Phenomenologist' (1999), p. 18.

19. Interestingly, Geertz later went on to call for a 'cultural phenomenology' himself, without an apparent awareness of Connor having proposed the same thing with reference to his own work. See p. 360 of Geertz's, 'Person, Time and Conduct in Bali' (2007).

20. Connor highlighted ethnography's reflexive orientation, in comparison with conventional scholarly writing, just as Jackson did, describing it as 'the impulse to acknowledge rather than to conceal the fact that writing is taking place, and that a particular person is doing the writing'. See Connor, 'CP' (1999), p. 18.

21. See, for example, Leavy, *Method Meets Art* [2008] (2015); Schneider and Wright (eds.) (2013); Pandian and McLean (eds.) (2018).

22. See I. A. Richards, *Practical Criticism* (1929).

23. See Roland Barthes, 'The Death of the Author' (1967).

24. Foucault bolstered this idea two years later in a talk, 'What is an author?', which also sought to deny the privileged status of the author when interpreting a text. See Michel Foucault, 'What Is an Author?' [1969] (1979).

25. See Stanley Fish, 'Is there a text in this class?' (1980).

26. Fish's idea would be echoed and developed with a wider socio-political perspective in Benedict Anderson's theory of *Imagined Communities* (1983).

27. See Gerard Genette, *Paratexts* (1997).

28. Genette called these 'peritexts'—see Genette (1997).

29. Genette called these 'epitexts'—see Genette (1997).

30. See Juliet Gardiner, 'Recuperating the Author' (2000).

31. See Gardiner (2000), p. 274.

32. See Gardiner (2000), p. 256.

33. Ibid. In this vein, Squires (2007) delved more deeply into ways in which the marketing of fiction fundamentally affects its reception.
34. See Lurie, 'Festival, Inc.' (2004), p. 12.
35. See Michael Meehan, 'The Word Made Flesh' (2005).
36. See Meehan (2005).
37. See Liana Giorgi, 'Between Tradition, Vision and Imagination: The Public Sphere of Literature Festivals' (2011), p. 34.
38. See Johanson and Freeman, 'The Reader as Audience: The Appeal of the Writers' Festival to the Contemporary Audience' (2012).
39. See Johanson and Freeman (2012), p. 312.
40. See Johanson and Freeman (2012), p. 313.
41. See Fuller and Rehberg Sedo, *Reading Beyond the Book: The Social Practices of Contemporary Literary Culture* (2013).
42. For more on this, see Danielle Fuller, 'Listening to the Readers of "Canada Reads"', in Fuller and Rehberg Sedo' (2013).
43. See Fuller and Rehberg Sedo (2013), p. 244.
44. See Driscoll (2014), p. 192. Criticisms that 'dismiss literary festivals as commerce driven and are snide about their predominantly female, middle class audiences', Driscoll argues, 'only reinforce the fact that festivals are middlebrow institutions, working outside the legitimate site of higher education and offering a *more accessible* kind of cultural experience'.
45. *Literary Festivals and Contemporary Book Culture* (2018). This book follows Weber's earlier article on 'Conceptualising the Audience Experience at the Literary Festivals' (2015).
46. See Weber (2018), p. 186.
47. See Weber (2018), p. 33. To experiment with another innovative approach to exploring audience experience at literary festivals, Driscoll went on to conduct a sentiment analysis of the Melbourne Writers' Festival using audience Twitter feeds—see Driscoll, 'Sentiment analysis and the literary festival audience' (2015). The results were limited; Driscoll's main conclusion was that emotion expressed through Twitter tends to be 'moderate'. See discussion in Weber (2018), p. 33.
48. See Lurie (2004), p. 12. Other sociological studies of literary festivals, many of which are outlined in more detail in Weber

(2018), include: Carolyn Bain, 'Searching for Tennessee: Performative Identity and the Theatrical Event. Tennessee Williams/New Orleans Literary Festival' (2007); Giorgi (2011); Cori Stewart 'We Call Upon the Author to Explain: Theorising Writers' Festivals as Sites of Contemporary Public Culture' (2010); Wenche Ommundsen, 'Literary Festivals and Cultural Consumption' (2009).

49. See Weber (2018), p. 10.
50. See James English's study of literary prizes (2008).
51. Bourdieu's texts expanding upon his theorisation of the literary field include: *Distinction: A Social Critique of the Judgement of Taste* (1984); *The Rules of Art* (1996); and 'The Field of Cultural Production' (2006).
52. See Weber (2018), p. 28.
53. Motivations are said to include 'people watching', having a 'shared experience', having 'interpersonal' and 'professional interactions', and having 'conceptual interaction with a community', and 'enhancing appreciation of literature', 'developing professional knowledge', 'intellectual engagement' and 'broadening cultural experiences'. See Weber (2018), pp. 63–53.
54. See Weber (2018), p. 155.
55. See Weber (2018), pp. 39–40.
56. See Weber (2018), p. 196.
57. See Weber (2018), p. 48.
58. See Weber (2018), pp. 95–6.
59. See Weber (2018), p. 77.
60. See Weber (2018), p. 37.
61. See Finkelstein and Squires (2019).
62. See Finkelstein and Squires (2019), p. 1 of Ch. 30.
63. See Finkelstein and Squires (2019), p. 2 of Ch. 30.
64. See Finkelstein and Squires (2019), p. 2 of Ch. 30.
65. See Driscoll and Squires (2018).
66. See Driscoll and Squires (2018), para. 18.
67. See Driscoll and Squires (2018), para. 16.
68. See Le Guin, 'Telling Is Listening' (2004), p. 199.

69. John Sutherland used this term to refer to Q. D. Leavis's work in his book, *Fiction and the Fiction Industry* (1978). Leavis herself called the project 'anthropological', in her introduction to the book (1932), p. xv.

70. See The Middlebrow Network of scholars' summary of Leavis's contribution, accessible online at: https://www.middlebrow-net work.com/Annotations/tabid/1061/articleType/ArticleView/articl eId/1459/Leavis-Q-D-Fiction-and-the-Reading-Public-London-Pimlico-2000-first-pub-1932.aspx (accessed 4 March 2019).

71. See Loren Glass, 'An Interview with Janice Radway' (2009), p. 92.

72. See Radway (1984), p. 210.

73. Radway herself has become increasingly interested anthropological approaches to understanding local and global dynamics and the 'micropolitics of subjectivity' in contemporary culture, but clearly considers herself to remain an outlier in this respect in relation to the fields in which she is established. See Glass (2009).

74. See Reed (2011), p. 27.

75. See Reed (2011), p. 193.

76. See Reed (2011), p. 195.

77. *Saffron Shadows and Salvaged Scripts: Literary Life in Myanmar Under Censorship and in Transition*, New York: Columbia University Press, 2015.

78. See Wulff, *Rhythms of Writing* (2017), p. xiii.

79. See Wulf (2017), p. xvii.

80. See Wulff (2008).

81. See Malinowski, 'The Problem of Meaning in Primitive Languages' [1923] (1989).

82. See Finnegan, *Oral Literature in Africa* [1970] (2012).

83. See Raymond Williams, *Culture and Society* [1958] (1983), p. 309.

84. Dennis Tedlock, for instance—see *Finding the Center the Art of the Zuni* (1972): a book of translations of Native American Zuni narratives.

85. See Bauman and Joel Sherzer (eds.), *Explorations in the Ethnography of Speaking* (1974).

86. See Bauman and Sherzer (eds.) (1974), Introduction: p. 12.

87. See Bauman (1975), p. 30.

88. See Bauman (1975), p. 21.
89. See Bauman (1975), p. 38.
90. See Bauman (1975), p. 42.
91. See Finnegan (1977), p. 3.
92. See Finnegan (1977), p. 2 (my emphasis added.) She went on to clarify: 'In the written form we set it apart typographically, but also by its setting or the way it is performed or read aloud: whatever its rhythmic properties may be, a poem is likely (even in a literate culture) to be delivered in a manner and mood which sets it apart from everyday speech and prose utterance'—p. 25.
93. Finnegan added: 'even when there is little or no change of actual wording in a given poem between performances, the context still adds its own weight and meaning to the delivery, so that the whole occasion is unique'—(1977), p. 28.
94. See Finnegan (1977), p. 26.
95. See Thiong'o, 'Notes Towards a Performance Theory of Orature' (2007).
96. See Ong, *Orality and Literacy: The Technologizing of the Word* (1982).
97. See Ong [1982] (2002), pp. 73–74.
98. See Ong [1982] (2002), p. 32.
99. See Ong [1982] (2002), p. 142.
100. See Connor (2009) for this critique of Ong, referenced earlier.
101. See Turner, 'Betwixt and Between: The Liminal Period in Rites of Passage' (1967).
102. See p. 129 of Sharon Rowe, 'Modern Sports: Liminal Ritual or Liminoid Leisure' (2008).
103. See Graham St. John', 'Introduction' in St. John (ed.), *Victor Turner and Contemporary Cultural Performance* (2008), p. 7.
104. Turner adapted the term 'liminal' to 'liminoid' when referring to Western contexts, on the basis that such performance events were less transformational; see Turner, 'Liminal to Liminoid, in Play, Flow and Ritual: an essay in comparative symbology' in Turner, *From Ritual to Theatre: The Human Seriousness of Play* (1982). This has been critiqued by later scholars; see, e.g., Rowe (2008), p. 141.

Turner would go on to expand upon these ideas in *The Anthropology of Performance* and *The Anthropology of Experience* (both 1986).

105. Schechner would go on to write *Between Theater and Anthropology* (1985): a direct consequence of his work with Turner.

106. See Schechner, *Performance Studies: An Introduction* (2002).

107. See St. John (ed.) (2008).

108. As Pollock put it: 'The struggle to write performance seems to me to give performative writing its depth and value, ethically, politically and aesthetically. In this struggle at least, performative writing seems one way not only to make meaning but to make writing meaningful'. See Pollock, 'Performing Writing' (1998), p. 95.

109. Recent scholarly publications in this vein include Tríona Ní Shíocháin, *Singing Ideas: Performance, Politics and Oral Poetry* (2018).

110. See, for instance, Laura Severin, *Poetry Off the Page: Twentieth-Century British Women Poets in Performance* (2017); Julia Virtanen, *Poetry and Performance During the British Poetry Revival 1960–1980* (2017).

111. The central importance of the body is explored, for example, in Adrienne Rich, *Of Woman Born* [1976] (1995).

112. See Merleau-Ponty, *The Phenomenology of Perception* [1945] (2013).

113. See Thomas Csordas, 'Somatic Modes of Attention' (1993), p. 138.

114. The book opens, not with a theoretical reflection, but with a scene, involving a conversation between two scholar friends over French toast about the contemporary resonances of an ancient Sufi story that explored the interconnectedness of the intelligible and the sensible. 'Stiffened from long sleep in the background of scholarly life', Stoller reflected, 'the scholar's body yearns to exercise its muscles… to restore its sensibilities… it wants to breathe in the pungent odors of social life, to run its palms over the jagged surface of social reality, to hear the wondrous symphonies of social experience, to see the sensuous shapes and colours that fill windows of consciousness. It wants to awaken the imagination and bring

scholarship back to "the things themselves". See Stoller (1997), pp. xi–xii.

115. Stoller here references the work of Kirsten Hastrup; see Stoller (1997), p. 91.

116. See Stoller (1997), p. 91.

117. To me, the word is too loaded with sexual implications.

118. A key example is Sarah Pink's book, *Doing Sensory Ethnography* (2009).

119. Echoing Stoller, they described the basic premise of the book as being that '*humans sense as well as make sense*'. See Vannini et al. (2012), p. 18.

120. See Vannini et al. (2012), p. 13.

121. See Vannini et al. (2012), pp. 53–54.

122. See Vannini et al. (2012), pp. 75–76.

123. See Vannini et al. (2012), p. 80.

124. See Ellis and Bochner, *Evocative Autoethnography* (2016).

125. See Michel de Certeau, 'Reading as Poaching', pp. 130–139 of Towheed, Crone and Halsey (eds.) (2010). He adds: 'Reading is… situated at the point where social stratification (class relationships) and poetic operations (the practitioner's constructions of a text) intersect' (p. 135). 'In earlier times, the reader interiorized the text; he made his voice the body of the other; he was its actor…. The withdrawal of the body… is a distancing of the text' (p. 137).

126. See p. 136 of De Certeau in Towheed, Crone and Halsey (eds.) (2010).

127. As Dariusz Gafijczuk puts it, reflecting on Back and Pawar's work in a special 'Live Methods' edition of *The Sociological Review*: 'the contemporary sociological imagination has proven remarkably resistant to duration as an active analytical dimension'; he describes sociology as having been 'starved of temporal sensibility'. See Gafijczuk, 'Vividness, Time and the Restitution of Sociological Imagination' (2017).

128. See Back and Pawar (2012), p. 8.

129. See Back and Pawar (2012), p. 13.

130. See Back and Pawar (2012), p. 21. This aesthetic disposition to sociological writing mirrors the approaches proposed by Stoller and by Vannini, Waskul and Gottschalk among others.
131. In the interests of reflexivity, I note that David Wiles is my dad. They say you always start to become your parents, whether you like it or not.
132. I note that Temporality, and especially rhythm, is another aspect of the 'feedback loop' of liveness that Fischer-Lichte describes as 'a principle based on the human body. The heartbeat, the blood circulation, and respiration each follow their own rhythm, as do the movements we carry out while walking… writing… The same goes for the sounds we make when speaking, singing, laughing, crying. The inner movements of our bodies that we are incapable of perceiving are also organized rhythmically', and have a 'particular capacity for perceiving rhythms and tuning our bodies to them'. Her notion of 'the autopoietic feedback loop', she suggests, 'can show whether and to what extent the performance succeeds in drawing the audience into its rhythm'. See Fischer-Lichte (2008), p. 140.
133. See D. Wiles (2014), pp. 47–48.
134. See D. Wiles (2014), p. 53.
135. D. Wiles references Eviatar Zarubavel's use of 'mnemonic communities' in *Time Maps: Collective Memory and the Shape of the Past* (2003).
136. See Anderson (1983).
137. Lerner et al. point out that 'many psychological scientists now assume that emotions are, for better or worse, the dominant driver of most meaningful decisions in life', and point out that scholarly papers on emotion and decision making doubled from 2004 to 2007 and again from 2007 to 2011. See Lerner et al. (2015), pp. 800–801. Helena Wulff interrogated the 'emotional turn' in scholarship early on in her edited volume, *Emotions: A Cultural Reader* (2007), and proposed that the neuroscience of emotion should be sufficient to 'close the traditional Western gap in which emotions are separated from rationality and thought: the heart vs mind debate' (see p. 1).

138. See Williams, *Marxism and Literature* (1978), p. 131.
139. See Behar, *The Vulnerable Observer* (1997).
140. As Fischer-Lichte puts it, describing the power and impact of the voice in performance: it 'leaps from the body and vibrates through space so that it is heard by both the speaker... and others. The intimate relationship between body and voice becomes particularly evident in screams, sighs, moans, sobs and laughter'. Voice can 'clarify the syntactic structure of what is spoken', 'accentuate and emphasize the intended meaning', and 'further reinforce its desired effect on the listener,' by creating a 'bridge' and establishing a 'relationship between two subjects'. See Fischer-Lichte (2008), pp. 125–126.
141. See, e.g., Sharma and Tygstrup (eds.), *Structures of Feeling* (2015). The Introduction (p. 2) acknowledges the belated revaluation of Williams's work in this area.
142. See Maffesoli, *The Time of the Tribes* (1996), p. 11. He notes here that the German Romantic idea of *Stimmung* (atmosphere) is being invoked more and more often, on one hand to describe relations between social micro-groups, and on the other hand to show the way these groups are situated in spatial terms (ecology, habitat, neighbourhood)': a reference to how emotions are connected to physical, spatial environments.
143. Lecture given by Georgina Born at the British Academy, 19th May 2015.
144. See Lofgren and Ehn, 'Emotions in Academia' (2007), p. 102.
145. See Lofgren and Ehn (2007), p. 102.
146. See Wilce (2009), p. 1.
147. See Wilce (2009), p. 2.
148. See Wilce (2009), p. 3.
149. See Wilce (2009), p. 190.
150. See Houen, 'Introduction: Affecting Words' (2011), p. 218.
151. See Houen (2011), p. 222.
152. See Attridge, 'Once More with Feeling: Art, Affect, and Performance' (2011).
153. Attridge elaborates this to propose that 'the affective event of a literary work arises as the tangible experience of an 'as if', which

'means we feel [the work's] emotions, but always as performances of language's powers', which are bound up with literary form. He demonstrates this through a close reading of a visceral, gory passage from Cormac McCarthy's novel *Blood Meridian* (1985), pointing out the difficulty of articulating the 'complex of feelings' of a reader engaging with this text, but describing how McCarthy's account of a horrifying event 'produces not just some mental simulacrum of affect, but a real feeling that is quite likely to register on the skin or in the pit of the stomach'. See Attridge (2011), pp. 392–393.

154. See Daniel W. Smith's introduction to Deleuze (1997), p. xxxiii.

155. Ibid., p. liii.

156. See Oxford English Dictionary entry, 'aesthetic', 3rd edition (2011).

157. See Gaut, *Art, Emotion and Ethics* (2007).

158. See, in particular, Georgina Born's article making this case: 'The Social and the Aesthetic: For a Post-Bourdieuian Theory of Cultural Production' (2010).

159. See Georgina Born, Eric Lewis and Will Straw (eds.), *Improvisation and Social Aesthetics* (2017), blurb.

160. See Born (2010), p. 8. See also Andrew Barry and Born (eds.), *Interdisciplinarity: Reconfigurations of the Social and Natural Sciences* (2013).

161. *Rationalizing Culture: IRCAM, Boulez and the Institutionalization of the Musical Avant-garde* (1995).

162. *Uncertain Vision: Birt, Dyke and the Reinvention of the BBC* (2006).

163. See Born, Lewis and Straw, 'Introduction: What Is Social Aesthetics?' (2017).

164. See Born et al. (2017), p. 9.

165. See Born et al. (2017), p. 3.

166. See Born et al. (2017), p. 4.

167. See Born et al. (2017), p. 46.

168. See Anjan Chatterjee, 'Neuroaesthetics: Researchers Unravel the Biology of Beauty and Art' (2014) and *The Aesthetic Brain: How We Evolved to Desire Beauty and Enjoy Art* (2015). Chaterjee calls neuroaesthetics a 'discipline dedicated to exploring the neural

processes underlying our appreciation and production of beautiful objects and artwork, experiences that include perception, interpretation, emotion, and action', which 'represents a convergence of neuroscience and empirical aesthetics' and is 'rooted in observation'.

169. See Chatterjee (2014).
170. See Chatterjee (2014).
171. See Starr (2013), p. 120.
172. See Starr (2013), p. 118.
173. Starr elaborates this, explaining that such reward values 'exist in comparison (for that is what reward value does, enabling us to compare choices, experiences, desires, and outcomes), so that pleasures, displeasures, and uneasiness combine in dynamic play. Any such configuration (laughter, discomfort, awe, longing, pleasure) is a unique one. And once made, it is not fixed but can decay over time or newly evolve, becoming available for new configurations and new evaluations. From the perspective of neural circuitry, she explains, this occurs through communication between reward regions (such as the nucleus accumbens) and the frontal cortex. See Starr (2013), p. 121.
174. See Starr (2013), p. 120.
175. See Starr (2013), p. 150.
176. See John Fiske, 'Audiencing: Cultural Practice and Cultural Studies' (1994).
177. See Eleonora Belfiore and Oliver Bennett, *The Social Impact of the Arts: An Intellectual History* (2008), p. 6, for an elaboration of this argument by reference to the history of debates around the social impact of the arts.
178. Penelope Woods, for example, through her study of audiences at Shakespeare's Globe Theatre, sought to foreground the role of 'the experiential, of the phenomenological, in audience studies', through 'critical engagement with affect and feeling', by recognising audience subjectivity through a new 'ethics of listening', largely through conversations with audiences before and after performances, based on a set of indicative questions. Woods proposes that, despite possibilities for engagement with audiences

through social media, such as Facebook, 'the discursive face-to-face sociality of the theatre may yet remain best served, in research terms, by methods that invoke and engage with this discursive sociality in an unmediated face-to-face context'. See Woods, *Globe Audiences: Spectatorship and Reconstruction at Shakespeare's Globe* (2011).

179. See Arts Council web page, 'The Case for Arts and Culture', https://www.artscouncil.org.uk/why-culture-matters/case-art-and-culture (accessed 21 February 2019).

180. See Arts Council England, 'The Value of the Arts and Culture to People and Society', 2014, www.artscouncil.org.uk/media/upl oads/pdf/The-value-of-arts-and-culture-to-people-and-society-An-evidence-review-Mar-2014.pdf.

181. See Arts Council England (2014), p. 47.

182. See Arts Council England (2014), p. 4.

183. See Arts Council England (2014), p. 47.

184. See Belfiore (2014).

185. See Heywood et al., 'Enriching Britain' (2015), p. 27.

186. See AHRC project report, by Geoffrey Crossick & Patrycja Kaszynska, 'Understanding the Value of Arts & Culture: The AHRC Cultural Value Project' (2016), Executive summary, p. 5.

187. AHRC (2016), p. 9.

188. AHRC (2016), p. 22.

189. AHRC (2016), p. 22.

190. AHRC (2016), p. 121.

191. AHRC (2016), p. 127.

192. AHRC (2016), p. 21.

193. AHRC (2016), p. 22.

194. AHRC (2016), pp. 52–54.

195. AHRC (2016), pp. 67–68.

196. AHRC (2016), p. 78.

197. AHRC (2016), p. 45.

198. One of the scholars who contributed to the AHRC report, and who has been seeking to explore experiential qualities of performance, is performance studies scholar Matthew Reason. Together with Anja

Mølle Lindelof, he edited an interdisciplinary volume called *Experiencing Liveness in Contemporary Performance* (2015), in which they argue, along the lines of the AHRC report, that audience research needs to be more phenomenological—and that it needs to include analyses of '*how do*—how do performances and audiences interact to construct a live experience', whereby the 'particular dynamic, the particular experiential qualities of these performances' are considered. The 'focus needs to shift away… from liveness and towards experiencing live', they proposed, because the 'challenge of engaging with, understanding and mapping experience seems fundamentally more vital than searching after an ontology'. This, they added, 'invites consideration of a *thickening* of our understanding of the experience of live performance'—a metaphor that resonates with the 'thick description' developed by ethnographers. See Reason and Lindelof (eds.) (2016), p. 5.

199. AHRC (2016), p. 141.
200. AHRC (2016), p. 142 and p. 150.
201. AHRC (2016), p. 145, citing Pink (2009) and Paterson (2009).
202. AHRC (2016), p. 145, citing Matthew Reason (2010).
203. See Ben Walmsley, 'Deep Hanging Out in the Arts' (2018), Abstract.
204. See Walmsley (2018), Conclusion.
205. See Walmsley (2018), Abstract.
206. See 'Funding announced for new collaborative centre for cultural value', AHRC, 9 August 2018: https://ahrc.ukri.org/newsevents/news/funding-announced-for-new-collaborative-centre-for-cultural-value/ (accessed 9 February 2019).
207. See Paul Benneworth, 'Putting Impact into Context (2015).
208. See the discussion of this issue in relation to arts policy in Ben Walmsley's article, 'Deep hanging out in the arts: an anthropological approach to capturing cultural value' (2018). For critiques of the broader 'impact agenda' in academia, see Collini (2012) and Ben R. Martin, 'The Research Excellence Framework and the 'Impact Agenda': Are We Creating a Frankenstein Monster?' (2011).
209. Susan Sontag, 2001 Jerusalem Prize acceptance speech (2013).

210. See, e.g., Charles A. Gallagher, 'Blacks, Jews, Gays and Immigrants Are Taking Over' (2014); Zachary Karabell, '(Mis)leading Indicators: Why Our Economic Numbers Distort Reality' (2014).

## Chapter 6

1. This echoes Weber's indicative conclusions about literary festival audiences, discussed in Chapter 2.
2. See discussion in Chapter 2.
3. Ibid.
4. See discussion in Chapter 2.
5. See discussion in Chapter 3.
6. See discussion in Chapter 2.
7. See conversation with James Daunt in Chapter 3.
8. See discussion in Chapter 3.
9. See discussion in Chapter 2.
10. See 'Coronavirus: Almost 500,000 stream first online Hay Festival', BBC News, 1 June 2020: https://www.bbc.co.uk/news/uk-wales-52875868 (accessed 8 June 2020).
11. See discussion in Chapter 2, with reference to the work of Tali Sharot among others.
12. See extended discussion of the notion of authenticity towards the end of Chapter 3.
13. See discussion in Chapter 2.
14. See discussion in Chapter 2.
15. See discussion of liminality and liveness in Chapter 2, with reference to Victor Turner's work.
16. See discussion in Chapter 2, with reference to Fischer-Lichte's work on feedback loops.
17. See discussion in Chapter 2, with reference to Joseph Devlin and colleagues' work on physiological responses to audience participation.
18. See discussion in Chapter 3.
19. See discussion in Chapter 2.
20. See discussion in Chapter 2.

21. See discussion in Chapter 2, and Helen Taylor's important book referred to there: *Why Women Read Fiction* (2019).
22. See Evan Williams, 'The art of asking a question to a literary festival panel' (2016).
23. See Le Guin (2004), pp.261–282.
24. See discussion in Chapters 2 and 3.
25. See discussion in Chapter 2.
26. See discussion in Chapter 2.
27. See discussion of Rubery's research in Chapter 2.
28. See Joanna Robinson: 'Neil Gaiman on His New Storytelling MasterClass, *Good Omens,* and the Upside of Twitter' (2019) in which he is quoted as saying: 'I know lots of novelists. Novelists are very nice people. But I'm not a novelist. I'm a storyteller who sometimes writes novels, and graphic novels, and short stories, and makes film or television'.
29. See discussion in Chapter 2.
30. See discussion in Chapter 2.
31. See discussion in Chapters 2 and 4.
32. See discussion in Chapter 2.
33. On this note, I realised with dismay, when editing this Hay ethnography, that I had only focused on a series of white male author-performers. This was partly due to programming, partly due to circumstance, and partly due to the loss of several recorded conversations with women author-performers whom I had intended to feature, including the magnificent Anne Enright. This book was pared down to feature only two ethnographies, when others that I had researched and sketched out would have featured more diverse author-performers including more women, adding to the sense of distortion. In future, I have resolved to attend more carefully to my own representation of diversity in my research.
34. See discussion in Chapter 3.
35. See Bradford Lit Fest website: https://www.bradfordlitfest.co.uk (accessed 1 October 2018).
36. See discussion in Chapters 2 and 3.
37. See discussion in Chapter 2, with reference to Gardiner's work on the resurrection of the author.

38. See discussion in Chapter 3.
39. See Cummins (2018) and discussion in Chapter 3.
40. See discussion in Chapter 3, with reference to Gatti (2016), Kirschgaessner (2016), and Orr (2016).
41. See discussion in Chapters 2–4.
42. See Armitstead (2019).
43. Lan Samantha Chang, 'Writers, protect your inner life' (2017).
44. Ibid.
45. See discussion in Chapter 2.
46. See Celeste Ng, Tweet posted on 12 July 2018, Twitter handle @pronounced-_ing. Accessed 2 Feb 2019 at: https://twitter.com/pronounced_ing/status/1017539391789654016?lang=en
47. Anon, ibid.
48. Ibid.
49. See discussion in Chapter 2.
50. See discussion in Chapter 2, with reference to Fischer-Lichte's work on feedback loops.
51. See Chapter 2.
52. See Chapter 3.
53. See Chang (2017).
54. See Lorrie Moore, 'It's better to write than be a writer' (2018)
55. See discussion in Chapter 2.
56. See discussion in Chapter 2.
57. See Chapter 3.
58. See discussion in Chapter 2.
59. Geertz (1973), pp. 5–6, 9–10.
60. Oswald's full statement is available online at: https://secure.ersvotes.com/V2-4-4/oxfordpoetry19/en/home?bbp=-1&x=-1 (accessed 30 May 2019).

## Chapter 7

1. See Le Guin, 'Off the Page: Loud Cows' (2004), which includes the full version of this performance talk and poem.

# Bibliography

Abdel-Magied, Yassmin, 'As Lionel Shriver Made Light of Identity, I Had No Choice but to Walk Out on Her', *The Guardian*, 10 September 2016.

Abrahams, Ian and Wishart, Bridget, *Festivalized: Music, Politics and Alternative Culture*, London: S.A.F. Publishing Limited, 2010.

Adams, Tony E., Holman Jones, Stacy and Ellis, Caroline (eds.), *Autoethnography: Understanding Qualitative Research*, New York: Oxford University Press, 2015.

AEA Consulting, *Thundering Hooves: Maintaining the Global Competitive Edge of Edinburgh's Festivals*, Scottish Arts Council, May 2006.

Aitkenhead, Decca, 'Confessions of a First-Time Festival-Goer', *The Guardian*, 1 June 2010.

Albera, Dionigi and Eade, John, *New Pathways in Pilgrimage Studies: Global Perspectives* (Routledge Studies in Pilgrimage, Religious Travel and Tourism), London: Routledge, 2016.

Alexander, Jeffrey C. and Reed, Isaac (eds.), *Meaning and Method: The Cultural Approach To Sociology*, London: Paradigm, 2009.

Anderson, Benedict, *Imagined Communities: Reflections on the Origin and Spread of Nationalism* (2nd ed.), London: Verso, 1991.

© The Editor(s) (if applicable) and The Author(s), under exclusive license to Springer Nature Switzerland AG 2021
E. Wiles, *Live Literature*, Palgrave Studies in Literary Anthropology,
https://doi.org/10.1007/978-3-030-50385-7

Anderson, Leon, 'Analytic Autoethnography', *Journal of Contemporary Ethnography*, Vol. 35, no. 4, 2006, pp. 373–395 (p. 375).

Anderson, Porter, 'Hay Festival 2018 Sets a Record, Selling 18,000 More Tickets Than in 2017', *Publishing Perspectives*, 4 June 2018.

Appiah, Kwame Anthony, 'Mistaken Identities: Creed, Country, Color, Culture', Fourth *Reith Lecture*. Transcript at: http://downloads.bbc.co.uk/radio4/transcripts/2016_reith4_Appiah_Mistaken_Identities_Culture.pdf (accessed 30 January 2019).

Armitstead, Claire, '"Identity Is a Pain in the Arse": Zadie Smith on Political Correctness', *The Guardian*, 2 February 2019.

———, 'Ali Smith: This Younger Generation Is showing Us That We Need to Change, and We Can Change', *The Guardian*, 23 March 2019.

Arts Council England, 'Literature in the 21st Century: Understanding Models of Support for Literary Fiction', 2017.

———, 'The Value of Arts and Culture to People and Society', 2014.

Atkinson, Sarah and Kennedy, Helen W., 'From Conflict to Revolution: The Secret Aesthetic, Narrative Spatialisation and Audience Experience in Immersive Cinema Design', *Participations*, Vol. 13, no. 1, 2016, pp. 252–279.

Attala, Jennifer, *Performing the Festival: A Study of the Edinburgh International Festival in the Twenty-First Century*, University of Glasgow: ETHOS, 2012.

Atkinson, Paul, 'Narrative Turn or Blind Alley?', *Qualitative Health Research*, Vol. 7, no. 3, 1997, pp. 325–344.

Attridge, Derek, 'Once More with Feeling: Art, Affect, and Performance', *Textual Practice*, Vol. 25, no. 2, 2011, pp. 329–343.

Auslander, Philip, *Liveness: Performance in a Mediatized Culture* [1999] (2nd ed.), Abingdon: Routledge, 2008.

——— (ed.), *Performance: Critical Concepts in Literary and Cultural Studies*, London: Routledge, 2003.

———, *Theory for Performance Studies*, Abingdon: Routledge, 2008.

Austin, J. L., *How to Do Things with Words*, eds. J. O. Urmson and M. Sbisa, Oxford: Clarendon Press, 1975.

Baker, Paul, *Polari: The Lost Language of Gay Men*, Routledge, 2002.

Bakhtin, Mikhail, *Rabelais and His World*, Indiana: Indiana University Press, 1984.

Bakke, Gretchen and Peterson, Marina (eds.), *Anthropology of the Arts: A Reader*, London: Bloomsbury, 2017.

———, *Between Matter and Method: Encounters in Anthropology and Art*, London: Bloomsbury, 2017.

Baillie Gifford, 'Reporting from Hay 2018', report online at: https://www.bai lliegifford.com/en/uk/individual-investors/sponsorship/hay-festival/report ing-from-hay-festival-2018/ (accessed 21 September 2018).

Bain, Carolyn, 'Searching for Tennessee: Performative Identity and the Theatrical Event. Tennessee Williams/New Orleans Literary Festival', in *Festivalising! Theatrical Events, Politics and Culture*, eds. Temple Hauptfleisch et al., Amsterdam: Brill, Rodopi, 2007.

Baldwin, Thomas (ed.), *Merleau-Ponty: Basic Writings*, New York: Routledge, 2004.

Bannet, Eve Tavor, *Transatlantic Stories and the History of Reading, 1720–1810: Migrant Fictions*, Cambridge: Cambridge University Press, 2011.

Barker, Nicolas (ed.), *A Potencie of Life: Books in Society. The Clark Lectures 1986–1987. The British Library Studies in the History of the Book*, London: The British Library, 1993.

Barry, A., Born, G. and Weszkalnys, G., 'Logics of Interdisciplinarity', *Economy and Society*, Vol. 37, no. 1, Taylor & Francis, 2008, pp. 20–49.

Barthes, Roland, 'The Death of the Author', First published in the American magazine, Aspen, 5–6 (1967). Available online at: http://www.ubu.com/ aspen/aspen5and6/threeEssays.html#barthes (accessed 28 February 2019). Also published in *Image-Music-Text*, London: Flamingo, 1977.

Bartie, Angela, *The Edinburgh Festivals: Culture and Society in Post-War Britain*, Edinburgh: Edinburgh University Press, 2014.

Barton, Fiona, 'Scandal of the "Gay" Asylum Seeker Rapist', *The Daily Mail*, 22 June 2006.

Bauman, Richard, 'Verbal Art as Performance', in Vol. III of *Performance: Critical Concepts in Literary and Cultural Studies*, London: Routledge, 2003.

——— (ed.), *Folklore, Cultural Performances, and Popular Entertainments*, New York: Oxford University Press, 1992.

———, *Story, Performance, and Event: Contextual Studies of Oral Narratives*. Cambridge, UK: Cambridge University Press, 1986.

Bauman, Richard and Sherzer, Joel (eds.), *Explorations in the Ethnography of Speaking*, Cambridge University Press, 1974.

BBC News, '20 Facts About Hay-on-Wye and Its Famous Festival', 27 May 2011, https://www.bbc.co.uk/news/uk-wales-13561739 (accessed 21 September 2018).

———, 'David Cameron Buys £25,000 Garden Shed "to Write in"', 30 April 2017: https://www.bbc.co.uk/news/uk-politics-39761410 (accessed 3 February 2019).

————, 'Coronavirus: Almost 500,000 Stream First online Hay Festival', BBC News, 1 June 2020: https://www.bbc.co.uk/news/uk-wales-52875868 (accessed 8 June 2020).

Behar, Ruth, *Lucky Broken Girl*, New York: Penguin, 2017.

————, 'Ethnography in a Time of Blurred Genres', pp. 145–155 of *Anthropology and Humanism: Art of Ethnography: Narrative Style as a Research Method*, 2007.

————, *The Vulnerable Observer: Anthropology That Breaks Your Heart*, Beacon Press, 1997.

Behar, Ruth and Gordon, Deborah (eds.), *Women Writing Culture*, Berkley: University of California Press, 1995.

Belfiore, Eleonore, '"Impact", "Value" and "Bad Economics"': Making Sense of the Problem of Value in the Arts and Humanities', *Arts & Humanities in Higher Education*, Vol. 14, no. 1, 2014, pp. 95–110.

Belfiore, Eleonore and Upchurch, A., *Humanities in the Twenty-First Century: Beyond Utility and Markets*, London: Palgrave Macmillan, 2013.

Bellaigue, Eric de, *British Book Publishing as a Business Since the 1960s*, London: British Library, 2004.

Benneworth, Paul, 'Putting Impact into Context: The Janus Face of the Public Value of Arts and Humanities Research', *Arts and Humanities in Higher Education*, Vol. 14, no. 1, 2015, pp. 3–8.

Bernstein, Charles (ed.), *Close Listening: Poetry and the Performed Word*, New York: Oxford University Press, 1998.

Berry, David M., *Understanding Digital Humanities*, New York: Palgrave Macmilan, 2012.

Bhaksar, Michael, *Curation: The Power of Selection in a World of Excess*, Piatkus, 2016.

Bindel, Julie, 'Paul Burston's Literary Event, Polari', *The Guardian*, 7 March 2012.

Birdwhistell, Ray L., *Kinesics and Context: Essays on Body Motion Communication*, Pennsylvania: University of Pennsylvania Press, 1970.

Born, Georgina, *The Ethnography of a Computer Music Research Institute: Modernism, Post Modernism, and New Technology in Contemporary Music Culture*, University of London: London, 1989.

————, *Rationalizing Culture: IRCAM, Boulez and the Institutionalization of the Musical Avant-Garde*, London: University of California Press, 1995.

————, *Uncertain vision: Birt, Dyke and the Reinvention of the BBC*, London: Vintage, 2005.

————, 'The Social and the Aesthetic: Methodological Principles in the Study of Cultural Production', in *Meaning, and Method: The Cultural Approach to Sociology*, eds. J. Alexander and I. Reed, London: Paradigm, 2007.

————, 'The Social and the Aesthetic: For a Post-Bourdieuian Theory of Cultural Production', *Cultural Sociology*, Vol. 4, July 2010, pp. 171–208.

———— (ed.), *Music, Sound and Space: Transformations of Public and Private Experience*, Cambridge: Cambridge University Press, 2013.

Born, Georgina and Barry, Andrew (eds.), *Interdisciplinarity: Reconfigurations of the Social and Natural Sciences*, London: Routledge 2013.

Born, Georgina, Lewis, Eric and Straw, Will (eds.), *Improvisation and Social Aesthetics*, Duke University Press, 2017.

Bosanquet, Theodora, *Henry James at Work*, University of Michigan Press, 2006.

Bourdieu, Pierre, *Distinction: A Social Critique of the Judgment of Taste*, trans. Richard Nice, London: Routledge, 1984.

————, 'The Forms of Capital', pp. 241–258 of *Handbook of Theory and Research for the Sociology of Education*, ed. J. Richardson, New York: Greenwood, 1986.

————, *The Field of Cultural Production: Essays on Art and Literature*, ed. Randal Johnson, London: Polity Press, 1993.

————, *Sociology in Question*, trans. Richard Nice, London: Sage, 1993.

————, *The Rules of Art: Genesis and Structure of the Literary Field*, trans. Susan Emanuel, Cambridge: Polity Press, 1996.

————, 'The Field of Cultural Production', pp. 99–120 of *The Book History Reader*, eds. D. Finkelstein and A. McCleery, London and New York: Routledge, 2006.

Brouillette, Sarah, *Literature and the Creative Economy*, Stanford: Stanford University Press, 2014.

Brown, Duncan (ed.), *Oral Literature and Performance in Southern Africa*, Oxford: James Currey Publishers, 1999.

Brown, Melinda and Lilton, Deborah L. 'Finding The "B" in LGBTQ+: Collections and Practices That Support the Bisexual and Pansexual Communities', pp. 143–165 of *LGBTQ+ Librarianship in the 21st Century: Emerging Directions of Advocacy and Community Engagement in Diverse Information Environments (Advances in Librarianship, Volume 45)*, ed. Bharat Mehra, Emerald Publishing Limited, 2019.

Brown, Stephen (ed.), *Consuming Books: The Marketing and Consumption of Literature*, London: Routledge, 2006.

Buliatis, Zoe, 'Measuring Impact in the Humanities: Learning from Account-ability and Economics in a Contemporary History of Cultural Value', *Palgrave Communications*, Vol. 3, no. 7, 2017.

Burston, Paul, 'Polari First Book Prize 2018', October 14, 2018: https://www.paulburston.com/single-post/2018/10/14/Polari-First-Book-Prize-2018 (accessed 10 March 2019).

Burton, Peter, *Parallel Lives*, Inland Womensource, 1985.

Carter, David and Ferres, Kay, 'The Public Life of Literature', in *Culture in Australia: Policies, Publics and Programs*, eds. Bennett and Carter, Cambridge: Cambridge University Press, 2001.

Callender, Craig (ed.), *The Oxford Handbook of Philosophy of Time*, Oxford: Oxford University Press, 2011.

Calvino, Italo, *The Literature Machine: Essays*, London: Secker and Warburg, 1987.

Calvino, Italo, *The Uses of Literature: Essays*, trans. Patrick Creagh, San Diego: Harcourt Brace Jovanovich, 1986.

Calvino, Italo, *Six Memos for the New Millennium*, Cambridge, MA: Harvard University Press, 1988.

Carr, Nicholas, *The Shallows: What the Internet Is Doing to Our Brains*, London: Blackstone, 2010.

Carroll, Joseph, Gottshall, Jonathan, Johnson, John A. and Kruger, Daniel J. (eds.), *Graphing Jane Austen: The Evolutionary Basis of Literary Meaning*, London: Palgrave Macmillan, 2012.

Chang, Heewon, *Autoethnography as Method*, Walnut Creek, CA: Left Coast Press, 2008.

Chang, Lan Samantha, 'Writers, Protect Your Inner Life', LitHub, August 7 2017: https://lithub.com/writers-protect-your-inner-life/ (accessed 5 March 2019).

Chatterjee, Anjan, 'Neuroaesthetics: Researchers Unravel the Biology of Beauty and Art', *The Scientist*, May 1 2014.

———, *The Aesthetic Brain: How We Evolved to Desire Beauty and Enjoy Art*, Oxford University Press, 2015.

Citton, Yves, *The Ecology of Attention*, trans. Barnaby Norman, Polity Press, 2016.

Clark, Alex, 'Drawn from Life: Why Have Novelists Stopped Making Things Up?', *The Guardian*, 23 June 2018.

Clifford, James and Marcus, George, *Writing Culture: The Poetics and Politics of Ethnography* [1986] (2nd ed.), University of California Press, 2010.

Clift, Stephen, 'Creative arts as a Public Health Resource: Moving from Practice-Based Research to Evidence-Based Practice', *Perspectives in Public Health*, Vol. 132, no. 3, 2012, pp. 120–127.

Clift, Stephen, Luongo, Michael and Callister, Carry (eds.), *Gay Tourism: Culture, Identity and Sex*, London: Continuum, 2002.

Cohen, Marilyn (ed.), *Novel Approaches to Anthropology*, Lexington Books, 2013.

Colclough, Stephen, *Reading Experience 1700–1840: An Annotated Register of Sources for the History of Reading in the British Isles*, Reading: Simon Eliot, 2000.

Colclough, Stephen, *Consuming Texts: Readers and Reading Communities, 1695–1860*, Basingstoke: Palgrave Macmillan, 2007.

Collini, Stefan, *What Are Universities For?*, 2012.

———, *Speaking of Universities*, Verso, 2017.

Collins, Derek, *Master of the Game: Competition and Performance in Greek Poetry*, Cambridge MA: Harvard University Press, 2005.

Comer Kidd, David and Castano, Emanuele, 'Reading Literary Fiction Improves Theory of Mind', *Science Express*, 3 October 2013, www.scienc emag.org.

Connor, Steven, *The English Novel in History, 1950–1995*, London: Routledge, 1995.

———, 'CP: Or, A Few Don'ts by a Cultural Phenomenologist', *Parallax*, Vol. 5, no. 2, 1999, pp. 17–31.

———, 'Writing The White Voice', Talk given at the *Sound, Silence and the Arts* symposium, Nanyang Technological University, Singapore, 28 February 2009: http://www.stevenconnor.com/whitevoice/ (accessed 15 February 2019).

———, *Beyond Words: Sobs, Hums, Stutters and Other Vocalizations*, London: Reaktion Press, 2014.

Conquergood, Dwight, 'Performing as a Moral Act: Ethical Dimensions of the Ethnography of Performance', in Vol. III of *Performance: Critical Concepts in Literary and Cultural Studies*, London: Routledge, 2003.

———, With Patrick E. Johnson (ed.), *Cultural Struggles: Performance, Ethnography, Praxis*, University of Michigan Press, 2013.

Copland, Fiona and Creese, Angela, *Linguistic Ethnography: Collecting, Analyzing and Presenting Data*, London: Sage, 2015.

Corder, Jim W., 'Academic Jargon and Soul-Searching Drivel', *Rhetoric Review*, Vol. 9, no. 2, 1991, pp. 314–326.

Cowdrey, Katherine, 'Nielsen Tracks Sales at Hay and Edinburgh for First Time', *The Bookseller*, 17 May 2016.

———, 'ALCS Survey finds 15% Drop in Average Author Earnings Since 2013', *The Bookseller*, 27 June 2017.

Cox, Martin, 'The Long-Haul Out of the Closet', pp. 151–173 of *Gay Tourism: Culture, Identity and Sex*, 2002.

Crawford, Matthew, *The World Beyond Your Head: On Becoming an Individual in an Age of Distraction*, Penguin, 2015.

Crossick, Geoffrey and Kaszynska, Patrycja, 'Understanding the Value of Arts & Culture: The AHRC Cultural Value Project', Arts and Humanities Research Council report, 2016.

Csikzentmihalyi, Mihaly, *Creativity: Flow and the Psychology of Discovery and Invention*, New York: Harper, 1997.

Csordas, Thomas, 'Somatic Modes of Attention', *Cultural Anthropology*, Vol. 8, 1993, pp. 135–156.

——— (ed.), *Embodiment and Experience: The Existential Ground of Culture and Self*, Cambridge: Cambridge University Press, 1994.

Culler, Jonathan, 'Philosophy and Literature: The Fortunes of the Performative', *Poetics Today*, Vol. 21, no. 3, Fall 2000, pp. 503–519.

Cummins, Anthony, 'The Struggles of Karl Ove Knausgaard—And Those of His Readers—Are Finally Over', *Prospect*, 11 December 2018.

Damon, Maria, "Was That 'Different', 'Dissident', or 'Dissonant'? Poetry (n) the Public Spear—Slams, Open Readings, and Dissident Traditions', in *Close Listening: Poetry and the Performed Word*, ed. Charles Bernstein, New York: Oxford University Press, 1998.

Darnton, Robert, 'First Steps Toward a History of Reading', pp. 23–35 of *The History of Reading*, eds. Towheed, Crone, and Halsey, London: Routledge, 2010.

Davis, Cynthia and Mitchell, Verner D. (eds.), *Zora Neale Hurston: An Annotated Bibliography of Works and Criticism*, Scarecrow Press, 2013.

De Certeau, Michel, 'Reading as Poaching', pp. 130–139 of eds. Towheed, Crone and Halsey, 2010.

Delany, Carol, with Deborah Kaspin, *Investigating Culture: An Experiential Introduction to Anthropology* [2004] (3rd ed.), Wiley, 2017.

Deleuze, Gilles, *Essays Critical and Clinical*, trans. Michael A. Greco and Daniel W. Smith, Minnesota University Press, 1997.

De La Fuente, E., 'In Defence of Theoretical and Methodological Pluralism in the Sociology of Art: A Critique of Georgina Born's Programmatic Essay',

*Cultural Sociology: A Journal of the British Sociological Association*, Vol. 4, no. 2, Sage, 2010, pp. 217–230.

Denis, P. A. and Aycock, Wendell M., *Literature and Anthropology*, Texas Tech University Press, 1988.

Denzin, Norman K., 'The Many Faces of Emotionality', pp. 17–30 of *Investigating Subjectivity: Research on Lived Experience*, ed. C. Ellis, London: Sage, 1992.

Denzin, N. K., *Interpretive Ethnography: Ethnographic Practices for the 21st Century*, London: Sage, 1997.

Derk, Peter, 'What an Author Reading Is and Why You Should Go to One', Column for Lit Reactor, 11 April 2016: https://litreactor.com/col umns/what-an-author-reading-is-and-why-you-should-go-to-one (accessed 7 March 2019).

Dewey, John, *Art as Experience*, New York: Capricorn Books, 1939.

———, *Democracy and Education* [1916], Hazelton, PA: Pennsylvania State University *Electronic Classics Series*, 2001: https://nsee.memberclicks.net/ass ets/docs/KnowledgeCenter/BuildingExpEduc/BooksReports/10.%20demo cracy%20and%20education%20by%20dewey.pdf.

Dickie, George, *Art and the Aesthetic: An Institutional Analysis*, London: Cornell University Press, 1974.

Di Piero, W. S., 'In the Flea Market of the Mind', *New York Times Book Review*, 8 March 1998.

Dissanayake, Ellen, *What Is Art For?* Seattle: University of Washington Press, 1988.

Dix, Hywel (ed.), *Autofiction in English*, Palgrave, 2018.

Dolar, Mladen, *A Voice Is Nothing More*, Cambridge, MA: MIT Press, 2006.

Dreyer, Benjamin, Tweet on 22 Feb 2019, *Twitter*, @BCDreyer: https://twi tter.com/BCDreyer/status/1098960200688635905 (accessed 22 February 2019).

Driscoll, Beth, 'Local Places and Cultural Distinction: The Booktown Model', *European Journal of Cultural Studies*, Vol. 21, no. 4, 2016, pp. 401–417.

———, 'Sentiment Analysis and the Literary Festival Audience', Continuum, Vol. 29, no. 861–873, 2015.

———, *The New Literary Middlebrow: Tastemakers and Reading in the Twenty-First Century*, London: Palgrave, 2014.

Driscoll, Beth and Squires, Claire, 'Serious Fun: Gaming the Book Festival', *Memoires du Livre*, Vol. 9, no. 2, Printemps, 2018.

———, '"Oh Look, a Ferry"; or The Smell of Paper Books', *The Lifted Brow*, 24 October 2018.

Duffy, Stella, 'Talking Books and Writing and Diversity and Stuff', 29 April 2018, https://stelladuffy.blog/2018/04/29/talking-books-and-writing-and-diversity-and-stuff/ (accessed 15 October 2018).

———, 'SOME Equality Is Not Equality', 25 March 2016, https://stella duffy.blog/2016/03/25/some-equality-is-not-equality/ (accessed 15 October 2018).

———, 'The Book Event—Thoughts for Authors', 3 January 2013, https:// stelladuffy.blog/2013/01/03/the-book-event-thoughts-for-authors/ (accessed 2 April 2019).

Durkheim, Emile, *The Elementary Forms of Religious Life*, Glencoe: Free Press, [1912] 1995.

Eagleton, Terry, *The Ideology of the Aesthetic*, Oxford: Blackwell, 1990.

Eco, Umberto and Carrière, Jean-Claude, *This Is Not the End of the Book*, London: Vintage, 2012.

*The Economist* (eds.), 'From Papyrus to Pixels: The Future of the Book', 11 October 2017.

Edemariam, Aida, 'Festival Fever', *The Guardian*, 28 May 2005.

Elfenbein, A., 'Cognitive Science and the History of Reading', *Publications of the Modern Language Association of America*, Vol. 121, no. 2, The Modern Language Association of America, 2006, pp. 484–502.

Eliot, Simon and Rose, Jonathan, *A Companion to the History of the Book*, Oxford: Blackwell, 2007.

Ellis, Carolyn, Evocative Autoethnography: Writing Emotionally About Our Lives', pp. 115–139 of *Representation and the Text*, eds. W. G. Tierney and Y. S. Lincoln, New York: State University of New York Press, 1997.

Ellis, Carolyn and Bochner, Art (eds.), *Composing Ethnography: Alternative forms of Qualitative Writing*, Walnut Creek, CA: Alta Mira Press, 1996.

———, *Evocative Autoethnography: Writing Lives and Telling Stories*, London: Routledge, 2016.

Ellis, Carolyn and Flaherty, M. G. (eds.), *Investigating Subjectivity: Research on Lived Experience*, London: Sage, 1992.

English, James F., 'Everywhere and Nowhere: The Sociology of Literature After "the Sociology of Literature"', *New Literary History: A Journal of Theory and Interpretation*, Vol. 41, no. 2, The John Hopkins University Press, 2010.

———, *The Economy of Prestige: Prizes, Awards and The Circulation of Cultural Value*, London: Harvard University Press, 2005.

English, Parker, *What We Say, Who We Are: Leopold Senghor, Zora Neale Hurston, and the Philosophy of Language*, Lexington Books, 2010.

Epstein, Jacob, Books: 'Onward to the Digital Revolution: A Review of *Merchants of Culture: The Publishing Business in the Twenty-First Century* by John B. Thompson', *New York Review of Books*, 10 February 2011.

Erickson, Rebecca, 'Our Society, Our Selves: Becoming Authentic in an Inauthentic World', *Advanced Development Journal*, Vol. 6, 1994, pp. 27–39.

Ermarth, Elizabeth Deeds, *Sequel to History: Postmodernism and the Crisis of Representational Time*, Princeton: Princeton University Press, 1992.

Eversmann, Peter, 'The Experience of the Theatrical Event', pp. 139–174 of *Theatrical Events: Borders, Dynamics, Frames*, eds. Cremona, Eversmann, Van Maanen, Sauter and Tulloch, Amsterdam: International Federation for Theatre Research, 2004.

Ewan, Paul (aka. Francis Plug), *How to Be a Public Author*, Galley Beggar Press, 2014.

Falassi, Alessandro, 'Festival: Definition and Morphology', pp. 1–10 of *Time Out of Time: Essays on the Festival*, ed. Falassi, Albuquerque: University of New Mexico Press, 1987.

Fassin, Didier, 'True Life, Real Lives: Revisiting the Boundaries Between Ethnography and Fiction', *American Ethnologist*, Vol. 41, no. 1, 2014, pp. 40–55.

Fawcett, Clare and Cormack, Patrick, 'Guarding Authenticity at Literary Tourism Sites', *Annals of Tourism Research*, Vol. 28, no. 3, 2001, pp. 686–724.

Fay, Elizabeth A., 'Author', Chapter 6, pp. 107–124 of *A Handbook of Romanticism Studies*, eds. Joel Faflak and Julia M. Wright, London: Wiley, 2012.

Ferguson, Susan, 'Dickens's Public Readings and the Victorian Author', *Studies in English Literature, 1500–1900*, Vol. 41, no. 4, The Nineteenth Century, Autumn 2001, pp. 729–749.

Fernyhough, Charles, *The Voices Within: The History and Science of How We Talk to Ourselves*, Profile Books, 2016.

Fine, E. C., *The Folklore Text: From Performance to Print*, Bloomington: Indiana University Press, 1994.

Finkel, Rebecca, 'McFestivalisation? The Role of Combined Arts Festivals in the UK Cultural Economy', *Journeys of Expression Conference*, published in Conference Proceedings: Sheffield Hallam University, 2004.

Finkelstein, Daniel and McCleery, Alistair, *The Book History Reader*, London: Routledge, 2006.

Finkelstein, Daniel and Squires, Claire, 'Book Events, Book Environments', in *The Cambridge History of the Book in Britain: Volume VII, The Twentieth*

*Century and Beyond*, eds. Andrew Nash, Claire Squires and I. R. Willison, 2019.

Finnegan, Ruth, *Oral Literature in Africa*, Oxford: Oxford University Press, 1970.

———, *Oral Poetry: Its Nature, Significance, and Social Context*, Cambridge University Press, 1977.

———, *Oral Traditions and the Verbal Arts: A Guide to Research Practices*, London: Routledge, 1992.

———, *Communicating: The Multiple Modes of Human Interconnection*, London: Routledge, 2002.

———, *Where Is Language?: An Anthropologist's Questions on Language, Literature and Performance*, London: Bloomsbury Academic, 2015.

———, *Black Inked Pearl: A Girls' Quest*, Garn Press, 2015.

Fischer, Stephen Roger, *A History of Reading*, London: Reaktion, 2003.

Fischer-Lichte, Erika, *The Transformative Power of Performance: A New Aesthetics*, trans. Jain, London: Routledge, 2008.

Fish, Stanley, 'What Makes an Interpretation Acceptable?', pp. 96–108 of *The History of Reading*, eds. Towheed, Crone, and Halsey, London: Routledge, 2010.

———, 'Interpreting the Variorum', *Critical Enquiry*, Vol. 2, no. 3, pp. 465–485, 1976.

———, 'Is There a Text in this Class?', Chapter 13, pp. 147–174 of *Is There a Text in This Class? The Authority of Interpretive Communities*, Harvard University Press, 1980.

Fisher, Alden L., *The Essential Writings of Merleau-Ponty*, New York: Harcourt, Brace and World, 1969.

Fisher, Tony and Katsouraki, Eve (eds.), *Beyond Failure: New Essays on the Cultural History of Failure in Theatre and Performance*, Routledge, 2018.

Fiske, John, 'Audiencing: Cultural Practice and Cultural Studies', pp. 189–198 of *Handbook of Qualitative Research*, eds. Denzin and Lincoln, Sage, 1994.

Flood, Alison, 'Booksellers 'behead' the King of Hay', *The Guardian*, 30 September 2009.

———, 'UK Publishing Industry Remains 90% White, Survey Finds', *The Guardian*, 6 September 2017.

———, 'Simon Armitage named UK's Poet Laureate', 10 May 2019: https://www.theguardian.com/books/2019/may/10/simon-armitage-poet-laureate.

———, 'US Publishing Remains "as White Today as It Was Four Years Ago"', *The Guardian*, 2020: https://www.theguardian.com/books/2020/jan/30/us-publishing-american-dirt-survey-diversity-cultural-appropriation.

Foster Wallace, David, 'Privilege', Oxford Dictionaries blog: https://blog.oxf orddictionaries.com/2015/07/31/reflections-on-language-david-foster-wal lace/ (accessed 26 February 2019).

——, 'Tense Present: Democracy, English, and the Wars over Usage', *Harper's Magazine*, April 2001.

Foucault, Michel, 'What Is an Author?' [1969], talk published in Josue V. Harari, *Textual Strategies*, Ithaca, NY: Cornell, 1979, pp. 141–160.

Freeman, John, 'Hay Festival: "The Woodstock of the Mind"', *The Guardian*, 1 June 2008.

Friedman, Jane, 'Author Income Surveys Are Misleading and Flawed—And Focus on the Wrong Message for Writers', Jane Friedman blog, 2 July 2018, at: https://www.janefriedman.com/author-income-surveys/.

Frieze, James (ed.), *Reframing Immersive Theatre: The Politics and Pragmatics of Participatory Performance*, London: Palgrave, 2017.

Fuller, Danielle, 'Beyond CanLit(e): Reading. Interdisciplinarity. Trans-Atlantically,' pp. 65–85 of *Shifting the Ground of Canadian Literary Studies*, eds. Smaro Kamboureli and Robert Zacharias, Waterloo, ON: Wilfrid Laurier University Press, TransCanada Series, 2012.

——, 'Citizen Reader: Canadian Literature, Mass Reading Events and the Promise of Belonging,' *The Fifth Eccles Centre for American Studies Plenary Lecture*, Pamphlet Series, print and online. London: Eccles Centre & The British Library. Also available at: http://www.bl.uk/eccles/pdf/bacs2010. pdf#zoom=80, 2011.

——, *Writing the Everyday: Women's Textual Communities in Atlantic Canada*. Montreal and Kingston: McGill-Queen's University Press, 2004.

Fuller, Danielle and Procter, James, 'Reading as "Social Glue"?: Book Groups, Multiculture, and Small Island Read 2007', 'Region/Writing/Home: Relocating Black, Migrant and Diasporic Writing in Britain', *Special Issue Moving Worlds: A Journal of Transcultural Writings*, eds. Corinne Fowler and Graham Mort, Vol. 9, no. 2, 2009, pp. 26–40.

Fuller, Danielle and Rehberg Sedo, DeNel, *Reading Beyond the Book: The Social Practices of Contemporary Literary Culture*, London: Routledge, 2013.

Funk, Wolfgang, Groß, Florian and Huber, Imtraud (eds.), *The Aesthetics of Authenticity*, Deutsche Nationalbibliotek, 2012.

Gabattiss, Josh, 'London Pride: Anti-trans Activists Disrupt Parade by Lying Down in the Street to Protest 'Lesbian Erasure'', *The Independent*, 7 July 2018.

Gafijczuk, Dariusz, 'Vividness, Time and the Restitution of Sociological Imagination', in 'Live Methods' special edition of *Sociological Review*, eds. Back and Pawar, 2017.

Gallagher, Charles A., '"Blacks, Jews, Gays and Immigrants Are Taking Over": How the Use of Polling Data Can Distort Reality and Perpetuate Inequality Among Immigrants', *Ethnic and Racial Studies*, Vol. 37, no. 5, April 2014, pp. 731–737.

Gallese, Vittorio, 'Mirror Neurons, Embodied Simulation, and the Neural Basis of Social Identification', *Psychoanalytic Dialogues*, Vol. 19, no. 5, 2009, pp. 519–536.

Gardiner, Juliet, 'Recuperating the Author', *The Papers of the Bibliographical Society of America*, Vol. 94, no. 2, 2000, pp. 255–274.

Gatti, Claudio, 'Elena Ferrante: An Answer?', *The New York Review of Book*, 2 October 2016.

Gaut, Berys, *Art, Emotion and Ethics*, Oxford University Press, 2007.

Geertz, Clifford, 'Person, Time and Conduct in Bali', pp. 357–367 of *Emotions: A Cultural Reader*, ed. Wulff, London: Bloomsbury, 2007.

———, 'Thick Description: Toward an Interpretive Theory of Culture', pp. 3–30 of *The Interpretation of Cultures: Selected Essays*, New York: Basic Books, 1973.

———, *Works and Lives: The Anthropologist as Author*, Cambridge: Polity Press, 1988.

———, *Local Knowledge: Further Essays in Interpretive Anthropology*, London: Fontana, 1993.

———, 'Deep hanging Out', *The New York Review of Books*, Vol. 45, no. 16, 1998, p. 69.

Gell, Alfred, *Art and Agency: An Anthropological Theory*, Oxford: Clarendon, 1998.

Genette, Gerard, *Paratexts: Thresholds of Interpretation*, trans. Jane E. Lewin, Cambridge: Cambridge University Press, 1997.

Giannachi, Kaye and Shanks (eds.), *Archaeologies of Presence: Art, Performance and the Persistence of Being*, London: Routledge, 2012.

Gibbs, Raymond W., *Embodiment and Cognitive Science*, Cambridge University Press, 2005.

Gilbey, Ryan, 'The Fresh Prince to the Crystal Maze: Standby for a Bizarre VHS Odyssey', *The Guardian*, 1 April 2015.

Giorgi, Liana, 'Between Tradition, Vision and Imagination: The Public Sphere of Literature Festivals', pp. 29–44 of *Festivals and the Cultural Public Sphere*, eds. Sassatelli, Giorgi and Delanty, Abingdon: Routledge, 2011.

Glass, Loren, 'An Interview with Janice Radway', pp. 91–104 of *Iowa Journal of Cultural Studies*, no. 10/11, Spring and Fall 2009.

Glassner, Andrew S., *Interactive Storytelling: Techniques for 21st Century Fiction*, Natick, MA: A.K.Peters, 2004.

Glavey, Brian, 'Poetry and the Attention Economy', pp. 423–429 of *Contemporary Literature*, Vol. 58, no. 3, Fall 2017.

Goffman, Erving, *The Presentation of Self in Everyday Life* [1956], London: Penguin, 1990.

———, *Interaction Ritual: Essays on Face-to-Face Behavior*, New York: Anchor Books, 1967.

Gold, Michael, 'The ABCs of L.G.B.T.Q.I.A.+', *The New York Times*, 21 June 2018.

Goody, Jack, *The Interface Between the Written and the Oral*, Cambridge: Cambridge University Press, 1987.

Goodman, Dana, *The Republic of Letters: A Cultural History of the French Enlightenment*, Ithaca: Cornell University Press, 1994.

Gottlieb, Alma and DeLoache, Judy, *A World of Babies: Imagined Childcare Guides for Eight Societies* (2nd ed.), Cambridge: Cambridge University Press, 2017.

Greco, A. M., Rodríguez, C. E. and Wharton, R. M., *The Culture and Commerce of Publishing in the 21st Century*, Stanford: Stanford University Press, 2007.

Griswold, Wendy, *Cultures and Societies in a Changing World* (4th ed.), London: Sage, 2013.

———, *Regionalism and the Reading Class*, London: University of Chicago Press, 2008.

———, *Bearing Witness: Readers, Writers, and the Novel in Nigeria*, Princeton: Princeton University Press, 2000.

———, *Cultures and Societies in a Changing World*, London: Sage, 1997.

Griswold, Wendy, Mangione, Gemma and McDonnell, Terence E., 'Objects, Words, and Bodies in Space: Bringing Materiality into Cultural Analysis', in *Qualitative Sociology*, 2013.

Gritten, Anthony, 'Music Before the Literary: Or, The Eventness of Musical Events', pp. 21–33 of *Phrase and Subject: Studies in Literature and Music*, ed. Delia da Sousa Correa, Legenda, 2006.

Habermas, Jürgen, *The Structural Transformation of the Public Sphere: An Inquiry into a Category of Bourgeois Society*, Cambridge: Polity [1962], trans. Thomas Burger with Frederick Lawrence, Cambridge, MA: MIT Press, 1991.

Hadley, Steven and Belfiore, Eleonora, 'Cultural Democracy and Cultural Policy', *Cultural Trends*, Vol. 27, no. 3, 2018.

Hale, Dorothy J. (ed.), *The Novel: An Anthology of Criticism and Theory 1900–2000*, Oxford: Blackwell, 2006.

Hall, Gary, *Digitize this Book! The Politics of New Media or Why We Need Open Access Now*, Minnesota: University of Minnesota, 2008.

Halsey, K., Swann, J. and Allington, D., 'Folk Stylistics' and the History of Reading: A Discussion of Method, *Language and Literature: Journal of the Poetics and Linguistics Association*, Vol. 18, no. 3, Longman, 2009, pp. 231–246.

Hansen, Anders and Machin, David, *Media and Communication Research Methods*, London: Palgrave Macmillan, 2013.

Harrison, Anthony Kwame, '"What Happens in the Cabin…": An Arts-Based Autoethnography of Underground Hip Hop Song Making', *Journal of the Society for American Music*, Vol. 8, no. 1, February 2014, pp. 1–27.

Harvey, David, *The Condition of Postmodernity*, 1990.

Hauptfleisch, Temple, Sauter, Willmar, Lev-Aladgem, Shulamith, Martin, Jacqueline and Schoenmakers, Henri (eds.) *Festivalising!: Theatrical Events, Politics and Culture*, Amsterdam: Rodopi, 2007.

Havelock, Eric A., *The Muse Learns to Write: Reflections on Orality and Literacy from Antiquity to the Present*, New Haven: Yale University Press, 1986.

Hawes, Leonard C., 'Becoming Other-Wise: Conversational Performance and the Politics of Experience', in Vol. III of *Performance: Critical Concepts in Literary and Cultural Studies*, London: Routledge, 2003.

Hay Festival, 2017 Report, https://www.hayfestival.com/portal/documents/Hay-Festival-2017-Report.pdf (accessed 22 March 2017).

Hayles, Katherine, *How We Think: Digital Media and Contemporary Technogenesis*, Chicago: University of Chicago Press, 2012.

Hayles, Katherine, *My Mother Was a Computer: Digital Subjects and Literary Texts*, Chicago: University Of Chicago Press, 2005.

Heidegger, Martin, *Being and Time*, London: Wiley-Blackwell, 1978.

Henry, Jo and Leslie, *Expanding the Book Market: A Study of Reading and Buying Habits in GB*, Book Marketing Limited: London, 2005.

Hensher, Philip, *The Missing Ink: The Lost Art of Handwriting, and Why It Still Matters*, London: Macmillan, 2012.

Heywood, et al., 'Enriching Britain: Culture, Creativity and Growth: The 2015 Report by the Warwick Commission on the Future of Cultural Value, 2015. Online: https://warwick.ac.uk/research/warwickcommission/

futureculture/finalreport/warwick_commission_final_report.pdf (accessed 1 April 2019).

Higgins, John (ed.), *The Raymond Williams Reader*, Oxford: Blackwell, 2001.

Hobart, Angela and Kapferer, Bruce (eds.), *Aesthetics in Performance: Formations of Symbolic Construction and Experience*, New York: Berghahn Books, 2005.

Hochman, B., 'The History of Reading and the Death of the Text', *American Literary History*, Vol. 21, no. 4, Oxford University Press, 2009, pp. 845–858.

Holdsworth, Rachel, 'Lit Preview: Homework @ Bethnal Green Working Mens Club', The Londonist, 20 July 2012: https://londonist.com/2012/07/lit-preview-homework-bethnal-green-working-mens-club (accessed 8 March 2019).

Holt, Fabian, 'The Economy of Live Music in the Digital Age', *European Journal of Cultural Studies*, Vol. 13, no. 2, 2010, pp. 243–261.

Houen, Alex, 'Introduction: Affecting words', *Textual Practice*, special edition: 'Affect, Text and Performativity', Vol. 25, no. 2, 2011, pp. 215–232.

Huey, Edmund Burke, *The Psychology and Pedagogy of Reading: With a Review of the History of Reading and Writing and of Methods, Texts and Hygiene in Reading*, New York: MacMillan, 1928.

Hurston, Zora Neale, *Mules and Men* [1935], Harper Perennial, 2009.

———, *Barracoon: The Story of the Last Slave* [1935] HQ, 2018.

———, *Their Eyes Were Watching God* [1937], Virago, 1986.

Husserl, Edmund, *The Phenomenology of Internal Time Consciousness*, Indiana: Indiana University Press, 1964.

Hynes, Deborah, *Bakhtin Reframed*, London: I.B. Tauris, 2013.

Iacoboni, Marco, 'Imitation, Empathy and Mirror Neurons', *Annual Review of Psychology*, Vol. 60, pp. 653–670.

Idhe, Don, *Listening and Voice: Phenomenologies of Sound*, New York: State University of New York Press, 2007.

*The Independent* (anon. eds.), 'Blagger's Guide to the Hay Festival', *The Independent*, 27 May 2012: https://www.independent.co.uk/arts-entertainment/books/features/the-balggers-guide-to-the-hay-festival-7791203.html (accessed 17 March 2019).

Ingold, Tim, *Being Alive: Essays on Movement, Knowledge and Description*, London: Routledge, 2011.

———, *Correspondences*.

Irwin, William (ed.), *The Death and Resurrection of the Author?* Raeger, 2002.

Iser, Wolfgang, 'The Reading Process: A Phenomenological Approach', pp. 80–92 of *The History of Reading*, eds. Towheed, Crone, and Halsey, London: Routledge, 2010.

Jackson, Michael D., *How Lifeworlds Work: Emotionality, Sociality and the Ambiguity of Being*, Chicago: University of Chicago Press, 2017.

———, *Dead Reckoning*, Auckland: Auckland University Press, 2006.

———, *Paths Toward a Clearing: Radical Empiricism and Ethnographic Inquiry*, Indiana: Indiana University Press, 1989.

Jaggers, Abbie, 'Interview with John Mullan: On Jane Austen and Reading Aloud', *Listening Books Blog*, 17 July 2017, http://listeningbooksblog.com/john-mullan-interview-jane-austen-reading-aloud/.

Jajdelska, Elspeth, *Silent Reading and the Birth of the Narrator*, Toronto: University of Toronto Press, 2007.

———, 'Pepys in the History of Reading', *Historical Journal*, Vol. 50, no. 3, Cambridge University Press, 2007, pp. 549–570.

James, Henry, 'Preface', *The Golden Bowl*, New York: Doubleday, 1978.

Janssen, Catherine Jo, 'An Ethnographic Study of The Moth Detroit StorySLAM', *Electronic Theses and Dissertations*, Digital Commons, East Tennessee State University, 2012.

Jenkyns, Richard, *Classical Literature: An Epic Journey from Homer to Virgil and Beyond*, New York: Basic Books, 2016.

Johanson, Katya and Freeman, Robin, 'The Reader as Audience: The Appeal of the Writers' Festival to the Contemporary Audience', *Continuum: Journal of Media & Cultural Studies*, Vol. 26, no. 2, 2012, pp. 303–314.

Johnson, E. Patrick, *Appropriating Blackness: Performance and the Politics of Authenticity*, Duke University Press, 2003.

Johnson, William A., 'Toward a Sociology of Reading in Classical Antiquity', *American Journal of Philology*, Vol. 121, 2000, pp. 593–567.

Jones, Paul, *Raymond Williams' Sociology of Culture: A Critical Reconstruction*, Basingstoke: Palgrave Macmillan, 2004.

Jordan, Jennie and Newbold, Chris (eds.), *Focus on World Festivals: Contemporary Case Studies and Perspectives*, Oxford: Goodfellow, 2016.

Joubert, Annekie, *The Power of Performance: Linking Past and Present in Hananwa and Lobedu Oral Literature*, Mouton de Gruyter: New York, 2004.

Kallendorf, Craig, *The Virgilian Tradition: Book History and the History of Reading in Early Modern Europe*, Aldershot: Ashgate Variorum, 2007.

Karabell, Zachary, '(Mis)Leading Indicators: Why Our Economic Numbers Distort Reality', *Foreign Affairs*, Vol. 93, no. 2, March–April 2014, pp. 90–101.

Keightly, Emily (ed.), *Time, Media and Modernity*, New York: Palgrave Macmillan, 2012.

Kennedy, A. L., 'The Voice on the Page', *The Essay*, Radio 3, first broadcast 6 February 2019.

Kirschenbaum, Matthew G., *Mechanisms: New Media and the Forensic Imagination*, London: MIT, 2008.

Kirschgaessner, Stephanie, 'Elena Ferrante: Literary Storm as Italian Reporter 'Identifies' Author', *The Guardian*, 2 October 2016.

Kivy, Peter (ed.), *The Blackwell Guide to Aesthetics*, Oxford: Blackwell, 2004.

Klaver, Elizabeth, 'Spectatorial Theory in the Age of Media Culture', in *Performance: Critical Concepts in Literary and Cultural Studies*, London: Routledge, Vol. II, 2003.

Kosslyn, Stephen M. and Matt, Ann M. C., 'If You Speak Slowly, Do People Read Your Prose Slowly? Person-Particular Speech Recoding During Reading', *Bulletin of the Psychonomic Society*, Vol. 9, no. 4, 1977, pp. 250–252.

Kuerti, L., Elkadi, H. and Kuechler, S., *Every Day's a Festival! Diversity on Show*, Sean Kingston Publishing: Wantage, 2011,

Kuzmicova, Anezka, 'Audiobooks and Print Narrative: Similarities in Text Experience', pp. 217–237 of *Audionarratology: Interfaces of Sound and Narrative*, ed. J. Mildorf, Berlin: De Gruyter, 2016.

Lakoff, George and Johnson, Mark, *Metaphors We Live By* (2nd ed.), Chicago: University of Chicago Press, 2003.

Langellier, K. M., 'Personal Narrative, Performance, Performativity: Two or Three Things I Know For Sure', *Text and Performance Quarterly*, Vol. 19, no. 2, 1999, pp. 125–144.

Lea, Daniel, 'The Anxieties of Authenticity in Post-2000 British Fiction', *Modern Fiction Studies*, Vol. 58, no. 3, 2012, pp. 459–476.

Leavis, Queenie Dorothy, *Fiction and the Reading Public* (1932), London: Pimlico, 2000.

Leavy, Patricia, *Low-Fat Love: Social Fictions*, Sense Pulblishers, 2015.

———, *Handbook of Arts-Based Research*, Guildford Press, 2017.

———, *Method Meets Art:* Arts-Based Research Practice [2008] (2nd ed.), Guildford Press, 2015.

Lee, Katja, 'Making Cents of Contemporary Intimacies: The Private in the Public', pp. 217–228 of *Contemporary Publics: Shifting Boundaries in New Media, Technology and Culture*, eds. Lee et al.

Le Guin, Ursula K., *Steering the Craft: A 21st Century Guide to Sailing the Sea of Story*, New York: Houghton Mifflin, 2015.

———, 'Telling is Listening', pp. 185–205 of *The Wave in the Mind*, Boulder: Shambala Press, 2004.

————, 'Off the Page: Loud Cows: A Talk and a Poem About Reading Aloud', pp. 117–126 of *The Wave in the Mind*, Boulder: Shambala Press, 2004.

————, 'Lost in Mindspace', *The Guardian*, 21 July 2007.

————, *The Language of the Night: Essays on Fantasy and Science Fiction*, Berkley: Berkley Publishing Group, 1985.

Le Poidevin, Robin and Macbeath, Murray (eds.), *The Philosophy of Time*, Oxford: Oxford University Press, 1993.

Lerner, Jennifer, Li, Ye, Valdesolo, Piercarlo and Kassam, Karim S., 'Emotion and Decision Making', *Annual Review of Psychology*, Vol. 66, 2015, pp. 799–823.

Lindblom, Charles, *Culture and Authenticity*, Blackwell, 2008.

Livingstone, Eric, *An Anthropology of Reading*, Bloomington: Indiana University Press, 1995.

Llewellyn, Sam, 'Hay Festival: A Town Set at a Slight Angle', *The Telegraph*, 18 March 2011.

————, 'Why a Weekend in Hay-on-Wye Should Be on Your Bucket List', *The Telegraph*, 4 April 2017.

Lo Dico, Joy, 'Celebrated Literary Feud Ends After Naipaul and Theroux Bury the Hatchet', *The Independent*, 20 May 2011.

Lofgren, Orvar and Ehn, Billy, 'Emotions in Academia', pp. 101–118 of *Emotions: A Cultural Reader*, ed. Helena Wulff, London: Bloomsbury, 2007.

Lowder, J. Bryan, 'Polari, the Gay Dialect, Can Be Heard in This Great Short Film "Putting on the Dish"', *Slate*, 28 July 2015.

Lowell, Lewis J., *The Anthropology of Cultural Performance*, London: Palgrave Macmillan, 2013.

Loxley, James, *Performativity*, London: Routledge, 2007.

Lurie, Caroline, 'Festival, Inc.', *Australian Author*, Vol. 36, no. 2, 2004, pp. 8–12.

Luyster, Brad, Twitter handle @zuph, Tweet, 4 March 2019: https://twitter.com/zuph/status/1102582420900114432.

Lyotard, Jean-Francois, *Peregrinations: Law, Form, Event*, New York: Columbia University Press, 1988.

Macdonald, D. L., 'One Moment in the History of Reading: Midnight, 18 June 1816', *Keats-Shelley Review*, Vol. 18, 2004, pp. 149–174.

Machon, Josephine, *Immersive Theatres: Intimacy and Immediacy in Contemporary Performance*, London: Palgrave, 2013.

Maddox, Brenda, 'Say Hay', *New York Times* online, 5 July 1998, https://archive.nytimes.com/www.nytimes.com/books/98/07/05/bookend/bookend.html (accessed 15 September 2018).

Madison, D. Soyini, *Critical Ethnography: Method, Ethics and Performance*, Los Angeles: Sage, 2012.

Maffesoli, Michael, *The Time of the Tribes: The Decline of Individualism in Mass Society*, trans. Don Smith, London: Sage, 1996.

Mah, Ann, 'Searching for Anne of Green Gables on Prince Edward Island', *New York Times*, 21 March 2014.

Malinowski, Branislaw, *Argonauts of the Western Pacific: An Account of Native Enterprise and Adventure in the Archipelagos of Melanesian New Guinea* [1922], London: Routledge & Kegan Paul, 1950.

———, 'The Problem of Meaning in Primitive Languages' [1923], pp. 296–336 of *The Meaning of Meaning: A Study of the Influence of Language upon Thought and of the Science of Symbolism*, eds. Charles K. Ogden and Ian A. Richards, London: Kegan Paul, 1989.

Manovski, Miroslav Pavle, *Arts-Based Research, Autoethnography, and Music Education: Singing Through a Culture of Marginalization*, Rotterdam: Sense Publishers, 2014.

Marche, Stephen, 'Literature Is Not Data: Against Digital Humanities', *LA Review of Books*, 28 October 2012.

Marcus, George E., 'Ethnography in/of the World System: The Emergence of Multi-Sited Ethnography', *Annual Review of Anthropology*, Vol. 24, 1995, pp. 95–117.

Marjanovic, Tatjana, 'The (In)Visibility of Academic Prose Writers: A Story of Scholarship Turning Human', *Changing English: Studies in Culture and Education*, Vol. 18, no. 4, 2011, pp. 437–442..

Martin, Ben R., 'The Research Excellence Framework and the 'Impact Agenda': Are We Creating a Frankenstein Monster?', *Research Evaluation*, Vol. 20, no. 3, 1 September 2011, pp. 247–254.

Mast, Jason L., *Social Performance: Symbolic Action, Cultural Pragmatics, and Ritual*, Cambridge Cultural Social Studies, Cambridge, 2009.

McCormick, Charlie T. and Kennedy White, Kim (eds.), *Folklore: An Encyclopaedia of Beliefs, Customs, Tales, Music, and Art* (2nd ed.), Santa Barbara, CA, 2010.

McDonald, Peter, 'The Challenge of *Diary of a Bad Year*', *Novel: A Forum on Fiction*, Vol. 43, no. 3, Fall 2010, pp. 483–499.

———, 'On Strong Opinions: Celebrity Authors in the Contemporary Agora', *Celebrity Studies*, Vol. 8, no. 1, 2017, pp. 172–175.

McGinnis, Jared, 'The Event's the Thing: A Provocation', *International Literature Showcase:* https://litshowcase.org/content/the-events-the-thing/, 2016 (accessed 20 April 2019).

McGuigan, Jim, 'The Cultural Public Sphere', *European Journal of Cultural Studies*, Vol. 8, no. 4, pp. 427–443, 2005.

McHoul, Alexander, 'Ethnomethodology and Literature: Preliminaries to a Sociology of Reading', *Poetics*, Vol. 7, no. 1, March 1978, pp. 113–120.

McLean, Stuart, *Fictionalizing Anthropology: Encounters and Fabulations at the Edges of the Human*, Minnesota: University of Minnesota Press, 2017.

McParland, Robert, *Charles Dickens's American Audience*, Lanham, MD: Lexington Books, 2010.

Meehan, Michael, 'The Word Made Flesh: Festival, Carnality and Literary Consumption', *Text*, 'Literature and Public Culture' special issue, October 2005.

Merleau-Ponty, Maurice, *Phenomenology of Perception* [1945], trans. Donald A. Landes, London: Routledge, 2013.

Middlebrow Network of Scholars, The, 'Q.D. Leavis: Fiction and the Reading Public': https://www.middlebrow-network.com/Annotations/tabid/1061/art icleType/ArticleView/articleId/1459/Leavis-Q-D-Fiction-and-the-Reading-Public-London-Pimlico-2000-first-pub-1932.aspx (accessed 4 March 2019).

Miles, Rebecca, 'Hay Festival Generates Millions for the Tourism Industry in the Area', *Hereford Times*, 1 October 2018.

Mills, Margaret Ann, *Oral Narrative in Afghanistan: The Individual in Tradition*, London: Garland Publishing, 1990.

Moore, Lorrie, 'It's Better to Write Than Be a Writer', 3 April 2018, LitHub: https://lithub.com/lorrie-moore-its-better-to-write-than-be-a-writer/ (accessed 10 March 2019).

Moore, Steven, *The Novel: An Alternative History: Beginnings to 1600*, New York: Bloomsbury, 2010.

Moran, Joe, *Star Authors: Literary Celebrity in America*, London: Pluto Press, 2000.

———, *First You Write a Sentence: The Elements of Reading, Writing… and Life*, London: Penguin, 2018.

Moretti, F., 'History of the Novel, Theory of the Novel', *Novel*, Vol. 43, no. 1, Brown University , 2009, pp. 1–10.

Morphy, Howard and Perkins, Morgan, *The Anthropology of Art: A Reader*, London: Wiley-Blackwell, 2006.

Moss, Steven, 'Making Hay', *The Guardian*, 31 May 2001.

Mullan, John, *What Matters in Jane Austen?: Twenty Crucial Puzzles Solved*, London: Bloomsbury, 2012.

Murray, Simone, *The Digital Literary Sphere: Reading, Writing and Selling Books in the Internet Era*, John Hopkins University Press, 2018.

————, *Mixed Media: Feminist Presses and Publishing Politics*, London: Pluto, 2004.

————, *The Adaptation Industry: The Cultural Economy of Contemporary Literary Adaptation*, Abingdon: Routledge, 2011.

————, 'Charting the Digital Literary Sphere', *Contemporary Literature*, Vol. 56, Part: 2, 2015, pp. 311–339.

Murray, Simone, and Weber, Millicent, "Live and Local'?: The Significance of Digital Media for Writers' Festivals', *Convergence: The International Journal of Research into New Media Technologies*, Vol. 23, no. 1, 2017, pp. 61–78.

Mussell, James, *The Nineteenth-Century Press in the Digital Age*, New York: Palgrave Macmillan, 2012.

Myers West, Sarah, 'Data Capitalism: Redefining the Logics of Surveillance and rivacy', *Business and Society*, Vol. 58, no. 1, pp. 20–41. Article first published online: 5 July 2017; Issue published: 1 January 2019.

Narayan, Karen, *Love, Stars and All That*, Simon & Schuster, 1994.

————, 'Tools to Shape Texts: What Creative Nonfiction Can Offer Ethnography', pp. 130–144 of *Anthropology and Humanism: Art of Ethnography: Narrative Style as a Research Method* (Vol. 2), San Jose, CA, Society for Humanistic Anthropology, 2007.

————, *Alive in the Writing: Crafting Ethnography in the Company of Chekhov*, Chicago: University of Chicago Press, 2012.

Neilsen, Morten and Rapport, Nigel (eds.), *The Composition of Anthropology: How Anthropological Texts are Written*, London: Routledge, 2018.

Nelson, Maggie, *The Argonauts*, London: Melville House, 2017.

Newbold, Chris, Jordan, Jennie, Maughan, Christopher and Bianchini, Franco, *Focus on Festivals: Contemporary European Case Studies and Perspectives*, Goodfellow, 2014.

Ng, Celeste, Tweet posted on 12 July 2018, Twitter handle @pronounced_ing. https://twitter.com/pronounced_ing/status/1017539391789654016?lan g=en (accessed 2 February 2019).

Nguyen, Viet Than, *Twitter* post, 14 February 2019:https://twitter.com/viet_t_nguyen/status/1096148948715065344 (accessed 15 February 2019).

Nightingale, Virginia (ed.), *The Handbook of Media Audiences*, Oxford: Wiley-Blackwell, 2011.

Niles, John D., *Homo Narrans: The Poetics and Anthropology of Oral Literature*, Pennsylvania: University of Pennsylvania Press, 2010.

Oatley, Keith, 'Fiction: Simulation of Social Worlds', *Trends in Cognitive Sciences*, Vol. 20, no. 8, August 2016, pp. 618–628.

O'Connell, John, *For the Love of Letters*: *The Joy of Slow Communication*, London: Short Books, 2012.

Office of National Statistics, 'Ethnicity and National Identity in England and Wales: 2011', 11 December 2012, https://www.ons.gov.uk/peoplepopula tionandcommunity/culturalidentity/ethnicity/articles/ethnicityandnationali dentityinenglandandwales/2012-12-11 (accessed 20 September 2018).

Ohmann, Richard M., *Politics of Knowledge: The Commercialization of the University, the Professions, and Print Culture*, Middletown, CT: Wesleyan University Press, 2003.

Okely, Judith, *Anthropological Practice: Fieldwork and Ethnographic Method*, Berg, 2013.

Ommundsen, Wenche, 'From the Altar to the Market-Place and Back Again: Understanding Literary Celebrity', pp. 244–255 of *Stardom and Celebrity: A Reader*, eds. Redmond and Holmes, London: Sage, 2007.

——, 'Literary Festivals and Cultural Consumption', *Australian Literary Studies*, Vol. 24, no. 1, 2009, pp. 19–34.

Ong, Walter J., *Orality and Literacy: The Technologizing of the Word* [1982] (2nd ed.), London: Routledge, 2002.

Orr, Deborah, 'The Unmasking of Elena Ferrante Has Violated My Right Not to Know', *The Guardian*, 3 October 2016.

Ortiz-Robles, Mario, *The Novel as Event*, Ann Arbor: University of Michigan Press, 2010.

O'Sullivan, Simon, 'The Aesthetics of Affect: Thinking Art Beyond Represen- tation', *Angelaki: Journal of the Theoretical Humanities*, Vol. 6, no 3, 2001, pp. 125–135.

Oswald, Alice, Statement for Oxford Professor of Poetry Elections 2019: https://secure.ersvotes.com/V2-4-4/oxfordpoetry19/en/home?bbp=-1&x=-1 (accessed 30 May 2019).

Page, Benedicte, 'Authors Call for Boycott on Non-paying Festivals', *The Bookseller*, 15 January 2016.

Page, Ruth and Thomas, Bronwen (eds.), *New Narratives: Stories and Story- telling in the Digital Age*, Chesham: Combine Academic, 2012.

Palmer, C., 'Ethnography: A Research method in Practice', *International Journal of Tourism Research*, Vol. 3 no. 4, Wiley 2001, pp. 301–312.

Pandian, Anand, and Mclean, Stuart, *Crumpled Paper Boat: Experiments in Ethnographic Writing*, Duke University Press, 2017.

Parker, Kevin, 'The Rise and Rise of Literary Festivals', 26 February 2015, http://www.literaryfestivals.co.uk/announcements/the-rise-and-rise-of-lit erary-festivals (accessed 5 August 2018).

Patterson, Tiffany Ruby, *Zora Neale Hurston and a History of Southern Life*, Temple University Press, 2018.

Pearson, Jacqueline, *Women's Reading in Britain 1750–1835: A Dangerous Recreation*, Cambridge: Cambridge University Press, 1999.

Peele, Thomas, 'Introduction', in *Queer Popular Culture: Literature, Media, Film and Television*, ed. Thomas Peele, Palgrave, 2011.

Perkins, Kathryn, 'The Boundaries of BookTube', *The Serials Librarian: The International Journal of Continuing Print & Electronic Resources*, Vol. 73, no. ¾, 2017, pp. 352–356.

Perrone-Bertolotti, Marcela et al., 'How Silent Is Silent Reading? Intracerebral Evidence for Top-Down Activation of Temporal Voice Areas During Reading', *Journal of Neuroscience* Vol. 21, no. 49, 2012, pp. 1754–1762.

Peterson, Eric E. and Langellier, Kristin M., 'The Performance Turn in Narrative Studies', *Narrative Inquiry*, Vol. 16, no. 1, 2006, pp. 173–180.

Petrelli, D. and Wright, H., 'On the Writing, Reading and Publishing of Digital Stories', *Library Review*, Vol. 58, no. 7, 2009, pp. 509–526.

Phelan, James, *Narrative as Rhetoric*, Ohio: Ohio State University Press, 1996.

Phelan, Peggy, 'The Ontology of Performance: Representation Without Production', pp. 146–166 of *Unmarked: The Politics of Performance*, London: Routledge, 1993.

Pink, Sarah, *Doing Sensory Ethnography*, London: Sage, 2009.

Poirier, Richard, 'The Performing Self', in Vol. IV of *Performance: Critical Concepts in Literary and Cultural Studies*, London: Routledge, 2003.

Pollock, Della, 'Performing Writing', pp. 73–103 of *The Ends of Performance*, eds. Peggy Phelan and Jill Lane, New York: New York University Press, 1998.

Ponting, David, 'Charles Dickens as Solo Performer', pp. 109–134 of *The Changing World of Charles Dickens*, ed. Robert Giddings, Vision Press, 1983.

Popova, Maria, *Figuring*, Canongate, 2019.

Prendergast, Amy, *Literary Salons Across Britain and Ireland in the Long Eighteenth Century*, London: Palgrave, 2015.

Prendergast, Christopher (ed.), *Cultural Materialism: On Raymond Williams*, London: University of Minnesota Press, 1995.

Pullman, Philip, Resignation Speech, quoted in 'Philip Pullman Resigns as Patron of Oxford Literary Festival Over Refusal to Pay Authors', *Society of Authors*, 14 January 2015, https://www.societyofauthors.org/News/News/2016/Jan/Pullman-OLF-Resignation (accessed 1 March 2019).

Purves, Alex C., *Space and Time in Ancient Greek Narrative*, New York: Cambridge University Press, 2010.

Rabkin, Gerald, 'The Play of Misreading: Text/Theatre/ Deconstruction', *Performing Arts Journal* Vol. 7, no. 1, 1985, pp. 163–173.

Radbourne, Jennifer, Johanson, Katya, Glow, Helen and White, Tabitha, 'The Audience Experience: Measuring Quality in the Performing Arts', *International Journal of Arts Management*, Vol. 11, no. 3, 2009, pp. 16–29.

Radway, Janice A., *Reading the Romance: Women, Patriarchy, and Popular Literature* [1984] (2nd ed.), University of Caroline Press, 1991.

———, *A Feeling for Books: The Book-of-the-Month Club, Literary Taste, and Middle-Class Desire*, Chapel Hill, NC: University of North Carolina Press, 1997.

Ramdarshan Bold, Melanie, 'The Eight Percent Problem: Authors of Colour in the British Young Adult Market (2006–2016)', *Publishing Research Quarterly*, Vol. 34, no. 3, pp. 385–406, 2018.

———, *Inclusive Young Adult Fiction: Authors of Colour in the United Kingdom*, London: Palgrave, 2019.

Raply, Timothy John, 'The Art(fulness) of Open-Ended Interviewing: Some Considerations on Analysing Interviews, *Qualitative Research*, Vol. 1, no. 3 2001, pp. 303–323.

Rapport, Nigel, *The Prose and the Passion: Anthropology, Literature and the Writing of E.M. Forster*, Manchester: Manchester University Press, 1994.

———, *The Transcendent Individual: Towards a Literary and Liberal Anthropology*, London: Routledge, 1997.

Raven, James, Helen, Small and Tadmor, Naomi, *The Practice and Representation of Reading in England*, Cambridge: Cambridge University Press, 1996.

Rayner, Alice, 'The Audience: Subjectivity, Community and the Ethics of Listening', in Vol. II of *Performance: Critical Concepts in Literary and Cultural Studies*, London: Routledge, 2003.

Rayner, Keith, Pollatsek, Alexander, Ashby, Jane and Clifton, Charles Jr., *Psychology of Reading* (2nd ed.), Psychology Press, 2013.

Reason, Matthew, 'Asking the Audience: Audience Research and the Experience of Theatre, *About Performance*, Vol. 10, 2010, pp. 15–34.

Reason, Matthew and Mølle Lindelof, Anja (eds.), *Experiencing Liveness in Contemporary Performance*, 2016.

Reed, Adam, *Literature and Agency in English Fiction Reading*, Manchester: Manchester University Press, 2011.

Reed, Jennifer, 'The Three Phases of Ellen: From Queer to Gay to Post-Gay', pp. 9–26 of *Queer Popular Culture: Literature, Media, Film and Television*, ed. Thomas Peele, London: Palgrave Macmillan, 2011.

Reed-Danahay, Deborah E. (ed.), *Auto/ethnography: Rewriting the Self and the Social*, New York: Berg, 1997.

———, 'Anthropologists, Education and Autoethnography", *Reviews in Anthropology*, Vol. 38, no. 1, 2009, p. 32.

Rees, Jasper, 'The Glastonbury of the Mind: Hay turns 25', *The Arts Desk*, 31 May 2012: https://theartsdesk.com/comedy/glastonbury-mind-hay-turns-25.

Reynolds, Peter (ed.), *Novel Images: Literature in Performance*, London: Routledge, 1993.

Ricardo, Francisco (ed.), *Literary Art in Digital Performance: Case Studies in New Media Art and Criticism*, London: Continuum, 2009.

Riley, Denise, '"A Voice Without a Mouth": Inner Speech.' *Qui Parle*, Vol. 14, 2004, pp. 57–104.

Rich, Adrienne, *Of Woman Born: Motherhood as Experience and Institution* [1976], New York: W.W. Norton, 1995.

Richards, I. A., *Practical Criticism*, Cambridge: Cambridge University Press, 1929.

Richardson, D., Griffin, N., Zaki, L., Stephenson, A., Yan, J., Hogan, J., Skipper, J. and Devlin, J. T., bioRxiv preprint https://doi.org/10.1101/351148, 20 June 2018.

Roase, Jonathan, *The Intellectual Life of the British Working Classes* (2nd ed.), Yale: Yale University Press, 2010.

Robertson, Robin (ed.), *Mortification: Writers' Stories of Their Public Shame*, London: Fourth Estate, 2003.

Robinson, Joanna, 'Neil Gaiman on His New Storytelling MasterClass, *Good Omens*, and the Upside of Twitter', *Vanity Fair*, 29 January 2019.

Robles, Mario Ortiz, *The Novel As Event*, Michigan: University of Michigan Press, 2010.

Ronström, Owe, 'What a Festival "Says" and "Does": Reflections on Festivals and Festivalisation', Visby: Gotland University, 2011.

Rosaldo, Renato, Narayan, Kirin and Lavie, Smadar (eds.), *Creativity/Anthropology*, Cornell: Cornell University Press, 1993.

Roth, Wolff-Michael and Jornet, Alfredo, 'Situated Cognition', *Wiley Interdisciplinary Reviews: Cognitive Science*, Vol. 4, no. 5, 2013, p. 463.

Rowe, Sharon, 'Modern Sports: Liminal Ritual or Liminoid Leisure', in *Victor Turner and Contemporary Cultural Performance*, ed. Graham St. John, 2008.

Rub, Guy A., 'Amazon and the New World of Publishing: Comments on Chris Sagers, Apple, Antitrust and Irony', *I/S: Journal of Law and Policy*, Vol. 14, no. 2, 2018, pp. 367–390.

Rubery, Matthew, *The Untold Story of the Talking Book*, Harvard University Press, 2016.

———— (ed.), *Audiobooks, Literature and Sound Studies*, London: Routledge, 2011..

Ryszik, Melena, 'The Comedy-Destroying, Soul-Affirming Art of Hannah Gadsby', *The New York Times*, 24 July 2018.

Saenger, Paul, *Space Between Words: The Origins of Silent Reading*, Stanford: Stanford University Press 1997.

Saha, Anamik, *Race and the Cultural Industries*, Polity Press, 2017.

————, 'The Rationalizing/Racializing Logic of Capital in Cultural Production', *Media Industries*, Vol. 3, no. 1, 2016.

Saha, Anamik, and van Lente, Sandra, 'Rethinking Diversity', London: Goldsmiths Press, 2020: https://www.spreadtheword.org.uk/wp-content/uploads/2020/06/Rethinking_diversity_in-publishing_WEB.pdf.

San Juan, E., *Critique and Social Transformation: Lessons from Antonio Gramsci, Mikhail Bakhtin, and Raymond Williams*, Lampeter: Edwin Mellen Press, 2009.

Sansom, Ian, *Paper: An Elegy*, London: Fourth Estate, 2012.

Santoro, M., 'From Bourdieu to Cultural Sociology', *Cultural Sociology: A Journal of the British Sociological Association*, Vol. 5, no. 1, 2011, pp. 3–24.

Sassatelli, Monica, Giorgi, Liana and Delanty, Derard, (eds.), *Festivals and the Cultural Public Sphere*, Abingdon: Routledge, 2011.

Saunders, Mark, Lewis, Philip and Thornhill, Adrian (eds.), *Research Methods for Business Students*, Harlow: Financial Times Prentice Hall, 2009.

Sauter, Willmar, *Eventness: A Concept of Theatrical Events*, Berlin: STUTS, 2008.

Savage Landor, Walter, *Imaginary Conversations*, 1909.

Schehner, Richard, *Between Theater and Anthropology*, University of Pennsylvania Press, 1985.

————, *Performance Studies: An Introduction*, London: Routledge, 2002.

Schlesinger, Philip, *Expertise, the Academy and the Governance of Cultural Policy*, Media, Culture and Society, Vol. 35, no. 1, 2013, pp. 27–35.

Schlesinger, Philip, 'Exiles and Ethnographers: An Essay', *Social Science Information*, Vol. 45, no. 1, 2006, pp. 53–77.

Schmid, Susanna, *British Literary Salons of the Late Eighteenth and Early Nineteenth Centuries*, London: Palgrave, 2013.

Schneider, Arnd and Wright, Christopher (eds.), *Anthropology and Art Practice*, Bloomsbury Academic, 2013.

Schwarz, D. R., 'Performative Saying and the Ethics of Reading: Adam Zachary Newton's Narrative Ethics, *Narrative*, Vol. 5, no. 2, 1997, pp. 188–206, Columbus: Ohio State University Press, 1997.

Secord, James A., *Victorian Sensation: The Extraordinary Publication, Reception, and Secret Authorship of Vestiges of the Natural History of Creation*, Chicago: University of Chicago Press, 2000.

Sedgwick, Eve Kosofsky, *Touching Feeling*, New York: Duke University Press, 2003.

Sedo, DeNel Rehberg (ed.), *Reading Communities: From Salon to Cyberspace* (pp. 181–199), Houndsmills: Palgrave Macmillan, 2011.

Self, Will, 'The Novel Is Absolutely Doomed', *The Guardian*, 17 March 2018.

———, 'Will Self's Rules for Reading Aloud', *The Telegraph*, 24 May 2013.

———, 'A Point of View: Nostalgia—It's Not Like It Used to Be', *BBC News Magazine*, 14 December 2012.

Severin, Laura, *Poetry Off the Page: Twentieth-Century British Women Poets in Performance*, London: Routledge, 2017.

Sexton, David and Urwin, Rosamund, 'Goodbye Ed Victor', *The Evening Standard*, 8 June 2017.

Seymour, Laura, *Roland Barthes's The Death of the Author*, London: Routledge, 2018.

Sharma, Devika and Tygstrup, Frederik (eds.), *Structures of Feeling: Affectivity and the Study of Culture*, De Gruyter, 2015.

Sharman, R. L., 'Style Matters: Ethnography as Method and Genre', pp. 117–129 of *Anthropology and Humanism: Art of Ethnography: Narrative Style as a Research Method* (Vol. 2), San Jose, CA: Society for Humanistic Anthropology, 2007.

Sharot, Tali, *The Influential Mind: What the Brain Reveals About Our Power to Change Others*, 2017.

Shaughnessy, Robert, 'Immersive Performance, Shakespeare's Globe and the "Emancipated Spectator"', *The Hare Online*, http://thehareonline.com/, issue 1, Friday, 4 May 2012.

Shíocháin, Tríona Ní, *Singing Ideas: Performance, Politics and Oral Poetry*, New York: Berghahn Books, 2018.

Shriver, Lionel, 'I Hope the Concept of Cultural Appropriation Is a Passing Fad', Speech Given at the Brisbane Writers Festival, published in *The Guardian*, 13 September 2016.

Sicherman, Barbara, *Well-Read Lives*, Chapel Hill: University of North Carolina Press, 2010.

Siegenthaler, Fiona, 'Towards an Ethnographic Turn in Contemporary Art Scholarship', *Critical Arts: South-North Cultural and Media Studies*, Vol. 27, pp. 737–752, 2013.

Siemens, Ray and Schribman, Susan (eds.), *A Companion to Digital Literary Studies*, Oxford: Blackwell, 2007.

Singh, J. P, Globalized Arts: *The Entertainment Economy and Cultural Identity*, New York: Columbia University Press, 2010.

Sobol, J., 'Oracy in the New Millennium: Storytelling Revival in America and Bhutan', *Storytelling, Self, Society*, Vol. 6, no. 1, 2010, pp. 66–76, London: Taylor & Francis.

The Society of Authors, 'Philip Pullman Resigns as Patron of Oxford Literary Festival Over Refusal to Pay Authors', *Society of Authors*, 14 January 2015, https://www.societyofauthors.org/News/News/2016/Jan/Pul lman-OLF-Resignation.

———, 'Where We Stand: Festivals, Teaching, Appearances': http://www.societyofauthors.org/Where-We-Stand/Festivals,-teaching-appearances (accessed 2 February 2019).

Somers-Willett, Susan, *The Cultural Politics of Slam Poetry: Race, Identity, and the Performance of Popular Verse in America*, Michigan: University of Michigan Press, 2009.

Sontag, Susan, 2001 Jerusalem Prize Acceptance Speech, published as 'The Conscience of Words' in *At the Same Time: Essays and Speeches*, Penguin, 2013.

Spillman, Lyn (ed.), *Cultural Sociology*, Oxford: Blackwell Publishers, 2002.

Spry, Tami, 'Performing Autoethnography: An Embodied Methodological Praxis', *Qualitative Inquiry*, Vol. 7, no. 6, 2001, pp. 706–732.

Squires, Claire, *Marketing Literature: The Making of Contemporary Writing in Britain*, Basingstoke: Palgrave Macmillan, 2007.

———, 'Marketing Literature: The Making of Contemporary Writing in Britain', pp. 115–118 of *Feminist Literary Theory: A Reader*, ed. Eagleton (3rd ed.), Oxford: Wiley-Blackwell, 2010.

———, 'The Book in Britain: 1914–Present', pp. 188–193 of *Oxford Companion to the Book*, eds. S. J. Suarez, M. F., H. Woudhuyse, Oxford: Oxford University Press, , 2010.

———, 'Taste and/or Big Data?: Post-Digital Editorial Selection', *Critical Quarterly*, Vol. 59, no. 3, October 2017, pp. 24–38.

Squires, Claire, Ray Murray, Morris, Lewis-McPhee and Preston, *The Book Unbound: Disruption and Disintermediation in the Digital Age*, eds. Taylor & Russell, http://www.bookunbound.stir.ac.uk, 2012.

Squires, Claire, and Ray Murray, Padmini, 'The Digital Publishing Communications Circuit', *Book 2.0*, Vol. 3, no. 1, 2013, pp. 3–23.

Squires, Claire, Fuller, Danielle and Rehberg Sedo, DeNel, 'Marionettes and Puppeteers? The Relationship Between Book Club Readers and Publishers', pp. 181–199 of *Reading Communities from Salons to Cyperspace*, ed. D. Rehberg Sedo, Basingstoke: Palgrave Macmillan, 2011.

St Claire, William, *The Reading Nation in the Romantic Period*, Cambridge: Cambridge University Press, 2007.

St. John, Graham (ed.), *Victor Turner and Contemporary Cultural Performance*, Berghahn, 2008.

Starr, G. Gabrielle, *Feeling Beauty: The Neuroscience of Aesthetic Experience*, MIT Press, 2013.

Steiner, Ann, 'Select, Display, and Sell: Curation Practices in the Bookshop', *Logos*, Vol. 28, no. 4, 2017, pp. 18–31.

Stephanides, S. and Lindberg-Wada, G., Translation and Ethnography in Literary Transaction, pp. 300–309, *Studying Transcultural Literary History*, New York, 2006.

Stewart, Cori, 'We Call upon the Author to Explain: Theorising Writers' Festivals as Sites of Contemporary Public Culture', *Journal of the Association for the Study of Australian Literature*, Vol. 10, pp. 1–14, 2010, Special issue: Common Readers.

Stewart, Michael, 'Review: *Uncertain Vision: Birt, Dyke and the Reinvention of the BBC* by Georgina Born', *The Journal of the Royal Anthropological Institute*, Vol. 15, no. 2, June, 2009, pp. 448–450.

Stille, Alexander, *The Future of the Past: The Loss of Knowledge in the Age of Information*, London: Picador, 2002.

St. John, Graham (ed.), *Victor Turner and Contemporary Cultural Performance*, Oxford: Berghahn, 2008.

Stock, B., 'Rosenbach Lectures: Minds, Bodies, Readers', *New Literary History: A Journal of Theory and Interpretation*, Vol. 37, no. 3, John Hopkins University Press, 2006, pp. 489–524.

Stoller, Paul, *The Taste of Ethnographic Things: The Senses in Anthropology*, Pennsylvania: University of Pennsylvania Press, 1989.

———, *Sensuous Scholarship*, Pennsylvania: University of Pennsylvania Press, 1997.

———, *Jaguar: A Story of Africans in America*, Chicago: University of Chicago Press, 1999.

Storr, Will, *The Science of Storytelling*, London: William Collins, 2019.

Sutherland, John, *Fiction and the Fiction Industry*, London: Athalone Press, 1978.

————, *Bestsellers: Popular Fiction of the 1970s*, London: Routledge & Kegan Paul, 1981.

————, *Reading the Decades: Fifty Years of British History Through the Nation's Bestselling Books*, London: BBC Books, 2002.

————, *How to Read a Novel: A User's Guide*, London: Profile, 2006.

————, *A Little History of Literature*, Yale University Press, 2013.

Sword, Helen, *Air and Light and Time and Space: How Successful Academics Write*, Harvard University Press, 2017.

Tassi, Phillip, 'Media: From the Contact Economy to the Attention Economy', *International Journal of Arts Management*, Vol. 20, no. 3, 2018, pp. 49–59.

Taylor, Charles, *The Ethics of Authenticity*, Harvard University Press, 1992.

Taylor, D. J., *The Prose Factory: Literary Life in England Since 1918*, Chatto & Windus, 2016.

Taylor, Helen, *Why Woman Read Fiction: The Stories of our Lives*, Oxford: Oxford University Press, 2019.

Taylor, Jodie, Bennett, Andy and Woodward, Ian (eds.), *The Festivalization of Culture*, Farnham: Ashgate, 2014.

Tedlock, Dennis, *Finding the Center the Art of the Zuni, 1972: A Book of Translations of Native American Zuni narratives* [1972] (2nd ed.), University of Nebraska Press, 1999.

Thiong'o, Ngũgĩ wa, 'Oral Power and Europhone Glory: Orature, Literature and Stolen Legacies', in *Penpoints, Gunpoints and Dreams: Towards a Critical Theory of the Arts and the State in Africa*, Oxford University Press, 1998.

————, 'Notes Towards a Performance Theory of Orature', *Performance Research*, Vol. 12, no. 3, 2007.

Thomas, Rosalind, 'Performance and Written Literature in Classical Greece: Envisaging Performance from Written Literature in Comparative Contexts', pp. 27–34 of *Anthropology of Performance: A Reader*, ed. Frank Korom, London: Wiley-Blackwell, 2013.

Thompson, David W. (ed.), *Performance of Literature in Historical Perspectives*, London: University Press of America, 1983.

Thompson, John B., *Books in the Digital Age*, Cambridge: Polity, 2005.

————, *Merchants of Culture: The Publishing Business in the 21st Century* (2nd ed.), Cambridge: Polity, 2012.

Thormählen, Marianne (ed.), *The Brontës in Context*, Cambridge: Cambridge University Press, 2012.

Tivnan, Tom and Richards, Laura, 'Business Focus: Literary Festivals', *The Bookseller*, 18 March 2011.

Todd, Richard, *Consuming Fictions: The Booker Prize and Fiction in Britain Today*, London: Bloomsbury, 1996.

Towheed, Shafquat, Crone, Rosalind and Halsey, Katherine (eds.), *The History of Reading*, London: Routledge, 2010.

Trilling, Lionel, *Sincerity and Authenticity*, Harvard University Press, 1972.

Turetzky, Phillip, *Time*, London: Routledge, 1998.

Turner, Edith, 'Introduction to the Art of Ethnography', pp. 108–116 of *Anthropology and Humanism: Art of Ethnography: Narrative Style as a Research Method* (Vol. 2), 2007.

Turner, Victor, *The Ritual Process: Structure and Anti-Structure* [1961], Pascataway: Transaction, 1995.

———, 'Betwixt and Between: The Liminal Period in Rites of Passage', pp. 93–111 of *The Forest of Symbols: Aspects of Ndembu Ritual*, Cornell University Press, 1967.

———, *From Ritual to Theatre: The Human Seriousness of Play*, PAJ Publications, 1982.

———, 'Liminality and the Performative Genres', pp. 19–41 *Rite, Drama, Festival, Spectacle: Rehearsals Towards a Theory of Cultural Performance*, ed. J. J. MacAloon. Philadelphia: Institute for Study of Human Issues, 1984.

——— (ed.), with Edith Turner, *On the Edge of the Bush: Anthropology as Experience*, Tucson: University of Arizona Press, 1985.

——— (ed.), with Edward M. Bruner, *The Anthropology of Experience*, University of Illinois Press, 1986.

———, *The Anthropology of Performance*, PAJ Publications, 1986.

———, *Celebration: Studies in Festivity and Ritual*, Washington, DC: Smithsonian Institution Press, 1982.

Van Kalmthout, T. et al., *The Sound of Literature: Secondary School Teaching on Reading Aloud and Silent Reading, 1880–1940*, London; Pickering & Chatto, 2011.

Van Maanen, John, *Tales of the Field: on Writing Ethnography*, Chicago: University of Chicago Press, 2011.

Vannini, Phillip, Waskul, Dennis and Gottschalk, Simon, *The Senses in Self, Society, and Culture*, London: Routledge, 2012.

Vannini, Phillip and Williams, Patrick J. (eds.), *Authenticity in Culture, Self and Society*, Routledge, 2009. Includes Vannini with Sarah Burgess, 'Authenticity as Motivation and Aesthetic Experience', pp. 103–119.

Vintage editors, *Stop What You're Doing and Read This!*, London: Vintage, 2011.

Virtanen, Julia, *Poetry and Performance During the British Poetry Revival 1960–1980: Event and Effect*, Switzerland: Palgrave Macmillan, 2017.

Vonnegut, Kurt, *Cat's Cradle* [1963], Penguin Modern Classics edition, London: Penguin, 2008.

Wade, Stephen, 'Introduction', in *Reading the Applause: Reflections on Performance Poetry by Various Artists*, eds. Paul Munden and Stephen Wade, Huddersfield: University of Huddersfield, 1999.

Wallman, James, *Stuffocation*, London: Penguin, 2015.

Walmsley, Ben, 'Deep Hanging Out in the Arts: An Anthropological Approach to Capturing Cultural Value', *International Journal of Cultural Policy*, Vol. 24, no. 2, 2018, pp. 272–291.

Warf, Barney, *Time-Space Compression: Historical Geographies*, London: Routledge, 2008.

Waterman, S., 'Carnivals for Elites? The Cultural Politics of Arts Festivals', *Progress in Human Geography*, Vol. 22, no. 1, 1998, pp. 55–74.

Waterson, Alisse, and Vesperi, Maria D. (eds.), *Anthropology Off the Shelf: Anthropologists on Writing*, New York: Wiley-Blackwell, 2011.

Weber, Max, (ed.) Guenther Roth and Claus Wittich, *Economy and Society: An Outline of Interpretive Sociology* [1951], University of California Press, 1978.

Weber, Millicent, *Literary Festivals and Contemporary Book Culture*, Palgrave, 2018.

Weidhaas, Peter, *A History of the Frankfurt Book Fair*, trans. and ed. Carolyn Gossage and Wendy A. Right, Read How You want, 2017.

Weissman, Dick, *Which Side Are You On? An Inside History of the Folk Music Revival in America*, London: Continuum, 2005.

Whitaker Long, Beverly and Hopkins, Mary Frances, *Performing Literature: An Introduction to Oral Interpretation*, Upper Saddle River, NJ: Prentice-Hall, 1982.

Whitington, Teresa, *The Syllables of Time: Proust and the History of Reading*, London: Legenda, Modern Humanities Research Association and Maney, 2009.

Wilce, James, *Language and Emotion*, Cambridge University Press, 2009.

Wiles, David, *Theatre and Time*, London: Red Globe Press, 2013.

Wiles, Ellen, *Saffron Shadows and Salvaged Scripts: Literary Life in Myanmar Under Censorship and in Transition*, New York: Columbia University Press, 2015.

———, *The Invisible Crowd*, London: Harper Collins, 2017.

————, 'Three Branches of Literary Anthropology: Sources, Style, Subject Matter' in *Ethnography*, 'online first', 28 March 2018, https://journals.sag epub.com/doi/abs/10.1177/1466138118762958.

Williams, Evan, 'The Art of Asking a Question to a Literary Festival Panel', *McSweeney's*, 26 September 2016: https://www.mcsweeneys.net/ articles/the-art-of-asking-a-question-to-a-literary-festival-panel (accessed 30 March 2019).

Williams, Raymond, *Culture and Materialism: Selected Essays*, London: Verso, 2010.

————, *Marxism and Literature*, 1978.

————, *The Sociology of Culture*, London: Schocken, 1982.

————, *Writing in Society*, London: Diane, 1983.

————, *Culture and Society* [1958], Columbia University Press, 1983.

————, *Drama in Performance*, Maidenhead: Open University Press, 1991.

Willingham, Daniel, 'Is Listening to an Audiobook Cheating?' (blog post, republished in the Washington Post), 24 July 2016. http://www.danielwil lingham.com/daniel-willingham-science-and-education-blog/is-listening-to-an-audio-book-cheating (accessed 30 August 2018).

Windscheffel, Ruth Clayton, *Reading Gladstone*, Basingstoke: Palgrave Macmillan, 2008.

Wright, Thomas, *Oscar's Books*, London: Chatto & Windus, 2008.

Wolf, Werner, 'Intermediality', pp. 252–256 of *Routledge Encyclopedia of Narrative Theory*, eds. David Herman and Marie-Laura Ryan, London: Routledge, 2005.

Wolf, Maryanne, *Proust and the Squid: The Story and Science of the Reading Brain*, Icon Books, 2008.

————, *Reader, Come Home: The Reading Brain in a Digital World*, Harper Collins, 2018.

Woods, Penelope, 'Globe Audiences: Spectatorship and Reconstruction at Shakespeare's Globe', PhD thesis, London 2012.

Worsley, Lucy, *Jane Austen at Home: A Biography*, London: St Martin's Press, 2017.

Worthington, Marjorie, 'Fiction in the "Post-Truth" Era: The Ironic Effects of Autofiction', *Critique: Studies in Contemporary Fiction*, Vol. 58, no. 5, 2017.

Wulff, Helena, *Rhythms of Writing: An Anthropology of Irish Literature*, Bloomsbury Academic, 2017.

———— (ed.), *The Anthropologist as Writer: Genres and Contexts in the Twenty-First Century*, Oxford: Berghahn, 2016.

————, 'Literary Readings as Performance: On the Career of Contemporary Writers in the New Ireland', *Anthropological Journal of European Cultures*, Vol. 17, 2008, pp. 98–113.

———— (ed.), *Emotions: A Cultural Reader*, London: Bloomsbury, 2007.

Yeganeh, Farah, 'Iranian Theatre Festivalized', *Theatre Research International*, Vol. 30, no. 3, October 2005, pp. 274–283.

Zunshine, Lisa, *Why Do We Read Fiction? Theory of Mind and the Novel*, Ohio State University Press, 2006.

# Index